GENDER

ON THE DIVIDE

J. A. M. Whistler, *Miss Rosa Corder*.
Copyright The Frick Collection,
New York

J. A. M. Whistler, *Robert, Comte de Montesquiou-Fezensac*.
Copyright The Frick Collection, New York

GENDER

ON THE DIVIDE

THE DANDY IN

MODERNIST

LITERATURE

JESSICA R. FELDMAN

CORNELL UNIVERSITY PRESS

ITHACA AND LONDON

For George

Yes is this present sun.

CONTENTS

Acknowledgments ix

Abbreviations xi

1. Introduction *1*

2. Paroles hermaphrodites: Gautier's Dandy *25*

3. Cette vie en l'air: Barbey's Dandy *54*

4. *Mundus Muliebris:* Baudelaire's Dandy *97*

5. On the Divide: Cather's Dandy *143*

6. The Intimidating Thesis: Stevens's Dandy *180*

7. The Abyssinian Maid: Nabokov's Dandy *220*

Afterword *269*

Select Bibliography *273*

Index *285*

ACKNOWLEDGMENTS

Without the generosity of Paul Barolsky—friend, scholar, flaneur, and above all, teacher—this book simply would not have been written.

Cecil Lang read the manuscript twice and succeeded equally in editing it and encouraging me. Janet Beizer not only responded to my work in progress but also continually inspired me—by her own scholarly example—to ask the questions I genuinely cared about. Michael Levenson read my work at a crucial moment and continued to support the project with departmental resources. As the book neared completion, Patricia Meyer Spacks, Alison Booth, Mark Edmundson, Jeanette Hudson, and David Kovacs helped in precisely the ways I most needed.

Jefferey Persels's translations and Virginia Germino's and Gena McKinley's editorial assistance were expertly and graciously delivered. The reference staff at Alderman Library was unfailingly professional and disarmingly cheerful. I am indebted to Bernhard Kendler and Teresa Jesionowski of Cornell University Press for their clear sight and exacting guidance. This volume itself is designed and typeset by Wilsted & Taylor.

Christine Taylor and LeRoy Wilsted have been my friends for twenty years; that their work should join my own in this way is a cause for celebration.

Ruth Barolsky, Susan Cutler, Mary McKinley, Maria Sistrom, Christine Taylor, and Mabel Timberlake supported me with their wisdom and good works during the writing of this book. Barbara Berring, Margot Baker, Nancy Himelstein, Mary Knutsen, Phyllis Leffler, Rachel Lilly, Kathryn Lynch, Elizabeth Ravdin, Joey Roberts, Elizabeth Scott, Beverly Simmons, and Margaret Stetz—all participants in the extracurricular seminar that stretches from my undergraduate days to the present—have helped to form my thinking and have given me a sense of place beyond mere geographical location.

Finally, and with profound gratitude, I acknowledge my family. Joan Simko was present at the other end of the line, unfailingly. My father's library and my mother's letter writing were my introduction to the literary life; parental support enabled me to continue living among books. Jonathan Feldman took an important photograph; Judy Cantil stayed in touch across many time zones. Ruth Levy taught me an important lesson about family that also applied to work. Susannah and Michael, small children when I began this book, repeatedly asked, "When will your story be done?" and thus reminded me that criticism should aspire to the condition of art. More important, they waited patiently for my answer while offering me the chief pleasures of my days. Writing of the decentered, I have learned to value even more the center: for constancy and inspiration, I thank my husband, George Rutherglen.

J. R. F.

ABBREVIATIONS

JULES-AMÉDÉE BARBEY D'AUREVILLY

DD	"Du Dandysme et de G. Brummell"
DO&DH	Le XIXe siècle: Des oeuvres et des hommes
L	Lettres à Trébutien
M	Memoranda
O&H	Le XIXe siècle: Les oeuvres et les hommes
PA	Premiers articles (1834–1853)

CHARLES BAUDELAIRE

CS	The Mirror of Art: Critical Studies by Charles Baudelaire
IJ	Intimate Journals
OC	Oeuvres complètes, ed. Dantec and Pichois
OC, Raymond ed.	Oeuvres complètes, ed. Raymond
SW	Baudelaire: Selected Writings on Art and Artists

WILLA CATHER

KA	The Kingdom of Art
MA	My Ántonia
PH	The Professor's House
SF	Collected Short Fiction, 1892–1912
WP	The World and the Parish

THÉOPHILE GAUTIER

JF	Les Jeunes-France: Romans goguenards
MM	Mademoiselle de Maupin

VLADIMIR NABOKOV

Comm	"Commentary" to Aleksandr Pushkin's Eugene Onegin
PF	Pale Fire
PRP	"Pushkin, or, the Real and the Plausible"
SM	Speak, Memory
SO	Strong Opinions

ALEKSANDR PUSHKIN

EO	Eugene Onegin

HOLLY STEVENS

SP	Souvenirs and Prophecies: The Young Wallace Stevens

WALLACE STEVENS

CP	The Collected Poems of Wallace Stevens
LWS	Letters of Wallace Stevens
NA	The Necessary Angel
OP	Opus Posthumous

ROBERT LOUIS STEVENSON

PO	Prince Otto

All English translations following French quotations are the author's own, or Jefferey Persels's with the help of the author, unless accompanied by a volume citation.

GENDER

ON THE DIVIDE

La femme est le contraire du dandy.

BAUDELAIRE

Paraître, c'est *être*, pour les Dandys comme pour les femmes.

BARBEY

1

INTRODUCTION

DEFINING DANDIES

The dandy is the riddle, the ever-expanding set of questions which forms about the changing answer of human identity itself. As students of the dandy ruefully discover, the urge to delimit dandyism by time, place, or coterie is both irresistible and contrary to dandyism's spirit, that of displacement. If a center must be named, the Regency period in England presents itself, with Beau Brummell the reigning beau on whom all other dandies necessarily model themselves.[1] According to this historical model, dandyism, originally an English phenomenon, crossed the channel to France when exiled French aristocrats, schooled in the ways of London high society, found it safe to return to Paris. Dandyism then developed simultaneously in London and Paris, each group of dandies looking across

[1]Every study of literary dandyism owes a debt to Ellen Moers, *The Dandy: Brummell to Beerbohm*. It offers an excellent historical background to the subject. For a list of other historical accounts of dandyism, see the bibliography in Carassus. Among the works most useful to me have been Creed, François, Prevost, and Kempf.

the channel for the very essence of "bon ton" (for the English dandy) or "le high life" (for the French *fashionable*). Thus, for the French, dandyism is an English phenomenon, an import. For stylish Londoners, "la mode," Parisian style, must set the standard. This international proliferation of dandyism suggests the very displacement crucial to "placing" dandyism: it exists in its purest form always at the periphery of one's vision, often in a foreign language or a text requiring decipherment.

But the phenomenon of displacement only begins there. It extends to every aspect of description and definition of that elusive figure, the dandy. If, for example, I discuss dandyism as it exists in poems and novels, it is with the certainty that I thereby fail to account for actual dandies of the coffeehouse and avenue. Are the "truest" dandies figures of pen and ink, or flesh and blood? If I try to capture dandies by studying pictures and accounts of actual, historical dandies, I am struck by these dandies' inevitable slide into fiction, for the "realer" the dandy, the more a product of (his own) make-believe he is. If a dandy is a person who plays the part of himself, how can the real be neatly culled from such fiction?

Once again, if I regard actual dandies as constitutive of dandyism, I am struck by their tendency to die into abstraction, to personify the idea of dandyism rather than to breathe as individuals. Yet if I begin with dandyism as a set of abstract qualities, if I roam the worlds of art and history in search of figures who fit the profile, I am chastened by the paradoxical quality of every "true" dandy: his success in eluding every category, every abstraction or generalization, among them the abstraction of "dandyism" itself. The chief rule of the brotherhood of dandies, strictly observed, is to evade conformity.

Jules Barbey d'Aurevilly's 1845 essay on Brummell, "Du Dandysme et de G. Brummell," scintillates with dandyism's paradoxical, centerless, mobile truth. Barbey's Brummell is both English and not English, a historical person and a legendary personage, an incarnate figure and a flight of rhetoric, an exercise in Barbey's *sprezzatura* but equally Barbey's intense attempt at personal salvation. If it is true that Brummell alone defines dandyism by perfectly personifying it, Barbey also believes that "le Dandysme a sa racine dans la nature humaine de tous les pays et de tous les temps, puisque la vanité est universelle" (DD 281; Dandyism has its roots in human nature of all places and all times, since vanity is universal). Hence the essay's postscript, "Un Dandy d'avant les Dandys," a portrait of two seventeenth-century French dandies, one male, one female, following on the central essay's claim that dandyism is a masculine phenomenon of nineteenth-century England. Of this more later.

Charles Baudelaire, who after Barbey is the other great nineteenth-century theorist of dandyism ("Le peintre de la vie moderne," 1863), expresses the shape of dandyism's definition in the opening line of his journal: "De la vaporisation et de la centralisation du *Moi*. Tout est là" (*OC* 1271; Of the vaporization and centralization of the Self. There is everything). The self was for Baudelaire always the dandy's self; to chart its expansions and contractions was to trace the very shifting contours of dandyism.

Certainly my book offers a "centralized" version of dandyism, a set of characteristics from which dandies have tended to choose, so that the type of the dandy is recognizable. The dandy is, for example, artificial in dress and deportment, always elegant, often theatrical. He creates "la mode," style itself. He requires an audience in order to display his hauteur, his very distance from that audience. Aloof, impassive, vain, the dandy has a defensive air of superiority that shades into the aggression of impertinence and cruelty. Military in bearing and discipline, the dandy is also as fragile and whimsical as a butterfly. Outwardly cool, he burns inwardly. A man, he pursues an ideal of charm and personal beauty which the dominant culture, against which he poses himself, labels feminine. He roams, occasionally, among the capitals of Europe or takes a trip to the Orient.

A list of dandies who would answer to this description includes Beau Brummell and other notable figures of the avenue such as "Silent" Hare, "Teapot" Crawfurd, and "Apollo" Raikes (Moers 58–59). The list grows longer and lusher when it encompasses the fictional creations of such writers as Chateaubriand, Eugène Sue, Stendhal, Honoré de Balzac, Alfred de Musset, Alfred de Vigny, Prosper Mérimée, Mikhail Lermontov, Aleksandr Pushkin, Benjamin Disraeli, Edward Bulwer-Lytton, Joris-Karl Huysmans, and Max Beerbohm. Surely dandies are most powerfully typified by the fictional creations of Lord Byron and Oscar Wilde, chief among them Byron and Wilde themselves. For such a list replicates itself when we recognize that the dandies of literature are often created by artists who are also dandies. The hall of mirrors is the dandy's ancestral home. In a dizzying reflexivity, the dandy created within the work of art—Pelham or Onegin or Don Juan—is actualized, rendered "real" in print by the living, breathing dandy-writer who chooses to make of himself and his daily life a fiction.

Such is the dandy "centralized." Vaporized, he is predictably much vaguer, less a product of any particular time or place. He is the figure who practices, and even impersonates, the fascinating acts of self-creation and presentation. He is the figure of paradox created by many societies in order to express whatever it is that the culture feels it must, but cannot, synthe-size.[2] This dandy is neither spirit nor flesh, nature nor artifice, ethical nor aesthetic, active nor passive, male nor female. He is the figure who casts into doubt, even while he underscores, the very binary oppositions by which his culture lives.[3]

The "vaporized" phenomenon of dandyism diffuses backward in time to the figures who inspired many nineteenth-century dandies. Alcibiades, the Athenian general of the fifth century B.C., would be the patriarch of all dandies, except that he deliberately feminized himself. Nineteenth-century writers in the dandy tradition would have read of Alcibiades in a variety of sources: Thucydides, Plato, Plutarch, Erasmus, Shakespeare. All the writers whom I treat refer to him: Barbey and Baudelaire directly and intensely; Théophile Gautier, Wallace Stevens, Willa Cather, and Vla-dimir Nabokov in passing. Alcibiades is dandylike in all his personal char-acteristics. He is aristocratic, wealthy, elegant, brave, skilled in oratory. Most striking are his chameleonic powers of self-transformation. Protec-tor of the Athenian democracy, he is also its nemesis, ready to deceive Ath-ens for personal gain or even for personal entertainment. He is insolent, given to socially outrageous behavior, and dissolute, yet the wisest man in Athens loves him.[4] A hoaxer on a grand scale, he is in the end—whatever his form, whatever his rhetoric—a challenger of hierarchies and systems. Of the long list of accusations lodged against him over his lifetime, the most serious involved his breaking of images and profaning of mysteries.

Once again, considering the dandy in his widest definition, I would in-clude Baldassare Castiglione's courtier, his *disinvoltura* a dandy's mix of ease, aplomb, and simplicity shading into coolness, impudence, hauteur.[5]

---

[2]See O'Flaherty, *Asceticism and Eroticism* for a discussion of Siva and androgyny, both of which have been central to my developing concept of dandyism.

[3]See Needham for a discussion of binary symbolism as it occurs in several cultures. His discussion of the nature of the relation between opposing things or qualities is especially helpful: "The contention that a table of opposites implies a total division of things and qualities into two opposed and mutually exclusive spheres, each characterized by one dis-tinctive quality, rests at once in a disregard of the function of analogy in a dual classification and also on a misunderstanding of the nature of analogy" (xxx). He explains that the two sides of the duality are related indirectly, analogically, in "a constant 'classificatory current,' as Dumézil puts it; the 'equilibria are unstable' and the symbolic categories are ascribed different values according to the 'perspectives' in which they are viewed" (xxix). Needham's discussion of the relational and contextual nature of binary systems helps explain the "cur-rent" or process of resemblance between male and female which I trace in this volume.

[4]This insolence, dissolution, and even criminality characterize a strain of dandyism which Green develops at length.

[5]See Mazzeo for a discussion of the courtier that is itself a model of scholarly elegance. I depend here heavily on his interpretation.

The courtier knows the importance of carriage, gesture, and clothing to the artistic fashioning of oneself. Castiglione views the self as a work of art, subject first to ennobling development, ever after to painstaking polishing. Such a concept of self provides the distance between the dandy and the crowd, since most men are content to assume ready-made lives, blunted sensibilities. Further, the courtier's dandyism reveals a late Renaissance turning inward occasioned by political defeat, a defensive movement paralleled by the nineteenth-century dandy's response to bourgeois culture.[6]

Dandyism expands backward in time, but it also reaches forward. Thus I argue that the tradition of dandyism, legitimately traced in ancient Athens and fifteenth-century Florence, is even more strongly present in twentieth-century America. I propose to study the nineteenth-century French dandy as an icon of modernism, to unfold Baudelaire's enigmatic pronouncements on the dandy, summarized in his "Il cherche ce quelque chose qu'on nous permettra d'appeler la *modernité*"(*OC* 1163; He seeks that certain something that one would permit us to call *modernity*). I propose as well to expand that search into the pages of the high modernist tradition of American letters, seeking the dandy in the works of three writers who worked self-consciously in the French tradition—Cather, Stevens, and Nabokov.

An anatomy of dandyism can occur as a process, but it can never be fixed by chart, map, or lexicon. If we fix dandyism's temporal center in nineteenth-century London or Paris, we do so only until we come to understand dandyism as an expression of anti-essentialism. There simply is no essential time, place, or figure of dandyism. There are only differences among dandyism's texts, chief among them the dandy's own painstakingly presented body. Dandies are skeptics who demand that their audiences recognize their status as human signifiers, freely moving about in a world that is always textual.

DANDIES AND GENDER

In this study I observe dandies as they impersonate some of the major struggles of the modernist arena: the gropings of Romantic subjectivity toward a classical, sculptured objectivity; the anguished pull between aesthetics and moralism; the understanding of human identity as vapor or

[6]For an account of the dandy as a figuration of the modern temper, see Benjamin.

diamond; and implicit in all these, the political choice between reaction and rebellion. The figure who emerges not only rehearses the thematics of modernity but also challenges "patriarchal thought." He replaces the my-thologies of "phallogocentrism" with something else. I place these terms in quotation marks to indicate their contingency, their status as cultural constructions. Before I can mark the dandy's place within feminist criti-cism, however, I must reveal the lie folded within this introduction—that the dandy is *he*.

Dandyism exists in the field of force between two opposing, irreconcil-able notions about gender. First, the (male) dandy defines himself by at-tacking women. Second, so crucial are female characteristics to the dandy's self-creation that he defines himself by embracing women, appropriating their characteristics.

To begin with the attack. The "actual" dandy courts women in order to cut them. If never allowing a woman the slightest bit of power over one means living a solitary (or even celibate) life, so be it. The six artists I have chosen all write out their misogyny; I have not hesitated in the following chapters to quote some of their most troubling statements. Perhaps the fiercest of these pronouncements belongs to Baudelaire:

> La femme est le contraire du dandy.
> Donc elle doit faire horreur.
> La femme a faim et elle veut manger. Soif, et elle veut boire.
> Elle est en rut et elle veut être foutue.
> Le beau mérite!
> La femme est *naturelle*, c'est-à-dire abominable.
> Aussi est-elle toujours vulgaire, c'est-à-dire le contraire du dandy.
>
> (*OC* 1272)

Woman is the opposite of the dandy. Thus she must inspire horror. Woman is hungry and she wants to eat. Thirsty, and she wants to drink. She is in heat and wants to be fucked. What fine merit! Woman is *natural*, that is to say, abominable. Thus she is always vulgar, that is to say, the opposite of the dandy.

But from Gautier, whose d'Albert objectifies women as statues, to Nabo-kov, who creates a host of threatening, vulgar, and sad women, all six of these writers express a range of negative feelings about women.

I have spoken of two opposing attitudes toward women. If the first is dislike, even fear and hatred, the second is an admiring yearning for the female. So crucial are female characteristics to the dandy's self-creation that he defines himself by embracing women, seeking to share their char-acteristics. I speak here not of a pseudoandrogyny, the male dandy improved or completed by taking on female characteristics in order to become a "supermale." Reconciliation, synthesis, complementarity are never the ways of dandyism.[7]

Rather, these writers both reject and pursue women because they engage in that most self-dividing of activities: living within dominant cultural forms while imagining new forms taking shape in some unspecifiable "beyond." Cultural change may certainly be charted as the result of social, economic, and religious phenomena as they impinge on the collective imagination of a society. Yet such change may, on the contrary, *begin* within those individuals in a culture who happen to see things in a new (and often illogical or even crazy-seeming) way.[8] I intend here neither the romanticization of mental illness nor a belated turn to the Romantic type of the mad artist, but instead a recognition of the troubling, disruptive shapes appearing in the visions of artists as they create against or beyond the stale visions of cultural "truths." From within their rich subjectivity, the writers I study both revile and celebrate women because through the energy generated by such self-contradiction they can imagine a challenge to the repressive system that divides people into two categories, male and female, and then announces in a myriad of ways the superiority of one group over the other. "La femme est le contraire du dandy" (Woman is the opposite of the dandy) meets "*Paraître, c'est être, pour les Dandys comme pour les femmes*" (DD 314; *To appear* is *to be*, for Dandies as for women) across a vast divide, created by a culture that polarizes gender. Dandies poise themselves precisely upon, or rather within, this divide: the violence of such self-placement generates the energy of dandyism as a cultural form. Perhaps an anecdote will help.

Barbey d'Aurevilly includes in "Un Dandy d'avant les Dandys," a long-delayed afterword to his essay on Brummell, a sketch of the court of Louis XIV. There the duc de Lauzun applies a dandy's powers in an attempt to capture in marriage Mademoiselle de Montpensier (la Grande Mademoiselle), cousin to Louis XIV and the richest woman in France. Lauzun is famous for his cruelty to women, Barbey reminds us:

[7]See O'Flaherty, *Women, Androgynes* (283–309), for a discussion of pseudoandrogyny.

[8] I intend here something like the point Rorty makes in his recent essay "Feminism and Pragmatism." There he discusses the need feminists feel to expand "logical space," to change people's feelings about the world by "provid[ing] new language which will facilitate new reactions. By 'new language' I mean not just new words but also creative misuses of language—familiar words used in ways which initially sound crazy" (233). Such language would often appear incoherent "with the rest of the beliefs of those who currently control life-chances and logical space" (240).

Rappelez-vous la scène (dans les *Mémoires de Saint-Simon*) où il met son talon sur la main d'une duchesse—les talons se portaient hauts, sous Louis XIV, comme celui des femmes d'aujourd'hui (1879),—et où il pirouette sur ce talon pour l'enfoncer dans la chair, comme un vilebrequin. C'est à faire crier le lecteur, s'il est nerveux.   (DD 282–83)

Recall the scene (in the Memoirs of Saint-Simon) where he places his heel on the hand of a duchess—heels were worn high, under Louis XIV, like those of women today (1879)—and where he pirouettes upon this heel to bury it in her flesh, like a brace and bit. This makes the reader moan, if he is sensitive.

How to regard this verbal blade of perversity?[9] Lauzun's power over women is defined in terms of women: without the foil of female vulnerability, Lauzun's "impitoyable vanité," his sadomasochistic cruelty, go unexpressed. Seeking the hand of la Grande Mademoiselle, he has wounded the hand of a duchess. Yet to do so is to lose his identity, to become more tool than man, "comme un vilebrequin." And it is the blood of a woman that sheathes a bloodless high heel, itself an emblem not just of pitiless phallic aggression but also of femininity itself, "comme celui des femmes d'aujourd'hui." By the act of announcing his dandyism—the elegance of dandies carries with it an impertinence tending toward a cool, criminal brutality—Lauzun throws into relief his assumption of female essence. His feminine heel, bathed in female blood, is the emblem of the dandy's paradox: his simultaneous attack on and blood tie to women.

Furthermore, the anecdote belongs to a history chronicled not just by Saint-Simon and by Barbey, but also by la Grande Mademoiselle herself. In "Un Dandy d'avant les Dandys," Barbey quotes and paraphrases her memoirs, her artful account of the love affair of the century, weaving it

---

[9]The anecdote in Saint-Simon's *Mémoires,* which describes Mme de Monaco, appears as follows: "Lauzun était fort jaloux et n'était pas content d'elle. Une après-dînée d'été qu'il était allé à Saint Cloud, il trouva Madame et sa cour assises à terre sur le parquet pour se refraîchir, et Mme de Monaco à demi-couchée, une main renversée par terre. Lauzun se met en galanterie avec les dames, et tourne si bien qu'il appuie son talon dans le creux de la main de Mme de Monaco, y fait la pirouette et s'en va. Mme de Monaco eut le force de ne point crier et de s'en taire" (Saint-Simon 8:625–26; Lauzun was quite jealous; he was not pleased with her. One evening in summer that he had gone to Saint Cloud, he found Madame and her court seated on the parquet floor to cool themselves off and Madame de Monaco half reclining, one hand resting palm up on the ground. Lauzun set about chatting gallantly with the women, and turned in such a way that he pressed his heel in the hollow of Madame de Monaco's hand, executed a pirouette there and left. Madame de Monaco had the strength not to cry out and to remain silent.)

into his own commentary. Like Gautier, Baudelaire, Cather, Stevens, and Nabokov, Barbey in his own way feminizes his text, uses a woman's words, in order to imagine a world beyond dichotomous gender. If we cry out at Lauzun's brutality, we must marvel at Barbey's redistribution of sexual roles. It is Lauzun in the end who is sterile, silenced, and passive and la Grande Mademoiselle who, by her unwavering sense of self-importance and by the power of art, earns a dandy's triumph over Lauzun. Her tale is a tragedy in which she takes the hero's part. *Her* words will help us here: "En arrivant à Tournay, je voulus en parler à M. de Lauzun. En descendant de carosse, je me voulus appuyer sur lui, il s'en alla; je pensai tomber" (Montpensier 127; Upon arriving at Tournay, I wanted to speak with M. de Lauzun. As I descended from the coach, I wanted to lean upon him, but he walked away; I thought I would fall). What she knows and fears is falling: descending from her high place to marry a (comparative) nobody. What we learn when she takes the masculine part, leading Lauzun on, speaking, acting, feeling, writing in order to re-create herself as a forty-year-old virgin in love, is the sense of free fall associated with an abandonment of rigid categories. Not just class but gender is hierarchical, and to challenge it is to step beyond a known culture toward chaos.

My study of the dandy-tradition anatomizes this step into *plein air*. These writers, in challenging dichotomous gender, exceed their cultures, open a new door through which their cultures might pass. That is, in living securely within what feminist critics have labeled phallocentric discourse, these writers have also, simultaneously and paradoxically, found a place within that discourse which is outside it. Stevens, borrowing the concept of novelty from William James's psychology, expressed this impossible position when he said that "we live in concepts of the imagination before the reason has established them" (*NA* 154). For Stevens—and he speaks for all the writers I treat—a true change of style implies the ability of genius to see, and by seeing to create, however dimly and intuitively, at the farthest reaches of culture and, blindly, one startling step beyond. Such is the creation of the new, modernism's raison d'être. La Grande Mademoiselle's free-fall is ours, as we begin to understand the meaning of gender implicit in the tradition of dandyism.

The common assumption is that dandies are male; female dandies such as la Grande Mademoiselle, la comtesse Dash, and Mathilde de La Mole, are the exceptions. For Albert Camus the dandy is a species of the rebel, "a man who says no." For Walter Benjamin, it is always the *flâneur*, never the *flâneuse*, who walks about the city, the man of the crowd. Emilien Carassus, in his anthologized excerpts from forty works concerning dandyism, includes not a single female dandy, as if the concept were a contradiction in terms. Perhaps Roland Barthes's statement best summarizes the truth of dandyism; it is, he reports, "un phénomène essentiellement masculin" (Carassus 315).

Yet femaleness hovers about the phenomenon from Alcibiades to Nabokov. At first it appears as a way to define dandyism negatively: Baudelaire's "La femme est le contraire du dandy"; Plutarch's suggestion that Alcibiades' success lay in avoiding womanly silliness. Barbey's Brummell punishes women, as his predecessor Lauzun has done. Camus instructs us in the (male) dandy's rebellion, so clearly different from and superior to woman's passive resentment (Camus 17).[10]

Yet—and with this "yet" I must begin to refer to the dandy as both "she" and "he"—dandies regularly internalize a woman's world, what Baudelaire refers to as the *mundus muliebris*. Baudelaire tells us he was a precocious dandy when as a child he inhaled the perfume of his mother's fur coat. Plutarch gossips of Alcibiades' long purple robes resembling a woman's. Just before his assassination, Alcibiades, we are told, dreams himself "arrayed in his mistress's habit," while she "painted his face as if he had been a woman" (Plutarch 262). Earlier, he has been accused of fighting like a woman. Barbey describes himself as "un efféminé de ma taille" and conceives of Brummell in part as an aristocratic woman. Castiglione's courtier possesses *grazia*, a female quality. When theoreticians of dandyism have reported such facts, they have taken pains to ignore them, dismiss them ironically, deny them. Roger Kempf, for example, engages in all three strategies, instructing us that "la femme ne pèse guère dans l'histoire universelle du dandysme. Lady Hamilton, la Grande Mademoiselle, la duchesse de Langeais, Mathilde de La Mole n'illustrent pas un sexe, mais une race" (Kempf 157; woman hardly matters in the universal history of dandyism. Lady Hamilton, la Grande Mademoiselle, the duchess of Langeais, Mathilde de La Mole illustrate not a sex, but a race).[11]

---

[10]Camus writes, "Resentment is very well defined by Scheler as an autointoxication— the evil secretion, in a sealed vessel, of prolonged impotence. Rebellion, on the contrary, breaks the seal and allows the whole being to come into play. . . . Scheler himself emphasizes the passive aspect of resentment and remarks on the prominent place it occupies in the psychology of women who are dedicated to desire and possession" (17).

[11]Kempf in fact lists many effeminate dandies, but consistently denigrates the female (e.g., after recognizing that Mlle de Montpensier is a dandy, he goes on to discuss only Lauzun, the male dandy, at length). Kempf attributes the effeminacy of dandies to their homosexuality; to label it is thus to "explain" it.

In fact the literature of dandyism challenges the very concept of two separate genders. Its male heroes, artists and their subjects alike, do more than punish women or dally with them—*they relocate dandyism within the female realm in order to move beyond the male and the female, beyond dichotomous gender itself*. How is dandyism displaced upon the female? By a variety of methods, each as distinctive as the artist who invents it. It is one of my major goals to lay bare these displacements. From Gautier's Mademoiselle de Maupin through Nabokov's Eugene Onegin, the dandy's distance from woman repeatedly collapses into direct resemblance to her, this resemblance itself generating a modern, analogical world in which women are *as* men, men are *as* women. This resemblance requires us to understand the dandy as neither wholly male nor wholly female, but as the figure who blurs these distinctions, irrevocably. The "incorrigible proposition" (Kessler and McKenna 77) that biological fact proves the natural status of two distinct genders is challenged throughout the literature of dandyism.

By now there is a rich critical literature exploring the possibility that what we see as the scientific, objective data underlying our notion of two distinct genders are in fact qualified by the educated, "cultured" eyes of those doing the looking. "Gender" we take to be the cultural fabrications we work upon "sex," the actual, naturally determined biological difference. In fact gender and sex are not so easily distinguishable from each other.[12] Since we tend to believe that distinctions between men and women

[12]In the third chapter of their book, Kessler and McKenna demonstrate that gender cannot always be determined by a person's sex, because sex itself is sometimes open to interpretation. "There is no question, genetically, whether an individual is female or male [one Y chromosome = male; no Y chromosome = female]. And yet even this dichotomy is not always so clear. There do exist individuals who are genetic mosaics. For example, they may have some cells with XO chromosomes and other cells with XXY. What is their genetic gender? As in the case of the scientific definition of death and life, such examples make obvious that attribution of gender, even in science, is sometimes a matter of making a decision" (52).

Kessler and McKenna argue that biologists' "criteria for gender are grounded in everyday gender attributions" (68). They continue: "No matter what the criteria, though, and no matter how contradictory or confusing the results of research have been [e.g., the idea of male versus female hormones has been called into question], at no time have biologists challenged the basic incorrigible proposition which they hold, not as biologists but as members of everyday society, that there are two genders" (74). Instead, "concepts of gender lead to the *discovery* of differentiating facts" (75, emphasis added).

Literary and social critics as well as anthropologists have explored the contingency of sex. Armstrong, for example, writes in essential agreement with the findings of Kessler and McKenna. She declares herself a follower of Foucault, who, in the first volume of *History*

are based on a biological substratum of truth (e.g., genitals or X and Y chromosomes), the melting of that firm substratum reveals that both sex and gender are stories whose plots are subject to change.

Thomas Laqueur, in *Making Sex*, gives us one recounting of that plot. He argues that the medieval and Renaissance belief in the "one-sex body"—the male body of which the female is a like, but lesser version— gave way by 1800 to a two-sex system. While the one-sex model thrived on similarities and analogies hierarchically arranged—all ultimately analogized to a cosmic order—the two-sex model seeks two rigidly separated categories, male and female, arrayed rather more horizontally than vertically (though men are still superior to women). In this later model, presumably the model reflected by the six writers I examine, "not only are the sexes different, but they are different in every conceivable aspect of body and soul, in every physical and moral aspect" (Laqueur 5).

Although I find Laqueur's larger argument—that sex, as well as gender, is a cultural construct—convincing, my book challenges the particulars of his two-sex model as a cultural monolith of the modern understanding. I demonstrate that from early in the nineteenth century, artists in the tradition of dandyism challenged the rigid separations of the two-sex system which Laqueur himself sees as dominant but not universal. They challenged this model in two ways: by questioning substratum and by questioning surface. The first involves a radical challenge to the power of so-called objective fact, "sex," to determine or even support one's gender. Here, by advertising the self as nothing but the sum total of powerful, premeditated, costumed poses, dandies announced the ascendance of fiction over fact. That male dandies were sometimes referred to as "she" suggests that the public, however cynically, got the dandies' message. To call a man "she" is not simply to mock effeminacy; it is to register the possibility of manipulating, causing to metamorphose, that most fixed of birth- and biology-determined "facts"—one's gender. And if sex is thus brought into question, surely other aspects of the self might quickly follow. The dandy's imperturbable and impervious demeanor, his encasement in flaw-

---

of Sexuality, "makes sex a function of sexuality and considers sexuality as a purely semiotic process" (11). For Armstrong, sexuality cannot be grounded in nature, because nature itself is constructed. "Along with Foucault, I would argue that the difference between nature and culture is always a function of culture, the construction of nature being one of culture's habitual tropes of self-authorization. . . . the idea of natural sex, it seems to me, poses a contradiction in terms that is without doubt the purest form of ideology" (262n.).

See also the work done in the scientific construction of race, such as Stepan, for its parallels with the scientific construction of gender.

lessly smooth clothing, announce to the world the inaccessibility not just of genital "proof" but also of substratum, of "essential" truth itself. Artificial, polished surface—cultural arrangements—he announces as primary, as constitutive of self. I am what I choose to appear to be.

The dandy challenges the two-sex model as well by questioning surface, what we might think of as gender roles or attributes. Men dress and act in a "masculine" way, work at certain jobs, assume certain responsibilities. Women inhabit other cultural expectations of "feminine" appearance and creativity. Dandies often choose to imagine themselves through the gender attributes of the so-called opposite sex. The chapters that follow describe the series of choices which dandy-artists make in an effort to appropriate the "other" sex: imagining that contradiction in terms, the female dandy;[13] adopting what they believe to be feminine modes and methods of creation; exploring the world of women as a sphere introducing the possibility of freedom from strict gender categories.

Laqueur's argument is most useful when it establishes the "living changingness," as Stevens would put it, of our truths about sex and gender. The tale of sex and gender I describe develops in the nineteenth century as a subplot, a story written against the grain of more clichéd gender arrangements. It is above all a tale of analogical relation: male as female, female as male, with emphasis on the energy of the relation. Sex and gender as sorting categories give way to the engulfment of sex by gender, especially gender as self-presentation, and the engulfment of gender as static category by gender as analogical process.

Dandies, by demonstrating that human identity is a matter of self-construction and presentation, have always self-consciously played with the construction of gender. It has been the work of twentieth-century ethnomethodologists to demonstrate that the "irreducible fact" of polarized gender is not decreed by biology but instead created, given its sense of objectivity and reality, through the course of social interaction (Kessler and McKenna vii). Yet dandies have long conveyed this possibility in their posing, strolling, being seen, being *taken for* what they "are." Both at the club and on the written page, they announce that the world of two distinct biological genders is not the only world. Dandies instruct us in the *primacy of the act of gender attribution*, a social act subject to the changing nuances of social intercourse. Social manner, self-presentation rather than genitals,

[13]I refer here not to the female version of dandies, which simply replicates cultural arrangements of female inferiority (e.g., the *lionne* as inferior version of the *lion*, as Matoré discusses them, 46–47), but the paradoxical figure of a "real" dandy (i.e., male) who is nevertheless female. I address this issue at length in Chapters 2–4.

determines our gender. As a social construct gender is subject to cultural manipulation, freed from its "necessary" division into biological males and biological females.[14] And that is precisely what writers in the tradition of dandyism demonstrate.

DANDYISM AND FEMINISM

The literature of dandyism suggests an orientation for feminist criticism as it seeks to expand beyond the "feminist critique" and "gynocriticism"— both of which are predicated on a polarized view of the sexes—to a model emphasizing the numerous but subtle *liens* between the male and female literary traditions.[15] Writers in the dandy-tradition suggest that the one

[14]Genitals are, after all, usually hidden, subject to change by medical operation, and, in the case of preoperative transsexuals, "incorrect," given their gender identities. Secondary sexual characteristics are too ambiguous in many cases to allow for a definitive gender attribution. Thinking of and presenting oneself "as," taking another person "as" male or female—these are the contextual acts which determine gender. A person lacking a penis may choose to be a man and be taken as such by those who read the series of subtle and not-so-subtle social cues that help us determine the gender of those we meet. Although genitals and gender identity usually coincide, *they need not*; therefore genitals cannot be considered the *essential* basis for gender. For the full argument supporting these necessarily brief statements, see Kessler and McKenna.

[15]I refer here to the progression of feminist approaches outlined by Showalter. As she argues in a still timely essay, feminist critics first learned to carry out the "feminist critique," to become critical readers of male texts, to understand how women were marginalized or silenced within the dominant discourse. Next, feminist literary critics learned to practice a "gynocriticism," defining a female tradition of literary practice rather than reading against the grain of masculine discourse. The problem then became one of relating the male and female traditions. Should we read male and female literatures separately? Become comparativists? Discover how they interact? Gender-based criticism suggests the last. A decade after Showalter's essay, we as feminist critics still grapple with the issue of polarized male and female traditions.

A survey of recent literary scholarship reveals a burgeoning interest in the construction of masculinity—in addition to femininity—as a crucial area within the field of gender criticism. Although this has been a vital field in anthropology (see, for example, Gilbert H. Herdt, *Guardians of the Flute: Idioms of Masculinity* [New York: McGraw Hill, 1981]), literary scholars have until recently assumed the masculine to be the given, the unproblematical. Essays such as Peter Schwenger, "The Masculine Mode," and Eve Sedgwick, "The Beast in the Closet: James and the Writing of Homosexual Panic" (both in Elaine Showalter, ed., *Speaking of Gender*); and David Van Leer, "The Beast of the Closet: Homosociality and the Pathology of Manhood," *Critical Inquiry* 15 (1989): 587–605, have at least begun to ask the questions that will complement the questions critics ask about the construction of femininity. Several collections of essays on this topic have also appeared recently, among them: Michael Cadden and Joseph Boone, *Engendering Men: The Question*

remaining monolith for most feminist critics—patriarchy itself—is not essentially alien to women, nor can we regard it as the solid basis for our oppression. Rather, in dismantling patriarchy, women might be re-creating themselves at the same time.

Certainly the concept of a "phallocentric reality" to which we cling seems real when we think about employment discrimination or rape or any of the myriad ways in which women are silenced. To speak of both maleness and femaleness as problematical appears to obfuscate the very real political disadvantages of women. Any theory that sees both women and men as "prisoners of gender" in interrelated ways (Flax 629) causes us, so the argument goes, to lose our focus on the still crushing subordination of women to men. Yet a misstatement of the problem cannot help us in our political struggle. Critics who have attempted the deconstruction of patriarchy itself have been at best ambivalent about the process. Toril Moi, for example, calls for "a more sophisticated account of the contradictory, fragmented nature of patriarchal ideology" (64) while continuing to refer to the "phallocentric order" that defines woman as marginal (163). With Hélène Cixous, I would caution, "Beware, my friend, of the signifier that would take you back to the authority of a signified!" (892).[16]

Certainly a belief in gender as dichotomy—a belief challenged by the writers I study—has helped to shore up our uncritical view of phallocentrism. For example, in an article discussing forms of dressing up, including transvestism, Sandra Gilbert describes male modernists' unwillingness to give up a conservative, hierarchical view of dressing up, while, she argues, female modernists gleefully subvert the patriarchal order in their postwar

---

of Male Feminist Criticism (New York: Routledge, 1990); Diana Fuss, *Inside Out: Lesbian Theories, Gay Theories* (New York: Routledge, 1991); Laura Claridge and Elizabeth Langland, *Out of Bounds: Male Writers and Gender(ed) Criticism* (Amherst: University of Massachusetts Press, 1990).

[16]Carolyn Heilbrun, however, in *Toward a Recognition of Androgyny*, manages example after example of the interpenetration of masculine and feminine qualities in literature. Although Heilbrun clings to a dichotomous view of gender ("androgyny" for her means the simple combining of male and female categories, not the challenging of gender categories themselves), we cannot afford to ignore the gender ambivalence of some patriarchal discourse which her study chronicles. And in her classic article on the "sex/gender system," Gayle Rubin points out that "from the standpoint of nature, men and women are closer to each other than either is to anything else. . . . the idea that men and women are two mutually exclusive categories must arise out of something other than a nonexistent 'natural' opposition. Far from being an expression of natural differences, exclusive gender identity is the suppression of natural similarities. It requires repression. . . . The same social system which oppresses women in its relations of exchange oppresses everyone in its insistence upon a rigid division of personality" (179–80).

fictions of costume. Thus Gilbert's "male modernist" seeks the "consolation of orthodoxy" while her "female modernist" wishes to "restore the primordial chaos of transvestism" (416).[17] Still to be considered, however, is the powerful counterargument to this lopsided claim: men, as well as women, have sought to challenge orthodoxy, have sought the chaos of transvestism. Male artists, far from simply speaking the privileged voice of the dominant culture, have felt themselves crushed by it, made to doubt the legitimacy of their own voices. Eventually a telltale sign of uncertainty enters Gilbert's argument: "Of course I am talking mainly about women," she cautions (416), and mentions in a footnote "a significant nineteenth-century tradition of writing about androgyny, hermaphroditism, transvestism, and even transsexualism" (407).[18]

My book reveals precisely that tradition as forbidding a simple "we versus they," "feminism versus phallocentrism" model of feminist analysis. Five of the authors whose work I examine are male, yet all six eschew the "consolations of orthodoxy" in favor of a radically rewritten tale of gender and hierarchy. Indeed the inclusion of one woman writer among the six serves to demonstrate that the gender of modernist artists in the tradition of dandyism no longer affords a useful basis for distinguishing between them as artists. Cather's early cross-dressing and adoption of a male pseudonym, or her later adoption of a male persona such as St. Peter or Jim Burden, tell the "female" half of the story to which a male such as Nabokov contributes when he seeks his artistic roots in an "Abyssinian maid" or identifies the very texture of his fictional world as female. Two genders in changing relation rather than fixed opposition: such is dandyism's shape. Within "patriarchal" thought itself, all six of these writers work in the name of Alcibiades, playing ends against the middle, teasing threatening metamorphoses of gender from their charming, elegant, elusive characters.

[17]Gubar writes, e.g., "the asymmetrical status accorded men and women in our culture is provocatively illuminated by the different attitudes we inherit toward cross-dressing in the two sexes" (483). She then classifies the goals of cross-dressing as clearly different for men and women. I would argue that some male artists experiment with women's clothing for reasons similar to those of women artists when they adopt men's dress. And just as Gubar's female writers adopt male narrators, so male writers adopt female narrators. "Patriarchal culture" has not yet successfully sorted artists into two distinct groups.

[18]Such polarization along gender lines has infused the feminist critique. For example, Smith-Rosenberg, echoing Gilbert and Gubar, refers to the "male sexual discourse which had begun in the nineteenth century precisely to defend gender conventions" (289).

Discussions of polarized, warring gender tribes imply gender as fixity: one is male or female, and therefore one has certain attitudes about, for example, cross-dressing and dressing up. I must ask instead *how* gender relations are created over time, never assuming that gender distinctions are simple, fixed, and wholly divisive. When Susan Gubar correctly characterizes Gertrude Stein as one who claimed "the right of self-creation with great wit and relish" and "evaded the gender categories that obsessed so many of her contemporaries" (495), her description applies to modernists of both sexes, Gautier, Barbey, Baudelaire, Cather, Stevens, and Nabokov among them. Writers "on the divide" are those who manage to escape, by the energies of genius, the prison of dichotomous gender. They are able to reveal the authority of patriarchal culture as neither monolith nor mirage, but a cultural construction like any other: contingent, riddled with inconsistency, existing in complex relation to its surroundings rather than simply ruling over them.

But how can men write beyond patriarchy if they are part of it? Here two notions apply. First, women as well as men are implicated in patriarchy, live within its linguistic forms. If Gilbert and Gubar's female modernists can escape the traces, find a language of words and clothing and gesture edging beyond the dominant discourse, so can male modernists. The force of my study, taken as a whole, indicates that one possible "Archimedes' Point" for feminist critics (Jehlen 576), a position from which to survey the culture, can exist within avant-garde art, whatever the gender of the artist. Indeed, that gender is often quite ambiguous. Second, most men cannot write beyond patriarchy, but some gifted artists can, those who deliberately seek the new. When they write beyond patriarchy—which is to say they display patriarchy's fragmentation, its holes and contradictions, its concatenated nature—they often do so unconsciously, inadvertently. I attempt to find them out as they found themselves out, within the dandy's mirror of their fictions. Shoshana Felman asks, "How can one speak from the place of the Other? How can the woman be thought about outside of the Masculine/Feminine framework, *other* than as opposed to man, without being subordinated to a primordial masculine model? . . . In other words, how can thought break away from the logic of polar oppositions?" (4). One answer is to look at both male and female artists who have been "other" by virtue of both their gender and their identity as artists within nineteenth- and twentieth-century bourgeois culture. Since female artists (always) and male artists (often) have had to question the same "primordial masculine model," male and female artists have on occasion adopted similar strategies, their responses to the same system of oppression serving to blur the line between them.[19]

AN ARCHAEOLOGY OF WOMEN

Literary critics who discuss a phallocentric cultural norm pitting men against women implicitly take man as the measure. Women are the way they are because men have controlled things. Even when women have created their own tradition, they have done so in reaction to or despite "phallogocentrism." I argue for a different model in literary criticism, one necessitating what I call an "archaeology of women." In the writers I treat, the vast shapes and delicate shards of the woman's world, *mundus muliebris*, can be made visible—if one knows where to look. This is a case of neither the woman behind the throne of male creativity nor a further polarization of gender. Such an archaeological search reveals, instead, that for a special group of artists who were willing to "feminize" their art because they saw their own gender as contingent, the reflexivity (male as female, female as male) rather than the dichotomy of gender became apparent. Cixous has designated such a notion of gender "the other bisexuality":

> To admit that writing is precisely working (in) the inbetween, inspecting the process of the same and of the other without which nothing can live, undo-

[19]I simply do not accept the scholarship which finds that male artists write freely and unselfconsciously while women artists have had to create themselves as writers before taking pen in hand. Jehlen, for example, analyzes women writers' need to "create their creativity," to construct "an enabling relationship with a language that of itself would deny them the ability to use it creatively" (583). She adds, "Since men (on the contrary) can assume a natural capacity for creation, they begin there" (583). Anyone who believes in a masculine assumption of a "natural capacity for creation" should read Baudelaire's journals, to name an example close at hand. In fact, almost the opposite might be argued: it is precisely in male fear of women's creative capacity that male writers have had to create themselves before putting pen to paper.

As I outline in this Introduction, although I disagree with some of his premises and conclusions, I believe that Frank Lentricchia (*Ariel and the Police*) has correctly pointed out the effects of something called patriarchy upon male as well as female writers. Insofar as male artists have had a new vision, they have often found themselves writing against the grain of their culture, unsure of who they are because their new vocabulary and vision remove them from comfortable self-definition. Unlike Lentricchia, I do not join with capitalist society in devaluing the feminine as a force in the creation of literature. Once again, my position does not preclude the recognition of the silencing of women artists, such as Tillie Olsen eloquently chronicles in *Silences*. It only recognizes that both male and female artists have suffered within repressive cultures.

ing the work of death—to admit this is first to want the two, as well as both, the ensemble of one and the other, not fixed in sequence of struggle and expulsion or some other form of death but infinitely dynamized by an incessant process of exchange from one subject to an other.   (883)

I label the tendency of modern artists who seek themselves to inhabit female structures "the feminization of art," but I mean this phrase to be read and then read beyond.[20] For when male artists seek the female—however awkwardly, tentatively—they begin to form the analogies that transform the very dichotomization of gender which they have earlier assumed.

The notion of the feminization of a literary text can be a troubling one for a variety of reasons, beginning with the objection that such feminization necessarily reasserts male power. To intrude on the woman's world, to arrogate female forms to male creation, is to retrace a sadly familiar trajectory. This objection I address specifically and repeatedly in the chapters that follow, for it describes an act of possession with which dandy-artists do indeed begin. Barbey, for example, shamelessly appropriates women to his creative needs (as he does men). Yet these six artists move beyond the objectification and possession of the female. As products of their culture, they engage in the "taking" of the female. As artists who accomplish the impossible—the long view beyond established culture—the taking of the female is not their way. Instead, they radically question male domination. This is the kind of reservation best dealt with not by *pronunciamento* but by a careful look at the evidence: specific artists, particular works of art, individual acts of appropriation. Such is the work of the following chapters.

But there is another kind of reservation which can take a relatively unsophisticated form: simple resistance to the idea that any male artist could possibly *want* to feminize his own work. I argue that male artists have wanted to do just that. This reservation, in its more sophisticated form, is symptomatic of a type of misogyny. Frank Lentricchia, in *Ariel and the Police*, presents a clear case of it: "Modernist poetics in Stevens is a feminization of the literary life motivated by capitalist values and, at the same time, a struggle to overcome this feminization which (in our culture) is more or less equivalent to the trivialization of literature and the literary impulse" (146).

Feminization is, by the fiat of cultural definition, failure. Stevens at-

---

[20]I mean it not as Ann Douglas does, as a weakening or sentimentalizing process, but instead as a process that enabled American modernist artists to avoid precisely the pitfalls Douglas convincingly describes.

tempts to "recover poetic self-respect, whose name was necessarily phallic, from poetic self-trivialization whose various names were 'Keats,' 'feminin-ity,' 'Christianity,' and 'ideality'" (Lentricchia 163). According to Lentric-chia, for an artist to feminize his art is to participate in his own humiliation as artist and in the weakening of culture in general. This is a perdurable form of misogyny because the reasons for labeling feminization as degra-dation can differ from critic to critic. For example, Ann Douglas, in *The Feminization of American Culture*, argues that feminization means senti-mentality and lies, the craven reaction of women (and some men) to a cul-ture that has marginalized them. For Douglas feminization marks the fall into slavish mass consumerism from a high-minded Calvinist heritage.[21]

For Lentricchia, who not coincidentally judges Douglas's book as "a major and (to me) persuasive account of the subject of her title" (252), the terms are different but the result, the devaluation of the feminine, is the same. While Lentricchia at first appears to criticize the capitalist culture that trivializes its male artists and urges them to be "real" men, getting and spending, he soon turns to his own version of misogyny, casting his dis-cussion in aesthetic terms. Where Douglas pits feminization against a Pu-ritan ideal, he pits feminization against a realist standard. He anatomizes Stevens's aestheticism, labels it feminine—that is, interiorized, passive, re-pressed, yearning—and blasts Stevens for caving into commodity fetish-ism as both a way of life (his possession of fine carpets) and a way of poetry (his possession of experience in fine poetic images). Lentricchia appears not to have considered that without such poetic images, without his sup-posedly wrong-headed and degraded aestheticist views, a Stevens still worthy of being read and endlessly explicated would not exist. He wants a Stevens who would drop his social elitism and champagne tastes, a Ste-

---

[21]Since Douglas's book appeared in 1977, several important studies in the feminization of American culture have appeared: Nina Baym, *Woman's Fiction: A Guide to Novels by and about Women, 1820–1870* (Ithaca: Cornell University Press, 1978); Mary Kelley, *Private Woman, Public Stage: Literary Domesticity in Nineteenth-Century America* (New York: Ox-ford University Press, 1984); Jane Tompkins, *Sensational Designs: The Cultural Work of Fic-tion, 1790–1860* (New York: Oxford University Press, 1985); Susan K. Harris, *Nineteenth-Century American Women's Novels: Interpretive Strategies* (Cambridge, England; New York: Cambridge University Press, 1990); as well as the introductory essays to Rutgers University Press's American Women Writers series and articles appearing in the journal *Legacy*. These and other critical works have deepened our understanding of the widespread dis-semination of nineteenth-century fiction by American women by asking why the works were written, for whom, how, and with what results. The partial answers to these questions reveal a body of literature which can be held up to a variety of critical standards and meth-odologies and found to represent an enriching and constitutive, not a degenerate (as Doug-las and Lentricchia would have it), strain in American culture.

vens more consonant with Lentricchia's own late-century political views. Although he begins by trying to describe what was bothering Stevens, Lentricchia gradually comes to use Stevens to mount an attack on Keatsian femininity in art wherever it may be found.

Lentricchia lapses into the archaic view of the feminine as the fallen. Chronicling Stevens's increasing movement into the female, for example, he describes in *Ariel and the Police* the poet's identification with a woman in the opening lines of "Notes toward a Supreme Fiction":

> At the moment of interiorization, when the speaker feels entered, the gender differentiation of speaker and addressee becomes confused at least and perhaps reversed. . . . Not a phallicizing of his poetic role in the anxious style of his earlier career, but a refusal of the phallic for an image also (to be sure) culturally bestowed but now not received defensively, not now trivialized in macho perspective—an image now empathetically assumed.
>
> Once "she" is *inside*, "I" becomes "we."   (222, emphasis added)

Lentricchia reveals a problem. Stevens seems, from early poetry to late, fascinated by the experiment of imagining himself as a woman. Far from denying Stevens's impulse to feminization, Lentricchia describes it with accuracy and sensitivity. But when it comes time to judge that impulse, Lentricchia is oddly damning. The key word in the quotation above is "inside": Lentricchia despises interiority, and he labels it feminine. Stevens's (feminine) world of imagination is trivial not just because capitalist society says it is, but because Lentricchia himself finds it weak, self-regarding, greedy, idealist, in chains. It is woman herself. In short, Lentricchia faults Stevens for feminizing his art.

In contrast, the writers I study, Stevens included, are, for all their misogyny, also genuine celebrants of the female. So deeply do they revere it that they transform it into their artistic method and into the very texture of their art. If the tableau is at times misogynist, the very weave of the tapestry reveals a profound admiration for women. This combination of feelings about women makes sense once we see that both misogyny and philogyny contribute to a process of questioning the very system that has divided women and men. By exploring the space between the categories of male and female, these dandy-artists ultimately sidestep the mire of misogyny.

SOME WORDS ABOUT STRUCTURE

This book presents two groups: nineteenth-century French writers and twentieth-century Americans who wrote self-consciously in the French tradition. I had a wide choice of French writers in the tradition of dandyism; I chose Barbey and Baudelaire because they explicitly theorize the dandy. I chose them too because, with Gautier, they provide clear examples of the three propelling forces of literary dandyism: metamorphosis, paradox, and analogy.

Gautier, a devotee of Ovid, expanded the received notions of dandyism by putting his images of dandies in metamorphic motion. Dandyism for him moves—among characters, between genders, across landscapes, among genres. Barbey likes to refine that motion into rapidly vibrating, sharply contradictory, even paradoxical positions. His dandies figure forth the truth of self-presentation which relentlessly contests itself, the vibrant stasis of eternally opposed positions. In contrast to Gautier's fluidities, Barbey's distinctions and hierarchical arrangements allow him to play the game of elegantly, obsessively stepping back and forth over the lines. His step across the gender line perhaps best defines his dandyism, for the dandy's special form of beauty—elegance—he characterizes as the feminized "petit sexe" of a masculine beauty.

With Baudelaire, metamorphosis and paradox, the poetics of license and control, join to suggest a third way: analogy. Baudelaire's dandy courts a primordial chaos by an unmaking of the world, a creative loosening of its rigid systems of classification in favor of the finding of resemblances. Like Barbey's "vie en l'air," these analogies are not based on or aspiring to any higher model. The dandy makes his truth as he makes analogies: between his home and his place of exile, between animals and people, between vision and will, between his gender and that of the women on whom he patterns himself and his art.

Metamorphosis, paradox, and analogy all help the dandy step across the divide between France and America. Cather, Stevens, and Nabokov share a view of French as a feminine language, one that provides in their own writing a female space through which they might find their way beyond the patriarchal limitations of their native tongue.[22] But the translation can never be complete: the dandy's journey across the divide of time and space is finally a journey to the divide conceived of as a wide space of cultural possibility.

What do the heirs of the tradition of dandyism do with their riches? They use them, I argue, to solve artistic problems, chief among them the conception of a precisely modern beauty. Cather, for example, searches for a "moral aestheticism," the artist's sensitivity to the finest nuances of ex-

---

[22]English was Nabokov's native literary tongue; he read and wrote English before he did Russian (*SM* 28).

perience and expression which reflects as well her responsibility to the human community. She makes use of nineteenth-century French writers' wresting of gender from two opposing categories to imagine an art that is itself freed from the opposing categories of the ethical and the aesthetic. For her, the French aestheticist power of sensation is feminine, the American moral power of sympathy is masculine, but the two can become analogically related within the effeminate "romance of temperament." In both *The Professor's House* and *My Ántonia*, Cather feminizes a male form, the romance of direct, "manly" action. By imagining such an intertwining of gender and aesthetics and personifying it as the figure of the dandy, Cather creates a new form of beauty.

Stevens has long been labeled a dandy, but usually in order to reduce him to the precious fop of American poetry. I reveal a Stevens who acts upon the dandy's hypothesis of the fictional nature of the self and thus feels free to experiment with his identity. I trace his chosen position outside of two native cultural givens, his gender and his language. Exploring the French and the female, he finds the energy to explode in his macaronic poetry the very notion of two distinct and immutable genders. When he reveals the masculine "figure of the youth as virile poet" claiming the woman's words spoken by the "sister of the minotaur" (*NA* 67), he writes in the finest tradition of dandyism. Male is as female, English is as French, disorder is as order: this, I disclose, is the message from Key West.

Although there have been a few studies of Aleksandr Pushkin's "influence" on Nabokov, Nabokov's relation to Pushkin is far more intense and complex than critics have dared acknowledge. Both Nabokov's translation of Pushkin's *Eugene Onegin* (a verse novel about a Brummellesque dandy) and his commentary on that novel are designed to establish that Nabokov is Pushkin, Pushkin is Nabokov. Believing that to pose is to be, Nabokov the dandy skirts madness. Like Cather and Stevens, he locates a special truth in the French and the female, but he does so because Pushkin did before him. In exploring Pushkin's rewriting of French poetry and in musing on Pushkin's mysterious ancestor, "the Blackamoor of Peter the Great," Nabokov locates the essence of all artistic truth in the decentered, unlocatable: a black woman who drowns, to be resurrected in "not text but texture" (*PF* 44). I demonstrate that throughout Nabokov's fiction, women are visionaries who, moored in reality, see beyond this patterned world to the infinitely patternable words of the modern understanding. They beckon to the rift through which we might escape to a world beyond dichotomous gender, beyond the forms of patriarchy, to the textures of modern beauty.

What I demonstrate in those writers working in the tradition of dandyism in the nineteenth century is a feminization of literary culture. By the twentieth century, this tradition has grown into something else: a certain trivialization of gender. Cather, Stevens, and Nabokov, as the heirs of Gautier, Barbey, and Baudelaire, move their characters freely between genders. The fluid movement of analogy cannot be frozen within the confines of either maleness or femaleness. What Virginia Woolf describes in *Orlando* across time, Cather, Stevens, and Nabokov achieve almost casually, at every moment of their narratives.

All this occurs because of the location of modernism's dandy: on the divide. Cather's "Divide" is the fertile farmland between the Republican and Little Blue rivers in Nebraska (Woodress 35). It is to such a divide, wide and rich, that my title refers. And it is to the elegant chaos of the dandy's mirror world, a floating groundedness, that I now turn.

2

PAROLES HERMAPHRODITES

———————❖———————

GAUTIER'S DANDY

Théophile Gautier (1811–1872) came of age as a Romantic artist not when he fought the battle of *Hernani* in 1830 but when he realized that, by its principles of energy and change, Romanticism required its own transformation. As a member of *le petit cénacle*, a second-generation circle of Romantic artists, Gautier seized on satire as a transforming device. In 1833 he published *Les Jeunes-France: Romans goguenards*, a collection of stories that mock *la vie bohème*, from its fanciful costumes and erotic practices to its artistic productions and pretensions.[1] Among his targets was dandyism, for the phenomenon that had been imported from London some fifteen years earlier had been naturalized in part by the Jeunes-France, young Romantic artists, themselves.[2]

[1] I translate *roman* as "story" or "tale," because these fictions are not novels. In titling the volume *Romans goguenards* (mocking novels), Gautier mockingly inflates their genre; they fall somewhere between *conte* (story) and *roman* (novel).
[2] For histories of dandyism, see Moers, Carassus, and Matoré.

A celebration of the elegance and aloofness of the wealthy English "sporting" gentleman, dandyism does not initially appear a useful form for the French Romantic poet or painter. Yet one aspect of dandyism—its principled rejection of the vulgarity of middle-class life—appealed to Gautier and his circle. For this was the era of Louis-Philippe, and the dandy's antibourgeois posture attracted the artists of the day.[3] Retrospectively, Gautier sees the Jeunes-France as followers of the high priest of the dandies, Lord Byron:

> Nous admirions fort les prouesses du jeune lord [Byron] et ses bacchanales nocturnes dans l'abbaye de Newstead. . . . Ces banquets où circulait, pleine d'une sombre liqueur, une coupe plus blanche que l'ivoire, effleurée par des lèvres de rose avec un léger sentiment d'effroi nous semblaient la suprême expression du dandysme, par l'absolue indifférence pour ce qui cause l'épouvante du genre humain.   (*Histoire du Romantisme* 50)

> We strongly admired the prowess of the young lord [Byron] and his nocturnal bacchanals in the abbey of Newstead. . . . Those banquets where circulated, full of a somber liquid, a chalice whiter than ivory, and touched by rosy lips with a slight feeling of fear, seemed to us the supreme expression of dandyism, by the absolute indifference to what causes fear in the human species.

In *Mademoiselle de Maupin*, Gautier's novel of 1835, he radically expands the notion of the dandy as merely a stylishly dressed, wealthy, and blasé man. Gautier begins with dandyism as a social pose and ends with a dandyism so aestheticized that it can be expressed only in works of art. He begins with the dandy as character—and here the cavalier d'Albert, that snob, aesthete, fop, comes to mind—but he leads us to enlarge our view of dandyism by presenting us with d'Albert's mirror image, Madeleine, who shares with d'Albert the dandy's mask. Indeed, such an enlargement is the subject of my book as a whole, for when Gautier imagines a woman with the characteristics of a dandy, or when he imagines a dandy as a man possessing the characteristics of a woman, he suggests a process in which the other five writers I examine also engage, with all the intensity of their genius. It is a process of feminizing art in order to challenge the very distinctions commonly made between male and female.

Gautier's dandyism grows beyond its embodiment in both sexes: he presents us with a dandyism not just of character but of novelistic texture itself. *Mademoiselle de Maupin* is a novel of and about metamorphosis; its

---

[3]For a still valid analysis of the relation between dandyism and the Jeunes-France, see Creed, especially the chapter "Le dandysme transplanté" (7–18). She further discusses Gautier and his circle in "Le costume" (60–80).

issues are those of structure and flux. In metamorphosis we may seek the etiology of that mythical creature, the dandy, the figure who has transformed himself. Gautier leads us to look beyond even metamorphic texture, to seek the dandy in an allegory of aesthetic belief. Gautier's dandy impersonates the Parnassian aesthetic credo as he takes his place in a modernist analogical universe: historical figure, fictional character, narrative technique, aesthetic belief all reveal one another, once the dandy appears to our eyes as the figure in the carpet. Because dandies are always fictional (both in books and on the avenue, where they create the fiction of themselves), they present special problems for critics. Stalking the dandy, we find him hovering between myth and history, among the incidents and coincidences of plot, the hazes and particularities of character, the echoes of allusion.

Gautier's story "Celle-ci et celle-là" ("This One and That One," included in the *Jeunes-France* collection of 1833) can provide us with a map of the at first bewildering landscape of *Mademoiselle de Maupin*. It locates us in the dandy's world; it asks us to pay special attention to narrative technique; and it instructs us in the art of reading allegory. Rodolphe, the dandy-hero of the tale, who consults the mirror as his first act of the day, passes the time in leisured ennui. Although he is a poet, he appears never to write, and his most blissful hours are those in which he and his friend Albert design an especially enchanting *gilet* (waistcoat). Rodolphe seeks a grand passion; but to his credit as a dandy it is "non une passion épicière et bourgeoise, mais une passion d'artiste, une passion volcanique et échevelée" (*JF* 98; not a shopkeeper's or a bourgeois's passion, but an artist's passion, a volcanic and frenzied passion); furthermore he wants it primarily "pour compléter sa tournure, et le poser dans le monde sur un pied convenable" (*JE* 98; in order to complete his image and present him to the world on a proper footing). The plot of the story grows out of Rodolphe's vain and shallow character: he finds the woman of his dreams, but in reality she cannot conform to the ideal. The lady, "celle-là" or Madame de M***, is willing, but Rodolphe fails repeatedly to raise the affair to a level of drama commensurate with his idealized version of himself. At last his pretty maidservant-mistress Mariette, "celle-ci," rebels, demanding that he replace his cold and artificial lover with her own honest and sweetly natural self. Rodolphe accepts her happy ending.

This is the tale of a dandy who gives up falsity to become a man without masks, loved for himself and capable of loving others. Yet, as the title announces, the story has another point to make, one about categories and relations between them. Gautier presents three principal sets of relations—

man over woman, human over animal, master over servant—in order to upset them. These hierarchical relations recognized, the story then offers itself in three versions: Rodolphe's interpretation of the events diverges utterly from the narrator's and ours. Our thick hero learns that his power over women is superficial and that a good woman will exercise a beneficial power over him. Animals—Rodolphe's cats appear frequently, especially when he is discouraged or sad—instruct him in the evil artificialities of "society." Likewise, Mariette teaches him that social hypocrisy blinds people to true virtue and true love. The narrator, however, undercuts each of these lessons, mocking the didacticism in art which Gautier will soon attack head-on in the preface to *Mademoiselle de Maupin*. By his unrelenting tone of ridicule, the narrator prevents us from believing in the possibility of Rodolphe's psychological or moral growth. From the narrator's cynical point of view, Rodolphe has merely traded one falsity (social power) for another ("natural" love). By the story's end Rodolphe, soon to become, we suspect, a dull husband, is no longer much of a dandy; the narrator, who has taken hold of our values and given them a sharp twist, *is*. He is particularly so because we have nothing but his tone upon which to pin our denunciation of Rodolphe. The narrator is a dandy in his masks—superior to Rodolphe certainly, but superior to the very act of telling the tale, given to satiric asides, parody, preaching, always with his elbow in our ribs. The narrator's persona is one of manic wit, defying us to take anything in the story seriously, especially and paradoxically defiance itself. The pose, then, is one of distance, impertinence, world-weary cynicism.

For the reader, the choice between Rodolphe's naiveté (*ci*) and the narrator's cynicism (*là*) seems a thematic red herring. Rather than a narrative that brings some truisms home, "Celle-ci and celle-là" presents as its uncomfortable burden *the necessity of questioning the very distinctions we make between ci and là, whatever the issue*. Gautier scrutinizes relations in general, particularly those that clearly involve power. If one should love the humble servant rather than the shallow society woman, perhaps it is equally true that one should love the humble cats rather than the humble servant. After all, Rodolphe often strokes his favorite (male) cat and Mariette simultaneously. And if one can entertain the notion of loving "celle-ci" rather than "celle-là" or both of them equally, perhaps Rodolphe should love his intimate friend Albert rather than his servant or his cats. If this were to come to pass, perhaps he could love women, cats, and men at once, and go beyond the bounds not just of propriety and morality but of control itself. The story's pat conclusion denies itself, leaving us with the faint but echoing promise of anarchy: personal, social, universal.

Added to the tale, as if to stem the tide of disorder, is a second ending, an allegorical interpretation of its characters and events: "Il y a un mythe très-profond sous cette enveloppe frivole: au cas que vous ne vous en soyez pas aperçu, je vais vous l'expliquer tout au long" (*JF* 199; There is a very profound myth underneath this frivolous envelope: in case you haven't noticed it, I will explain it to you at length). Here Gautier plays with the idea of personifying aesthetic ideas:

> Madame de M*** représente la poésie classique, belle et froide, brillante et fausse, semblable en tout aux statues antiques. . . . Mariette, c'est la vraie poésie, la poésie sans corset et sans fard, la muse bonne fille qui convient à l'artiste . . . qui vit de la vie humaine, etc. (*JF* 199)

> Madame de M*** represents classical poetry, beautiful and cold, brilliant and false, similar in all respects to ancient statues. . . . Mariette is true poetry, poetry without a corset and without makeup, the well-behaved muse appropriate to the artist . . . poetry that lives on human life, etc.

While the narrator here nonchalantly offers us some near-nonsense (what *is* poetry that "vit de la vie humaine"?), he is also rehearsing a set of allegorical relations that extend throughout the tale: cold statue/warm flesh, classical/romantic. Gautier mocks aesthetic allegory in this "roman goguenard" but finds it important enough to repeat, on a grander scale, in *Mademoiselle de Maupin*. In the novel as in the story, Gautier disembodies the dandy as he stands in his favorite position, contemplating his mirror image. He examines category and relation, especially those of gender. Erotic interest vivifies aesthetic statement. Thus Gautier forms the complex contours of modernism's dandy: figure, texture, aesthetic creed.

"UN AIR DAMOISEAU": CROSSING THE GENDER LINE

Critics have analyzed at length the many doublings, mirrorings, echoes, and masks of *Mademoiselle de Maupin*.[4] The novel is indeed a vast *mise en*

---

[4]The critical literature on the subject is well developed but limited; it does not address the topic of d'Albert and Madeleine as the masked and mirrored dandy, nor does it analyze the novel's style and rhetoric as textual dandyism.

For detailed surveys of the novel's masks and mirrors, see, for example, Bouchard and Savalle.

Albouy, in an extremely useful article, links the novel's sexual doubling to aesthetic issues, arguing that Madeleine's "false androgyny" reveals Gautier's willingness to dwell in

abyme; all characters operate within a system of mirrors. Among these
mirrors, that of the dandy—the glass before which he poses, first to create
and then to judge himself—reflects the greatest urgency. There he expects
to see both self and not-self; only the purest paradox of identity will suffice. In *Mademoiselle de Maupin*, Gautier places before the dandy's mirror
the cavalier d'Albert. We watch d'Albert scrutinizing his image, finding it
perhaps a bit too effeminate, certainly not beautiful enough, obviously the
most interesting image in the wide world. It is only gradually that Gautier
lets us see the image staring back at him: that of Madeleine. Like Rodolphe, who fails as a dandy from the first paragraph of his tale, when he
looks into his mirror "pour se constater à lui-même qu'il n'était pas un
autre" (*JF* 96; to prove to himself that he was not someone else), d'Albert
seems to fall short of some unspecified standard. Like Rodolphe, d'Albert
cannot accept the paradox of the mask in which *je* is always *un autre*; Madeleine thrives upon it. D'Albert is finally an egotist and an aesthete, but
he lacks power, will, superiority, grace—the attributes which Madeleine
certainly possesses. Yet, without d'Albert's yearnings and disquisitions,
without his concentrated stare into the glass, Madeleine is but an amusing
lady swashbuckler. Let us begin, as Gautier means us to, with d'Albert's
dandyism, and then seek its translation in Madeleine. Just as French dandies translate the English code of dandyism into their native tongue, creating a language neither French nor English ("les happy few," "le sportsman," "le fashionable," etc.), so Gautier translates a male into a female
figure, seeking a third way for the dandy. It is the act of translation, not the
"arrival" at the female, which interests Gautier. His dandyism begins in
the space between d'Albert and Madeleine, between male and female; it is
from the first neither *celle-ci* nor *celle-là*, but instead a challenge to polarized thinking.

Gautier withholds his title character and opens the novel with an epistolary self-portrait of the cavalier d'Albert. D'Albert moves strangely in
and out of focus as a dandy. Certainly his daily life would qualify him for
the role; wholly free of economic pressures, his daily task appears to be the

ambiguity and to entertain opposing notions of aesthetic idealism and Parnassian materi-
alism. Lloyd ("Speculum Amantis," 86–87) joins Albouy in questioning earlier interpre-
tations of the novel as "mimetically reproducing the life of an actual individual," corroborating my view that the dandy in literature must be read allegorically. Lloyd's focus on the
novel as a "web of cracks," a "*mise en abyme*" that breaks down the barriers between the
real and the artificial, supports both her view of the novel's "duplicity" and my notion of
dandyism as paradoxical in nature.

graceful conquering of empty hours. He suffers from ennui, takes pains with his costume and coiffure even though he is aware that people find him effeminate:

> mes cheveux étaient bouclés et lustrés avec plus de soin qu'il ne convenait; que cela, joint à ma figure imberbe, me donnait un air damoiseau on ne peut plus ridicule . . . je ressemblais plus à un comédien qu'à un homme.
>
> (*MM* 112)
>
> my hair was curled and shined with more care than was seemly; and that, together with my beardless face, gave me the most ridiculous air of a young pageboy. . . . I resembled more an actor than a man.

An actor more than a man, d'Albert admits to his correspondent Silvio what he would never, as a dandy, admit publicly—that he desires a mistress. The publicly self-satisfied fop is privately the insecure male: "Une maîtresse pour moi, c'est la robe virile pour un jeune Romain" (*MM* 79; A mistress for me is as the virile toga for a young Roman). Yet as a dandy he does not seek out or encourage women, because they fall short of his vision of pure beauty. Furthermore, he fears that his own lack of beauty and his limited wealth preclude an ideal love affair. Although he may appear to possess a dandy's *froideur*—"j'ai la réputation d'un jeune homme tranquille et froid, peu sensible aux femmes et indifférent aux choses de son âge" (*MM* 76–77; I have the reputation of being a cold and tranquil young man, little interested in women and indifferent to the trappings of his age)—in fact his coldness hides from the world a richly smoldering emotional life.

Slowly we take our bearings in d'Albert's verbiage. Gautier gives us enough clues to enable us to identify d'Albert: he is dandylike in his vanity, foppishness, lethargy, nonchalance, and ennui. Short of living in Paris, he is a dandy on the pattern of the comte d'Orsay; a lesser, provincial version, perhaps, but a dandy nonetheless. Yet Gautier floods us with much more information about his character than the type seems to require. Nothing that we learn about d'Albert disqualifies him as a dandy; rather, it complicates and deepens the very concept of dandyism. Gautier re-creates through d'Albert the psychological history which would lead a man to join the ranks of the dandy-brotherhood. As Gautier writes a novel, he creates a mythic being: the dandy who is also aesthete and would-be artist. D'Albert's self-appointed task, throughout the novel, is to find and possess the ideal mistress, but he serves as well Gautier's *programme*, to claim the dandy as a type of the modern aesthete. The model is no longer to be the

British sporting gentleman, shallowly self-satisfied, but the prisoner of his
own consciousness, the martyr of his own complicated sensibility. Chief
among the dandy's complications are those of gender. Gautier tags the
gender of his dandy-aesthete with a question mark, and then distributes
between d'Albert and Madeleine his meditations upon that very act. Thus
in Gautier begins the artist's argument with himself on the subject of
gender, an argument that is to characterize the literature of dandyism
throughout the nineteenth century.

Although d'Albert rails against the solitude and ennui that trap him in
himself, he lacks neither the beauty nor the funds necessary for approaching women. Instead, d'Albert describes himself as simply estranged from
society in general, "une goutte d'huile dans un verre d'eau" (*MM* 122; a
drop of oil in a glass of water), or as slowly hardening, "la volupté même
. . . ce feu dévorant qui fond les rochers et les métaux de l'âme . . . n'a jamais pu me dompter ou m'attendrir" (*MM* 122; sensual delight, even . . .
that devouring fire that melts the rocks and metals of the soul, . . . never
could subdue me nor soften me). Although women initially promise a focus outside himself, he cannot melt in their presence because he really
wishes to borrow or, better, to possess their beauty for his own. He begins
by claiming to seek an ideal of female beauty, but the movement toward
another is, in his mind, always one in which he will engulf the other, take
on her beauty, rather than merge with her:

> J'ai aimé les armes, les chevaux et les femmes: les armes, pour remplacer les
> nerfs que je n'avais pas; les chevaux, pour me servir d'ailes; les femmes, pour
> posséder au moins dans quelqu'une la beauté qui me manquait à moi-
> même.   (*MM* 166–67)

> I loved arms, horses, and women: arms, for replacing the nerve I did not
> have; horses, for giving me wings; women, in order to possess in at least one
> of them the beauty that was lacking in myself.

Albert perceives himself, like a woman, to lack nerve. He loves women because he can, by possessing them, hope to take on their beauty. The statement presents a characteristic blend of vanity and defensiveness; in it d'Albert imagines himself swift, sure, and beautiful, but the accent falls on the
wish to repair deficiencies rather than the image of power. What this statement lacks, to render it the wholly characteristic statement of a dandy, is
impertinence. While it insults women by placing them on a par with animals and objects, d'Albert probably means it as complimentary. A dandy's
impertinence must be at least wielded as a weapon, if not received as a
blow.

From the inability to possess a mistress because he wants in some sense to incorporate female qualities, it is but a brief step to the dandy's preference for women depicted in art rather than possessed in the flesh:

> je me suis rejeté sur les tableaux et les statues;—ce qui, après tout, est une assez pitoyable ressource quand on a des sens aussi allumés que les miens. Cependant il y a quelque chose de grand et de beau à aimer une statue, c'est que l'amour est parfaitement désintéressé, qu'on n'a à craindre ni la satiété ni le dégoût de la victoire, et qu'on ne peut espérer raisonnablement un second prodige pareil à l'histoire de Pygmalion.   (*MM* 167)

> I fell back on paintings and statues;—which, after all, is a relatively pitiful resource when one has senses as inflamed as mine. However, there is something grand and beautiful in loving a statue, in that the love is perfectly disinterested, in that one need fear neither the satiety nor the disgust of conquest, in that one may not reasonably hope for a second wonder equal to the story of Pygmalion.

For the dandy, physical love is vulgar and ugly. Erotic victory disgusts him, because it means losing a vital, composed isolation. If the dandy is cold and pure, why not "mate" with his own kind: a statue. The statue will not metamorphose into life, because the dandy's imperturbability freezes all movement. Yet a certain kind of change does occur. When *volupté* does not melt him, when he cannot find a living woman who will complete his own beauty and prove herself worthy of the possessing, he can claim these failings as victories, seek only "l'amour désintéressé" (disinterested love), and cultivate his sangfroid. Such is the maneuver of the dandy, who traditionally lives out his day in the wholly male society of club, restaurant, and private gambling circle. Women are publicly ignored; the dandy's womanizing occurs with the utmost discretion. A real woman is someone to hide, and Gautier tells us why this is so. As a dandy, d'Albert seeks a center within himself, turning away from life and toward art, cultivating internally his darker self, externally a posture of superiority and disdain.

D'Albert relentlessly pursues love, even as, dandylike, he denies its place in his life. While Gautier carefully displays the vanity involved in this desire, its centrality to the plot and the vast number of pages dedicated to its exploration throw it into a kind of prominence that appears to belie the dandy's asexual pose. D'Albert even goes so far as to take the second-best Rosette as a mistress and to leave society for the pleasures of her company alone. For all his egotism, he looks longingly outward and upward, seeking the incarnation of his vision of perfect beauty. He never ceases to pursue that vision, even when he half believes Madeleine to be a man. Gautier appears to close d'Albert out of the kingdom of the dandies, by virtue of his most unseemly lust for beauty.

We gradually recognize, on the contrary, that d'Albert's yearning for Madeleine strengthens his image as a dandy. He sees in her the embodiment of his vision of beauty because she is his mirror image. Not merely Echo to his Narcissus, Madeleine complements d'Albert's strengths and reverses his weaknesses. The novel demands that we consider the two characters together, as versions of each other. The figure of the dandy multiplies and blurs.

The similarities between the two characters begin with the very substance of the novel: they write the letters of which it is primarily constructed. Furthermore, the recipients of their letters, Graciosa and Silvio, are doubles. Both d'Albert and Madeleine dislike social hypocrisy and the social institutions of courtship and marriage followed inevitably by adultery. Both vow to travel in search of a better kind of love. They share a Platonic view of love, although d'Albert has only imperfectly grasped Diotima's wisdom and Madeleine has emphasized perhaps too heavily the moral element in love. Both stage events and view their lives in dramatic terms. Both succumb to Rosette's sexual charms while denying the possibility of loving and living with her on into the future. D'Albert sees in Madeleine "[l]a beauté de l'ange, la force du tigre, et les ailes de l'aigle" (*MM* 166; the beauty of an angel, the force of a tiger, and the wings of an eagle); in possessing her, d'Albert would be able to claim for himself her strength, nerve, birdlike speed, and beauty.

Madeleine's undeniable personal beauty, her power and elegance in sword fighting, her mask, and her disdain for vulgar, hypocritical men make her, as well, a dandy. Her very being contradicts but completes d'Albert: he searches for beauty, she for truth. She glories in power, he flounders in sensibility. He wishes to become, like Tiresias, a woman, but the desire is shallow and fleeting. Madeleine's wish to "become" a man for the purpose of educating herself in the ways of love spurs her to cross-dress and set in motion the plot of her own life. Her search for a man worthy of her life and her continual disappointment (not to mention her frequent attempts to disentangle herself from the webs of others' lustful attractions to her) lead her not into despair, but into a sense of increasing distance from the erotic fray. Her penultimate act in the novel is to lose her virginity, but her ultimate act is to disappear. After dividing a night of love between Rosette and d'Albert, she leaves forever, preventing erotic victory from degenerating into the futility of repetition, the vulgarity of satiety.

Both Madeleine's gender and her masquerade make her defensive, but she transforms that defensiveness into superiority, just as dandies on the avenue transform lack of exalted social standing, imperfect beauty, and laziness into a dramatic persona which either hides these failings or claims them as victories. Madeleine's defensive duel with Alcibiades and her continued dueling thereafter are emblematic of her ability to turn threats against her person and her persona into triumph. Such a triumph, and not erotic triumph, is the dandy's goal, even if he duels with pointed words more often than with swords. Not that Madeleine lacks the dandy's verbal acuity. Her speech, spilling over with double entendres and verbal feints, enables her to evade the erotic clutches of those who believe her to be male and those who know her to be female.

Madeleine arrives in d'Albert's life not to fulfill his desire but to echo it. She impersonates the dandy's desire because she cannot or will not find a resting place in any human breast. Her ambiguous gender and her bisexuality suggest that her needs are too great for social fulfillment: the social taboos that cluster about her character represent the radical disjunction of personal needs and social fulfillment. Like the dandy's strolling, her picaresque story will not admit of conclusion. Both accept the impossibility of closure. Embodying a total, voluptuous yearning, a sinking into the self treasured for its very masochistic intensity, Madeleine gives the lovelorn Rosette a dandy's counsel:

> Hélas . . . la meilleure partie de nous est celle qui reste en nous, et que nous ne pouvons produire.—Les poètes sont ainsi.—Leur plus beau poème est celui qu'ils n'ont pas écrit.   (*MM* 180)

> Alas . . . the best part of us is that which remains in us, and that we cannot produce.—Poets are thus.—Their most beautiful poem is the one they have not written.

Both love and creation must be a yearning toward the impossible, an accepted, even cherished, sterility. The other alternative for the dandy in the throes of love or creative yearning is the attraction to the dark realm, here suggested by homoeroticism, a strand taken up several decades later by the dandy's descendants, the decadents. Decadent love and creation, by virtue of their twisted tableaux of dangerous possibilities, act as an antidote to society's sentimental farce of vulgar sexual and pseudoartistic activities.

Madeleine's transvestism allows Gautier to express his view of dandyism as revolutionary. After dressing as a man in a self-initiated rite de passage, Madeleine sees the world turned, not upside down, but back to front.[5]

---

[5]For a useful anthropological account of the phenomenon of "the world turned upside down," see Babcock, especially the introduction (13–36), and Davis (147–90).

What is usually hidden from women during courtship—men sniggering at the very women they court—takes its place on the stage of her drama; backstage all the temporarily eclipsed forms of sentimentality and polite sexual posturing proceed without director or audience. Madeleine sees the debased side of men, but instead of sharpening her skills in choosing a good man for a husband (her initial plan) she learns that husbands and marriage are, for her, impossible. Indeed, her female identity itself is now called into question:

> j'étais un homme, ou du moins j'en avais l'apparence: la jeune fille était morte. . . . il me sembla que je n'étais plus moi, mais un autre, et je me souvenais de mes actions anciennes comme des actions d'une personne étrangère auxquelles j'aurais assisté, ou comme du début d'un roman dont je n'aurais pas achevé la lecture. (*MM* 238)

> I was a man, or, at least, I had the appearance of a man: the young girl was dead. . . . it seemed to me that I was no longer myself, but someone else, and I remembered my former actions as a stranger's actions that I'd witnessed, or like the beginning of a novel I'd yet to finish reading.

If rites de passage are intended as experiences of monstrosity, in which the initiate learns to see, understand, and value the structures of society, this rite de passage has failed.[6] Instead, Gautier has created a figure who, in finding herself constitutionally unable to reenter the categories of gender, will call those categories themselves into question. A dandy in privilege, beauty, will, superiority, aloofness, Madeleine, we begin to recognize, is perhaps more a dandy for her paradoxical gender status: a woman dressing as a man who feels herself to be neither male nor female. She achieves this state first by forgetting for long periods of time that she is female:

> j'oubliais insensiblement que j'étais femme;—mon déguisement me semblait mon habit naturel . . . je ne songeais plus que je n'étais au bout du compte qu'une petite évaporée qui s'était fait une épée de son aiguille. (*MM* 310)

> I forgot imperceptibly that I was a woman;—my disguise seemed to me my natural dress. . . . I no longer thought that I was, all things considered, only a little scatterbrain who'd made a sword of her needle.

She no longer believes herself to be a "petite évaporée," a bit of nothingness, but she chooses to be a nobody, pure incognito, if personhood must involve gender.

---

[6]For a discussion of rites de passage and their importance in conserving cultural values, see Turner.

And it is this last claim which Gautier explores with special care. First, he offers us d'Albert, a dandy manqué, an effeminate male who wishes to possess feminine Beauty. Next, he displays d'Albert's double, a woman whose mask of superiority and powers of self-creation reveal her as a dandy not so manqué. Then Gautier has Madeleine question the concept of gender. While d'Albert is "un peu éffeminé" (a little effeminate), Madeleine/Théodore de Seranne's effeminate appearance hides, paradoxically, a person who is no longer, by "her" own account, either male or female: "*Je ne suis plus une femme, mais je ne suis pas encore un homme*" (*MM* 319, emphasis added; I am no longer a woman, but I am not yet a man). Madeleine has learned what every dandy of my study announces: gender is a creation of self-presentation and social attribution, not of god-given or genetically fixed biological "fact."[7]

Finding herself outside the categories of gender, Madeleine responds sexually to both men and women, but her marginal position causes her always to hold back, to assess, to judge. She becomes the spectator of her own sexual experience, the reader of the novel that is her life. She is simultaneously novelist and critic, consciousness and self-consciousness, hedonist and strict moralist. She may be physically expansive, but she must always control herself. Gautier, in creating Madeleine's problematical gender, imagines not just a sexual, but an aesthetic, stance toward the world. Cool without and volcanic within, coldly judgmental and open to sense impression, the double being of the dandy-aesthete here is born in an extended sexual conceit which will serve Gautier, Barbey, and Baudelaire equally well.

From the point at which she recognizes the strange status of her gender, Madeleine's letters read as a dandy's daybook. She gives up her plan to seek a good man, recognizing that the fulfillment of her desire is impossible. She raises this understanding to a law of human nature: "c'est le propre des plans que l'on a de n'être point exécutés, et c'est là que paraissent principalement la fragilité de la volonté et le pur néant de l'homme" (*MM* 358; it is the nature of the plans that one makes not to be carried out, and it is therein that appears chiefly the fragility of the will and the pure nothingness of man). The dandy may have a daily routine, but never a plan. The dandy's will may be strong, but directed inward; the kingdom of the self may perhaps be ruled, but the outer world of nature and public affairs, symbolized by the mob, never. Language must be divorced from emotion,

---

[7]I explore this idea more fully in following chapters; I allude here to an argument which I base on the work of Kessler and McKenna. See, too, my Introduction.

once hope of realizing desire is abandoned; Madeleine notes that her epigrams "brillaient par un mérite d'exactitude" (*MM* 360; shone with the
merit of exactitude) because her invective, in contrast to that of men, is un-
mixed with love.

Mademoiselle de Maupin is not, however, the tale of a transsexual, a
woman "becoming" a man. It is a novel about "crossing over" in which
Madeleine's gender masquerade stands for change in general, especially
change within pairs of opposing terms: human/animal, self/other,
masked/naked, object/image, day/night, artificial/real. The novel is satur-
nalian; the festivities merely begin with the upsetting of sexual arrangements. A glorious disorder gradually emerges. At its center stands the
dandy, perfectly attired, superciliously smiling, and ready to explode.

Madeleine and d'Albert rhyme as characters. The pattern of doubling
in which they find their fictional being is as crucial to their meaning as the
measure of psychological realism Gautier has invested in them. They are
fictional people, but Gautier means for us to read them as textures as well.
The figure of the dandy, already split between Madeleine and d'Albert,
fragments even further when we consider the other doublings in the text:
Rosette and d'Albert mirror one another, as do Rosette and Madeleine.
This three-way mirror opens even wider, to include the reflections of Isnabel and Alcibiades. Figure everywhere gives way to such dizzying reflection that the novel's meaning finally inheres more firmly in its texture
and tone than in the comforts of plot, setting, or characterization. The figure of the dandy, dissolved by the power of the mirror, recrystallizes not
as a single person, but as a series of rhetorical strategies. We can find this
dandy lurking everywhere, from the novel's very structure to its weave of
literary allusion and its characteristic metaphors. What makes such diffusion artistically possible for Gautier is at once a theme and a mode of writing: metamorphosis. *Mademoiselle de Maupin* is a novel of and about
metamorphosis, and the dandy constituted by such a text is "him"self a
metamorphic figure.

GENDER'S OVIDIAN METAMORPHOSIS

Gautier writes *Mademoiselle de Maupin* through many literary ancestors:
E. T. A. Hoffmann, Shakespeare, Ovid, Dante, and Pierre Laclos, among
others.[8] Chief among these is Ovid. Not only does Gautier frequently al-

[8]Lloyd, in "Rereading *Mademoiselle de Maupin*," usefully catalogues and comments on
the writers informing Gautier's novel. She comes to see, in "Speculum Amantis," the *Meta-*

lude to figures from the *Metamorphoses*—Pygmalion, Bacchus, Hermaph-roditus, Ianthe, Thetis and Achilles, Venus and Adonis, Apollo and Daphne—but he borrows Ovid's narrative style of continuous change, of fluidity that eddies and pools, loops easily backward, moves forward, seemingly to no particular end. Just as Ovid's myths often provide etiolo-gies, so the novel offers us an etiology of the dandy.[9] He is a figure who has suffered and enjoyed transformation, even if he is now frozen into a cos-tume, a routine, a fixed place in the world. The rolling quality of Ovidian metamorphosis brought the dandy to his current state; at close range we can even see that his static demeanor is in fact the product of many tiny adjustments. Gautier chooses to rewrite in particular the Ovidian myths, like that of Tiresias, in which the sexual impulse reveals itself as strange and threatening, capable of transporting individuals from one "layer" of the universe, society, family, or self to another.

Gautier's characters in *Mademoiselle de Maupin*, like Tiresias, never fully escape solitude. It is for them as final a judgment as his blindness. Like Tiresias, they suffer for their explorations of gender, but they expe-rience as well the rewards of challenging the systems of order in which gender is enmeshed. Although the novel's plot unfolds in a tale of roman-tic intrigue and the confusions of gender, it is, again like the myth of Tiresias, a tale of hierarchically arranged classifications—animal and human, divine and human, female and male, natural and artificial—and of the losses and gains we register in questioning these sets of relations.

Mademoiselle de Maupin is a novel of metamorphosis not just because Madeleine takes on masculine power even as d'Albert languishes but also because all characters discover the fluidity of categories and experience the terrors and pleasures of roaming up and down the hierarchies of their own personalities, families, and society. They learn the lesson that categories need not dissolve, they need only be questioned, to set the world in motion toward chaos. When Gautier moves his characters toward—and occasion-ally over—those lines Tiresias crossed, such movement is experienced as a troubling but satisfying exercise of freedom. Spinning the many sexual *liens* among Rosette, Isnabel, Alcibiades, d'Albert, and Madeleine, Gau-

---

morphoses as the "novel's true model." While Lloyd's focus is the novel's seduction and ed-ucation of the reader, my analysis establishes the meaning of metamorphosis both for the dandy—the figure of self-transformation—and for the dandy-text, with its Ovidian nar-rative structure.

[9] I am indebted to Barkan's interpretation of the *Metamorphoses*, particularly his notions of "levels" of transformation and Ovidian etiologies. I am also indebted to his readings of specific myths, those of Tiresias and Narcissus.

tier becomes Arachne, a challenger of the gods of nineteenth-century bourgeois culture.

To the extent that the dandy is a figure of rebellion, the pleasures or, in Gautier's term, the "caprices" of metamorphosis provide him with a mode for challenging the structures of authority. To the extent that the dandy is a figure conservative of tradition and authority, the terrors of the meta-morphic temptation counsel restraint, even to the point of paralysis. Once again, Gautier draws us to the mirrored and opposing images of d'Albert and Madeleine in order to impersonate these two positions.

For d'Albert, the controlling Ovidian myth of metamorphosis is that of Narcissus. Not only is d'Albert given to staring into pools and mirrors, but he is a brother of the Jeunes-France: self-dramatizing and egotistical. Gautier supplies him with crushingly long speeches about himself, medi-tations revealing that his vision of pure beauty is but a version of himself, prettier than he is, not evil and twisted as he believes himself to be, female though he is male, but himself nonetheless. He is, we know, doomed to die unfulfilled, entranced not only by his own beauty but also by the shadowy rewards of remaining utterly fixed. He fittingly will die by the force of ne-gation. The process of cooling and hardening has, as he frequently tells us, already begun.

D'Albert has much to say about hierarchy and levels of being, but his mood is always conservative rather than rebellious. Like Rodolphe in "Celle-ci et celle-là," surrounded by cats whose affection, like that of Mari-ette, he takes for granted, d'Albert associates women with animals. The impulse here is to weaken categories, but only in order to assert with more strength his own position in a hierarchy he jealously guards. Gautier is often rather cruel to d'Albert: he has d'Albert name his horse after a no-torious rapist of the day (*MM* 78 and 411, n. 1) and his mistress after a fa-vorite dog. He blurs the categories of women, animals, and things— "J'avais ce que je désirais depuis si longtemps, une maîtresse à moi comme mon cheval et mon épée" (*MM* 145; I had what I had desired for so long— my own mistress, just like my own horse and my own sword)—but the re-sult is a kind of moral smudge rather than the freeing of one order of being to become another. The weight of the novel mocks d'Albert and his priggish attempts to fulfill himself; certainly Madeleine shows us that if women are to be considered as animals, one had better think of stallions and lions rather than fillies and cats.

D'Albert, like Madeleine, cross-dresses, but the category he challenges is that of species rather than gender. He dons a lavish bear costume, com-plete with headpiece, and makes love to Rosette, who wears, as instructed, ballgown and diamonds. The purpose of the staged scene, d'Albert tells us, is to prove to himself, through bizarre and therefore memorable experience, that he does, in fact, have a mistress because "simplement je ne me sens pas l'avoir, voilà tout" (*MM* 116; I simply didn't feel that I had one, that's all).

D'Albert stages the scene in order to excite both Rosette and himself; he takes on a beastly persona, while Rosette assists in ripping off her elaborate costume. Turning the world upside down, the fop lumbers about in a furry animal skin while the beautiful courtesan gaily destroys her laces and feathers. While he becomes less of a man, Rosette takes on his cast-off masculinity: "Rose a déployé dans cette occasion un héroïsme tout à fait au-dessus de son sexe" (*MM* 117; Rose demonstrated on that occasion a heroism completely above her sex). During the drama, she becomes the aloof dandy, "un témoin désintéressé" (*MM* 117; a disinterested witness) of the sacking of her toilette, while d'Albert later melts in an infantile appreciation of her erotic performance:

> Il y avait quelque chose de si maternel et de si chaste dans son regard que j'oubliai totalement la scène plus qu'anacréontique qui venait de se passer, et me mis à genoux devant elle en lui demandant la permission de baiser sa main; ce qu'elle m'accorda avec une gravité et une dignité singulières.
>
> (*MM* 118)

> There was something so maternal and so chaste in her look that I forgot completely the more than Anacreontic scene that had just happened, and I went down on my knees in front of her and begged her permission to kiss her hand; which she granted me with singular gravity and dignity.

In playing beast to her antique hero, d'Albert experiences some of the ecstasies yielded by this fleeting escape from his place in the hierarchy. Rosette plays human to his beast, male to his female, mother to his son, and he submits to her, gaining thereby a brimming measure of sexual pleasure. Both strip themselves of their masks—bear and ballgown—in order that d'Albert experience the deepest intimacies of which he is capable.

The scene fails for d'Albert in its very successes. He tells us that it is merely one of twenty or more staged sexual events, and that when it is over, he cannot believe it really happened, worrying instead that it has been dream, illusion, "fantasmagorie." He cannot, either in reality or through artifice, believe he has a lover because events teach him that he lacks *any* feeling of connection to another: "L'existence ou la non-existence d'une chose ou d'une personne ne m'intéresse pas assez pour que j'en sois affecté d'une manière sensible et convaincante" (*MM* 121; The existence or the nonexistence of a thing or a person does not interest me enough to affect me in a perceptible and convincing way).

D'Albert can turn the world upside down, but his very being rebels against the upset. The world upside down is but unconvincing dream or illusion, while "reality" for d'Albert means men above women and animals alike, mothers embraced securely outside the incest zone, and a distance kept between the heights of his superior self and the swarming plains below. His frustration at this distance is matched only by the sense of superiority he thereby gains. Narcissus, unable to grasp his own beautiful image, cannot develop the least genuine interest in others.

The scene fails to effect any genuine transformation of the self. In its metamorphic texture—rapid vacillations between animal and human, high and low, control and victimization, narration and interpretation, humor and pathos, sexual titillation and moral reflection—it takes its place in the metamorphic flux of the novel as a whole. D'Albert reveals himself as a rigid, sticklike man, bobbing along the watery flow of Gautier's narrative, a dandy moving to meet his reversed image in the mirror of Madeleine's supple transformations.

For d'Albert the goal is only and always a mimetic realism; no price in imaginative anarchy, in staged sexual scenes or dramatic caprices such as the "théâtre fantasque," is too high to pay for the exact rendering of "la vie réelle, sous ses allures fantasques" (*MM* 263; real life, in its fantastical aspects). D'Albert celebrates the aesthetic *via negativa*: attracted to the fantastic, he allows disorder because it yields order. And in this way, as well, he reads *As You Like It*, "une pièce qui me ravit" (*MM* 263; a play that delights me).

His fascination with the play echoes Gautier's own, for it informs the entire plot of half-veiled identities in *Mademoiselle de Maupin*. D'Albert's interest in the play lies in the power of metamorphosis to reveal a character's true, that is, original or essential, identity. As director of the amateur theatrical group, he reads the play for its secret message which will reveal the "actual" gender of Rosalinde/Théodore/Madeleine: "à travers le voile de ces expressions empruntées, sous ce masque de théâtre, avec ces paroles hermaphrodites, il [Théodore] faisait allusion à son sexe réel et à notre situation réciproque" (*MM* 287; through the veil of those borrowed expressions, under the theatrical mask, with those hermaphroditic words, he [Theodore] alluded to his real gender and to our mutual situation).

For all his previous talk of a "théâtre fantasque," of mushrooms as spectators, green skies, curtains made of butterfly wings, and the absence of cause and effect, d'Albert uses Shakespeare's play to escape from the mysterious, free-floating, and bizarre. He reads *As You Like It* for its clear, if at first hidden, message, and he reads it as a mirror of his own experience. The play, he tells us, "était en quelque sorte une autre pièce dans la pièce, un drame invisible et inconnu aux autres spectateurs que nous jouions pour nous seuls, et qui, sous des paroles symboliques, résumait notre vie complète et exprimait nos plus cachés désirs" (*MM* 293; was a sort of play within a play, a drama invisible and unknown to the spectators, that we played for ourselves alone, and which, in symbolic words, summed up our whole life and expressed our most hidden desires). Narcissus, gazing into the waters, once more sees the world right side up, with its hierarchies in order and its plot moving steadily toward the wished-for dénouement. While d'Albert believes in an objective and fixed truth to which language and art can be made to correspond, Madeleine offers a pragmatist's vision of truth. For her, truth, especially that of gender, is made through experience, not discovered behind the veil of appearances. And it is through her exploration of her own gender that she arrives at the understanding that challenges the very notion of essentialism.

"TOUJOURS EN L'AIR": MADELEINE'S IDEA OF ORDER

When, late in the novel, d'Albert gathers the courage to declare his love to Madeleine, he writes with certainty, "vous êtes une femme; nous ne sommes plus au temps des métamorphoses;—Adonis et Hermaphrodite sont morts" (*MM* 336; you are a woman; we are no longer in the time of metamorphoses;—Adonis and Hermaphroditus are dead). Certainly Madeleine's sexual ambiguity has attracted d'Albert. He is never quite sure he wants to accept what he knows almost immediately upon seeing her: that she is a woman in man's clothing. Rather than reading the text of her swelling chest as authoritative, he looks to Shakespeare for the secret message of truth, the way to remove Madeleine from sexual flux and place her squarely in a category she has long since learned to question.

Madeleine, on the other hand, desires escape from gender and from classification in general, a goal not without its own hazards. Perhaps the Ovidian myth that best illuminates her metamorphic qualities is that of Salmacis. I begin with a coincidence of utmost importance: just as we intuitively (if wrongly) believe that *Mademoiselle de Maupin* is d'Albert's story, so the Salmacis myth is more commonly referred to as the story of Hermaphroditus. In both narratives, the woman half appears and half disappears throughout, only to disappear as a person completely at story's end: Salmacis is transformed into transparent water, and Madeleine plans to disappear permanently from the scenes of the narrative she has just galloped, dueled, and dissembled her way through. Salmacis challenges Hermaphroditus's place as divinity, male, son, lover, foreigner. Once he enters Salmacis's watery medium, she joins him there, literally. The gods grant her prayer that the two may never be separated, and the embrace yields a being who is "no longer two beings." But who is left? The being is "no longer man and woman, / But neither, and yet both" (*Metamorphoses* 4.379–80). Not only does the paradoxical statement here deny and affirm at once—surely an order-destroying rhetoric—but it is Hermaphroditus who lives on. Certainly he is but "half a man, with limbs all softness," but "he" is somehow intact. Even though Salmacis supplies half of the hermaphroditic body, it is Hermaphroditus, a complicated male, who remains. A figure of cosmic fluidity desiring the chaos of complete union, Salmacis is gone; her transformation from water nymph to water, her transparency, her powers of contamination only figure forth what she essentially is: absence.

Madeleine's story, like that of Salmacis, is one of physical desire aroused and fulfilled, of gender at once merged and altogether denied, of social arrangements challenged and often destroyed. Unlike Salmacis, she paradoxically gains in presence as she gradually effaces all: herself as Mademoiselle de Maupin; male superiority in duels; the forms of courtship and marriage; heterosexual love as the norm; the certainties of home and hearth; the very notion of place, of the fixed location of the unitary self in the world.

D'Albert reads *As You Like It* for its secret meaning, which restores order to his world. Gautier gives us, in contrast, Madeleine's reading of a tapestry in Rosette's chateau:

> De grands arbres à feuilles aigues y soutenaient des essaims d'oiseaux fantastiques; les couleurs altérées par le temps produisaient de bizarres transpositions de nuances; le ciel était vert . . . les chairs ressemblaient à du bois, et les nymphes qui se promenaient sous les ombrages déteints de la forêt avaient l'air de momies démaillotées. . . . Des rocailles capricieusement dentelées, d'où tombaient des torrents de laine blanche, se confondaient au bord de l'horizon avec des nuages pommelés.   (*MM* 303)

> Tall trees with sharp leaves supported flocks of fantastical birds; the colors, altered by time, produced bizarre transpositions of nuances; the sky was green . . . the flesh resembled wood, and the nymphs who strolled under the faded shadows of the forest looked like unwrapped mummies. . . . Whim-

sically jagged rocks, from which fell torrents of white wool, blended with
the fluffy clouds on the horizon.

Madeleine looks at a dusty, fading tapestry and sees "ce monde fantas-
tique créé par les ouvriers de haute lisse" (*MM* 304; that fantastical world
created by tapestry weavers). The line between artifice and reality fades;
the tapestry becomes for her a world in which the organic processes of
time work their changes, in which actual water and the weaver's art merge
in "des torrents de laine blanche" (*MM* 303; torrents of white wool). She
sees a world in which metamorphosis rules, serenely joining one kind to
another, wool becoming flesh, flesh becoming wood. Nymphs, borrowed
from mythology and given a second artistic life, this one visual and tactile,
resemble mummies, the walking dead. Art, reality, life, death, shining,
fading, appearance, disappearance: Madeleine half studies, half creates
their subtle transformations.

The tapestry offers, along with its texture of transformation, a tale of
arrested metamorphosis as well. In one woven section, we see a huntress
who has loosed an arrow, aiming at a bird in the next panel. But the tapestry turns a corner of the room, and the arrow "décrit un grand crochet"
(takes a sudden turn) so that it can never hit the bird. Nor does the bird
reach what it seeks, the safety of a nearby branch. Madeleine muses, "Cette
flèche empennée et armée d'une pointe d'or, toujours en l'air et n'arrivant
jamais au but, faisait l'effet le plus singulier" (*MM* 303; That arrow, feath-
ered and armed with a golden point, always in the air and never reaching
its goal, caused the most singular effect).

She has some trouble assigning a story to this tableau. Perhaps it is a sad
symbol of human destiny, or perhaps it is an emblem of the artist who dies
before writing the work on which he hopes to base his reputation, his im-
mortality. There is no final story told by the tapestry, for its meanings mul-
tiply even as the spectator views it: "plus je la regardais, plus j'y découvrais
de sens mystérieux et sinistres" (*MM* 303; the more I looked at it, the more
I discovered there mysterious and sinister meanings). What *is* fixed is the
mood it generates; Madeleine is the reader of a Symbolist text as it reverberates with threatening, sad, nostalgic meanings.

Gautier's tapestry is perhaps a precursor of Baudelaire's "Correspondances" (1846), where "des forêts de symboles" (forests of symbols) observe
the observer "avec des regards familiers" (with familiar looks). Madeleine
writes:

> Toutes ces figures debout contre la muraille, et auxquelles l'ondulation de
> l'étoffe et le jeu de la lumière prêtent une espèce de vie fantasmatique, me

semblaient autant d'espions occupés à surveiller mes actions pour en rendre
compte en temps et lieu. . . . Que de choses ces graves personnages auraient
à dire, s'ils pouvaient ouvrir leurs lèvres de fil rouge. . . . De combien de
meurtres, de trahisons, d'adultères infâmes et de monstruosités de toutes
sortes ne sont-ils pas les silencieux et impassibles témoins!   (MM 304)

All those upright figures against the wall, and to which the undulation of the
fabric and the play of light lent a sort of visionary life, seemed to me as so
many spies occupied in keeping an eye on my actions in order to report on
them in due course. . . . What things those grave characters would have to
tell, if they could but open their lips of red thread. . . . Of how many mur-
ders, treacheries, vile adulteries and monstrosities of all sorts are they not the
silent and impassive witnesses!

She sees in the tapestry the meeting place of spirit world and physical
world, of nature and artifice, time and timelessness, aesthetics and morality, creation and criticism. All of these intersections are blurrings, dangerous infringements upon order. The fountain of Salmacis beckons in order
to entrap men, lessen their hold on the world, drown their certainties in the
depths of Symbolist waters. D'Albert reads *As You Like It* as sign; Madeleine reads the tapestry as symbol.

Surely the most troubling blurring of categories in the novel is that of
gender. For all Gautier's playful pronouncements, ironic speechifying, blatant coincidences of plot, and mirror games, the novel possesses a resid-
uum of, if not horror, deep discomfort. Women within their gender are
heterogeneous creatures: one has "un corps de vierge et une âme de fille de
joie" (*MM* 104; the body of a virgin and the soul of a prostitute); another
has "la beauté de l'ange, la force du tigre. . . . un beau masque pour sé-
duire et fasciner sa proie" (*MM* 166; the beauty of an angel, the strength
of a tiger. . . . a beautiful mask for seducing and fascinating her prey). Female gender alone is threatening enough, but the novel constantly pushes
toward description of that paradox, the hermaphrodite, "no longer man
and woman, but neither and yet both" (*Metamorphoses* 4.379–80). Here we
must pause for classification. What, exactly, is Madeleine?

D'Albert, having seen her, imagines a statue of Hermaphroditus, "une
des chimères les plus ardemment caressées de l'antiquité idolâtre" (*MM*
226; one of the most ardently caressed chimeras of idolatrous antiquity).
After a lengthy description of hermaphroditic ambiguity—"le ventre est
un peu plat pour une femme, un peu rond pour un homme," etc.—he decides that in Madeleine/Théodore "la portion féminine l'emporte chez lui,
et qu'il lui est plus resté de Salmacis qu'à l'Hermaphrodite des *Métamorphoses*" (*MM* 226; the belly is a little flat for a woman, a little round for a

man, . . . the feminine portion prevails in him, and that there is more in him of Salmacis than of the Hermaphroditus of the *Metamorphoses*). As Ovid's hermaphrodite is male, d'Albert's is female; hermaphrodites paradoxically retain a primary gender: we refer to them as "he" or "she," thus denying their monstrosity. Yet for all the talk of Madeleine as hermaphrodite, she is not so. She does not, like Hermaphroditus, possess the bodily characteristics of both sexes. Nor would we label Madeleine an androgyne, for androgynes are equally male and female, and, for all her transformations, Gautier's character is somehow a woman primarily. Gautier simply cannot imagine a single figure wholly outside dichotomous categories of gender. We can more accurately label her a "pseudoandrogyne," because she has "some sort of equivocal or ambiguous sexuality that disqualifies [her] from inclusion in the ranks of the straightforwardly male or female." These figures include "the eunuch, the transvestite . . . the figure who undergoes a sex change or exchanges his sex with that of a person of the opposite sex" (O'Flaherty, *Women*, 284).

But perhaps the most accurate label of all would be "psychological androgyne," for Madeleine herself tells us that she has the heart and body of a woman, but the "esprit" of a man. She is thus masquerading no matter how she appears; dressed as a woman she denies "esprit," dressed as a man she denies "corps." Her transformation "therefore entails no removal of the physical or social trappings of the 'wrong' sex . . . but a removal of the psychological trappings of any particular sex, a realization of one's wholeness" (O'Flaherty, *Women*, 293). Or, we might add, a recognition of one's fragmentation. For androgyny can be judged in two vastly different ways (294–96). It can appear as a fusing, a completion, an experience of the *coincidentia oppositorum* (Eliade 113), that is, a return to an original, undifferentiated unity that yields an increase of power. Alternatively, androgynes may appear as unmade, unformed, and chaotic beings who will, like Salmacis, unmake the fixities of society if given the chance.

Gautier himself appears divided on the subject of androgyny. Certainly he fills his *Histoire du Romantisme* with praise of the heterogeneous; one striking characteristic of each young Romantic artist is the mingling of categories he embodies. Jules Vabre is a Frenchman who emigrates and lives, breathes, and drinks in England in order to become the perfect translator of Shakespeare into French. He acquires an English soul. Petrus Borel has beautiful eyes, half Spanish, half Arab. Gérard de Nerval conflates reality and art, living his life as if it were a long band of paper that he inscribes with experience. Célestin Nanteuil has the fair complexion of a young girl; his beard is silky white.

For Gautier, heterogeneity of nationality, language, even male gender never threatens so profoundly as heterogeneity of gender in women. In one of his *Portraits contemporains* (1837), Gautier describes the actress Fanny Elssler as hermaphroditic.[10] Beginning in praise of her beauty, the essay shades into an attack on her "mixed" appearance:

> On a appelé mademoiselle Elssler une *Espagnole du Nord*, et en cela, on a prétendu lui faire un compliment: c'est son défaut. . . . Deux natures et deux tempéraments se combattent en elle; sa beauté gagnerait à se décider pour l'un de ces deux types. Elle est jolie, mais elle manque de race; elle hésite entre l'Espagne et l'Allemagne.   ("Mademoiselle Elssler" 374)

> Someone once called Mademoiselle Elssler a northern Spaniard, and by that he meant to compliment her: it's his mistake. . . . Two natures and two temperaments war within her; her beauty would gain from deciding between the two types. She is pretty, but she lacks pedigree; she hesitates between Spain and Germany.

Eventually Gautier arrives at Elssler's sexual ambiguity:

> Et cette même indécision se remarque dans le caractère du sexe: ses hanches sont peu développées, sa poitrine ne va pas au delà des rondeurs de l'hermaphrodite antique; comme elle est une très-charmante femme, elle serait le plus charmant garçon du monde.   ("Mademoiselle Elssler" 374–75)

> And this same indecision is noticeable in the characteristics of her sex: her hips are only slightly developed, her breasts do not exceed the curves of the ancient hermaphrodite; as she is a very charming woman, so she would be the most charming boy in the world.

Clearly disapproving of heterogeneity in *this* artist, Gautier ends by finding her facial expression "de malice sournoise peu agréable" (375; of sly malice hardly pleasant). Mlle Elssler metamorphoses within the portrait; she begins as beautiful and ends, specifically because of the heterogeneity of her race and gender, as unpleasant, indecisive.

In Madeleine as well, Gautier gives us a disturbing mix. He appears to enjoy her masquerade, just as he is initially attracted to Mademoiselle d'Aubigny-Maupin, the historical transvestite upon whom Madeleine is loosely based. Yet wherever she rides, Madeleine draws behind her on the page a pattern of chaotic innuendo, as if her androgyny spilled from her person into the fictional space she inhabits. She sprinkles the dust of suspect sexual practices throughout the narrative she has helped create. Is she mother or sister to Isnabel? And what sex is the pretty page? Why does

---

[10] Gautier's portrait of Elssler was brought to my attention by Albouy (602).

Madeleine find her little charge sexually adorable? Has Madeleine "caused" Rosette to become a lesbian? How early in the text does Madeleine herself become bisexual? If she and d'Albert share so many qualities, is his love for her incestuous? Masturbatory fantasy? Is the "baiser équestre" (equestrian kiss) a sodomic moment? Is Alcibiades' appearance at each of his sister's seduction scenes a coincidence or an incestuous gesture?

As the sexual fabric of the text unravels, the novel becomes, truly, *Mademoiselle de Maupin* and not the *Chevalier d'Albert* it might have been. Yet the two characters are unthinkable apart from one another, because they organize between them its texture of opposition. Madeleine celebrates metamorphosis but trails chaos. She claims the regenerative powers of dissolution even as she fears them. D'Albert clings to the paralyzing safeties of order and fixity, but saves the notion of tradition, nesting identity safely within it. Together they are *thèse* and *antithèse*: the mythic figure of the dandy who denies synthesis in favor of paradox, the figure Barbey will immortalize in Beau Brummell.

Gautier softens the sharp edge of paradox in his novel by the cushioning effect of verbiage, the dizzying effect of many mirrors. We want to know where Gautier stands in this world of opposing and mirrored ideas. If the dandy is a character, is she/he closer to Madeleine or d'Albert? If we want to seek the dandy in style and texture, is it metamorphic or fixed, symbol or sign? In order to answer these questions, we must consider Gautier's aesthetic belief. This we may find in the dandy as the impersonation of Gautier's Parnassian credo.

"QUI NOUS DÉLIVRERA DES HOMMES ET DES FEMMES?"

Gautier sketches, in his *Histoire du Romantisme*, two opposing sets of aesthetic characteristics: Romantic subjectivity, which allies itself with ideas and poetry, as against classical objectivity, which lives in images and sculpture (18, 29). D'Albert impersonates objectivity and instructs us in its limitations. As he approaches his mineral ideal, with his "songes de pierre" (*MM* 224; stone dreams), his "nonchalance" (*MM* 204), his heavy "trésor de haine et d'amour" (*MM* 205; treasure of hate and love), he becomes a man of stone himself: "Je comprends parfaitement une statue, je ne comprends pas un homme; où la vie commence, je m'arrête et recule effrayé comme si j'avais vu la tête de Méduse" (*MM* 268; I understand a statue perfectly, I do not understand a man; where life begins, I stop and draw back, frightened as if I had seen the head of Medusa). Gautier's attempt to rescue art from the blind alley of Romantic subjectivity, from its bohemian posturing and verbal excess, leads him to imagine an ascesis so extreme as to approach death itself. D'Albert personifies a position beyond classicism; the objectivity he seeks is Eastern in its extremity. The blank stare of the statue reveals no personality; its temperament impinges not at all on the world that passes before its eyes, ears, fingertips. "Objectivity," in the aesthetic sense of registering the "given" facts of the external world, in the sense of locating authority and truth outside and above the self and subordinating subjectivity to other forces, is for Gautier an aesthetic position that moves beyond allegory to the possibility of actually objectifying the self.[11] Such a self retreats from the world of flux and sensation, leaving behind only a stony stare. Such is the stare of the dandy when he "cuts" the vulgar mob; such is the frozen core of the dandy's impertinence, his chilly recoil from sexual contact, his utter impassivity.

Certainly Madeleine's association with flux, change, and genuine feeling suggests that she impersonates subjectivity. D'Albert's expository emotion, his objective distance from his feelings, and his sense that he never really has a mistress contrast with the potency and immediacy of Madeleine's emotional life, the heat of her erotic experience. Her ideal—a good man—may be as distant as d'Albert's vision of female beauty, but it does not prevent her from nurturing her feeling, connecting, transforming self. As soon as she escapes her social mask of young virgin, to don the costume that paradoxically expresses her true self, Madeleine begins to see the world differently. Although she wants to see into the very tissue of man, "l'anatomiser fibre par fibre avec un scalpel inexorable" (dissect him fiber by fiber with an inexorable scalpel), she wants him, in the end, "tout vif et tout palpitant sur ma table de dissection" (*MM* 235; alive and palpitating on my dissecting table). Her story is of a quest for knowledge that will allow her to reject received wisdom and begin to take in the world through awakened senses. Her "effervescence subite . . . bouillon de sang" (*MM* 253; sudden effervescence, rush of blood) fuel her imaginative pursuit of the world in which she is variously and serially detective, hopeful virgin, gentil knight, androgyne. The image of the tapestry huntress with her arrow gone astray reverberates once again, this time as sad emblem of the self always desiring, but on occasion failing, to reach an elusive world.

[11]For a full discussion of the issues of subjectivity and objectivity in modernist art, see Levenson. Chapter 5 (63–79) and chapter 7 (103–36) in particular have influenced my interpretation of Gautier's aesthetics.

Yet Gautier mocks the subjective ideals of Romanticism in *Les Jeunes-France*, satirizing artists with their vast, explosive egos and minuscule, implosive volumes of verse, their delusive trust in the imagination to remake the world, and even their botched suicides when the imagination wavers in its appointed task. Romantic subjectivity, if not attacked in *Mademoiselle de Maupin* as it is in the earlier work, is subjected to critical scrutiny. Certainly the doctrines of the Parnassian school suggest a challenge to Romanticism in general and subjectivity in particular.

The preface to *Mademoiselle de Maupin*, often read as an independent document and a seminal statement of *l'art pour l'art*, in fact establishes the terms of the post-Romantic, antisubjectivist critique which Gautier then allegorizes within the novel itself. The moralistic, utilitarian, and blasé critics whom he attacks are straw men for the purposes of this critique; arguing them down allows Gautier to pose for himself the question of what can follow upon Romantic subjectivity. For the terms of *l'art pour l'art* are still those of subjectivity: not only must art not serve a moral purpose, preach a lesson, or effect social progress, but its sole end is to express and to deliver pleasure through the refinement of the senses. The individual judges art by his nerve endings; the artist creates it by taking his pleasure of the muse:

> Dieu l'a voulu ainsi, lui qui a fait les femmes, les parfums, la lumière, les belles fleurs . . . et les chats angoras, lui qui n'ai pas dit à ses anges: Ayez de la vertu, mais: Ayez de l'amour. (*MM* 58)

> God wanted it so, he who made women, perfume, light, beautiful flowers . . . and angora cats, he who did not say to his angels, "Have virtue," but rather, "Have love."

The creative urge and the proper appreciation of art echo each other, and they reside in an erotic aestheticism, a sensual swooning into the world. But Gautier urges as well an art that seeks its source and goal beyond the feeling individual, for human nature is still fallen, and a human being's needs, including sexual imperatives, are "ignobles et dégoûtants, comme sa pauvre et infirme nature" (*MM* 58; base and disgusting, as his poor and infirm nature). Art must serve nothing but beauty; art that brings us pleasure is already suspect. The preface is, of course, more polemic than reasoned argument, but it does suggest that *l'art pour l'art* arises out of Gautier's need to square the aesthetic circle. He argues that art's standard is always as private and absolute as one's experience of pleasure, while at the same time art has an internal and self-referential code of beauty, independent of the individual and his shameful needs.

Examples of objectivity proliferate as the essay pushes toward a pure, mimetic art it cannot fully grasp. Artists, Gautier states, merely record the world rather than create it: "Les livres suivent les moeurs et les moeurs ne suivent pas les livres" (*MM* 54; Books follow manners and manners do not follow books). Images of cannibalism, of "anthrophagie," recur, as if Gautier would see human consciousness devouring itself in order to leave the primacy of the world intact. Gautier further counsels readers that the author removes himself from the work and lets the characters speak; the two must never be confused. Images of the writer as sexual master of the muse, taking his pleasure in order that Beauty might increase, give way to a celebration of adolescent innocence and virginity (Burnett 42–44). Sexual pleasure and aesthetic value, once linked, are here sundered, as Gautier coyly asks, "Qui nous délivrera des hommes et des femmes?" (*MM* 64; Who will deliver us from men and women?).

Who, indeed? D'Albert is centered, absolutist, controlled, but deathlike in his separation from the world. Madeleine is fertile and sensual, but dangerously close to sacrificing gender, social position, and selfhood itself for the many connections she makes to the world and its inhabitants. Just so the artist may choose a (masculine) deathlike classical restraint or a (feminine) life-exploding Romantic freedom. Unless there is a third way.

Gautier creates a third possibility in the very texture of the novel and impersonates it in the dual figure of the dandy, d'Albert/Madeleine. The novel is in one sense quite subjective: it places us within the motions of a mind or consciousness we are forced to posit in order to explain to ourselves why this is a novel and not a set of letters. Yet for all its subjectivity, this mind presents no temperament, no particular fix on the world. Rather, it glories in its distance: "je vois froidement . . . ma position est aussi parfaitement désintéressée que possible" (*MM* 319; I see coldly . . . my position is as perfectly disinterested as possible). When we try to give it a body, puppeteers and invisible men come to mind. The novel has a sterile, cold feeling about it; its games, its deliberate conflation of art and reality, its sex scenes doubling as aesthetic commentary—all these aspects of the novel chill it. We may read *about* emotional immediacy in Madeleine's character, but she is, finally, more a set of positions than a person. And so it is with every character. Distance rules, *liens* attenuate, and the wholly subjective text is, at the same time, quite objective. Impersonality is that third way, neither objective nor subjective, but an attempt to rescue the strengths of both. The mythic dandy is reborn in Gautier's narrative creation. Impersonality—the notion of an artist who is present and absent in his own text, the dandy who is present and absent in his own person—is an idea that will vivify literature for a century and more, if we begin counting in 1835, at the publication of *Mademoiselle de Maupin*. So Gautier's dandy strolls, creating not much but modernism itself.

What will become the aesthetic doctrine of impersonality, refined throughout the remainder of the nineteenth century, begins to flourish on the divide between Gautier's male and female dandies. It is no accident that Gautier invests transformative power in the figure of a woman; since Eve, woman has personified the energy of cultural chaos. As a Romantic, Gautier challenges hierarchy and category; for him the feminization of art means the exploration of potentially chaotic cultural forces. That he tempers such an impulse with the controlling powers of masculinity only marks him as a man of his time. That he imagines a woman who feels herself to be neither male nor female marks him as a visionary. The metamorphic quality of the novel frees it to cross and recross not just the divide of gender but of other gaps in a binary world: symbolism and realism, novel and essay, subjectivity and objectivity, romanticism and classicism. Escorted by the dandy himself or herself through a narrative textured by dandyism's elegantly ordered but shattering set of possibilities, we learn to check the very ground beneath our feet. Gautier creates the distrustful reader who will be capable of withstanding Barbey's narrative assaults. Ironically enough, it will be the Royalist and reactionary Barbey, not the revolutionary Gautier, who will dare speak words that challenge polarized gender at the root: "Le dandy est femme par certains côtés" (The dandy is woman in certain aspects).

3

CETTE VIE EN L'AIR

BARBEY'S DANDY

L'HABIT RÂPÉ

"Du Dandysme et de G. Brummell" (1845), a sixty-page essay, stands at the imaginative center of Jules-Amédée Barbey d'Aurevilly's (1808–1889) vast writings, an oeuvre that he, from the first, thought of as "collected." His is a characteristically nineteenth-century effort, the essay surrounded by novellas and multivolumed novels, letters beyond counting, hundreds of journalistic articles ranging from literary reviews to political polemic and fashion hints, private journals called *Memoranda*, and volumes of poetry. While he wrote furiously to eke out an inadequate settlement from his fading aristocratic family in Normandy, he was, as he proudly proclaimed, "aussi Dandy qu'on peut l'être en France" (*L* 1:124; as much a Dandy as one can be in France). Although he announced from time to time that his days as a dandy were over, Barbey dressed as a dandy throughout his life and lived, as time permitted, the dandy's leisured life. This meant hours devoted to his toilette and to society. Barbey's journals and letters convey the image of a man who lost mornings to hangovers, afternoons to ennui and neurasthenic headaches, evenings to society, but who nevertheless claimed long periods of time in solitude and creation. The life thus appears as a perpetual self-contradiction. As a dandy, Barbey solaced himself with long sessions at the baths, opium, fine meals. He designed his own clothing, posed at the rail before Tortoni's, strolled the boulevard, womanized discreetly enough. Yet throughout the years 1831 to 1888, in a state of mingled fury and coquetry, he wrote. "Du Dandysme et de G. Brummell" was a project of genius, for it enabled Barbey to juxtapose his two lives, to explain how the dandy's *froideur*, lethargy, "je ne sais quoi" related to the writer's *tourbillon*, the vortex of his passionate, verbal creation.

To call "Du Dandysme" an essay is a necessary inaccuracy. A butterfly's wing, it scintillates among many generic possibilities: history, biography, autobiography, memoir, eulogy, jeremiad, gossip column, satire, tragic tale. It is as if genre were for Barbey a matter of tint rather than structure. As Barbey adds a significant body of notes (all of which appeared, along with a preface, in the second edition, 1861) and incorporates another essay, a kind of afterword entitled "Un Dandy d'avant les Dandys" ("A Dandy before Dandies"), in the third edition (1879), even the textual integrity of "Du Dandysme" is debatable. Did the essay stop growing, or did Barbey's death alone give it a final form?

The essay's elusive quality arises not only when we try to identify its genre, but, mistlike, from whatever element the reader happens to examine. Its narrative is puzzling, its tone shifting, its imagery mysterious, often threatening a violence that never erupts. Like its subjects, dandyism and a famous dandy, the essay itself is difficult to capture. Insolently it puts us in our place, as if Barbey intended to see his readers fall short of the act of comprehension.

Barbey did, however, very much want to be read, to be claimed. His correspondence reveals him as a man at times desperate for recognition, planning to advertise, angered by editors' rejections and the public's ignorance of his works. At the same time, he deliberately antagonized editors and readers alike, attacking literary lions, celebrating evil, practicing a poetics of indignation and blasphemy. After Barbey's journalistic attack on Victor Hugo, graffiti in Paris read "D'Aurevilly idiot."[1]

To achieve the conflicting goals of being understood without being fully grasped, of being appreciated without being liked, of acquiring fame without pandering to a vulgar audience, Barbey seized upon one strategy and held to it throughout the essay. Just as his life as a dandy contradicted

[1] For biographical studies of Barbey, see Berthier, Creed, Girard, and Liedekerke.

his life as an artist, he would contradict himself, deliberately and fundamentally, in this work. There would be no "pinning down" of his argument, no formula for dandyism, no simple portrait of Brummell. When
Barbey's contradiction and antithesis reached a heightened pitch of energy, they would become paradox. What metamorphosis was to Gautier, a
means of reconstruing the world, paradox was to Barbey. Let us, then, approach this essay, which would seduce us with its very coldness, gingerly,
obliquely, by examining its first substantive note.

The dandies, Barbey tells us in this "historical" note, acted on a whim
to create "l'habit râpé," the threadbare costume. Because Barbey wants to
develop an argument he makes in the body of the essay, that dandies are
not merely fops, he develops the "fantaisie" at length:

> C'était précisément sous Brummell. Ils [dandies] étaient à bout d'imperti-
> nence, ils n'en pouvaient plus. Ils trouvèrent celle-là, qui était si *dandie*! (je
> ne sais autre mot pour l'exprimer), de faire râper leurs habits, avant de les
> mettre, dans toute l'étendu de l'étoffe, jusqu'à ce qu'elle ne fût plus qu'une
> espèce de dentelle,—une nuée. Ils voulaient marcher dans leur nuée, ces
> dieux! L'opération était très délicate et très longue, et on se servait pour l'ac-
> complir, d'un morceau de verre aiguisé. Eh, bien, voilà un véritable fait de
> Dandysme! L'habit n'y est pour rien. Il n'*est* presque *plus*.
>
> (DD 307–8, n. 2)

> It was precisely under Brummell. They [dandies] had run out of imperti-
> nence, they couldn't go on. They found that which was so "dandy" (I know
> no other word to express it), to tear their clothes before putting them on, the
> entire length of the cloth, until it was nothing more than a sort of lace,—a
> cloud. They wanted to walk in their cloud, those gods! The operation was
> very delicate and very long, and to accomplish it they used a piece of sharp-
> ened glass. And, well, there's a true example of dandyism! The clothes
> themselves are not important. They practically no longer *exist*.

The whim is certainly freakish enough to trouble us. The image of dandies wielding (or causing others to wield) sharpened glass to turn cloth into
lace webs convinces us that they are indeed beings apart, strange, obsessed.
Equally unsettling is Barbey's use of the image. If we have trouble understanding that clothes do not the dandy make, he will show us, imperti-
nently enough, the unmaking of clothes; he will teach by literalized metaphor. Lest we resist the lesson, he suggests that "ces dieux" achieve their
state by controlled violence. That sharpened glass might wound others.
Barbey swells the hints of sadism with reverberations of masochism: the
"longue" and "délicate" operation sounds dangerous, leaves the dandy ex-
posed to a slip of the glass, to the elements, places him in the nightmarish

situation of walking nearly naked down the street. Barbey insists, however, that for dandies the "fantaisie" is ultimately beautiful as well. Dandies are dressed in a kind of lace, floating together in a cloud of delicate thread-work. Together, in their imaginations, they have all but excised the heavy stuff of corporeal life—if clothes do not make the dandy, neither do bod-ies. Their fancy has nearly dissolved the armor of clothing and has joined them into a kind of unity; they share a cloud: "Ils voulaient marcher dans leur nuée, ces dieux!"

The note offers us an imagined act and an actual achievement, an im-pertinent prank and an exercise in spirituality, a threat and a blessing. It refuses to offer us a single vantage point from which to choose between these alternatives. I take this note to be characteristic of Barbey in two cen-tral ways. First, it challenges the notion of fixed identity, offering an image of the *unmaking* of self—"L'opération est très délicate et très longue"— and its *reconstitution* in or among other selves, the shared cloud of "ces dieux." Second, this metamorphic act occurs not for the sake of change or flux, but to reach the moving fixity of pitched contraries, the paradoxical, vibrant stasis of eternally opposed, struggling, evenly matched positions: clothed yet naked, capricious yet serious, impertinent, though vulnerable.

Barbey possessed, throughout his life, an appropriating eye. It gave his life a cloudlike quality, because he pulled so many others into his sphere, read himself metamorphically into and out of others' personal styles and words and actions so frequently, that only a ferocious, willed insistence on his own fixed identity, "ce terrible égoïsme," prevented what Baudelaire would so aptly call this "vaporisation . . . du *Moi*" (that terrible egoism . . . that vaporization of the I). Reading Barbey's journals, letters, and articles, we see a man both passionate and patient, painstakingly weaving the strands of his lacelike identity into those of others: friends, strangers, his-torical figures, authors, fictional characters.

Much of the substance of this chapter consists of a catalogue of these others: "exemplary portraits" of people who contribute to Barbey's dandy, who is in the end Barbey himself. Barbey created others that he might form himself, all the while insisting upon his own integrity, his own sov-ereignty over the world of shadowy figures he commanded. Stepping forth from Barbey's gallery of appropriated figures, insistently and with increas-ing powers of autonomy, is the figure of the woman. Barbey begins in fas-cination with an aristocratic woman, among other exemplary figures, and proceeds to a Brummell who is comprehensible only in terms of women: "*Paraître*, c'est *être*, pour les Dandys comme pour les femmes" (DD 314, n. 32; *To appear* is *to be*, for Dandies as for women). Even the form of his essay on Brummell is feminized, along with Brummell's own personal style of beauty, (feminine) elegance. Despite his avowed misogyny, Barbey tells the story of his appropriation of the female, his version of what Baudelaire will call the *mundus muliebris*, the world of women. Barbey's very acts of taking enable him to conceive of modern beauty: modernism develops along gender's lines as Barbey, like Gautier, redraws them.

CONCEIVING THE DANDY: EXEMPLARY PORTRAITS

If we study Barbey in the act of seeing others, we begin to appreciate "Du Dandysme's" mysteries, chief among them the ritual of being seen. Barbey is above all a portraitist; however seductive his plots and atmospheric his settings, they lead back to the contours of the human figure. Barbey saw others that he might see himself; he depicted what he saw in order that he, himself, might be seen. Out of a wealth of portraits in his letters and journals I have chosen four and labeled them "exemplary." They are portraits demonstrating the types of people to whom Barbey was strongly attracted and the ways in which he explained to himself that attraction. The argument here is not developmental: I do not present a chronology of portraiture growing deeper and more complex in time and "culminating" in Brummell. Such an argument is foreign to Barbey's methods. He did not move from the simple to the complex; rather he worked in palimpsests, layering one portrait over another, retaining some characteristics and removing others. The palimpsests thickened over time, but the "final" image toward which they all bore a family resemblance seems to have been intact in Barbey's imagination from the very beginning. Thus I may discuss a portrait as "constitutive" of Brummell even though it was written after "Du Dandysme," because through its surface we may detect the face of Brummell, at once surprising and familiar.

The first "exemplary portrait" is that of a group of men, not dandies, but madmen. On a visit to Normandy in 1856, Barbey accompanied a Dr. Vatel on a tour of the mental wards of a hospital:

> Ce qui m'a le plus frappé, le plus pénétré, ce qui m'a paru *inoubliable* d'impression, ce sont les fous tristes. . . . Quelles poses inouïes à étudier pour un sculpteur! Quelles admirables cariatides! . . . Tout cela marqué d'un caractère que je nommerai, mais que je n'exprimerai pas comme je viens de le voir: *l'intensité surhumaine de la douleur*.   (M 3:61)

> What struck me most, what penetrated me most, what seemed to me an *unforgettable* impression, were the sad madmen. . . . What unheard of poses to

study for a sculptor! What admirable caryatids!... All of it marked with a
character that I will name, but that I will not express as I have just seen it:
the superhuman intensity of suffering.

Given the range of inmates, Barbey chooses the catatonics, those so victim-
ized by an unspeakable sorrow that they have become living sculpture.
The "palimpsestuous" quality of all Barbey's figures begins to make itself
felt; for the shadow of Brummell, who died insane, darkens this portrait.
In fact, Barbey notes that he sees from this ward the windows of the pa-
vilion that Brummell himself inhabited during his final madness (*M* 3:62).
Barbey, uncharacteristically, feels pity for the inmates, for their self-
absorption is total, "tragique, épouvantable, dévorante" (*M* 3:62; tragic,
horrifying, overwhelming). They simply take no notice of the exterior
world. Such an image fascinates as it repels, for Barbey—and the dandies
he creates, Brummell first among them—will always strive for total impassivity, or at least strive to *appear* utterly unmoved by the world. Yet Barbey is well aware of the root meaning of "idiocy," in "self," individual isolation which has here reached solipsistic paralysis. What separates Barbey's
impassive dandy from grotesquerie will be, perhaps, just this residue of
horrified sympathy. Somewhere in the arrogant figure of the dandy lives
the victim of his own closed identity. Brummell dies a madman because
he lives, in part, as a madman.

During the same sojourn in Normandy, Barbey sees, in a private collection, a portrait of St. Sebastian by Van Dyck. Once again, the subject for
Barbey is agony, torture, and how it registers on the human countenance.
The insane reveal hidden and cataclysmic emotions by the utter immobil-
ity of their pose. St. Sebastian, as Van Dyck depicts him, is much harder
for Barbey to read, to see. If St. Sebastian's face and body reveal so much
pain, Barbey wonders, why isn't his chest bristling with arrows: "Pourquoi
l'expression d'un homme déchiré qui n'a pas une seule blessure, un seul dé-
chirement sur tout son corps presque convulsé cependant? Est-ce une contradiction? Est-ce un oubli?" (*M* 3:53–54; Why the expression of a torn
man who has not a single wound, a single tear on all his body, yet nevertheless almost convulsed? Is it a contradiction? Is it an oversight?). Barbey,
having spotted a paradox, "le supplice sans le supplice" (the torture without torture), in fact reads the entire portrait as a set of surprises or contradictions. He sees in St. Sebastian "l'élégance dans la force presque massive,
l'élégance dans la plus physique des douleurs!" (*M* 3:40; The elegance in
the almost massive strength, the elegance in the most physical of suffer-
ings). Unlike the madmen, St. Sebastian is both powerful and in pain, and
his power is itself both "massive" and "élégant." He is a particular kind of

martyr, a defeated soldier and an athlete. Although Barbey does not mention Alcibiades, the ghost of this aristocratic, duplicitous soldier hovers
over the portrait, to emerge explicitly in Barbey's portrait of Brummell.

Still wondering why no bleeding is depicted, Barbey deduces an answer
not from the painting but from the painter. Van Dyck is too aristocratic to
paint the gore: "Son *élégance* suprême lui a-t-elle conseillé de supprimer
la vue du sang comme trop physique et trop horrible? . . . Son *aristocratie*
qui ne l'a pas abandonné, même en peignant ce corps robuste de soldat Romain" (*M* 3:54; Did his supreme *elegance* lead him to suppress the sight
of blood as too physical and too horrible? . . . His *aristocracy* that did not
abandon him, even in painting this robust body of a Roman soldier). Van
Dyck held a paintbrush as he "retroussait" (curled upward) his moustache.
The artist's personal elegance is transferred, translated, to the elegance of
his subject; St. Sebastian himself is simply too soigné to bleed in public:
"Le Saint Sebastien est de l'élégance aristocratique de cette *moustache re-
troussée* qui a dans le talent, trait pour trait, ce qu'elle avait dans la figure!"
(*M* 3:39; Saint Sebastian has the aristocratic elegance of [Van Dyck's]
curled-up moustache, which has the same effect in [Van Dyck's] art of portraiture as it had on his face). Barbey clearly likes the impertinence of this
answer to a rather serious question; in essence, he says, a gentleman artist
never bleeds in public, nor do his subjects. There is, however, always a serious intent in the dandy's impertinence. Catatonic madmen show the effects of superhuman anguish: they are stone from the inside all the way
out. Van Dyck does not hide St. Sebastian's feelings, but presents us with
a blatant lie about them. Barbey's Van Dyck is an artist who deliberately
hides the bloody horror within the figure, not trying to deny its existence
or cover his own tracks, but to claim, paradoxically, that the horror both is
and is not there. We can see it and not see it, this "supplice sans le supplice."

The more Barbey examines the portrait—he returns on a second occasion—the more evidence of Van Dyck's elegance he finds. He notices, for
example, that Van Dyck, instead of painting St. Sebastian on a trampled,
bloodied hillock of torture, leans him against a flag, thus giving "l'illusion
d'un champ de bataille!" (*M* 3:54; the illusion of a battlefield!). The ex-
clamation point is Barbey's; he loves the openly illusionary act, finds it enchanting that Van Dyck would, in St. Sebastian, paint a self-portrait, a personification of his own "aristocratie," not even attempting to tell the "true"
story of how his martyr actually died to earthly life. Elegance, force, arrogance, lie, pose, purity, agony: through this mesh of abstraction Barbey
sees and appropriates the double figure of Van Dyck/St. Sebastian, reading into and out of the portrait the necessary elements of artistic dandy-

ism. As Van Dyck appropriates St. Sebastian in order to express his own aristocratic elegance, Barbey appropriates Van Dyck *and* St. Sebastian, recognizing in them the dandy's complex martyrdom.

Between his two viewings of the painting, Barbey, his journal reveals, buys a "limousine," a common, heavy cloak that Norman carters wear, and has it lined with black velvet. It is this limousine "dans laquelle je veux envelopper mon dandysme cet hiver" (*M* 3:52; in which I want to envelop my dandyism this winter), he writes; his costume, like Van Dyck's depiction of St. Sebastian, is an elegant, opaque "lie" from within which he will flaunt the naked truth of his superiority.

In discussing just how he knows that the unwounded Sebastian is vanquished, Barbey points to one detail: "les genoux portent en dedans comme les genoux d'une femme" (*M* 3:39; his knees turn inward like the knees of a woman). The return to the female in the male is, like Sebastian's bloodlessness, like Barbey's black velvet, truth spoken by a lie. It is a lie he tells with enough frequency that it merits a portrait of its own.

The third exemplary portrait is, then, that of a woman, a Mlle de G... who is Eugénie de Guérin, sister of Barbey's close friend, the poet Maurice de Guérin. Barbey meets her in 1838. Just as St. Sebastian embodies the wounded without a superficial wound, so Mlle de G...'s entire appearance has been created by her "combats intérieurs." She is, figuratively speaking, the expression of hidden fires: "Elle, c'est plus beau, c'est un holocauste" (*M* 2:339; As for her, she's more beautiful, she's a holocaust). Yet Mlle de G... has achieved a privileged state: unlike the idiots and St. Sebastian, she is a martyr without being a victim. If she is slowly refined by fire, giving off a "lueur purifiée, mais ardente encore" (*M* 2:339; purified, but still ardent, glow), the blaze is all her own, there is no victim's pyre. She is "un brasier de passions éteintes seulement parce qu'elles ne flambent plus" (a furnace of passions, extinguished only because they no longer flame). We cannot know the emotional history of her burning and dying passions; they extinguish themselves simply because they cannot burn forever. Yet, phoenixlike, "tout, tout n'est pas consommé" (*M* 2:339; all, all is not consumed), and she is, paradoxically, all potential.

In Mlle de G... Barbey sees female aristocracy. She is, from the first, patrician; although Barbey compares her to Christian martyrs, he insists that this aspect is continually cast into doubt by her aristocratic identity. She is "la femme essentiellement *comme il faut*. . . . La *patricienne* est encore plus forte que la chrétienne" (*M* 2:339–40; the essentially decent and well-bred woman. . . . The patrician in her is yet stronger than the Christian). She is not a maudlin, bourgeois Christian girl, but a noblewoman. In fact, as Barbey portrays her, she is a worldly ascetic, and she mirrors his own elegance unsupported by a lavish income, the austerity of his life which he must consume in the act of self-creation. Both he and she burn with a hard, gemlike flame; they devour self in their natively "aristocratic" (read intense, refined) standards for knowing the world.

Here Barbey creates a portrait as he imagines Van Dyck did, expressing his own elegance, his own hidden aristocracy, in the interior fires of another. Barbey hesitated not at all in "fictionalizing" real people in this way, in claiming them as representations of, or even better, parts of, what he called an "indéguisable [moi]" (the undisguisable [I]). Mlle de Guérin represents purity with the potential for depravity ("*le démon* . . . pourrait être encore le plus fort dans cette âme") (*M* 2:339; the demon . . . could still be the strongest in that soul). She represents as well, and in parallel, a "lady" with a woman's body. In the act of self-creation through another, Barbey would rather see the lady than the woman. Mlle de G...'s breast, like her mother's, is specialized to one task only—the passing on of the sacred fluid of elitism. Barbey wrote earlier, "une aristocratie personnelle n'est plus une aristocratie.—Il n'y a pas aristocratie sans transmission" (*M* 1:158; a personal aristocracy is no longer an aristocracy.—There is no aristocracy without transmission). Mlle de G... has breasts in order to nourish an abstraction, "aristocracy," not to fulfill the physical desires of men or babies, much less her own. What the brush is to Van Dyck, the breast is to the aristocratic woman, the means of making exterior, of objectifying, the abstract elegance of aristocracy circulating within her. This is, to borrow an image from Hindu mythology, "the breast that feeds itself."[2] It is a powerful image for the dandy-artist who would present the world with aesthetic offspring that only the privileged few of aristocratic lineage can claim. The dandy, in giving birth to himself, is the ultimate aristocrat, nourishing his own abstract offspring, personal sublimity. The vulgar world, "la foule," may shrivel and die.

Barbey turns to this vulgar world in his fourth exemplary portrait. It is a "self-portrait," a term that, for Barbey, is more a matter of degree than kind. For the portraits of the insane men, St. Sebastian, and Mlle de G... both are and are not self-portraits. Barbey, seeing himself in certain ways, seeks in others his own reflection and lives out the paradox of escaping subjectivity by enhancing it. In the case of the fourth portrait, he practices

---

[2]For a discussion of this image as well as an analysis of Hindu myths in which contradiction plays an essential role (as it does in the nineteenth-century mythology of dandyism), see O'Flaherty, *Asceticism and Eroticism*.

an even tauter form of paradox: even the sketch of himself both is and is not self.[3] He is writing a "private" journal, intended from the first to be read by Maurice de Guérin; he recounts his appearance in provincial society during a trip home. The mirrors are thus neatly arranged to create the *mise en abyme* that every dandy-writer loves: Guérin is to see Barbey as Barbey sees himself being seen by his provincial company.

The portrait proceeds by contraries; it is a series of exploding terms, a playful smokescreen from which the dandy emerges nonchalantly. In fact, the entire portrait is presented as a set of instructions for the cosmopolitan gentleman, the dandy who resides for six months in a small town:

> qu'il soit un peu et même extrêmement singulier dans ses opinions, mais très convenable dans ses manières . . . dur jusqu'à la férocité dans ses jugements sur les choses et encore plus sur les personnes, mais froid jusqu'au plus complet dédain (tuant avec la parole comme avec la balle, sans se passionner), grave et intellectuel (il faut cela au dix-neuvième siècle) dans les habitudes de la matinée sur lesquelles on vous fait une réputation, mais homme du monde en mettant son habit, le soir, et faisant la guerre au pédantisme de toutes les sortes,—exprimant des opinions austères en morale avec des paroles légères et railleuses . . . ne faisant jamais comme les autres, parce que les autres manquent presque toujours de distinction et qu'il faut marquer la sienne non pour soi-même, mais contre eux. (*M* 1:76–77)

> let him be a little or even extremely singular in his opinions, but very proper in his manner . . . tough to the point of ferociousness in his judgments of things and even more so of people, but cold to the point of disdain (killing with a word as with a bullet, passionless), grave and intellectual (it's necessary in the nineteenth century) in his morning habits, upon which one builds a reputation, yet a man of the world as to dressing in the evening, and waging war on pedantry of all sorts,—expressing austere moral opinions with light and mocking words . . . never doing anything as the others do, because the others almost always lack distinction and it is necessary to mark his own not for himself, but against them.

I quote at length in order to convey the portrait's quality of *sprezzatura*. Barbey could effortlessly continue to produce contrasts, or he could just as easily stop. The general rule seems to require that the dandy establish his own social balance by upsetting that of others. Out of the particulars, a familiar portrait emerges.

The dandy is "grave et intellectuel" but "homme du monde" in a way that suggests Mlle de Guérin's patrician asceticism. Like her, he is "aus-

[3]See Colie's discussion of "Epistemological Paradoxes," chap. 4.

tères en morales," but his mocking words suggest that he is capable of cruelty, capable of harboring, as she might, "le démon." Not quite so patrician
as she, Barbey's dandy must deliberately act against the grain, "ne faisant
jamais comme les autres, parce que les autres manquent presque toujours
de distinction." He should be, as Mlle de Guérin is, "dur jusqu'à la férocité
dans ses jugements . . . mais froid jusqu'au complet dédain"; he must be,
like St. Sebastian, a soldier, "tuant avec la parole comme avec la balle . . .
faisant la guerre au pédantisme." The dandy's entire sojourn in the prov-
inces is a six-month martyrdom; he suffers, like St. Sebastian, "le supplice
sans le supplice."

But where, we might ask, are "les fous"? We might look for them in
Barbey's instructions to act like a fool, especially around women, "se po-
sant hardiment absurde parce qu'il y a très souvent du génie dans l'absurdité . . . tout ce qu'on possède perdant de sa valeur immédiatement et les
thèses égoïstes étant ridicules à soutenir" (M 1:77; to pass oneself off as absurd because there is often genius in absurdity . . . all that one possesses
losing its value immediately and selfish theses becoming ridiculous to
defend).

Yet such a figure, while he will be incorporated, complete with cap and
bells, in Barbey's Brummell, is not the precursor of Barbey's tragic figures
of the mental ward.[4] Rather, that precursor appears in the final lines of this
"self-portrait." If such a man, Barbey writes, is not a successful woman-
izer, "j'accepte le nom d'imbécile et me crache moi-même à la figure
comme observateur" (M 1:77; I accept the name of imbecile and spit in my
own face as an observer). This "figure" is both the dandy's own face and
the figure he cuts in society, always observing himself. Triply reflexive (me
crache moi-même à la figure), it is as well Barbey, who in this passage engages in the dandy's act, that of observing himself. Since everything his
subject has done is brought to bear on his success as "ravageur" of the female sex, we are asked to judge this dandy as a whole, not merely his power
in the boudoir. "J'accepte le nom d'imbécile": Barbey suggests, with this
closing line, the possibility that the entire pose of impudence, distance,
contradiction, folly, and self-observation might make him an imbecile,
someone who spits on himself, or a pariah, someone to be spat upon. Barbey bursts the iridescent bubble of verbal bravado and ferocity; perhaps
there is something terribly painful about the entire pose, making him kin
to "les fous tristes."

---

[4] See Kaiser (59–83) for a discussion of the transvaluation of values represented by the
Renaissance Fool. The nineteenth-century dandy comes from the best of families.

After an actual evening spent in provincial society three months earlier, the defensiveness of the posture is made even clearer:

> J'ai joué l'Alcibiade tout le temps. J'ai bu plus que ces Normands grands buveurs. Ils s'étonnaient qu'un efféminé de ma taille, un damoiseau de Paris, résistât mieux qu'eux aux liqueurs fortes. (M 1:69)

> I played Alcibiades all the time. I drank more than those great Norman drinkers. They were astonished that an effeminate man of my size, a dainty fop from Paris, could hold strong liquor better than they.

What makes his feat impressive is precisely his feminine quality; Barbey admits that quality even as he proudly displays his ability to "overcome" it. The dandy's attacks on women are always, in part, attacks on himself, "un efféminé de ma taille," however tongue in cheek his self-characterization as female might appear. Perhaps this figure as dissembler, *poseur*, artist of opacity, is paradoxically utterly transparent; his sadness and fear, the idiocy of his absolute solitude, the feminization of his being, are his most strikingly apparent characteristics. Like the Sileni of which Alcibiades speaks in the *Symposium*, the dandy's "inner truth" might be made visible. We must look to Brummell himself, Barbey's central figure, to determine whether this paradox of vulnerable invulnerability, too, must be accepted in our search for modernism's dandy.

THE TRÉBUTIEN SOLUTION

Barbey appropriates qualities from both actual and fictional people. Mlle de G... and St. Sebastian seem curiously similar, for Barbey's purposes of self-portraiture—one "created" by aristocratic lineage, the other by an aristocratic painter. All of his portraits, of those living and dead, made of words or paint or stone, bear a family resemblance that ultimately converges on "le Dandy." The individual, accumulative gestures of appropriation that he carried out both before and after the central portrait demonstrate how he slowly came to furnish the empty abstraction of "dandyism" with a passionately felt series of human qualities. To ask, for example, why Barbey's dandy must be fiercely vain is to ask whom Barbey has noticed, and how, rather than what the phenomenon of dandyism is.

What I find in Barbey, so frequently as to suggest compulsion, is the story of appropriation. Barbey recounts, across all the years and genres of his writing, a tale of embrace. This embrace takes different forms, from the mildest of fantasizing to full-scale invasion and subjugation of another identity. For the critic who witnesses the repeated scene, an array of metaphors suggests itself. Barbey empathizes with others, or adopts them; annexes, colonizes them; fastens parasitically or vampirishly upon them. Yet this "taking" involves always an act of creation as well; Barbey presses others with the stamp of his own personality before impressing them into the service of his own personal drama. He teaches them to speak the *lingua barba* before he arrogates them to the empire of self.

If this sounds morally suspect, it is, and consciously so on Barbey's part. Intent on self-creation, he softens the line between lie and fantasy, criminality and poetic license, plagiarism and creation. To the extent that his portrait of Brummell has a center or heart, it is one of scandalous but satisfying license, and a strong sense of pride. In describing to his old friend Trébutien a literary hoax that he imagines carrying out, he confesses, "J'avoue que c'est pour moi un de ces profonds plaisirs d'ironie solitaire qui exaltent le sentiment de la puissance et qui sont de plaisanteries de Dieu" (*L* 1:223; I confess that this is for me one of those profound pleasures of solitary irony that exalt the feeling of power and that are God's jokes). The hoax itself reveals just how far toward the fraudulent Barbey can imagine moving.

In a letter to Trébutien, swearing him to secrecy, Barbey writes that he has patterned the central character of his novel, *L'amour impossible*, after an actual society woman, the marquise du Vallon. But the real secret is this: she has agreed to sign her name to his most current novel, soon to appear in installments in *Le Constitutionnel*. "Ne trouvez-vous pas cela *inattendu* . . . prendre des jupons pour écrire comme George Sand prit un pantalon à braguettes" (*L* 1:221; Do you not find that *unexpected* . . . putting on a skirt to write as George Sand put on button-fly trousers). The letter is a performance of vivacity and wit in which Barbey first presents as fact, and slowly reveals as fantasy, a plan to give over his writing, his self-expression, to a woman. It is the verbal equivalent of cross-dressing; the voltage Barbey feels is the thrill of being, however briefly, Barbey and not Barbey, male and not male, creative and passive. Yet the passage as a whole is about power; the power he would gain by being able to fool the public he would lose in allowing the woman to "become" him. He reasserts his power; the plan is, happily, unworkable because of the very strength of, in "her" words, "votre terrible et indéguisable vous." Taking the real marquise du Vallon and making her a fictional character was a kind of hoax that felt good. Taking her up again, this time to make her not a character in a novel, but a character in an "actual" plot (both novel and hoax are fictions, meant to fool), seems at first an exciting act of remanipulation, until we see Barbey unwilling to be appropriated, to relinquish his work to another's name.

In fact, this letter itself takes its place in an extended action of appropriation, one that fed Barbey's imagination during the years he created the palimpsest that **was** Brummell. This was his simultaneous creation and destruction of Guillaume-Stanislaus Trébutien, bookseller, scholar, and antiquarian in Normandy, a process that spanned their correspondence (1832–58) and ended when Trébutien could accept such double abuse no longer. While it continued, Barbey, Brummell, and Trébutien formed a *mise en abyme*, and the prose of "Du Dandysme" developed as a set of mirrors rigged to catch the reflection of the correspondence surrounding it.

In these letters, Barbey carries out on a grand scale the art of self-portraiture, continuously creating a Trébutien who exists as a version of Barbey himself. That this portrait takes shape in a series of letters addressed to its subject is of significance, because it is a portrait more of a process than of a person. It is an epistolary portrait of an influence: of Barbey's describing, teaching, cajoling, controlling another. As the portrait of the growth of a relationship between two people, it demonstrates, in practice, what Barbey believes to be the essence of his project on dandyism and Brummell: to show Brummell not, primarily, as a historical figure, existing as a peak among the foothills of his society, someone merely stronger and wittier and better dressed than the others, but as an *influence*, as a man whose greatness inhered in his relation to his society. Barbey confides to Trébutien that he intends not to base his study on facts and anecdotes:

> J'ai cherché à m'expliquer une influence, j'ai marqué les besoins que cette influence révélait, je l'ai circonscrite, etc., etc. En d'autres termes, j'ai fait de si haut de l'histoire que ce n'en est presque plus.   (*L* 1:119)

> I sought to explain to myself an influence, I noted the needs that that influence revealed, I circumscribed it, etc., etc. In other words, I became so removed from the history that it practically no longer is one.

From this point of view—and for Barbey, a point of view is seldom preclusive of others—Brummell came into existence to fill a void, to serve a society peculiarly in need of his gifts of caprice, elegance, and force. Yet at the same time, he dominated the society that gave him power ("J'ai marqué les besoins que cette influence révélait"), rescuing it from ennui, spurring it to flee vulgarity, teaching it a new standard of success. Barbey's Brummell is, then, paradoxically both the necessary expression of a puritanical society's repressed impulses of whim and beauty, and vividly his own man.

With this paradox in mind, we turn back to the letters and enter Barbey's world of analogy. Just as Brummell and English society existed in a circular relation to each other, so do Barbey and Trébutien. The correspondence is a record of Barbey's influence over Trébutien, his re-creation of Trébutien as foil, mirror, sounding board, factotum. Because it exists as a work in progress,[5] the correspondence is mildly horrifying. It is one thing to see Barbey reflecting his preoccupations in his exemplary portraits; it is quite another to watch him forcing an actual person to participate in his self-portraiture. Barbey transforms a living person into an image of himself, and in the process drains him of life: "Pardonnez-moi cette abusive correspondance," he writes (L 1:199; Forgive me this abusive correspondence). Barbey abused Trébutien in order to construct a scale model of a relationship: as Trébutien is to Barbey—an active, if unwilling participant in the drama of dandyism—so society would be to Brummell. For dandyism, the cult of the individual, requires spectators. As Barbey the dandy creates Trébutien, he creates the notion of Brummell's relation to English society, which he will echo in the essay.

Seen in this light, "Du Dandysme et de G. Brummell" truly loses its boundaries; it grows seamlessly out of the correspondence. Letters and essay appear as versions of each other, as do Barbey and Trébutien, as do Brummell and his public. The categories of art and life begin to merge.

From the beginning, it is a chronicle of power, of Barbey's gradual encroachment upon Trébutien, first claiming his sympathy and friendship, then his time, energy, and professional expertise, and eventually his very identity. Barbey feels himself, typically, "fou de sensations vives" (L 1:178; mad with vibrant sensations), but counts on his friend to rescue him: "vous me soutiendrez dans ce travail qui me réfléchit le passé comme dans un miroir concentrique et me le renvoie dévorant" (L 1:178; you will support me in this work which reflects the past back to me, as in a concentric mirror, and sends it devouring back to me). If Trébutien must be stalwart, he must also be comforting, yielding: "Vous êtes pour moi un oreiller de satin rose orné de dentelles sur lequel j'endors tous mes scrupules" (L 1:182; You are for me a rose satin pillow decorated with lace on which I put to sleep all my scruples). The agreement is always one-sided: in exchange for being what Barbey needs, Trébutien will receive Barbey's undying friendship, itself a guarantee of more demands, unceasing needs. Description in the letters inevitably gives way to command: intimacy becomes encroachment.

[5]For a thorough, if jargon-ridden, reading of Barbey's letters and journals as literary creations, see Dodille. Although he traces the growth of Barbey's obsessions in these texts, their sheer volume and complexity have prevented him from carrying out a specific search for the figure of the dandy within them.

Barbey creates in the correspondence the fiction of their collaboration. Time and again, Trébutien the scholar is called on to provide facts and information which Barbey will then transform, in the furnace of imagination, to art itself. Trébutien is cold while Barbey is hot; he contrasts "les turbulences, les agitations, les ardentes indigences de ma vie!" (*L* 2:208; the excitement, the agitation, the ardent destitution of my life!) to his friend's careful research among his books, "au sein de ces livres dont il est l'usufruitier, comme une abeille dans sa maison d'or" (*L* 2:208; at the heart of those books of which he is the usufructuary, as a bee in its house of gold). Yet it is Barbey who methodically makes use of Trébutien's scholarly wealth, Barbey the vampire who unceasingly sucks at Trébutien's energies. Imperatives punctuate the flow of Barbey's peculiar epistolary style, half rant, half chat: aidez, soutiendrez, ecririez, faites, ramassez, pressez, occupez, assurez, n'oubliez (help, support, write, do, collect, hasten, occupy, assure, do not forget).

All of the tasks assigned Trébutien become, in the end, one great task, that of observing Barbey, and by observing, giving him life: "Vous seul êtes mon témoin et mon juge et je vis en votre présence mieux qu'en présence de personne. Je me VOIS VU" (*L* 4:102; You alone are my witness and my judge and I live in your presence better than in the presence of anyone. I SEE myself SEEN). The act, the primal favor every dandy demands, is faithful observation. It allies the dandy to his audience in a never-ending circle of domination and subservience. Just as Barbey needs Trébutien, yet believes himself his superior as artist and man, so Barbey's Brummell, standing at the apex of English society, courts his audience even as he reviles it. In exile in Caen toward the end of his life, Brummell would rather die than remain invisible to London society.

But how to keep the victim from turning on him? Barbey attempts to claim Trébutien's loyalty by describing him as part of the family: as spouse, jointly creating his books, "je suis sûr que votre ou plutôt *notre* livre sera adorable de *mise*" (*L* 1:198; I am sure that your, or rather *our*, book will have an admirable *appearance*); as mother, "merci, mon cher ami, de toutes les maternelles anxiétés de votre lettre" (*L* 1:128; thank you, my dear friend, for all the maternal anxieties of your letter); as father, uncle, brother, friend, only confidant. But metaphors of intimacy, however sincere, slide inevitably into acts of possession. We can only wonder how Trébutien felt, receiving letters in which Barbey claims him as a (subordinate) double: "cette âme échoïque et que j'ai appelée mon clavier" (*L* 1:32; that echoing soul I have called my keyboard) or, even worse, imagining him as a twin Christ: "de croix à croix, vous de la vôtre, moi de la mienne, nous

nous aimerions toujours" (*L* 1:138; from cross to cross, you from yours, I from mine, we will love each other always). There they hang in Barbey's fantasy, forever a pair of martyrs.

The distance between the two as they hang on their crosses is, however, a necessary gap. Were Barbey no longer able to engage in the creation of a Trébutien who increasingly resembles Barbey himself, he would lose his influence, his only power, the dandy's defining quality. "Je serai le lapidaire de votre esprit" (*L* 1:274; I will be the lapidary of your wit), he promises Trébutien. Like the image of the dandy who turns cloth into lace, this is an image of refinement by reduction. Yet were he to polish Trébutien's wit too far, his prey would elude him. In crafting the portrait of Brummell, Barbey will insert the lesson he learns over time with Trébutien: that the dandy who would create his own sense of superiority through imperialistic relations with others must take care not to efface wholly the native population, since his only source of being lies in their eyes. Barbey's Brummell dies not through alcoholism or gambling debts, but because of a monstrous egotism which, as it shades into madness, the world no longer cares to witness.

Among the letters to Trébutien we excerpt a series that treats specifically the writing and publication of "Du Dandysme." No other single work of Barbey's makes so frequent or so intense an appearance in the correspondence. Barbey himself suggests to Trébutien the idea of publishing an edition of "Du Dandysme" which would include the letters as annotation. While the correspondence as a whole displays Barbey's influence over Trébutien, this group of letters presents the contrary record of Trébutien's influence over Barbey. This tale completes the story of the dandy's relation to his audience, for, if his is a pose of utter, spiritual superiority—"ils voulaient marcher dans leur nuée, ces dieux" (they wanted to walk in their cloud, those gods)—it is as well a posture of martyred submission to the vulgar, material world: clothing, people, facts. The foremost fact is this: "Du Dandysme" would have been neither written nor published without Trébutien's help. He supplied Barbey with virtually every fact about Brummell's life which appears in the essay, and, when Barbey could not find a publisher, Trébutien took on the project.

The language of command still dominates these letters, yet what Barbey requires goes beyond Trébutien's willingness to echo, support, *become* Barbey, to matters far more solid: information, paper, ink. Barbey sends Trébutien a list of questions about Brummell's life which reveals that the essay is wholly present in his mind, in germ. Yet Barbey's conception of Brummell as a figure who must be captured in terms of his physiology, temperament, and influence lacks empirical support. It is Trébutien who must seek out the material to make true the shapes of Barbey's ideas. When Barbey discovers that a Captain William Jesse is completing a biography of Brummell, it is Trébutien who must write to him, see him, act as a conduit for Jesse's mere information about Brummell. And finally it is Trébutien upon whom Barbey must register the very act of creation: "Je vous écris avec une plume qui fume encore de mon *Brummell*. Je viens de l'achever" (*L* 1:118; I write to you with a pen that still smokes with my *Brummell*. I have just finished it).

In asking Trébutien to perform the functions of researcher, audience, and publisher, Barbey is really asking of him a more profound favor: to act as intermediary between himself and the world: "Ce qui m'a manqué jusqu'ici, c'était un moyen de publicité, un large et puissant intermédiaire entre mon esprit et beaucoup d'esprits à la fois" (*L* 1:109; What I was missing up to now was a means of publicity, a large and powerful intermediary between my mind and a lot of minds at a time). Barbey seeks fame and needs publicity, but, in parallel, he cultivates an egotism so great that it would deny the world. Barbey guides Trébutien toward two paradoxical limits: becoming the idea of Barbey himself, that is, losing his, Trébutien's, own identity; and, conversely, becoming "not-Barbey"—the world, other people, plain facts. The dandy's drama develops in just this conflict between extremes. Like Falstaff, the dandy embodies utter egotism aspiring to utter worldliness.

PARADOX AND DECEPTION: "DU DANDYSME" ITSELF

Barbey's passion for (self)portraiture begins in the ache of *mal du siècle*, in his efforts to escape ennui: "Je ne sais pas ce que j'aurais donné ce soir pour ne pas être moi-même" (*M* 1:198; I do not know what I would have given this evening not to be myself). Society teaches him how little masking matters: "le monde n'est plus pour moi qu'un vieux masque démasqué, remasqué, et démasqué cent fois" (*L* 1:190; the world is no longer for me but an old mask unmasked, remasked and unmasked a hundred times). As a frequent guest in the world of masks, he too might assume other identities. Yet the problem of ennui only reasserts itself through the mask, which, after all, separates one from others. He fears solitude and, even when he meets others, cannot lose the crushing sense of self-entrapment in relations that are tied and untied "like a garter." His is a dandy's paradoxical solution: only through the intensification and complication of his sense of himself can he hope to escape that self. Hence the series of exemplary portraits, all of them depictions of intensity: deeply felt sadness, purity, elegance, suffering, friendship.

We have missed the source of Barbey's genius if we stop at this point, describing him as one who made portraits of others, the better to mirror, aggrandize, escape himself. Throughout his writing there is a strain of comment on the act of self-portraiture, in which Barbey claims actually to have experienced himself as divided, as existing in multiple versions. He describes himself as branching, forking: "Ma vie bifurque et trifurque de tant de côtés . . . comprenez cette vie en l'air" (L 1:239; My life splits in two and in three on so many sides . . . understand this life up in the air). Or he enters a psychological state that is divided, and even uses two languages to express it: "*It is not dream and not reality*, mais je sortirai de cette position *bicéphale*" (M 1:10; but I will quit this bicephalous position). When he imagines possessing others by extending the self past its own permeable limits, such an imaginary "taking," physical or spiritual, can be, for Barbey, real: "à un certain degré dans le désir, la force de l'imagination corporise, et il y a possession réelle" (L 2:299; to a certain extent in desire, strength of imagination is incarnated, and there is real possession). Imaginary and "actual" possession merge. We begin to see that if his appropriation of others is sometimes, as in the case of Trébutien, cruel or selfish, it is not necessarily cynical. He imagines Trébutien so acutely that he possesses him by the very act of portraiture: "deux têtes sur un même corps, un *bicéphalisme* d'intelligence" (L 1:291; two heads on the same body, a bicephalous intelligence). And if one is double, why not multiple, feeling one's many faculties as both *moi* and as so many separate but equal selves:

> Dieu m'a pétri de je ne sais combien de limons! . . . Je suis double et triple et multiple, mais tout ce faisceau de facultés . . . tout cela, c'est moi. Faut-il casser son *moi* comme on casse un bouchon de cristal, et des dix mille facettes où se jouait la lumière n'en prendre qu'une?   (L 2:199)

> God formed me from I do not know how many dusts! . . . I am double and triple and multiple, but this whole bundle of faculties . . . all of it is I. Must one break one's *I* as one breaks a crystal stopper, and of the ten thousand facets on which the light plays take but one?

First conceiving of the self as a whole made of many parts, Barbey metaphorically breaks the fragile shell of self and then exults in its prismatic qualities. Since no single quality can take precedence over another, the self is irreducibly multiple. Barbey's recurring images of kaleidoscopes and chameleons metaphorically capture his sense of self as both multiple and in flux, as reflecting, capturing the changing patterns that are other people.

Paradox lies at the heart of this imaginative world. Barbey begins with a self that is *moi,* as sturdy and opaque as dried mortal clay. Yet this self is unstable because multiple; the *moi* is also crystalline, sharp, and capable, like the shards of glass wielded by the dandies, of delicately unmaking the self identified with the physical body. The self in fragments prismatically absorbs and refracts light from many sources: marble busts, paintings, friends, passersby. Self is other. This paradox is the first among many for Barbey; it will be refined and restated, eventually, by an equally powerful paradox: that male is female. In moving from the first paradox to the final paradox, Barbey creates his greatest portrait: George Bryan Brummell. Let us, then, reapproach the work about which we have been circling: "Du Dandysme et de G. Brummell."

The facts of Brummell's life as Barbey states them are easily recounted; the facts of dandyism, for reasons which I explore, resist paraphrase. To begin with Brummell himself: he was born in 1778 to a middle-class father, who made a fortune as private secretary to Lord North and spent much of it in entertaining celebrities of the day, including Charles James Fox and Richard Brinsley Sheridan. Brummell attended Eton, where he evidently shone as a proto-dandy, and earned the name Buck Brummell. After a short period at Oxford, he came down to enter the Tenth Hussars under the command of the Prince of Wales. It is here that his brilliant story really begins, for he captured the eye of the Prince of Wales (who was to become George IV). The prince's many favors appeared only to bring out the young man's native gifts of elegant dress and deportment, impertinence, vanity, and wit.

Before long, Brummell was the arbiter of taste, the sovereign of opinion. He resigned from the military, set up an elegant household in Chesterfield Street, and commenced a life of exquisite leisure. Never a libertine, Brummell, according to Barbey, in fact held himself aloof from women, preferring to find his pleasures in drink and gambling. He was a great artist whose work of art was himself. He charmed and terrorized, ruling London society from 1799 to 1814. Then he began to fail. He was too impertinent in his behavior toward the prince, he ran up crushing gambling debts, and eventually he had to leave England, in 1816. While he was setting up an elegant establishment in Calais, his personal belongings were auctioned off in London. For a time he continued, in his exile, to receive English society. The visitors came less and less frequently, he was unable to speak French fluently, and this master of conversation languished. His talents simply would not translate into French. After several years, William IV created a consulate at Caen and awarded it to Brummell, but this act precipitated the final stages of his downfall. His meteoric rise was balanced by his deeply miserable and protracted final years in Caen. Mad, starving, filthy, and inarticulate, he eventually entered the Bon Sauveur Hospital and in 1840 ended his days there, a charity case.

Such a biographical synopsis rings false to anyone who has read "Du Dandysme," because it implies that the essay may be divided into parts, one about dandyism, the other about this particular dandy. Barbey sees the essay in more organic terms: "Je dirai, en le précisant, ce que c'est que Dandysme; j'en montrerai les caractères, j'en ferai la législation, et enfin je complèterai l'idée par l'homme qui personnifia le plus cette idée, dans sa magnifique Absurdité" (L 1:77; I will say, in defining it, what Dandyism is; I will show its characters, I will make its laws, and finally, I will complete the idea through the man who most personified this idea, in his magnificent Absurdity). This account of the project, directed to Trébutien, bristles with implied and stated contradictions, not the least of which is the repeated use of *je* when the letter itself attests to the relationship, the collaboration, which has all along been seminal to the project. There is, further, the problem of conceiving of Brummell as a fulfillment, a personification of dandyism. For Brummell is a historical figure, an actual man. Brummell the man and Brummell the abstraction, the type of the dandy, pursue one another, endlessly, dizzily, throughout the essay. The more Brummell personifies dandyism, the less human and more universal he is. Yet dandies are exceptional, striking, unique human beings; it is precisely their goal to be sui generis. Barbey is thus forced at times to portray Brummell as the superior man from whom the notion of dandyism may be inferred, rather than as a personified abstraction. The work's title, yoking abstraction and man, points out the contradiction that generates much of the essay's electricity; a dandy may never, as Barbey plans, merely fulfill "legislation," display characteristics, stand for ideas. Yet without the idea of dandyism, without its mysterious code, Brummell would be nothing but a fop. Dandy and dandyism cannot exist separately; nor can they merge. Their modus vivendi is paradox.

Paradox suited Barbey. "Je suis inquiet, inquiet, inquiet. . . . Il n'y a que la vaste fixité de l'inquiétude en moi," he writes (L 2:218; I am worried, worried, worried. . . . There is only the vast fixity of worry in me). "Du Dandysme et de G. Brummell" is a work enacting such uneasiness, asking us to keep a steady eye on ideas that, yoked together in troubling ways,

strain against each other. Paradox involves the juxtaposition of two conflicting meanings, neither of which can triumph.[6] Is dandyism better captured deductively or inductively, through the abstraction or through the
man? Paradox asks us to decide between two meanings that, precisely because they reflect each other, cannot be judged separately; paradoxes "do
two things at once, two things which contradict or cancel each other"
(Colie 8).

The paradoxes in Barbey accumulate: the paradox of Brummell's portrait, which is always to a degree Barbey's self-portraiture; the irreducible
conflict between the specific dandy and dandyism; the paradoxes generated when it is a dandy (a lying, posing, hoaxing Barbey) who writes about
dandyism, itself the art of lying, posing, hoaxing, etc. Indeed, Barbey
writes self-consciously in the tradition of literary paradox which Colie has
mapped. When, for example, his critics label his latest work paradoxical,
he responds:

> Des paradoxes! Ah! parbleu! . . . Ils verront—J'ai tellement la haine du
> commun que la vérité m'ennuie et me dégoûte du moment qu'elle se répand.
> Fâcheuse disposition, mais c'est la mienne. Je ne suis point un sage, non!
> morbleu! mais la folie incarnée, surtout depuis quelque temps. Je trouve une
> volupté dans la déraison, et le diable m'emporte.   (M 2:254)

> Paradoxes! Ah! for God's sake! . . . They will see—I have such hatred for
> the common that truth bores me and disgusts me from the instant it takes
> hold. An unfortunate disposition, but it is mine. I am not a sage, no! for
> God's sake! but madness incarnate, particularly of late. I find sensual delight
> in insanity, and may the devil take me.

Barbey sees paradox as an antidote to fixed, accepted truth; like Erasmus's
Dame Folly, he must seek a superior truth through "déraison."[7] He sees
paradox in relation to lie, but the saving lie: "Quand je ne mens pas tout à
fait, je ne dis vrai qu'à moitié," he asserts (M 2:282; When I don't lie completely, I only tell half-truths). Lying and truth-telling, hyperbole and
delphic silence: the essay's coupled ideas struggle before our eyes. The
dandy forces us to take notice, to see, to see him.

What we see is strangely familiar, a prolonged déjà vu. Like Barbey's

---

[6]For a superb account of the tradition of paradoxy in Renaissance literature, see Colie.
I have adopted her descriptions and definitions of literary paradox, implying the continuity
of nineteenth-century and Renaissance paradox, although a full study of that continuity is
beyond the scope of my study.

[7]See Kaiser (92–100) for a germane discussion of Stultitia's paradoxical nature.

madmen, Brummell is a "cariatide," petrified, made stony, by an excess of emotion. Like St. Sebastian, he is a wounded martyr who yet appears unbloodied, natively aristocratic; like Mlle de G... he has a feminine, opulent austerity, a paleness reflecting an inner, possibly demonic, holocaust. Like Barbey himself, Brummell is a wasp-waisted *damoiseau*, superior to the vulgar people who surround him, yet in need of a pose to impress and control them. Like all of these portraits, Brummell is Barbey's self-portrait paradoxically masquerading as biographical essay.

Certainly Barbey's work is not the first to build its foundations on the fault lines of paradox. Yet earlier creators of paradox erected their structures to the greater glory of God; John Donne, Erasmus, François Rabelais, even Cervantes, imagined a place in which the eternal contradictions of paradox might find a final point of convergence. Barbey, though a Royalist and a Catholic, creates in his works worlds both built on paradox and aspiring toward it; they are works that exist "en l'air," with only a suggestion of moorings. They are a series of transformations, collages in progress, infinitely layerable palimpsests.[8] Barbey constructs them of trickery, ruse, caprice, even lies.

Dandyism, whether it strolls by on the street or the printed page, creates a particular kind of audience. Barbey's essay, from the moment it begins to contradict itself, from the moment its mocking lightness of tone suggests we take it with more than a grain of salt, forbids us to suspend disbelief as we are accustomed to doing. In this world turned upside down, we cannot ignore lies in order to seek the truth. Rather we must choose to seek the truth inhering in contradiction and deception. This can be difficult, painful. In reviewing Richelieu's *Memoirs* (*O&H* 14:139–51), Barbey quotes approvingly the witticism of Madame du Deffand: "Il n'y a dans ce monde que trois sortes de gens: les trompeurs, les trompés, et les trompettes" (*O&H* 14:141; There are only three sorts of people in the world: the deceivers, the deceived, and the instruments). Barbey writes of Richelieu (who appears throughout "Du Dandysme" as almost as fine a dandy as Brummell): "Il fut le trompeur, il est la trompette, et nous, nous serions les trompés" (*O&H* 14:141; He was the deceiver, he is the instrument, and we, we will be the deceived). A general principle of literary dandyism emerges: if we evade the deception, we miss the essence of the dandy's work. A corollary: there is always another angle of deception. How, then,

---

[8]I read Barbey as an *ironist*, much as Rorty (*Contingency, Irony, and Solidarity*) has described this modern figure. Yet, as my argument indicates, Barbey opposes his view of the contingency of the labyrinthine self with the image of a palace of self, a center, from which his posturings flow.

to read a work in which one man hides another: "la défiance devient ici la sagesse" (*O&H* 14:143; distrust here becomes wisdom).

Certainly the distrustful reader may find in "Du Dandysme" the record of one man (Barbey) devouring another (Brummell), the attraction of mystery and lie, the pleasure of discerning hints of Barbey's face in the mirror of his language. Certainly defiant readers have always felt the lure of this game; the essay was a popular success even though Barbey meant it for "le petit nombre des Elus" (*L* 1:255; the small number of the Elect). Barbey has some further advice for the critic of his works. In an essay describing the worthy critic, he states:

> En religion, nous sommes pour l'Eglise, en politique, pour la monarchie; en littérature, pour la grande tradition du siècle de Louis XIV, unité et autorité! . . . Et encore nous ne faisons pas la guerre; nous faisons des dénombrements et des discernements, voilà tout. (*DO&DH* 1:33)

> In religion, we are for the [Catholic] Church, in politics, for the monarchy; in literature, for the great tradition of the age of Louis XIV, unity and authority! . . . And yet we do not wage war; we take count and make distinctions, that is all.

The distrustful and defiant citizen, critic, reader: all make discernments, not war. In the case of "Du Dandysme," this reader discerns, gradually, the complicated pattern of modernism itself emerging from the essay's texture of paradox.

CETTE VIE EN L'AIR

Barbey manages at every moment in "Du Dandysme et de G. Brummell" to set linked antitheses in motion. It was the antithesis of self and other which propelled the project into being, and it is antithesis which keeps it so violently alive for the space of its sixty pages. Barbey's notion of dandyism quivers with contraries: it is English, but French; silenced, but eloquent; ardent, but cold; diffused, but centered. In exploring these oppositions, we achieve the only understanding Barbey is willing to yield to us.

Brummell, according to Barbey, was a man of few words. Barbey further silenced him, rarely quoting Brummell in the course of the essay. We have to take on faith Barbey's statements that Brummell's impertinence had too much breadth to be condensed into epigrams. Barbey portrays him always as a man who has gone *beyond* the merely verbal, a man who communicated by "l'intonation, le regard, le geste, l'intention transparente, le silence même" (DD 257; . . . intonation, look, gesture, transparent intention, even silence). He is a figure of neither words nor action, but influence, which is itself a kind of paradoxical demi-action and demi-language, a series of passive "acts" which one does not commit, but rather embodies. In fact, most of Brummell's actions are of this variety—half passive, half active: he reigns, influences, pleases, ignores, has, is.

Barbey goes so far as to say that "sa vie entière fut une influence, c'est-à-dire ce qui ne peut guère se raconter" (DD 232; his entire life was an influence, that is to say, what can hardly be told in its fullness). Here, the passive/reflexive "can hardly be told" suggests the relation of biographer to subject: by virtue of his very being, Brummell cannot tell his own story; he needs Barbey. Barbey locks himself in a far closer relationship with his subject than most biographers; like the "fous," Brummell cannot speak for himself. But there is an even greater depth of silence within Brummell; not only can he not speak for himself, but what he was, a social influence, cannot be captured in words by anyone:

> ce que l'on appelle exclusivement *esprit*, dans les produits de la pensée, tenant essentiellement à la langue, aux moeurs, à la vie sociale, aux circonstances, qui changent le plus de peuple à peuple, doit mourir dépaysé dans l'exil d'une traduction.   (DD 257)

> what one calls exclusively "wit"—in the products of thought, essentially attached to language, to custom, to social life, to circumstance, those aspects which change most from people to people—must die disoriented in the exile of translation.

Words cannot translate "esprit," linked as it is to the particular and the ephemeral; here, "l'exil de traduction" applies not just to the difficulty of capturing a French phrase in English, but of capturing experience in words.

Here is a central Barbeyan paradox of portraiture repeated and intensified: only in his silence, his voicelessness within the essay, is Brummell present. "Il plaisait avec sa personne, comme d'autres plaisent avec leurs oeuvres" (DD 254; He pleased by his appearance, as others please by their works), Barbey instructs us; among these "others" who use the word rather than the language of bodily gesture is Barbey himself. In his unwilled silence, in his absence which is presence, Brummell plays female to Barbey's male; of Barbey's transformation of such time-honored, misogynistic constructions of gender I have more to say below.

Brummell's wit perishes, if only to be reborn in Barbey's wit. The man, Brummell, has been translated into words; the words have flowed into

Barbey's self-portraiture, to constitute Barbey himself, the man made out of words. Barbey will not, of course, admit to this act of appropriation; its power for him resides in the hiding of all the necessary clues of the theft on the very face of the essay. As it becomes increasingly important to deflect suspicion, Barbey stresses the ways in which Brummell differs from himself. Short of creating the portrait of a female dandy—and his next project is, in fact, projected as an essay about Lady "Beauty" Hamilton—the best way of distinguishing Brummell from Barbey is to emphasize, literally, his foreignness, his very English nature. Throughout "Du Dandysme," Barbey takes great care to distinguish French from English dandyism, claiming that true dandyism can only be English. Yet in writing to Trébutien, Barbey confides, "Je prétends, dans *Brummell*, que le Dandysme ne s'acclimatera jamais parfaitement dans ce pays" (*L* 1:124; I claim, in *Brummell*, that Dandyism will never fully adapt itself to this country). Even had we no external evidence of Barbey's duplicity, the essay itself, in celebrating French dandies of earlier centuries, or in explaining at such length why d'Orsay was not *really* a dandy, suggests that the distinction between English dandyism and French dandyism manqué is not so easily made. In fact, several pages later in the essay, he casually announces that the ancestors of the English are the Normans; if Brummell is untranslatable into French, it is not for lack of a common stock.

Throughout the essay, Barbey distinguishes the English from the French only to collapse the distinction. For every example of dandyism's absolute dependence on all things British, Barbey supplies a counterexample linking it to the French. Dandyism is fundamentally English, although "tout porte à penser que cette origine [du dandysme] est française" (DD 237; everything leads one to believe that this origin [of dandyism] is French). Describing Brummell's characteristically English qualities to a French audience is for Barbey an exercise in cultural translation. It is the issue of *translation*, rather than national character per se, which fascinates him. He conceives of dandyism as English precisely because he wants to consider its transformation in France.[9] Words may be translated, however imperfectly. People, too, undergo translation, though at great personal risk: Brummell, exiled to France, dies of translation. Even worlds undergo translation, as they move from "reality" to printed pages, or from one work of art to another.

Barbey conceives of dandyism as English but French because he wants

[9] For a social and literary history of the importation of English dandyism into Paris, see Creed.

to imagine, once again, an other that is self. The common tongue is to be none other than Barbey's own. Further, he characterizes dandyism itself as, in essence, a translation. French frivolity crossed with English utilitarianism always yields paradox: one culture, one language, one self, expressed only by the power of another, "un genre de traduction" (DD 240; a type of translation). Translation is both impossible and inevitable. Nabokov, heir to the dandy tradition, demonstrates just such a logic throughout the extended meditation on translation which unites his oeuvre.

To ask why Barbey engages in self-contradiction within the essay is to step outside of it. One answer lies in his political views. Just as Gautier attempted a revolutionary reading of human institutions by exploring the metamorphic mode, so Barbey thinks in paradox for political reasons. He is a high reactionary—a monarchist who, even as he writes "Du Dandysme," is returning to the Catholic church. He believes in tradition and unity, the authoritarian grandeur of the past, not the democratic mediocrity of the present. In order to re-create France along these lines, nothing less than a counterrevolution will do. Yet every revolution is, for him, a Terror; his journals reveal that he hopelessly awaits the simple man of action who will turn France back to the ways of the seventeenth century. His heroes are those who show us, tell us, how to act: Machiavelli, Napoleon, Byron. Paradox as a mode allows Barbey to hold in his mind the contradictory, mutually effacing notions of rebellion and reaction, of individual will and overarching authority. It allows him to consider making France new in order to reclaim the past. To paradox Barbey joins restrained rage; his is a tone of indignation, blasphemy, a tone refined and intensified by his efforts to maintain a superior distance from the men whose vulgar self-expression carries the day in France.

Dandyism is an aggressively defensive pose, the pose of a man who feels isolated and threatened within a society he loathes. Brummell's life as Barbey chooses to tell it is the story of an island fortress too weak to repel the pressures of economic reality. Debts impinged. Exile from London hastened his end.

Yet we have evidence that Barbey intended to create the image of the dandy as impregnable fortress. Brummell's irony, Barbey explains, gave him the air of a sphinx, so useful in repelling others by mystifying them and causing them to reveal their own grotesque natures, no matter how carefully hidden. To these statements he adds a note:

"Vous êtes un palais dans un labyrinthe," écrivait une femme, impatientée de regarder sans voir et de chercher sans découvrir. Elle ne se doutait pas qu'elle

exprimait là un principe de Dandysme. A la verité, n'est pas *palais* qui veut,
mais on *peut* toujours être *labyrinthe*. (DD 311, n. 24)

"You are a palace in a labyrinth," wrote a woman, made impatient by looking
without seeing and seeking without finding. She did not suspect that she was
expressing a principle of Dandyism. In truth, not everyone is a *palace* who
wants to be, but one *can* always be a *labyrinth*.

To be a palace within a labyrinth is to be almost grotesquely overdefended;
Barbey criticizes this presumptuous woman (who is actually Eugénie de
Guérin) by dispensing with the palace. He likes, however, the idea of self
as labyrinth in which people die by either losing their bearings or meeting
the fearful monster at the center. The image is, for Barbey, one of the powerful enigmas of self: the best defense is a carefully planned series of false
leads.

The image of the branching labyrinth flatters Barbey because it echoes
his own experience of life as bifurcating and trifurcating. It offers, as well,
an image for Barbey's related concern: whether "cette vie en l'air" can or
should be moored, limited by a gravitational center, or whether the self is
to disperse throughout all available space. Is the dandy only a series of infinitely branching, enigmatic paths, or does he possess a royal "throne
room" of identity? "Du Dandysme" provides us with two answers. In images of light, energy, and grace, it describes the dandy as living his life *en
l'air*, engaged in incessant self-replication. In images of shells, carapaces,
and violence, it describes the self as unitary, inviolable, a volcanic crucible
of self-consciousness from which only an occasional puff of smoke
emerges. This self, because it cannot meander into the identities of others
and emerge again, rejects a wide but vaporous empire. And it has been
there all along, for the exemplary portraits depict people who are just this
way, armored against the world, self-contained, whether by madness, aristocracy, mask, or marble itself.

Brummell lives, paradoxically, both in stone and in air, in palace and in
labyrinth. We learn few facts about his appearance; Barbey hastens to take
his body away, so eager is he to register dandyism as a spiritual or intellectual phenomenon. Dandyism, Barbey insists, is a "manière d'être" (DD
229; a way of being) rather than a way of dressing; lest being remain invisible, Barbey describes it as "entièrement composée de nuances" (DD
229; entirely composed of nuances), a nuance being a kind of demi-
gesture, half movement, and half thought, half visible to the eye and half
intuited. Barbey carries the process of disembodiment even further in a
vocabulary of energy: the dandy is a series of sparks, ephemeral "jouis-

sances," light waves, abstract qualities which, by their intermingling, create the dandy's being. A process rather than an artifact, he radiates his being, "ces impressions vivantes, ineffaçables" (DD 260; these living impressions, ineffaceable), wavelike, upon his audience. Barbey characterizes the entire essay as "cette histoire d'impressions plutôt que de faits" (DD 261; this history of impressions rather than facts).

While Barbey celebrates energy over matter, he recognizes the dangers of the ephemeral personality. Just as Brummell dies, in the terms of the essay in which he has been given life, by exile into a French translation, he dies when the circuitry is broken. Not only does he make impressions on others, but he is dependent on them for the renewal of his own charge. Simply stated, his light burned out. "Ne remuons pas, ne comptons pas ces grains de sable qui furent des étincelles, et que le temps dispersa après les avoir éteints" (DD 258; Let's not move, let's not count those grains of sand that were stars, and that time dispersed after having blown them out), Barbey counsels. Since he existed in radiant relation to others, in the circular making and registering of impressions, he is, like Tinker Bell, especially in need of an audience. Barbey describes even his death in relational terms: "l'heure à laquelle on ne l'est plus pour personne, l'heure du malheur, allait sonnait pour Brummell" (DD 266; the hour at which one exists no longer for anyone, the hour of misfortune, was going to ring for Brummell). No longer "pour personne," he ceases to be.

Brummell's death is especially troubling because his way of life established for Barbey himself a description, even a rationale, for his own "vie en l'air." This is a life created in the motion to and from other people, what he describes in Brummell as his "ondoyante étendue" (undulating reach), and it is curious that this story is one not just of defeat, but of an especially humiliating defeat. Brummell loses his humanity—his language, mind—before he loses his life.

Barbey's account of Brummell's life is, in fact, a twice-told tale. If the first tale is one of relation, disembodiment, "ondoyante étendue," the second tale is its opposite. He begins it, uncharacteristically, with an anecdote, reporting Brummell's escalating impertinence toward the Prince of Wales, culminating in an insult directed to the prince's all-too-corporeal body. Thus he points out the superiority of his own wasp-waisted, elegant presence. This version of Brummell is not radiant, but cold, armored: "cette élégante froideur qu'il portait sur lui comme une armure et qui le rendait invulnérable" (DD 264; that elegant coldness that he carried upon him like a suit of armor and which rendered him invulnerable). A man in armor has no "ondoyante étendue," unless he walks as a paradox. Armored superiority suggests an impression made on others, but it exists to keep them at a chilly distance rather than to establish the alternating currents of social influence. It has to do, instead, with sterility and a military readiness to engage with the enemy in order to defeat him. It is a matter of impassivity rather than passivity.

This version of the self is layered upon the first. Brummell both shocks and amuses, insults and seduces: "Il versait à doses parfaitement égales la terreur et la sympathie, et il en composait le philtre magique de son influence" (DD 256; He poured forth terror and sympathy in perfectly equal doses, and concocted of them the magic philter of his influence). Barbey superimposes these two Brummells by means of tone, rhythm, and diction as much as by image. Reading Barbey the dandy's self-referential text, one is forced to swallow just this magic potion of sympathy and terror. The language, like the man it describes, has a kind of coldness at the heart "que rien n'occupe et que rien n'égare" (DD 254; which nothing occupies and nothing distracts). Not a single note of tenderness enters Barbey's hyperbolic praise of Brummell; rather, Brummell appears at times as the victim, not the object, of Barbey's admiration, as the beautiful butterfly, cruelly pinned, sectioned, and labeled.

A vocabulary of power sharpens the essay: "une grande force de vanité . . . audacieuse dictature . . . toute-puissance individuelle . . . ses mots crucifiaient. . . . il pliait tout sous sa dictature. . . . aspect charmant et cruel . . . il asservissait, etc." (a great force of vanity . . . audacious dictatorship . . . individual omnipotence . . . his words crucified. . . . he made all bow to his dictatorship. . . . a charming and cruel appearance . . . he enslaved, etc.). *This* dandy wants to make war, not discernments, to subjugate others openly: "Il était avant tout un Dandy, et il ne s'agit que de sa puissance. Singulière tyrannie qui ne révoltait pas!" (DD 255; He was above all a Dandy, and the only thing that matters is his force. Strange tyranny that repels no one!). If the self is a palimpsest, one image must wholly dominate the other. If the artist exists in fragile circuitry with his audience, he wants energy ultimately to flow his way, until the lights of others may be extinguished at his will. Drawing on the audience he despises for its failure to recognize him, he seeks his consolation in the intensity of a "cold" energy that, Medusa-like, freezes others. The dandy can best struggle against the softened brains and hearts of the day by exercising a power that is self-consciousness burning coldly within: "Savoir qu'on est une force console de bien des choses cruelles, amères, trompées, brisées, et qui sont la vie. La conscience de soi vaut mieux que la gloire" (O&H 13:42; To know that one is a force consoles one for many things that are cruel, bitter, deceived, broken and part of life. Self-consciousness is worth more than glory). Thus is Barbey's diabolism born in the glories of self-consciousness. In the form of impertinence, it is a stronger weapon for Brummell than bons mots. All of Barbey's works overflow with the imagery of concentration, intensity, passion. When the dandy becomes a writer—and we examine the feminizing moment when this occurs for Barbey—he wields himself, cold of demeanor, burning within, as his own best weapon against the world. Swords, sheaths, armor, birds of prey, military instincts: this is the violence within pressing back against the violence without, defense that is aggression.

Words of violence enable Barbey to free himself and his Brummell from charges of decadence. If the book is a weapon and not a flirtation, it can be wielded to effect change, and precisely the change he wills: "L'homme mesure tout à lui-même et . . . c'est le battement de son coeur qui donne le branle à l'univers!" (DO&DH 1: 275; Man measures everything according to himself and . . . it's the beating of his heart that gives the shock to the universe!). Will, not wit, matters.

Barbey's intensity issues in action, as he raises the flaming sword of his literary works, the challenge to the century's Philistine culture. Brummell, however, appears never to exercise his will other than negatively. He will not be moved emotionally or geographically. He will not submit. He will not work, nor, in the end, will he choose to live. He is neither a silent man who acts (Napoleon) nor a man of words wielding a sword (Barbey), nor a combination of the two (Byron). He is a silenced man who goes mad. The universe trembles not at all when George Bryan Brummell's pulse quickens. For he is only half a man.

FEMME PAR CERTAINS CÔTÉS

Barbey closes his essay on Brummell in a fanfare of antitheses:

> Natures doubles et multiples, d'un sexe intellectuel indécis, où la grâce est plus grâce encore dans la force et où la force se retrouve encore dans la grâce, androgynes de l'Histoire, non plus de la Fable, et dont Alcibiade fut le plus beau type chez la plus belle des nations!   (DD 278)

> Double and multiple natures, of undecided intellectual sex, in which grace is yet more graceful in its strength and in which strength still finds itself in grace, androgynes of History, not more than of Fable, and of whom Alcibiades was the most beautiful type in the most beautiful of nations!

Grace and power, male and female, history and myth are paradoxical pairs—not merely contrasting—because Barbey sees antithesis, not synthesis, as their highest form of expression. Significantly, the oppositions of the passage come to rest in Alcibiades, a figure of pitched contraries: soldier but lover, duplicitous but sincere, lethargic but active, tender but brash, statesman but hooligan. The essay finds its final focus in Alcibiades because his image forces the mind to dwell in equivocation, precisely where Barbey wants it to be. He requires a habit of mind which associates and analogizes contraries rather than effacing them. Only Philistines grasp at the closure of half-truths. Alcibiades himself is the model for equivocal thinking, because he offers, through his self-presentation at the Symposium, a convincing alternative to Socrates' essentialist notion of love. Socrates espouses the received wisdom of Diotima, viewing love as a process that ends in a fixed, abstract goal: the vision of love and truth as one. Alcibiades, in contrast, creates his argument in the process of speaking; the exploration of a particular love, his love for Socrates, is as far as that argument takes him. Alcibiades' experience of love is a compound of distance and intimacy; his love is a current of analogy between self and other, of savoring what is particular in Socrates and in his changing feelings toward him, rather than what might be viewed as universal in their relationship. As Alcibiades experiences it, intimacy never finds a grounding in essences or moves subtly toward an overarching truth; it exists in ever-collapsing, ever-renewing acts of connection between lover and beloved.[10]

In closing his essay on dandyism with the image of Alcibiades, Barbey raises, by implication, the question of what love is. For Barbey, that issue involves not only questions of human identity and its truth-making faculties, but questions of gender as well. Like all his recurrent antitheses—silence and speech, French and English, original and translation, portrait and self-portrait, ardent and cold—the antithesis of male and female allows Barbey to "play back and forth across terminal and categorical boundaries" (Colie 7).

What develops, when Barbey offers us, repeatedly, antitheses that neither merge into synthesis nor melt into an anarchical flow, is a world of analogy. The items within the antithesis come to be related to each other, associated with each other. In such a world, nothing simply is. Everything is *as* the other. What is true of, for example, the French "pseudo"-dandy (Richelieu) and the English "true" dandy (Brummell)—that they are par-

---

[10]See Nussbaum (165–99) for a reading of the *Symposium* which addresses these issues, so central to understanding dandyism.

adoxically both disjunct from each other and joined by common proper-
ties—is true of men and women. Barbey's androgynous dandy is located
within the antithesis of male and female. Yet Brummell is male. Isn't this,
we must ask, the familiar limitation of androgyny once again—that
Brummell is primarily male, with secondary female characteristics, and
not equally masculine and feminine? If Brummell is indeed such a "male
androgyne," Barbey may, in imagining him, explore the mysteries of gender while remaining safely tied to the accepted, unstated constructions of
gender within his society.

Such is not the case. Barbey demonstrates that gender, like identity, exists "en l'air." He is made to feel at times "sur la limite des deux sexes" (*L*
1:82; at the boundary of the two sexes). Surely a man who feels his life bifurcating, one who writes of "ma moitié mâle (l'autre moitié qui n'est pas
mâle, je l'ai aussi!)" (*L* 2:298; my male half (the other half which is not
male, I've got it also!), experiences an internal split. He might then chronicle that split in his portraits of women—Mlle de G..., the marquise du
Vallon, and others—or in the endless assigning of imaginary gender roles
within his letters to Trébutien. But he tells us of the relation of the female
with the male in another, more discursive way as well.

In the 1840s, under the female pseudonym Maximilliènne de Syrène,
Barbey published a series of fashion articles for *Le Moniteur de la Mode*
(*PA* 85–94). In them he throws a few sops to his editors, such as where to
buy the best corsets, or which color is "in" this season, but the articles are
in fact aesthetic meditations. In "De l'élégance" (1843) Barbey distinguishes between beauty and elegance along gender lines. Elegance, he begins, is less than beauty, but more than grace. In a characteristic Barbeyan
shift, however, he states that elegance is not just a diminution of beauty. It
has its own life. Beauty and elegance are as different as man and woman.
Invoking Balzac, who called women "le petit sexe," Barbey announces,
"l'élégance est le petit sexe de la beauté (*PA* 86; elegance is the lesser sex of
beauty). Elegance is, for Barbey, "inférieure à la beauté," but being different in kind as well as in size is "par cela même absolue comme la beauté"
(*PA* 87; even by that absolute like beauty).

For Barbey, elegance is both inferior to beauty and (powerfully) *other*
than beauty. We see him struggling toward a modern redefinition of
beauty which will go by the name of elegance. Furthermore, this redefinition of beauty is *associated* with the female. Just as women, "le petit
sexe," are smaller than, more capricious than men, yet incommensurable,
so elegance is related to and wholly other than beauty. "La Mode" is,
throughout the nineteenth-century vocabulary of fashion, depicted as a ca-

pricious queen, but she, too, must be taken seriously: "la Mode [est] une chose très grave sous son apparente légèreté" (*PA* 91; fashion [is] a very serious thing under its apparent frivolity). Caprice, for Barbey a defining characteristic of both elegance and fashion, is also a defining characteristic of the dandy. Brummell, whom Barbey describes as "ni beau ni laid," is above all elegant; his is a form of elegant beauty which Barbey conceives of in relation to the female gender. It is important to note that neither Brummell nor elegance is essentially female; they are associated with the female, and association is as close as we may come to Barbey's modern version of identity. We cannot recognize elegance (female) without measuring it against a greater beauty (male); yet elegance provides its own measure. Hierarchy is antihierarchy. Brummell, as the personification of elegance, is also the personification of a basic antithesis and association—that of male and female.

Not only does the paradoxical relation of elegance to beauty mirror the paradoxical relation of female to male, but elegance carries within itself a paradoxical antithesis. Elegance claims the lawless freedom of caprice, but it depends on a set of rules, "lois immuables" (immutable laws). The elegant one, the dandy, impersonates paradox, a movement of the mind which demands closure while it depends on process. Elegance is caprice within a code, female within male, movement within structure, radiance within marble. This is the equivocal beauty of the high modern: "When the blackbird flew out of sight, / It marked the edge / Of one of many circles" (*CP* 94). This, too, is Brummell's beauty.

The opening chapters of "Du Dandysme" place women at the center of a phenomenon whose center Barbey is at pains to deny. The dandy's necessary vanity, he explains, bears the same relation to pride that a queen bears to a king. Vanity, to borrow a term from Barbey's *Moniteur de la Mode* article, is thus the "petit sexe" of Pride: feminine, the power behind the throne. Just as we have seen earlier that the distinction between French and English is always collapsing in order to be reconstructed, so distance from, rejection of, women collapses into direct resemblance to them. And this resemblance itself collapses, at times, into something like identity. Dandies are, perhaps, women, although they are men.

The dandy's vanity associates him with queens, but the story of the female in "Du Dandysme" only begins there. It is a tale told on every page of the essay, in figurative language, in delicate nuances of diction, in anecdote and abstraction. It is a tale told, as we shall see, in the very structure of the essay. Barbey likens Brummell to coquettes, courtesans, and muses. Women never forgive him for being as graceful as they. His vocation is to please: the Prince of Wales's courtship of Brummell is as simple as the conquest of woman. Even the dandy's characteristic aggressive coldness, his defining aloofness from women, is itself a female characteristic: "sa vanité ne trempait pas dans un sang brûlant. Les Sirènes, filles de la mer à la voix irrésistibles, avaient les flancs couverts d'écailles impénétrables, d'autant plus charmantes, hélas, qu'elles étaient plus dangeureuses" (DD 245; his vanity was not soaked in burning blood. The Sirens, daughters of the sea, with irresistible voices, had sides covered with impenetrable scales, all the more charming, alas, because they were more dangerous). Barbey especially savors the comparison of the masculine *raffiné* (refined) with the feminine *fauve* (wild). When Brummell is not himself a siren, he is closely associated with the "amazon" Lady Stanhope. His is the only image which solaces her when she is alone and frightened in the desert. Just as Barbey personifies vanity as a queen, he personifies impertinence, the dandy's strongest weapon, as a woman: "Fille de la Légèreté et de l'Aplomb— deux qualités qui semblent s'exclure,—elle est aussi la soeur de la Grâce, avec laquelle elle doit rester unie" (DD 256–57; Daughter of Frivolity and of Aplomb—two qualities that seem mutually exclusive—she is also the sister of Grace with whom she must remain united). Barbey, in associating the dandy with women, takes care to secure him within women's roles: queen, mother, sister, daughter.

Brummell is not a coquette, courtesan, siren, or amazon, but he is like them, and as Barbey suggests of Brummell, the line is hard to draw. Barbey's antithetical association of male and female always threatens to take on a life of its own, similar to that of metamorphosis in Gautier. While Madeleine gallops full tilt at social institutions, d'Albert reins in every impulse. Barbey, combining both of these impulses, personifies them in the single figure of Brummell. "L'analogie s'arrête-là" (DD 226; The analogy stops there), he writes of the similarities between Brummell and Richelieu. Barbey is concerned that such analogizing and equivocation not run out of control. Even as he is engaged in imagining himself a feminized Brummell, he is equally adamant that all remain under control, that he know women stereotypically. To Trébutien he writes,

> Excepté la Vierge Marie, la mère de Notre Dieu et deux ou trois saintes qui sont bien et dûment en paradis, je vois dans les femmes des instruments de volupté ou de souffrance et des enfants gracieux.   (L 2:19)

> Except for the Virgin Mary, the mother of our God and two or three women saints who are well and duly in paradise, I see in women the instruments of sensual pleasure or of suffering, and graceful children.

Women are either innocent virgins and children or seducers and destroy-
ers of men, sirens and amazons. They are to be protected, avoided, or tri-
umphed over by men. Yet Barbey finds himself associating the female with
the male, and in association men's stereotypical power dissipates. When he
sees a particularly admirable woman, he compares her not just to any man,
but to one of his heroes, Byron (*M* 2:356). And in Byron himself he finds
a "female" quality, "la volonté *contredisante* de la femme" (*M* 2:273; the
contradicting will of woman).

  Women encountered in society resemble male dandies; male dandies
created in essays resemble women. In resemblance and analogy begins a
profound association. The vectors of reference to gender are so varied
within the essay, and extend so fully throughout the correspondence, journals, and novels, that the effect is one of a finely woven complexity of the
masculine and the feminine. Just as Gautier presents Madeleine with a
Symbolist tapestry that explains to her the tapestry of her own life, so Barbey creates Brummell within a texture of paradox that suggests the ultimate significance of both the dandy and the dandy-artist's self-creation.
They evince nothing less than the reweaving of a world in tatters. The
dandy lives before the mirror, constructing himself out of paradox, in order to reconstruct the fallen world:

> L'art s'y trouvait d'abord et s'y résumait de main divine; mais depuis que
> l'abus de la liberté a précipité le monde en chute, la création n'a plus été que
> le miroir brisé dans lequel les objets se déforment, s'interrompent et trem-
> blent. Et l'art a été fragmenté comme elle.   (*DO&DH* 1:303)

> Art was there first and was embodied there by divine hand; but since the
> abuse of liberty precipitated the world into its fall, the creation was no longer
> but the broken mirror in which objects deform themselves, interrupt them-
> selves and tremble. And art was fragmented like creation.

The world in history has been broken into shards, art along with it. The
contemporary artist must attempt, echoing God, to remake the world, yet
he cannot ignore the fragmentation of which he and his art are a part. Attempting the impossible, he adopts as his method the paradoxical. He
seeks by the sheer force of thought, the powers of association and equivocation, to join at least some of the larger fragments: male and female,
outer and inner, self and other.

  The writer must both reflect a shattered reality and remake it; Barbey
attempts to do so in "Du Dandysme" by writing an essay unified in texture
but discontinuous in structure. The discontinuity of the essay appears
most clearly in the distance the eye must travel from the body of the essay

to the forty-six appended notes. This distance is farther than it appears to the eye, for it is a distance not just from the central to the peripheral, from the important to the less important, but also from self to other, Paris to Caen, abstract to particular, history to anecdote, male to female. The notes allow Barbey to practice the paradoxist's art spatially and temporally, and we should not underestimate their importance either to Barbey—"selon moi, la meilleure part du *Brummell* sont les notes" (*L* 2:57; in my opinion, the best part of *Brummell* is the notes)—or to the distrustful reader who would grasp the essay in its acts of elusiveness.

Barbey begins to send the notes to Trébutien as soon as he has offered to publish the text. They take their place in Barbey's campaign to appropriate Trébutien: they cause Trébutien to pay further attention to the creations of Barbey's mind, to enter even further into dialogue that inevitably degenerates to monologue. Also, Barbey sees the notes as additions having their own artistic integrity, almost as a genre related to the prose poem or to the medieval illumination: "Elles ressemblent à des onyx et à des camées gravés avec une assez grande subtilité de burin, et toutes, elles ont été écrites à la marge de l'épreuve" (*L* 2:57; They resemble onyxes and cameos carved with a fair amount of engraver's subtlety, and all of them were written in the margin of the galley proofs). At the margins, they are both highly polished gems and capricious scribbles, frame and afterthought. So, too, is their content: what Barbey speaks of in the notes is both superior and subordinate to the body of the text.

The notes, like the essay as a whole, equivocate and associate, pose antitheses and collapse them. Most of them can be read independently of the text, as cameos of thought, but it is in juxtaposition with the text that Barbey's art of paradox takes on a new dimension of complexity. The notes equivocate with an already equivocal text. Let us return to a note we encountered early on, that of the "habit râpé" (see first section of this chapter). It begins ostensibly as a gloss on the textual statement that dandyism has little to do with toilette and material elegance. The example, as we have seen, communicates more uneasiness than certainty. Although Barbey writes to Trébutien that he loves the notes, which he likens to golden nails pinning down the billowing text, this note fixes almost nothing. Who are the dandies, we wonder. In what sense, how seriously, does Barbey call them gods? Just how threatening are those shards of glass? As if to provide some ballast to the note, Barbey expands it, offering another "concrete" example of the textual generality that dandies do not care primarily about their costume. The point of Brummell's gloves is not their perfect fit, but their fabrication by four separate craftsmen, three for the hand

and one for the thumb. This whimsical use of "evidence" does not fully prepare us for what follows in the note, which is in fact another note, embedded within the original. This note-within-note simply *contradicts* the text. It glosses the textual statement that the true dandy is English with an example of an Austrian dandy, the Prince de Kaunitz. And it does so anecdotally.

To the apparent equivocation between text and note, Austrian and English, Barbey thus adds another order of equivocation, that between generalization and anecdote. Anecdote is for Barbey a "feminine" mode, that of women who can speak only of their own experience: "généraliser c'est impossible à des êtres si sensibles et si personnels!" (*L* 1:21; to generalize is impossible for such sensitive and personal beings). The notes offer, in far greater proportion than the text, anecdote. Anecdote is gossip captured in print, and it is the life's blood of the notes, just as the quality of fable suffuses the text. Thus we learn, for example, that the Prince de Kaunitz disdained women to such an extent that he would not allow the death agonies of Marie-Thérèse to affect his *lever* or his *toilette*. The siren-text, sheathed in scales of often impenetrable, impersonal abstraction, gives way in the notes to a far greater range for the "feminine" modes of gossip, feelings, personality. Thus the central male text associates with marginal female notes; this structural androgyny intensifies the thematic association of male and female within the essay.

Many of the notes associate dandyism with women in a more direct way. Women are mentioned as antidandies or as embodying the very traits of dandyism. The notes, far from putting to rest the textual vacillations of gender, only quicken and syncopate the rhythms. The most characteristically Barbeyan performances are those in which he attempts multiple equivocations with the text. It is just because the lines among fable, history, and anecdote are so ambiguous that Barbey can polish his notes, offering a glittering, slippery "aid" to the floundering reader.

In the notes Barbey can state directly, using the word "woman"—"un Dandy est femme par certains côtés" (DD 316, n. 38; a Dandy is a woman in certain ways)—what he clothes in figurative language in the text. There, dandies have the talents of the courtesan; in the notes, they suffer behind masks, stoics of the boudoir, for *"paraître*, c'est *être*, pour les Dandys comme pour les femmes" (DD 314, n.32; to *appear* is *to be* for Dandies as for women). Yet, lest we think that the "truth" of the dandy's female qualities can at last find direct expression in the notes, Barbey intersperses notes of intense misogyny with notes acknowledging female dandyism. After writing a nasty note on the subject of Mme de Staël, whom he despises as he does all bluestockings, Barbey confides to Trébutien, "voilà une bonne note. Diablement hardie, mais bonne" (*L* 1:184; there's a good note. Devilishly bold, but good). Vanity reigns as a queen, but her subject continually rebels against female authority. Barbey tells us both that no woman may truly be a dandy, and that almost all women are in part dandies, since "natural" women, those who are not posing coquettes, are rare creatures.

Barbey feminizes dandyism, then, in several ways: by comparing Brummell to the androgynous Alcibiades (and to coquettes, courtesans, sirens, and amazons); by analogizing the dandy's elegance to the female sex; by structuring his essay, text and notes, along gender lines. Throughout "Du Dandysme" Barbey erects antitheses in order to half collapse them; by the essay's end, gender announces itself as the native ground of paradox.

Yet by the essay's end, one crucial antithesis remains wholly implied—that of dandy and artist. Brummell simply is no artist, Barbey insists. Brummell must be appropriated as such, however, if he is to be fully arrogated to Barbey's empire of self: this portrait of the dandy must figure forth the self-portrait of the artist who creates it. Dandies as elegant people can only be "des artistes de second degré" (*PA* 86). True artists create epic poems or symphonies; artists of elegance, like Brummell, create only themselves. Yet throughout "Du Dandysme," Barbey favorably compares Brummell's qualities to those of Shakespeare, Byron, Machiavelli, Stendhal: second degree is first degree; hierarchy is a net of relations.

The answer to the dilemma of dandy and artist lies locked within the stronghold of dichotomous gender, a fortress Barbey repeatedly attacks within his essay on dandyism. Finding the answer depends on Barbey's ability to achieve once more, but with the fiercest and most unrelenting of energies, what he has achieved all along. He must discover in woman his own truest artistic self, appropriate her so fully that henceforth "dandy," "woman," and "artist" are three terms that, taken together, describe one being, Barbey's own. This he does as afterthought to "Du Dandysme."

THE LOVE AFFAIR OF THE CENTURY

When, many years after initial publication of "Du Dandysme," Barbey writes "Un Dandy d'avant les Dandys," he appears to elaborate on the misogyny of the preceding essay and its notes. At the heart of dandyism lie two irreconcilable sets of facts about gender: first, that dandies create themselves by denying women, freezing them out of their ken, punishing them when they seek intimacy; and, second, that dandies resemble women, that female characteristics are necessary to the dandy's persona.

Although "Un Dandy d'avant les Dandys" tells the story of a "love" affair that occurred in the court of Louis XIV, that between Mademoiselle de Montpensier, "la Grande Mademoiselle," and Antonin de Caumont, duc de Lauzun, we may more profitably read it not as a historical sketch but as the two final exemplary portraits of this study. The framing story is pathetic. At the age of forty-three, the Bourbon princess, cousin to Louis XIV, is an old maid. Immensely wealthy and exalted in rank, she has failed to marry. She and her family have given up hope when she sees the duc de Lauzun, an officer of the King's Guard, and suddenly adores him. Though he is five years younger and far poorer than Mademoiselle, as well as socially her inferior, she sets out to attract him. Barbey now pursues the narrative of dandyism with a vengeance, as he writes the tale of Lauzun's triumph over Mademoiselle, a triumph of negative power. He enters upon an elaborate anticourtship, fanning the sparks of her initial interest by utter coolness. He "respectfully" evades, ignores, repulses her every gesture of intimacy. And it is precisely in his Machiavellian program of seduction by withdrawal that he wins the impossible prize. His conquest is a masterpiece of sadism; she suffers while he enjoys her pain. The princess approaches the king, who agrees to let the marriage take place. When family members, who have their eyes on the princess's fortune, intervene, the king goes back on his word. The princess is crushed, Lauzun is imprisoned. He returns to court ten years later, his freedom purchased with Mademoiselle's funds, and eventually marries another.

The epilogue to "Du Dandysme" is on its face a misogynistic account of a man who becomes a dandy in the process of torturing a woman. His "système" (DD 294), although Barbey describes it anecdotally at length, can be easily summarized: the more a proud woman of rank becomes tender toward one, the more one must retreat behind an impenetrable shield of "respect." This first principle is his only principle. It becomes, as the tale progresses, more satisfactory, from Lauzun's point of view, as a guide to action, but less satisfactory, from the reader's point of view, as the tale's center of interest. If Barbey set out to illustrate a dandy's campaign of coldness, he would have done better to shape it into a lengthy note rather than a short essay.

Barbey had, however, a much more interesting goal in mind. He wished to demonstrate that "le Dandysme a sa racine dans la nature humaine de tous les pays et de tous les temps, puisque la vanité est universelle" (DD 281; Dandyism has its roots in human nature of all countries and all times, since vanity is universal). No more flutterings over nationality, no more widening definitions of the dandy tucked away in notes. Barbey is ready to approach dandyism as a phenomenon as timeless and widespread as vanity itself, and one just as female as this queen of emotions. He is prepared, too, to take a step which he only tentatively prepares in "Du Dandysme." In this epilogue, the dandy whose portrait we receive is both a woman and an artist. In 1845, when Barbey initially published "Du Dandysme," he stated that the true dandy could be neither an artist nor a woman, even if he had some creative or feminine characteristics. Brummell wrote poetry, but Barbey hastens to explain that it was mediocre. The true dandy gives of neither his person nor his creative powers.

Artist, man of complex nature, generous soul—d'Orsay cannot be a dandy. Nor can Lady Hamilton, even though Barbey admires her dandy-like qualities. As the best sculptor England ever produced, she is disqualified by both her sex and her artistic gifts. She herself is "statuaire étrange, qui était aussi la statue, et dont les chefs d'oeuvre sont morts avec elle" (DD 318, n. 46; strange sculptor, who was also the statue, and whose masterpieces died with her). La Grande Mademoiselle shares the traits of both d'Orsay and Hamilton. She, too, is a statue. At her advanced age and station, Barbey tells us, she has a marble heart, a soul moved only by etiquette and ceremony. She is a virgin in every way, possibly even of curiosity. But like Lady Hamilton and d'Orsay, she is also a statuary, a maker, an artist. For it is in her *Mémoires*, liberally quoted throughout the piece, that Barbey finds his story, and it is through her *Mémoires* that Mademoiselle recreates herself as she creates the only Lauzun worthy of her attentions. Once again, and for the last time, we watch Barbey reading himself into and out of another portrait. The stakes are higher now, for in this return to the subject of Dandysme, Barbey finally, explicitly, joins the artist and the dandy. Dandies create themselves and artists create works of art, but the modern artist must do both.

La Grande Mademoiselle is a woman of words, of voice. No longer must the dandy be silent. A feminized Brummell has been silenced, but this woman triumphs over her opponent by the strength of her voice, broadening the very concept of dandyism in the process. Through her, Barbey integrates dandy and artist. Barbey quotes frequently and with evident pleasure passages from her journals, and although he asks us to snicker at the vision of maidenhood deluded, he asks us as well to admire it. As the tale progresses, we find it impossible to sneer, as Mademoiselle's complex nature seeks and finds self-expression. Barbey taunts the princess by saying that Lauzun had no need to write his *Commentaries* as did Caesar, because his conquest, an unhappy and lovelorn princess, did the job for him. Yet Barbey not only praises her account of the affair—"cela vaut un roman de Stendhal" (DD 283; that's worth a novel by Stendhal)—but also explains how she, by the power of the word and by her native nobility, gains ascendancy over Lauzun, the cold dandy, precisely by creating him: "Elle grandit l'homme qu'elle aime" (DD 286; She magnifies the man she loves). It is evident, Barbey tells us, that it was impossible in her eyes for any man who had so impassioned her to be anything other than superior to all other men. Barbey's twisted syntax suggests the tortured turnings of the princess's mind as she reaches the only possible conclusion of which she is capable: by his wit, manners and beauty—by his incomparable style— Lauzun exceeds any man at court. She creates him as he must be for her, and if reality (scheming relatives, an indecisive king) presses back, her image of Lauzun is not thereby damaged. Lauzun himself is all but silent; as Barbey robs Brummell of words, Mademoiselle robs Lauzun. *She* forces him to silence, if he would win his goal. She is the author of a romance "inouï"; the consummate dandy, she shocks those around her. Barbey is so moved by admiration that he writes of her: "Elle avait deviné le Dandysme moderne, cette femme-là!" (DD 289; That woman had deciphered modern Dandyism!).

Her life, like Barbey's, bifurcates. She lives it "en l'air," creating by her actions the very events she must then interpret, re-create in her journals. Lauzun's life remains tracked on its narrow path. She is two persons at once—a comic, infatuated old maid who will heap humiliation upon her own head, and the tragic artist-dandy whose celestial vision, conceived as it must be in the fallen world, puts her at that world's mercy. Like Barbey, that other writer of journals meant to be read by others, of private letters whose ultimate publication he wishes to secure, Mademoiselle wishes Lauzun would read her journal and know her heart. The vastness of her pride is redeemed by the sound of her voice in her journals. In a narrative of adversaries, the dandy-artist is a victim, a martyr, and a victor. The dandy Lauzun is a mere doll, wound up to commit cruel, self-serving acts. La Grande Mademoiselle's journal is the "Traité de la Princesse" which, over the years, Barbey imagines writing, but the content is "des choses charmantes comme n'en ont écrit que des écrivains de génie" (DD 293; those charmings bits like those written of only by writers of genius). The writing is subtle, artful: "C'est merveilleux de grâce voilée et de passion hypocritement montrée—de cette passion *qui veut qu'on la voie*, mais qui ne veut pas se faire voir . . . Situation piquante!" (DD 293; It's wonderful in its veiled grace and hypocritically shown passion—of that passion that wants to be seen but that does not want to show itself. . . . Piquant situation!).

In the mirror of Mademoiselle's tragicomedy Barbey finds his most intensely paradoxical, and therefore his "truest," self. She sums up Barbey's yearnings for innate aristocracy and self-possession. She shocks and enrages, challenges hierarchy and sets in motion an unheard of sequence of events, while she embodies tradition and hierarchy themselves. She is a woman whose words make the world true to her inner vision, even as she suffers at the world's hands.

Barbey's portrait of the dandy Mlle de Montpensier is in itself no more definitive a portrait than any of the others. It does not summarize, resolve, or replace the essay to which it is appended; rather, it displaces it for a moment. In the space between Brummell and Montpensier, between the dandy as sterile, silenced male and creatively voiced female, the modern artist emerges. Paradox is the tool, the translation and displacement of ideas and sensations the goal. To see a world of association and analogy in which self is as other, dandy is as artist, female is as male, is to see with a fine, modern eye.

As a dandy writing about dandyism, Barbey parsed the central paradox of identity: its need to take in the identities of others—whatever their nationality, personality, native tongue, gender—even as it contracts to a formidably private crystalline core. This is the insight Gautier personified in the characters of Madeleine and d'Albert; this is the insight Baudelaire was to codify in the opening lines of his journal: "De la centralisation et de la vaporisation du *Moi*. Tout est là" (*OC* 1271; Of the centralization and vaporization of the *Self*. There is everything). Barbey, a Napoleon of letters, established the borderless land of identity, itself ruled over by an insatiable *Moi*. In doing so, he challenged most of the sacred boundaries of his culture, crossing and recrossing the lines between polarized categories, choosing to live in the exile of translation, the unreason of paradox. There Barbey's dandy embodies the seeming, which is the only being, of the female world of elegance, modern beauty itself.

4

MUNDUS MULIEBRIS

━━━━━━━━━━━━━━━━

BAUDELAIRE'S DANDY

During the years 1857 and 1858, Charles Baudelaire (1821–1867) created his version of Thomas De Quincey's *Confessions of an English Opium-Eater* (1821) and *Suspiria de Profundis* (1845). De Quincey's works combine autobiography, polemic, and psychological thriller. In them he recounts his childhood, spent partly in the shelter of a loving family and partly as a street child in London; then his harrowing opium addiction, complete with transcribed visions; and finally his unsuccessful attempts to break the addiction permanently. Baudelaire's version, titled *Un mangeur d'opium*, was the work of a dandy and an artist. Just as Barbey created "Du Dandysme" by appropriating others' personalities, appearances, and labors, so Baudelaire seized on De Quincey's work and made it his own. The process by which *Confessions* became *Mangeur* combined translation, paraphrase, plagiarism, quotation, excision, and addition.[1] Baudelaire invented its

---

[1]For a complete account of the transformation of *Confessions* to *Mangeur*, see Wulf, in Baudelaire, *Mangeur* (28–97).

form partly because his editors clamored for ever shorter versions of De Quincey's original and partly because he saw in De Quincey a writer who told his, Baudelaire's, story. He wanted to lend his own voice to a tale that, though it chronicled the life of an English opium addict, seemed coincidentally to describe the life of a French artist and dandy.

Late in the work, De Quincey relates an opium vision he had as a young man at Oxford. Frequently he sees a dream figure whom he calls Levana, from the Latin *levare*, to raise in the air, to hold elevated. She is, De Quincey explains, and Baudelaire translates, the Roman goddess who presides over infancy and confers human dignity upon the child:

> Au moment de la naissance, quand l'enfant goûtait pour la première fois l'atmosphère troublée de notre planète, on le posait à terre. Mais presque aussitôt, de peur qu'une si grande créature ne rampât sur le sol plus d'un instant, le père, comme mandataire de la déesse Levana, ou quelque proche parent, comme mandataire du père, le soulevait en l'air, lui commandait de regarder en haut, comme étant le roi de ce monde, et il présentait le front de l'enfant aux étoiles, disant peut-être à celles-ci dans son coeur: "Contemplez ce qui est plus grand que vous!" Cet acte symbolique représentait la fonction de Levana.   (*OC* 453)

> At the very moment of birth, just as the infant tasted for the first time the troubled atmosphere of our planet, it was laid on the ground. But immediately, lest so grand a creature should grovel there for more than one instant, either the paternal hand, as proxy for the goddess Levana, or some near kinsman, as proxy for the father, raised it upright, bade it look erect as king of all this world, and presented its forehead to the stars, saying, perhaps, in his heart, "Behold what is greater than yourselves!" This symbolic act represented the function of Levana.
>
> (De Quincey, quoted in Baudelaire, *Mangeur*, 247, with minor correction)

The vision offers no less than an etiology of the dandy, as Baudelaire had been gradually coming to understand the type. He is a figure born in a dream—this vision has been vouchsafed only to the intoxicated opium eater—and destined never to draw a happy breath in the all-too-waking world of France under Louis-Philippe. Like the child who briefly tastes the atmosphere of our troubled planet, the dandy suffers on earth. He soon feels himself, however, lifted high above it. He never loses this sense of superiority, even though he realizes the shakiness of its foundation, for it is not the powerful goddess herself who elevates the child, but only a parent or bystander. Levana works only by proxy, by "mandataire." Further, the dandy, like the child, never reaches the stars and develops his blasé, impassive persona in an attempt to deny any possibility of fulfillment in the mere things of the earth. Creating his persona is the "work" he does to maintain his sense of elevation. Like the rest of us after the fall, even this "unemployed Hercules" (as Baudelaire later describes the dandy) must labor.

Doubly insecure in his elevation—the foundation questionable, the goal of utter superiority unattainable—the dandy, like the child, masters two lessons. First, he learns he must survey creation "comme étant le roi de ce monde," *as* king of the world. Such a role cannot be lightly played or easily rejected. Once Levana has claimed him, he must forever dramatize himself. Second, he must learn the satisfactions available to one who is distant from the ideal, but who nevertheless is moving toward it. Virtually every detail of the vision involves a separation beginning to be bridged, as the dreamer works his way toward union but never arrives there. The infant's mother is wholly absent; Baudelaire has excised one of De Quincey's "digressions" in which he discusses how "children torn away from mothers and sisters" at too early an age "not unfrequently die" (*Mangeur* 337). Separated from his mother, the child is adopted by Levana. Yet she herself will not rear the child, instead delegating this responsibility to the three women who will direct his education in pain and suffering: Our Ladies of Sorrows, Tears, and Sighs. It seems that the child is to be punished for the father's sin of pride when he tells the stars, as he holds the child aloft, "Behold what is greater than yourselves!"

In fact, it is the dream vision's concern with distance and proximity, separation and reconnection, which distinguishes it from the portrait of the high Romantic artist, damned from birth, superior in his very suffering, shaking his fist at the heavens as he establishes his dominion over hell. Baudelaire sees in the *Confessions* a "post-Romantic" story: that of a tortuous proximity to the ideal rather than a rebellious fall from it.

"Levana" is a vision, then, of the need to consider ourselves in painful relation to, rather than banishment from, the heavens. The dreamer is not a child of his mother or of his father, or of the earth or the stars. He is a child of Levana, but only through her agents. Connected to all, he is placed with none. He learns the anguish of a life lived in neither independence nor belonging.

The dream vision itself, as De Quincey wrote it, is an attempt at forming connections, the only redemptive activity permitted the dreamer. The first of these connections relates De Quincey himself to his persona, the narrator of *Confessions*, a relation that echoes the relation of the narrator to the dreamer. These three "selves" are paradoxically the same person and three different people. They are so closely related we cannot extract from the passage any one of them unaccompanied by the other two. In parallel, the passage portrays neither a wholly dreaming nor a wholly waking world: it is De Quincey's translation of the images of the addict's phantasmagoria into the structures of language. Further, the subject of the passage, the opium addict himself, combines two people: one lives in the dark solitude of addiction, the other in the enlightened community of health, and he presents himself as wishing to move from the former place to the latter, though he can never arrive. When Baudelaire enters De Quincey's hall of mirrors, the complexity increases exponentially. Baudelaire "translates" De Quincey's translation, transforming English to French, connecting his own experience and identity (as dreamer, as one "abandoned" by his mother, as sick soul, as writer) to De Quincey's experience and identity.

Baudelaire's "Levana" draws us into a world of complex and disorienting relations. This sense of displacement—who and where, exactly, is the central character?—is intrinsic to the dandy's experience, as Baudelaire wished to portray it. Baudelaire's dandy, as we shall see in some detail, is the man elevated from the earth, but distant from the stars. He is the man chosen for suffering who dreams as an antidote for the sickness of modern life. Further, he is the man who finds his place by losing it. His is a world of proximity. Like a king, but not a king, he rules by the power of analogy, not identity. It is the kingdom of analogy we must explore if we are to know Baudelaire's dandy.

DE L'AIR DANS LA FEMME: CONSTRUCTING THE DANDY

"En relisant le livre *Du Dandysme*, par M. Jules Barbey d'Aurevilly, le lecteur verra clairement que le dandysme est une chose moderne et qui tient à des causes tout à fait nouvelles" (*OC* 951; "If the reader will reread M. Jules Barbey d'Aurevilly's *Du Dandysme* he will see at once that dandyism is a modern phenomenon and owes its existence to a wholly new set of causes" [*SW* 106]). Thus writes Charles Baudelaire, who never achieved any of the extended works on the subject of dandyism he so often projected: "Le Dandysme littéraire ou la Grandeur sans convictions," "Le Dandysme dans les lettres," "Chateaubriand, père des dandies, et sa postérité," "Les Raffinées et les Dandies," etc. (Kempf 56, 122; "Literary Dandyism or Grandeur without Convictions," "Dandyism in Literature," "Chateaubriand, Father of the Dandies, and His Posterity," "The Sophisticated and the Dandies"). Baudelaire explicitly mentions dandyism, that "chose moderne," in several mysterious journal entries, in passing throughout the inspired body of criticism he wrote from 1845 to 1863, and in one concentrated chapter, "Le dandy," within "Le peintre de la vie moderne" (1863). In "Peintre" Baudelaire presents us, as Barbey has done before him in "Du Dandysme," with an essay about dandyism which expands into the entire oeuvre of which it forms a part. Unlike Barbey, Baudelaire sees from the very first the figure of the modern artist entwined with that of the dandy. They appear in the journals, *Fusées* and *Mon coeur mis à nu*, tantalizingly juxtaposed with the extraordinary man, "*le plus grand des hommes*" (*OC* 1296).

Like Barbey's Brummell, Baudelaire's dandy is far more exalted than a fashion-conscious fop; throughout the criticism he is associated with the word "génie," as, for example, when Baudelaire writes that "E. Delacroix, quoiqu'il fût un homme de génie, ou parce qu'il était un homme de génie complet, participait beaucoup du dandy" (*OC* 1130; "[E.] Delacroix, although a man of genius, or because he was a complete man of genius, had much of the dandy about him" [*SW* 377]). One journal entry after another implies the dandy's mysterious superiority—"Le Dandy doit aspirer à être sublime sans interruption; il doit vivre et dormir devant un miroir" (*OC* 1273)—without explaining it: "Eternelle supériorité du Dandy. Qu'est-ce que le Dandy?" (*OC* 1276; "The Dandy should aspire to be uninterruptedly sublime. He should live and sleep in front of a mirror. . . . Eternal superiority of the Dandy. What is the Dandy?" [*IJ* 56, 62]).

Gradually a composite portrait of the superior man and the "chose moderne," dandyism itself, emerges, a portrait that, while it provides a list of some of the dandy's characteristics, presents him as a shimmering locus of human sublimity, a mystery rather than a model. But is the extraordinary man of the journals—"Être un grand homme et un saint *pour soi-même*, voilà l'unique chose importante" (*OC* 1289; "To be, *before all else*, a *great man* and a *saint* according to one's own standards" [*IJ* 73])—the dandy himself?

The relation between the two is always close, though never identical. In the course of his critical writing, Baudelaire repeats a single literary gesture when he wishes to discuss dandyism. He first describes and praises an extraordinary man, and then states that dandyism is an element of his glory. Yet what occurs, over time, is that all Baudelaire's figures of greatness, all their qualities of sensitivity and will, artistic technique and inspiration, spiritual superiority and emotional suffering, Stoicism and Epicureanism, all participate in one immense, vaporous concept: the dandy.

Here is an example of that characteristic literary gesture, from the "Salon of 1859":

Jules César! quelle splendeur de soleil couché le nom de cet homme jette dans l'imagination! Si jamais homme sur la terre a ressemblé à la Divinité, ce fût César. Puissant et séduisant! brave, savant et généreux! Toutes les forces, toutes les gloires et toutes les élégances! . . . il n'est pas puéril, d'ailleurs, de rappeler que le dictateur avait autant de soin de sa personne qu'un dandy raffiné.   (*OC* 1058)

Julius Caesar! What a sunset splendour this name sheds upon the imagination! If ever a man on earth has seemed like God, it was Caesar. Powerful and charming, courageous, learned and generous, he had every power, every glory, and every elegance! . . . it is by no means silly to recall that the dictator took as much care of his person as the most refined dandy.   (*CS* 255)

At the same time as the "Salon" from which this passage is quoted was published, Baudelaire was working on the chapter of "Le peintre de la vie moderne" titled "Le dandy." Notice the phrases from "Le dandy" which either repeat or resonate with this passage on Caesar: "Le dandysme est une institution . . . très-ancienne, puisque César, Catiline, Alcibiade nous en fournissent des types éclatants . . . celui enfin qui n'a pas d'autre profession que l'élégance [*OC* 1177]. . . . [l]e dandysme est le dernier éclat d'héroïsme [*OC* 1179] . . . un soleil couchant" (*OC* 1180; "Dandyism . . . goes back a long way, since Caesar, Catiline, Alcibiades provide us with brilliant examples of it. . . . These beings have no other status but that of cultivating the idea of beauty in their own persons. . . . Dandyism is the last flicker of heroism . . . a setting sun" [*SW* 419–21]). These passages call to mind the conundrum Barbey made so evident: that we cannot know what dandyism is without knowing particular dandies, and (vice versa) that we cannot recognize a true dandy without a general notion of dandyism. The description of Caesar, while it implies that to know dandyism (as *la vie élégante*) is to recognize it in Caesar, suggests just as insistently that only when we know Caesar, only when we add his qualities to our notion of the dandy, will we appreciate the full complexity of the type. If we wish to know, for example, how and why the dandy despises the crowd, Caesar's life will instruct us. The dandy is defensive because the crowd is bloodthirsty.

As a reader of Gautier's *Mademoiselle de Maupin* and Barbey's "Du Dandysme," Baudelaire recognized that dandyism was a phenomenon that could expand to meet its creator's needs. Gautier found there the possibility of continuing artistic revolt against social structures and the aesthetic *via media* of artistic impersonality. Barbey discovered in dandyism the means of multiplying and fragmenting human identity while protecting it from dissolution. And both Gautier and Barbey, wanting to challenge comfortable bourgeois notions of order, chose to examine the concept of gender.

By writing of androgyny and transvestism, by assigning traditionally masculine roles to women (Madeleine as gentil knight, la Grande Mademoiselle as artist), Gautier and Barbey asked their audiences to consider some unsettling possibilities that extend beyond a mere change in sexual roles.[2] Madeleine sees, and we see with her, that by acting as a male and dressing as a male, not only is she accepted as a male by others, but she herself feels somewhat masculine. Further, having seen the power of creating a sense of gender, she understands that, had she remained a woman, she would likewise have been playing a role. This role would have necessitated a change in costume and script, tone of voice and gesture, but it would have been no more or less an activity of self-presentation than that of dressing as a young nobleman. More expected, yes, but "truer," "realer," no. In stepping outside of a dichotomized system of gender, she has stepped off the edge of the "common sense" world into free fall. She cannot imagine a place in which she can be. Her failure is Gautier's: he cannot yet imagine this modern place.

Baudelaire can. He imagines a place in which gender is a matter of self-presentation rather than absolute decree ("it's a girl!" etc.) by considering gender as a special case of self-presentation in general. And here the figure of the dandy must take center stage, for he flaunts self-presentation, reminding us that we, too, choose our clothing, posture, facial expressions, and daily activities in order to present a particular self to the world. Further, the dandy is for Baudelaire a figure who destroys the power of clichéd roles he sees about him, mocking the bourgeois "set piece" of chaste wife or responsible professional man or portrait painter, etc. In the process of creating the elegant dandy, the man whose toilette is sacred and whose waist is tiny, the notion of two separate genders itself is revealed as cliché. The dandy (fragile as a flower, forceful as a general) reveals that a simple dichotomy of female and male does not capture the elusive ways of gender, and that gender in fact is socially constructed, occurring in the experience of creating a sense of oneself as male or female (or both, or neither) and in being apprehended as such by others.

Throughout his works, Baudelaire self-consciously explores the issue of gender as self-presentation, as social phenomenon, as continuum rather

[2] I am indebted to Kessler and McKenna for their arguments establishing the primacy of gender attribution, rather than any "irreducible fact" of gender, in our understanding of what gender means. Of particular usefulness to my discussion is their demonstration that the existence of two separate sexes is not an essential "truth," but a social construction.

than dichotomy. He chooses the dandy, that ultimate actor of himself, as the figure through whom he carries on his experimentation. From early on, women and dandies seem to hover about one another in his musings. Here is an entry from *Fusées*:

> *De l'air dans la femme.*
>
> Les airs charmants et qui font la beauté sont:
> L'air blasé,   L'air de domination,
> L'air ennuyé,   L'air de volonté,
> L'air évaporé,   L'air méchant,
> L'air impudent,   L'air malade,
> L'air froid,   L'air chat, enfantillage, nonchalance et malice mêlés.
> L'air de regarder en dedans,   (*OC* 1256)

> *Of airs in Woman.* The charming airs, those in which beauty consists, are: The blasé, The bored, The empty-headed, The impudent, The frigid, The introspective, The imperious, The capricious, The naughty, The ailing, The feline—a blend of childishness, nonchalance and malice.   (*IJ* 35)

Any of these is an air Brummell would have been proud to claim. And there is that intriguing space between "l'air dans la femme" and "les airs charmants." Is this a list of female or male airs, or both? Such vagueness serves Baudelaire well when he considers the relation of gender to dandyism.

ANALOGY: RECAPTURING THE FEMALE IDEAL

In the process of reinventing dandyism and reconstruing gender, Baudelaire reexamines his idealist metaphysics. He cannot develop his pragmatic view of gender without considering what he thereby places in question: an idealist dualism of heaven and earth, spirit world and material world, form and appearance. The dandy is a superior man, a man higher than the others. Just how high (or sublimely low) is he, and upon what realms does he touch? Baudelaire attempts through his oeuvre to *place* the dandy. Yet he despises systems. He begins and ends not with a metaphysics, but with a set of responses to particular works of art and their creators. Like Barbey, Baudelaire works at a palimpsest, the layers of which contain images of both the artists he most admires and their works. And from the first, Baudelaire admires artists who are themselves dandies, whose very persons are works of art.

In a study of Edgar Allan Poe, he praises, for example,

sa haute distinction naturelle, son éloquence et sa beauté, dont, à ce qu'on dit, il tirait un peu de vanité. Ses manières, mélange singulier de hauteur avec une douceur exquise, étaient pleines de certitude. Physionomie, démarche, gestes, air de tête, tout le désignait, surtout dans ses bons jours, comme une créature d'élection. Tout son être respirait une solennité pénétrante. Il était réellement marqué par la nature, comme ces figures de passants qui tirent l'oeil de l'observateur et préoccupent sa mémoire.   (OC, Raymond ed., 727)

his great air of natural distinction, his eloquence, his physical beauty, about which, so it was said, he was not a little vain. His manner displayed an unusual mixture of *hauteur* and exquisite sweetness, together with an easy self-assurance. Expression, bearing, gestures, carriage of the head, everything about him, especially on his good days, marked him out as one of the elect. His whole being produced a penetrating sense of solemnity. Nature's finest stamp was truly upon him, like those passers-by who draw the observer's attention and linger on in his memory.   (SW 177)

Baudelaire creates a Poe who is a dandy—beautiful in his person, aristocratic, superior to the crowd, nonchalant—and then leaves open the question of how he came to be so. "Créature d'élection": surely not in the Christian sense of election. "Marqué par la nature": surely artifice, Poe's own hand, corrected nature.

In fact, Poe's very appearance implies a metaphysics. Baudelaire sees in him the product of invisible and superior, but quite vague, spiritual forces. The effect of solemnity is created by forces working through the man, but what are they? Poe's writings themselves suggest to Baudelaire the aura of otherworldliness he assigns to Poe's person. Poe's *Marginalia*, a favorite text of Baudelaire's, claims, for example, that we are in "no condition to banquet upon those supernal ecstasies of which music affords us merely a suggestive and indefinite glimpse" (Poe 16:6). Poe's literary accounts of transcendent realms, hidden by nature's opacity, but revealed from time to time to the spiritually aware artist, entice Baudelaire by their very vagueness, by their atmosphere of an otherworldly, sorrowful beauty. Poe is superior, a dandy; the legend of his person and the compelling quality of his tales, intimating an idealist metaphysics without tediously explicating it, inhabit together their portion of the vast literary space that Baudelaire early on sets aside for dandyism. He fills that space, slowly, inexorably, as he contemplates the works of other artists and creates his own in response. The Baudelaire with whom we have grown comfortable is the poet of "Correspondances," an idealist who believes that an inferior, material world echoes a superior, spiritual world, and that the poet's ear is finely tuned to hear that echo, to experience the "universal analogy." He locates this world in an idealist universe in which one absolute order arches above all creation, determining the order here below.

Yet in the "Salon of 1846" Baudelaire writes, "L'idéal absolu est une bêtise" (*OC* 912; "the absolute ideal is a piece of nonsense" [*CS* 84]). He imagines here a vastly different sort of ideal:

> Ainsi l'idéal n'est pas cette chose vague, ce rêve ennuyeux et impalpable qui nage au plafond des académies; un idéal, c'est l'individu, redressé par l'individu, reconstruit et rendu par le pinceau ou le ciseau à l'éclatante vérité de son harmonie native.   (*OC* 914)

> Thus the ideal is not that vague thing—that boring and impalpable dream—which we see floating on the ceilings of academies; an ideal is an individual, set right by the individual, reconstructed and restored by brush or chisel to the dazzling truth of its native harmony.   (*CS* 85)

The ideal is not that vague thing, the eerie spiritual whispers of a disembodied spiritual world. The ideal is not a system, such as pedants in all walks of life cling to. Rather, it is an individual remade not to fit a divinely established template, but to fit simply itself, its "native harmony." And it is the artist who restores the individual to his own, unique, and always harmonious truth.

Throughout his criticism, Baudelaire veers between statements of universal hierarchy and statements questioning that fixity of design. What brings these two views together in Baudelaire's mind is the force of analogy. For, as we learn in "Correspondances," "Les parfums, les couleurs et les sons se répondent" (*OC* 11; Perfumes, colors and sounds respond to one another). Not only does the realm of the ideal correspond to the realm of the material, but it provides the structure within which one earthly phenomenon may correspond to, form an analogy with, another earthly phenomenon. The perfection of the idealist's heaven ironically makes possible a vast fluidity among the things of earth, since all material things are continuously involved in the one universal harmony. Or, as Baudelaire describes the phenomenon late in his life, "les choses [sont] toujours exprimeés par une analogie réciproque, depuis le jour où Dieu a proféré le monde comme une complexe et indivisible totalité" (*OC* 1213; "all things always have been expressed by reciprocal analogies, ever since the day when God created the world as a complex indivisible totality" [*SW* 330–31]).

All the freedoms of synesthesia, all the ravishing notions of plants that gesture to man of moral concepts, or of scents that are as rich as ideas, Baudelaire pins on "the complex, indivisible totality" of Creation. Baudelaire's

God has created a world for the poet, indeed for any type of artist or thinker whose passion is finding likenesses, connections. Yet Baudelaire considers as well, and with increasing enthusiasm, an art that creates, rather than merely discovers, analogies. The change in emphasis, the interest in making analogies rather than corroborating the universal analogy, has enormous consequences. It opens the way to the modernist conception of the autonomous artist. Baudelaire shifts emphasis from universal analogy to what I call artistic analogy, by noting, for example, that "quoique le principe universel soit un, la nature ne donne rien d'absolu, ni même de complet; je ne vois que des individus" (*OC* 913; "although the universal principle is one, Nature provides no example of something absolute nor even of something complete; around me I see only individuals" [*SW* 77]). And he adds a footnote: "Rien d'absolu:—ainsi, l'idéal du compas est la pire des sottises; —ni de complet:—ainsi il faut tout compléter, et retrouver chaque idéal" (Nothing absolute:—thus the ideal of the compass is the worst of stupidities; nothing complete:—thus, all must be completed, and each ideal rediscovered). Baudelaire feels the need to capture what has been lost, what is distant. Nature presents him with nothing absolute, nothing even complete. But the artist, heir to Levana, who begins by trying to recapture an ideal unity, to work his way toward an Ideal he can never wholly grasp, soon discovers himself at play in the fields of analogy. At a distance from indivisible totality, a distance he can only reduce, never eliminate, he experiences the glory of multiplicity, movement, and correspondence in and of themselves, unmoored. No system of universal hierarchy can capture Nature's complexity and change, "le beau multiforme et versicolore, qui se meut dans les spirales infinies de la vie" (*OC* 955; the multiform and multicolored beauty that moves in the infinite spirals of life). Whereas for the idealist, full revelation of the universal analogy is possible only after death,[3] for the analogist, total revelation simply loses its attraction.

The analogist's imagination, committed as it is to reestablishing, by chisel or brush, the harmony intrinsic to each individual, is a potentially chaotic power. No authority outside the artist determines what that harmony should look like. Baudelaire registers his unease at Goya's monsters or the caricaturist Grandville's bizarre visual world. Grandville, Baudelaire tells us, died in the effort to "elucidate the law of the association of ideas" (*SW* 227). Yet there are forces that check artistic lunacy. Baudelaire is uninterested in anarchy and utter chaos, because they simply do not

[3]See Balakian (51–53).

strike him as beautiful. The equivocal harmony he seeks to re-create, the almost recaptured ideal, is best characterized in one of his own images, from *Mon coeur mis à nu*:

> Ce que j'ai toujours trouvé le plus beau dans un théâtre . . . c'est *le lustre*— un bel objet lumineux, cristallin, compliqué, circulaire et symétrique.
>
> (*OC* 1276–77)

> The thing which I have always thought most beautiful about the theatre is the chandelier—a fine, luminous, crystalline object with a complex spherical symmetry.
>
> (*IJ* 62)

The crystal chandelier is a harmony, a complicated combination of tiny parts, each reflecting the light. Each part is in motion, however subtly, so that the sparkling unity and plenitude of its beauty is the result of a continuing process of capturing the light. It is a beautiful symmetrical pattern created by no template, but by the random motions of a multiplicity of pieces of glass as they are struck by fleeting currents of air, random waves of light. Disorder continuously giving rise to a pattern that is not absolute: a modern thing.

While Baudelaire the idealist must satisfy himself with glimpses of the spiritual world, Baudelaire the analogist may turn to his own inner truth and study it at his leisure. The gifted idealist stands between heaven and earth, the analogist between inner and outer realities: "Qu'est-ce que l'art pur suivant la conception moderne?" he asks. "C'est créer une magie suggestive contenant à la fois l'objet et le sujet, le monde extérieur à l'artiste et l'artiste lui-même" (*OC* 1099; What is pure art, according to the modern conception? It is creating a suggestive magic containing both the object and the subject, the world outside the artist and the artist himself). However dark his poetry, Baudelaire proclaims the artist who is "l'homme hyperbolique" (*OC* 736), he who lives ardently, his imagination burgeoning with the new.

Baudelaire never fully abandons idealist language. As late as the 1861 essay on Wagner he speaks of universal hierarchy and (like Coleridge) of imagination in two tiers: the Creator above, the creator below. Yet a curious word begins to appear when he discusses the artist's creation: "concatenated." So well are all the parts of Wagner's music integrated that they are "concaténées" (*OC* 1232). Poe's style, too, he characterizes as "serré, comme les mailles d'une armure" (*OC*, Raymond ed., 734; close-woven, like the chain mail of armor). These words marks a unity that is discontinuous, a unity in linked pieces. If the artist is one who decomposes creation and then reforms it with the articulations of his analogies evident, his works introduce a certain amount of disorder into the world. He offers us a beautiful pattern with intimations of chaos, for what has been linked may be sundered.

The notion of a chaotic unity suggests the presence in Baudelaire's thought of what Eliade sees across world cultures: the desire to reenact, through ritual, the *coincidentia oppositorum*, the "reunion of opposites, the totalisation of fragments" (Eliade 122). Baudelaire's willingness to consider chaos as an element of order suggests that the ideal to which he aspires is not that of a Platonic or Christian transcendence, but the chaotic ideal of the homogeneous "void" preceding creation. The notion of a *coincidentia oppositorum* would have been familiar to Baudelaire not only from Genesis, but from Ovid's *Metamorphoses*, in the very lines to which, as I will demonstrate, Baudelaire alludes in "Le cygne":

> Before the ocean was, or earth, or heaven,
> Nature was all alike, a shapelessness,
> Chaos, so-called, all rude and lumpy matter,
> Nothing but bulk, inert, in whose confusion
> Discordant atoms warred.
>
> *(Metamorphoses* 1.5–9)

God steps in, separating heaven from earth, and "out of blind confusion / Found each its place bound in eternal order." In moving from utter confusion to God-given order,

> . . . something else was needed, a finer being,
> More capable of mind, a sage, a ruler,
> So Man was born, it may be, in God's image,
> · · · · · · · · · · · ·
> All other animals look downward; Man
> Alone, erect, can raise his face toward Heaven.
>
> *(Metamorphoses* 1.74–82)

Man, in God's image, can create order; yet in doing so he challenges the very notion of hierarchy, of God's utter superiority. His art is one of decreation of God's universe, that he might make it anew according to the lights of his own imagination. Baudelaire's decreative art, still alive a century later in deconstructionist criticism, is implicitly an art that yearns toward an era before time, when God had not yet made the world. It is an art in which humanly imposed form flirts with a conception of chaos. And who better to carry out the dangerous experiment of remaking the world than the heir to Levana's powers, he who has been raised toward the stars, the dandy: "All other animals look downward; Man / Alone, erect, can raise his face toward Heaven." The dandy-artist, as we shall see in some detail, raises his face to heaven in the name of Beauty, but a beauty that unweaves the fine cloth of the created universe in order that it might re-weave it as a loosely textured web, as a series of strands connecting, often in surprising ways, part to part, incorporating lacunae into its chaotic order.

LE DANDY

Baudelaire, when he came into his inheritance in 1842, escaped the bohe-mian life of the Latin Quarter and set himself up as a dandy on the Ile Saint Louis. He eventually settled handsomely in the Hôtel Pimodan, which had its own history of dandyism: it had belonged to the duc de Lau-zun, Barbey's "Dandy d'avant les Dandys," and it also provided the setting for Gautier's tale "Club des Hachichins."[4] Baudelaire's friends were more often than not dandies; he himself began, according to the account of Charles Asselineau, one of his close friends, as an "ultra-fashionable." He had long hair, a full, curled beard, and a costume of black with touches of pristine white:

> l'on vit alors apparaître sur le boulevard son fantastique habit noir, dont la coupe imposée au tailleur contredisait insolemment la mode, long et bou-tonné, evasé en haut comme un cornet et terminé par deux pans étroits et pointus.   (Asselineau 81)

> one then saw appear on the boulevard his fantastic black coat, whose cut, prescribed to the tailor, insolently contradicted the fashion, long and but-toned, flared at the top like a trumpet and ending in two narrow and pointed coat tails.

If Gautier and Barbey shocked with scarlet and bright blue, Baudelaire shocked by the purity of line, the absence of color. His costume seemed to form the man inside it. As the years passed and Baudelaire faced with in-creasing desperation an array of financial and emotional debacles, he moved from the Hôtel Pimodan, shaved the beard, clipped the hair, muted the line of his jacket, and settled in for the period of mourning which Na-dar's famous photograph reveals. Here was a dandy whose spirit, in the end, fully merged with his costume. Echoing Barbey, Baudelaire explains:

[4]See Starkie (70–83) for a succinct account of Baudelaire's personal dandyism.

Le dandysme n'est même pas, comme beaucoup de personnes peu réfléchies paraissent le croire, un goût immodéré de la toilette et de l'élégance matérielle. Ces choses ne sont pour le parfait dandy qu'un symbole de la supériorité aristocratique de son esprit.   (*OC* 1178)

Contrary to what a lot of thoughtless people seem to believe, dandyism is not even an excessive delight in clothes and material elegance. For the perfect dandy, these things are no more than the symbol of the aristocratic superiority of his mind.   (*SW* 420)

For *his* superiority of spirit, only the purest expression of *le gouffre*—the simple black coat, the physiognomy of nervous pain—would suffice. Catulle Mendès called him "His Eminence Monsignor Brummell" (Williams 15), capturing the aura of sanctity with which this dandy, by contemporary accounts, surrounded himself. "Il n'y a de grand parmi les hommes que le poète, le prêtre, et le soldat," Baudelaire writes in his journal, "l'homme qui chante, l'homme qui bénit, l'homme qui sacrifie et se sacrifie" (*OC* 1287; There are no great men save the poet, the priest, and the soldier. The man who sings, the man who blesses, and the man who sacrifices others and himself). Dandy that he was, a connoisseur of wines and leather bindings, antique furniture and elegant gloves, his dandyism was from early on so aesthetically meaningful a pose that, far from conflicting with his art, it sustained it. He intended to write, to bless, and to sacrifice himself (and others if necessary) in the name of Beauty. If the dandy's life contradicted the artist's, the practice of dandyism—and its definition—would have to change. Let us begin the search for Baudelaire's dandy at what appears to be its center, the chapter of "Le peintre de la vie moderne" titled "Le dandy." Before we are done, we will have examined two poems, "A une passante," and "Le cygne," an essay on Delacroix, and the penultimate section of "Peintre," "Les femmes et les filles." This far-ranging tour—Baudelaire praised the "cosmopolitan"—will reveal that appearances are deceptive. "Le dandy" is not the center of Baudelaire's literary dandyism, because it has no center. It exists somewhere between heaven and earth, somewhere between male and female, but its center, like that of the chaos to which it aspires, is nowhere at all.

"Le peintre de la vie moderne" (1860) is a thirteen-chapter essay celebrating the life, works, and milieux of Constantin Guys, a draughtsman of great talent who, pursuing a life of adventure, traveled to the Crimea to cover the war for an illustrated London newspaper. Along with drawings of military life, he produced many studies of highlife (and lowlife) in Paris and London. In the essay's ninth chapter, "Le dandy," Baudelaire answers the question posed in his journal, "Qu'est-ce que le dandy?" It is a study so concentrated that each of its sentences calls for a lengthy gloss. A compendium of statements about the dandy, it distills vast areas of Baudelaire's opinion, knowledge, and experience. It contains, in essence, a record of his lifelong contemplation of visual art, music, literature, and theology. The chapter is an intellectual autobiography, with the names of his personal sages removed: in it he appropriates the ideas of Stendhal, Denis Diderot, Joseph de Maistre, Poe, Eugène Delacroix, Eugène Fromentin, Francisco Goya, Chateaubriand, Paul de Molènes, and others.[5]

The reader of Barbey and Gautier discovers in "Le dandy" some familiar ideas in an agonizingly taut rhetorical presentation. Before these truths, Madeleine would quail, Brummell would retreat. Like Barbey, Baudelaire finds paradox a useful mode; while dandyism is "avant tout le besoin ardent de se faire une originalité, contenu dans les limites extérieures des convenances" ("above all, the burning desire to create a personal form of originality, within the external limits of social conventions"), and although it is a "culte de soi-même" (OC 1177; "cult of the ego" [SW 420]), it is also an institution, a brotherhood, a religion. It exists outside the law, but it possesses its own laws. An ancient institution—as we have noted, Caesar, Catiline, and Alcibiades practiced it—it also expresses the modern moment. It is a "soleil couchant," "le dernier éclat d'héroïsme dans les décadences" (OC 1180, 1179; "setting sun . . . the last flicker of heroism in decadent ages" [SW 420]), but it is also a movement of energy, of opposition and revolt, a sign of aristocratic strength and superiority of spirit. Although it is a full-time occupation, it involves only passive activity: the dandy is a "Hercule sans emploi" (OC 1180; unemployed Hercules), rich, blasé, and used to having others oblige him. At the same time, it is an ascetic brotherhood, stoical, demanding, grave even in its frivolity. Recipient of celestial gifts, the "born" dandy nevertheless can fail for lack of earthly funds or from an inability to fulfill the dandy's code.

The dandy is, finally, inseparable from the world of art, for not only does he create himself as a beautiful being, but in order to do so he must first possess an idea of Beauty: "Ces êtres n'ont pas d'autre état que de cultiver l'idée du beau dans leur personne, de satisfaire leur passions, de sentir et de penser" (OC 1178; "These beings have no other status but that of cul-

---

[5]This list is not exhaustive. Kempf and Gilman both, for example, discuss throughout their books these and other figures whom Baudelaire imaginatively claimed. Any serious book-length study of Baudelaire eventually assembles a partial list of his intellectual and artistic forebears.

tivating the idea of beauty in their own persons, of satisfying their passions, of feeling and thinking" [*SW* 419]). The dandy is nothing less than the most exquisitely sentient of beings in whom feeling and thought mingle.

Toward the end of "Le dandy," Baudelaire defends the chapter against those who might call it a digression from the essay's subject, Constantin Guys. "Le dandy" is not really a digression, Baudelaire claims, but a means of translating Guys the man and his works into words. Perhaps the most "accurate" translation, Baudelaire suggests, lies in transcribing the reveries inspired by Guys's works. Baudelaire defends himself against those who would seek a more unified work of criticism, perhaps the standard "life and works" format. What is an essay on the dandy doing in a study of Guys? Baudelaire's self-defense in fact comes too late, for "Le peintre de la vie moderne" exploded long before it reached this, its ninth chapter. It contains, beyond a brief biography of Guys and a survey of his works, long passages of poetic prose that, based on a particular drawing by Guys, soar into works of art in their own right, cadenzas on Guys's themes. Tale, philosophical essay, prose poem, "Salon," novella, biography, and operetta, "Peintre" describes fashion through the ages, the recent theaters of war, the class structure of Paris, and English highlife. What ostensibly binds these diverse subjects is the fact that Guys drew or painted them all. Baudelaire's hymn of praise to the Wagnerian *Gesamtkunstwerke*, the essay swells into pictures so rich as to appear painted in oils rather than words, into atmosphere and plot suitable to the tale or novel, into the stage setting of drama and the leitmotif of music.

Despite its variety of subjects and modes, "Peintre" is a "unified" work. We experience it as such not only because Baudelaire's voice and Guys's drawings weave throughout its pages, but also because of Baudelaire's method. We experience Baudelaire's processes of thought as neither a disorganized, chaotic stream of consciousness nor a systematically organized collection of thoughts. Rather, it is an essay held together by "la mémoire du present." It contains all the fleeting, vital, chaotic activity of the modern urban scene, and it contains as well the ordering connections that memory makes among the chaos. Another dichotomy—chaos versus order—is here successfully challenged. The assumptions underlying such a vision of order we must seek outside "Peintre" itself, returning to it only after we have examined some of Baudelaire's other works in which his notions of gender and metaphysics develop in tandem, each informing the other. One of the first forms of established, hierarchical order to be challenged is that of gender. Male and female, no longer held suspended in two distinct categories, may merge at the maker's will as he seeks a primordial ideal. And so, in "A une passante," Baudelaire wills it.

"UNE FEMME PASSA": ANALOGY AS ANDROGYNY

Ovid's man is like a god ("So man was born, it may be, in God's image") but not a god, and this is the first of many analogies in the *Metamorphoses*. The work as a whole depends on analogy, for however striking the metamorphosis from one type to another, from one "level of creation" to another, the transformation is never complete. Niobe turns to stone, but, *as* a human being, she weeps a mother's tears. Analogy removes us from the world of firm category: Niobe is both mother and statue, and neither. Metamorphosis can solidify into paradox; both depend on analogy's power to link not only like to like, but like to similar, and like to unlike.

Once again, we arrive at the question of gender, for our power to see likeness and difference might well be moored in our bodily experience of sexual characteristics.[6] For Gautier and Barbey, questions of gender, of analogizing female and male, provide the foundations of aesthetic questions. In order to imagine the relation between classical restraint and romantic energy, Gautier imagines Madeleine, a transvestite who suggests androgyny. In order to solve the problem of how a dandy might become an artist, Barbey first imagines himself, in his exemplary portraits, into and out of men and women alike. Barbey then creates a Brummell whom he silences and subordinates as if he were a woman, and presents la Grande Mademoiselle, a woman, as the type of the dandy artist.

We need not look far in Baudelaire's poetry and prose to find images that challenge our notion of an absolute disparity between male and female. Baudelaire's interest in analogizing, rather than distinguishing, female and male runs subtly through works in which overt images of the androgyne do not necessarily appear. Perhaps one of Baudelaire's sonnets about the relation of a man to a woman might help us to see how he explores the notion of gender itself:

A une passante

La rue assourdissante autour de moi hurlait.

Longue, mince, en grand deuil, douleur majestueuse,

[6]See Johnson for a discussion of the mooring of metaphors in bodily experience.

Une femme passa, d'une main fastueuse
Soulevant, balançant le feston et l'ourlet;

Agile et noble, avec sa jambe de statue.
Moi, je buvais, crispé comme un extravagant,
Dans son oeil, ciel livide où germe l'ouragan,
La douceur qui fascine et le plaisir qui tue.

Un éclair... puis la nuit! —Fugitive beauté,
Dont le regard m'a fait soudainement renaître,
Ne te verrai-je plus que dans l'éternité?

Ailleurs, bien loin d'ici! trop tard! *jamais* peut-être!
Car j'ignore où tu fuis, tu ne sais où je vais,
O toi que j'eusse aimée, ô toi qui le savais!

(*OC* 88–89)

To a Passer-by
Amid the deafening traffic of the town,
Tall, slender, in deep mourning, with majesty,
A woman passed, raising, with dignity
In her poised hand, the flounces of her gown;

Graceful, noble, with a statue's form.
And I drank, trembling as a madman thrills,
From her eyes, ashen sky where brooded storm,
The softness that fascinates, the pleasure that kills.

A flash . . . then night! O lovely fugitive,
I am suddenly reborn from your swift glance;
Shall I never see you till eternity?

Somewhere, far off! too late! *never*, perchance!
Neither knows where the other goes or lives;
We might have loved, and you knew this might be!

(*Flowers of Evil*, 118; trans. C. F. MacIntyre)

The dramatic action of the sonnet, a chance encounter, is deceptively simple. The speaker is a man who, out strolling in the city, is suddenly struck by the appearance of one member of the crowd. He is "reborn" by her glance, but does not approach her, celebrating the fugitive quality of the encounter. The two part ways, most likely forever, leaving us to examine the relation of the speaker to the beautiful fugitive, the relation of male to female.

Donald Aynesworth, in a thorough and learned essay, articulates the sonnet's complex power. He convincingly establishes the *passante* as "an avatar of the dandy."[7] Her funereal elegance (all dandies are in mourning for a better era), her power to astonish, and her refusal to be moved are "signs of sublimation . . . characteristic, in Baudelaire's eyes, of the reticence of dandyism" (Aynesworth 333–34). Thus we have two figures: the modern *flâneur*, jostled by the crowd, experiencing love as a shock in the loneliness and tumult of the modern city, and the female dandy, who seems "crisis-proof,"[8] an image of how to remain impervious to the crowd and the individual alike. Personal beauty is modern armor.

Aynesworth's argument here takes an interesting turn. The sonnet chronicles the entry of this female figure into the speaker's consciousness. When he is "reborn," Aynesworth tells us, "he is possessed by the thing he sees. To that extent he becomes, androgynously, the *passante*. She is his better half, while the crowd is his worse or lesser half" (332–33). He is, according to Aynesworth, "androgynously perfected" (335) through his aesthetic and erotic appreciation of the passerby. But what, we may ask, has happened to the woman in this reading? She simply disappears as she completes the male, makes him the dandy she has been. As Aynesworth correctly points out, Baudelaire reports in his journal that his early attraction to the feminine made him "un dandy précoce." His more mature attraction now reveals him as less a *flâneur*, more a dandy.

Critics, Aynesworth included, have been too eager to locate Baudelaire's understanding of the fluidity of gender in its most familiar—and, I would add, its most limited—form: the male who takes on female characteristics. The "pseudoandrogyne" who is thus created is a *man* who has simply reached over from Column A (penis, beard, Adam's apple, strength, will, etc.) and chosen a few extra items, usually those we label as secondary sexual characteristics, from Column B (vagina, breasts, wide hips, delicacy, passivity, etc.). He is thus a kind of supermale. Because gender is an either-or proposition, he is still he and she disappears. Such a use of the word "androgyny" reveals one of its weaknesses as a concept: the notion that gender comes in two discrete packages, one of which is considered dominant by our culture.

Baudelaire's notion of gender is more subtle and certainly more challenging to our "common sense" notion of gender. Let us try another read-

---

[7]Neither Aynesworth nor I wish to argue that the "passante" is any of the female versions of the dandy who made their way through the Paris of Louis-Philippe. She is not, for example a *lionne*, a woman who deliberately sought, *as* a woman, the life of a *fashionable*. It is, instead, the passerby's sexual ambiguity that interests me.

[8]See Benjamin (44–46).

ing of the poem.[9] A "je" whom we know to be male (based on the masculine endings of "crispé" and "extravagant") sees a beautiful woman passing by. Her characteristics could be those of a male, especially a male who is also a dandy: "longue . . . mince . . . en grand deuil . . . douleur majestueuse . . . main fastueuse . . . agile et noble . . . sa jambe de statue." With the sole exception of "balançant le feston et l'ourlet" (and even here, we might imagine an especially delicate male dandy holding out, e.g., a cloak), every one of these qualities could be attributed to either a male or a female. The sonnet gives an account of the speaker's *attribution* of gender, which we as readers must take on faith. We can only follow the speaker's lead, and *assume* that she is female. He says that this is "une femme" and proceeds to have a love affair with her, as brief, distanced, and painful as the modern moment. There is no narrator beyond this limited "je" to comment in an authoritative way on the gender of either of these figures, much less that "she is his better half," and that, along with his lesser half, the crowd, serves him by making him what he is. I am not questioning his attribution, arguing that "she" is really "he," but pointing out that it *is* an attribution. The poem is about the assigning of gender; the world it implies is one in which the notion of absolute gender—whether it be based on divine decree, genitals, sex roles, etc.—is not a possibility. There is only the social taking *as* female or male, the constructing of gender in actual social situations.

Furthermore, Aynesworth's conception of androgyny, dependent as it is on a dichotomy of male and female (with the male initially at a disadvantage, but eventually assuming his superiority to the female), neglects a central fact of the poem: its title, "To a [female] Passer-by." Perhaps the central figure of the poem is this being, whom he has labeled "femme." What has happened from her point of view? Nothing. Impassive, rubbing elbows with the crowd, she is above it. A member of the crowd has reacted strongly to her, but she does not know, nor would she care to know. Far from completing him androgynously, she remains completely distant from him. The "regard" is, in this reading, his, not hers.

This woman is "the dandy" of the poem's scene; the speaker is a disorganized member of the crowd who impinges on her not at all. The sonnet dramatizes an act of classification in which Baudelaire attributes to the type of the dandy a female gender, asking us to hold in our minds two no-

---

[9]Here, too, I am indebted to Kessler and McKenna as I argue for a reading of the poem that takes into account its drama of gender attribution.

tions that will not slide easily into the comforts of synthesis. He asks us to consider the dandy ("common sense" tells us he is male) in juxtaposition to the woman. Perhaps the only way of describing this paradoxical figure—*passante*, but not female, because "dandy"; dandy, but not male, because *femme*—is to decide that the two categories of gender simply will not suffice here. To be an androgyne is to sacrifice one's own gender in order to exist outside gender category, neither wholly male nor wholly female, but paradoxically both or neither. Once again, we must shift from gender, which is for Baudelaire the central instance of analogy—women and men are alike, but different—to analogy itself.

The second way in which "A une passante" is a poem about the analogy between male and female, the linking of that which we commonly understand as divergent, involves Baudelaire's understanding of the very act of making an analogy, any analogy. In Baudelaire's poetics, *analogy is itself characterized as female*, just as, for example, elegance, or modern Beauty is female, "le petit sexe" of beauty, for Barbey. The very filaments of Baudelaire's analogical web are associated with the female, even when the pattern depicted in it does not portray images of gender.

Baudelaire characterizes analogy as a female mode in one of the few passages in which he explicitly discusses androgyny. It appears in his version of De Quincey's *Confessions*, though the passage is Baudelaire's addition to, rather than translation, paraphrase, or condensation of De Quincey's words. De Quincey has just begun to describe his difficult childhood, mentioning that he is grateful for having been reared in the country, in solitude, and among gentle sisters rather than "horrid pugilistic brothers." Baudelaire then adds:

> En effet, les hommes qui ont été élevés par les femmes et parmi les femmes ne ressemblent pas tout à fait aux autres hommes. . . . Le bercement des nourrices, les câlineries maternelles, les chatteries des soeurs, surtout des soeurs aînées, espèce de mères diminutives, transforment, pour ainsi dire, en la pétrissant, la pâte masculine. L'homme qui, dès le commencement, a été longtemps baigné dans la molle atmosphère de la femme, dans l'odeur de ses mains, de son sein, de ses genoux, de sa chevelure, de ses vêtements souples et flottants . . . y a contracté une délicatesse d'épiderme et une distinction d'accent, une espèce d'androgynéité, sans lesquelles le génie le plus âpre et le plus viril reste, relativement à la perfection dans l'art, un être incomplet. Enfin, je veux dire que le goût précoce du *monde* féminin, *mundi muliebris*, de tout cet appareil ondoyant, scintillant et parfumé, fait les génies supérieurs.
>
> (*OC* 444–45)

Indeed, men who were reared by women and among women resemble other men not at all. . . . The rocking of wet nurses, maternal caresses, the wheedling ways of sisters, especially elder sisters, a type of diminutive mother, transform, so to speak, in moulding it, the masculine stuff. The man who, from the first, was bathed in the soft atmosphere of the woman, in the odor of her hands, her breast, her knees, her hair, her flowing and supple clothing . . . there developed a delicacy of skin and a distinction of accent, a type of androgeneity, without which the hardest and most virile genius remains, in comparison to the perfection of art, an incomplete being. In a word, I mean that the precocious taste for the feminine *world, mundi muliebris*, for all that undulating, scintillating and perfumed display, makes superior geniuses.

The passage is nothing less than a relocation of the ideal realm, from its place beyond the material world to the center of a female society. The ideal realm of "Correspondances" whispers to the human figure as he wanders through forests; this feminine world chatters, croons, rocks, and nurses him to a state of intense, infantile pleasure. The man reared by and among women, in "la molle atmosphère de la femme," learns a wisdom of the body which will later make him an artist of genius who remakes his world in an effort to return it to this feminized state. As one among many— mothers, sisters, nursemaids—he learns the joys of multiplicity in unity, the necessity of seeking an atmosphere in which the hard core of identity may slowly melt and stream into a bath of odors, shapes, textures, tastes, colors. From within this earthly paradise, this vast concatenated unity of breast and suckling child, self and other, female and male, infant and boy, body and clothing, the budding artist learns well the power of analogy, learns to associate beauty itself with the atmosphere of a world thoroughly caught up in flowing and intimate connection. Significantly, Baudelaire uses "je" (rather than *Mangeur*'s usual "il") to describe himself in this passage. It is as if Baudelaire simply inserted into his translation of *Confessions* a prose poem of his own and asked us not to mind its appearance in another's text: for the man with the "délicatesse d'épiderme," self and other may merge, must merge. His experience and De Quincey's, his narrative and De Quincey's: are they not versions of each other?

It is the precocious love of the feminine world that makes him both a dandy and an androgyne. To write from within a world of tender, subtle, world-creating connection is to write *as* an elder sister mothers a younger brother, *as* a woman, and her scent, and her clothing and belongings, merge into a cloud of beauty. To write as a poet who creates rather than apprehends analogies is to write *as* a woman. A man writing as a woman is neither male nor female; if we imagine Baudelaire's world as a web of analogy, we might visualize this person as walking a slender thread between the strong knots of "male" and "female." As observers wary of this dangerous position, we may still choose one gender or the other. But with every metaphor, simile, image, with every attempt to analogize word, self, and world, the artist of the *mundus muliebris* rejects our choice, weaves an ever finer net of connections among all the points of his world, not just those of gender. The "dandy précoce" of Baudelaire's journal, who early on exults in the smell of his mother's furs, in her feminine elegance, is the type of artist who can create analogies, who can move from encradlement in the feminine to his own feminine transformation of the world. *Like* a woman himself, he understands the concept of likeness which blends toward, but never fully into, unity. Giving up Levana's stars, he seeks the earthly grace of the female, not as an absolute, but as an orientation. To find those likenesses among the discords of the modern city is to be the mature dandy-artist's work. Baudelaire refers explicitly to the *mundus muliebris* only once again, in "Le peintre de la vie moderne." Let us, then, follow Baudelaire to the world of women.

THE TALKING SWAN: DANDIES AND ANALOGY

"Le cygne" (*OC* 81–83) is a poem about the dandy and his ability to seek his salvation through acts of analogy. The speaker of "Le cygne," like the subject of "Le dandy," lives in a troubled epoch, feels himself exiled from the center, déclassé, disgusted, idle, but nonetheless "riche[s] de forces natives," ready to reclaim what he has lost (*OC* 1179; rich in native forces). The poem enacts a drama of reclamation. Because Baudelaire has conceived of a dandy who creates himself in response to feelings of displacement and pain, the dandy's usual nonchalance and impertinence are overshadowed by his regret, intensity, and self-absorption. It is as if Baudelaire took the *fashionable* and figuratively revealed his inner life so that we no longer see the impeccable clothing, but the acuity of emotion which the clothing and blasé manner are designed to conceal from the world. Further, Baudelaire wants to determine whether modernity possesses a specific beauty, intrinsic to the emotions elicited by the traumas of contemporary life. If classic beauty is serenely radiant, perhaps modern beauty will be convulsive, tortured.

The tale of modern beauty is a tale of failure, since the dandy must fail when success is measured in empty, bourgeois terms. The speaker of "Le cygne," wandering through the place du Carrousel, thinks about the sadness of exile. The "place" has been changed to "le nouveau Carrousel" by urban renewal, causing him to feel exiled from a place and a time. He thinks of Andromache, exiled from Troy, and he remembers another exile he actually observed some years earlier—a swan escaped from its menagerie cage, dipping its wings in the dust of the Carrousel, exiled from its native lake. This image now oppresses the speaker, causing him to think again of Andromache, then of a "négresse," exiled from Africa to the mud and fogs of Paris, and finally of all exiles, "à quiconque a perdu ce qui ne se retrouve / Jamais, jamais!" (of whosoever has lost what can never be recovered / Never, never!). The poem ends with a list of some of these unfortunates, fading into a mental mist, "et bien d'autres encore!" (and many others besides!).

Although the poem describes suffering, it offers a tale of gravity, majesty, and violence which slowly gathers power: the fall of Troy, the continuous disintegration and rebuilding of Paris since ancient times, the movements of people over the vast face of the earth as lonely sailors or slaves. The dandy may embody failure, but failure on such a grand scale as to reveal sublimity.

At the center of the poem stands the swan, "ce malheureux, mythe étrange et fatal" (that unfortunate, strange and fatal myth), itself an aristocratic, dandylike bird, "dressed" in pure white or black, considered superior in its civilized grace and beauty to other birds. But here we must pause for a bit of historical background.

In 1856 Baudelaire read a work by the Fourieriste and naturalist Alphonse Toussenel, *Le monde des oiseaux, ornithologie passionnelle.* He so liked the book that he wrote a letter to Toussenel, praising it as "philosophically moving: especially in its treatment of analogy." Baudelaire explains to Toussenel that "imagination is the most scientific of faculties . . . for it alone can understand the *universal analogy,* or what a mystic religion calls *correspondence*" (*Selected Letters* 79–80). Toussenel's book in fact contains many ideas which Baudelaire would have found similar to his own, as well as some abhorrent notions of Progress, of the spiritual reduced to the material.

Toussenel, in *Le monde des oiseaux,* writes of the swan as the superior aristocrat of the birds, displaying as it does "l'amour du luxe et de la distinction et le respect exagéré de soi-même" (the love of luxury and of distinction and exaggerated self-respect). The swan glides over the waves with no apparent effort; it displays the blasé manner and "la galanterie raffinée" (Toussenel 274; refined politeness) of the consummate dandy. Toussenel does not merely liken the swan to human beings; he also reverses the analogy: humankind will, as it increasingly models itself on the glorious animal world, move toward ultimate "Harmony." The swan is an animal with human qualities who can teach us how to improve ourselves: "Voici une bête qui symbolise l'Edile des eaux, qui doit être un miroir de pureté, de distinction, d'élégance, d'atticisme, et à qui l'on ose faire un crime de ne pas savoir se plaire dans la société des lourdauds!" (Toussenel 278; Here is an animal who symbolizes the Councillor of the waters, who must be a mirror of purity, of distinction, of elegance, of atticism, and to whom one dares commit [*sic*] the crime of not knowing how to be happy in the company of oafs). Classifying all birds according to the shape of their feet, Toussenel finds in the swan not just "un simple *palmipède*," but a being whose very color, white, signifies "unitéisme," aspiration toward social Truth. What does Toussenel's exquisite bird have to do with Baudelaire's swan, "ses *pieds palmés* [emphasis added] frottant le pavé sec" (its *webbed feet* rubbing the dry pavement)?

Baudelaire's swan, like the principal speaker of the poem, is a dandy of extreme sensitivity, a dandy separated from the very harmony Toussenel's swan, a good Fourieriste bird, works toward. Although Baudelaire praises the Swedenborgian universal analogy in his letter to Toussenel, "Le cygne" is not another "Correspondances" in which an idealist aesthetic finds poetic expression. Baudelaire's swan, Andromache, and speaker are all beings exiled from harmony, operating outside the universal analogy, but they are not pathetic failures. Rather, they figure forth nothing less than Baudelaire's conception of modern Beauty:

> quelque chose d'ardent et de triste . . . des besoins spirituels, des ambitions ténébreusement refoulées,—l'idée d'une puissance grondante, et sans emploi—quelque fois l'idée d'une insensibilité vengeresse (car le type idéal du Dandy n'est pas à négliger dans ce sujet) . . . et c'est l'un des caractères de beauté les plus intéressants—le mystère, et enfin . . . *le malheur*.
>
> (*OC* 1255)

> something intense and sad . . . spiritual longings—ambitions darkly repressed,—powers turned to bitterness through lack of employment—traces, sometimes, of a revengeful coldness (for the archetype of the dandy must not be forgotten here) . . . and this is one of the most interesting characteristics of Beauty—of mystery, and last of all . . . of Unhappiness.   (*IJ* 32–33)

The figure of the dandy embodies the characteristics of a new beauty—a beauty of frustration, mystery, and *malheur*. The classical ideal, the marble brow bespeaking serene satisfaction, is to be replaced by the modern brow pulsing nervously with desire and sorrow. Swan, speaker, and Andromache all possess a "puissance grondante" which allows them to challenge their world.

Thus Baudelaire creates an analogy among man, woman, and animal.

Certainly the poem's immediate visual focus is not Andromache, since we can only "see" her in the mind's eye as we recall the relevant passage of the *Aeneid*. The narrator himself is invisible, a pair of eyes seeing for us. As its title establishes, this is a poem about a swan, in this case, a talking swan: "Eau, quand donc pleuvras-tu? quand tonneras-tu, foudre?" (Water, when, then, will you rain down? when will you crash, thunder?). Although Baudelaire considered the bizarre to be an element of beauty, we need to consider further just why he has so personified the bird.

The poem presents a kind of "salon," similar to Baudelaire's "Salons" of 1845, 1855, and 1859 in which the critic strolls from one painting to the next, pausing to describe, and thereby judge, what he sees. Here in "Le cygne" is a series of tableaux: of Andromache at Epirus, of "le nouveau [place du] Carrousel," of the Carrousel in years gone by, and, centrally, of the swan, bathing in the dust, "ridicule et sublime." Perhaps Baudelaire writes as a painter because his favorite painter, Delacroix—whom he studied, praised, and explicated over a longer period and in greater depth than any other single figure—painted, Baudelaire believed, like a poet. In an early analysis of Delacroix's paintings, he asks us to notice that in many of them there is one figure who epitomizes all the surrounding anguish—a crushed and stricken woman. Delacroix does not paint pretty women: "Presque toutes sont malades, et resplendissent d'une certaine beauté intérieure. Il n'exprime point la force par la grosseur des muscles, mais par la tension des nerfs. . . . Cette haute et sérieuse mélancolie brille d'un éclat morne" (*OC* 898; "Almost all of them are sick, and gleaming with a sort of interior beauty. He expresses physical force not by bulk of muscle, but by nervous tension. . . . This lofty and serious melancholy of his shines with a gloomy brilliance" [*CS* 68]).

The swan resembles the solitary woman in Delacroix's paintings, and so does Andromache. Both of them epitomize the anguish that grows until Baudelaire extends it to "la négresse," and then to a host of others. Baudelaire's swan is placed within the poem *as* female, both because it is another Delacroix-like figure of anguished beauty and because it exists in such close analogy to Andromache, a figure whom we do not hesitate to describe as female. Yet the swan is male according to other criteria: it is characterized as the masculine "ce malheureux," and it resembles the dandy, usually considered male.

To grasp the full implications of the analogy between Andromache and swan, we must examine the figure of Andromache herself. Baudelaire develops in "Le cygne" one particular aspect of the dandy, his sense of exile. The speaker feels exiled not just from the old Paris, but from the sources of beauty and meaning, whatever they may be. He turns to tradition, in the form of the classical Andromache, to try to reestablish connections. His drama within the poem—to refer once again to the vision of Levana—is that of feeling his way back to the stars toward which he was once raised, only to be lowered into the human world of anguish. Or, as Baudelaire expresses it in "Le cygne," the swan raises its face "vers le ciel quelquefois, comme l'homme d'Ovide" (toward the sky now and then, like Ovid's man), referring to the Ovidian creation myth I discussed above.

Andromache's story, as Baudelaire read it in the *Aeneid*, makes of her an emblem of the exiled person who manages to restore meaning to her world through acts of analogy. After her husband Hector has been killed by Achilles, she is sold to Pyrrhus, Achilles' son, who eventually gives her to the Trojan Helenus, Priam's son. When Aeneas meets her, she lives in exile in Epirus, on the banks of a dry stream which she pretends is the Simoïs, Troy's river. Her husband Helenus has built an imitation Troy nearby. Certainly Baudelaire would have seen in her a luxuriant sorrow, the ardent and sad face of modern beauty. But she is more than an icon of perpetual mourning. She is a figure who discovers in exile not just defeat but an opportunity to find her way back, if not to Troy itself, to a sense of being placed, of feeling "at home" in exile. Although it is tempting to see Andromache as frozen in grief, Virgil describes her as one who actively seeks redemption through the power of memory.[10] She does not sink into the living death of exile; she defies it.

Pleasure may be felt in the arrangements of exile, in a false Troy, as well as in the "real" Troy. As Helenus has, by remembering the old, made a new Troy, so Andromache has woven a scarf and presented it to one who resembles her lost son. Exiles may mourn, but they may also, through the acts of memory and creation, make of exile a place in which to live, not just slowly die.

Aeneas has apparently learned the lesson Helenus and Andromache embody, for his parting speech promises that if he succeeds in establishing a city in Italy, "I pray these shores,/Italy and Epirus, shall be one,/The life of Troy restored, with friendly towns/and allied people. A common origin/A common fall, was ours. Let us remember,/And our children keep the faith" (Virgil, Canto 3, p. 78). Just as Andromache and Helenus's city is joined by memory to the Asian Troy, so Aeneas's city will be joined by memory to the "Epirean" Troy.

---

[10]See Nelson (333), who argues that Andromache is "pathetic and unfulfilled, abandoned and cut off."

In Baudelaire's poem, it is Andromache's majesty, her "false Simoïs," which "a fecondé soudain ma mémoire fertile" (suddenly made fertile my memory). Her memory flows into the speaker's memory; he too must learn to work to redeem his existence. The dandy is one who, realizing that exile is our inevitable state, sees and makes resemblances (Epirus *as* Troy), one who makes gestures when grand actions are no longer possible.

"Le cygne" enriches the concept of dandyism by conceiving of its dandylike figures—speaker, swan, Andromache—as creatures of analogy. When the swan raises its head to the sky, Baudelaire analogizes its face to "le visage humain, qu'Ovide croyait façonné pour refléter les astres" (*OC* 1249; the human face, that Ovid thought fashioned for reflecting the stars). This is the Ovid we have seen, of the creation myth in which "all other animals looked downward; Man, / Alone can raise his face toward heaven" (*Metamorphoses* 1.81–82).

After he alludes in journal, essay, and poem to the passage from Ovid which serves to distinguish man from the rest of the animal kingdom, why does Baudelaire create a swan who, like "man alone," looks up? Precisely because he is creating his own world of analogy, through the exercise of remembering the swan. "Andromaque, je pense à vous" (Andromache, I think of you), the poem begins. In this grand gesture of imagining his way toward a mythical figure, the speaker frees himself of the sharp distinction between animal and human, present and past.

Baudelaire's analogy extends to gender as well. To the extent that the speaker imagines himself through Andromache, their difference in gender makes no difference. Once again, as in "A une passante," it is not a question of the dandy figure's completing himself by "identifying" with a woman. Rather, we have a male speaker telling us of a woman whose characteristic activities—remembering, re-creating—differ not at all from the epic's heroic men. When defining characteristics such as nobility, stoicism, and creativity are assigned equally to "male" and "female," the notion of two divergent genders weakens. Gender conceived of as "either male or female" simply does not matter very much in "Le cygne." Baudelaire now inhabits so fully a world of analogy that, by the end of the poem, the speaker empathizes equally with the feminine "négresse," the masculine "matelots oubliés" and "orphelins," and with those who cannot be distinguished by gender (or indeed by any categorization): "bien d'autres" (*OC* 83; negress, forgotten sailors, orphans, and many others).

In a modern analogical world, we might expect distinctions between orders of animals to blur as well. Baudelaire frequently thinks analogically of women and animals, sometimes in full-blown misogyny (see *Pauvres*

belgiques), but sometimes too with the kind of profound sympathy captured in "Les petites vieilles." The tenderness of the *mundus muliebris* is a
feeling he would extend not just to the child who, bathed in the feminine,
will ever afterward be incapable of seeing himself as wholly male, but even
to part of the animal world:

> Dans les pages suivantes . . . nous trouvons encore le même esprit de ten-
> dresse féminine appliqué maintenant aux animaux, ces intéressants esclaves
> de l'homme, aux chats, aux chiens, à tous les êtres qui peuvent être facile-
> ment gênés, opprimés, enchaînés.   (*OC* 449)

> In the following pages . . . we find again the same spirit of feminine tender-
> ness applied now to animals, those interesting slaves of man, to cats, to dogs,
> to all beings who can be easily troubled, oppressed, chained up.

As the *mundus muliebris* acts to shelter the child in a world of tender association, so it might take in animals as well. Baudelaire writes to reclaim
this world; Andromache and the swan echo and intensify each other in
"Le cygne" not just because Baudelaire has personified an animal—a talking swan—but because he has "animalized" a person: the speaker shares
in the swan's aristocratic elegance, entrapment in the bourgeois world of
the "new" Paris, and anger at the heavens. Both are waiting for the rains.

   "Le cygne" offers neither a world of utter loss, in which the self is irre-
mediably exiled from whatever was felt to be the center, nor a world of full
reclamation, in which a dialectic of decomposition and reconstruction
(Brombert 261) finds its backdrop of stability in universal analogy. Rather,
this is a world in which the very notion of fixity, of absolute source or goal,
is challenged. There is only exile from the already displaced center, or
from the center we choose *as* center. Similarly, the speaker wants to take
old Paris as the "true" Paris, but Andromache's presence in the poem reminds us that "old" Paris was for some but a place of exile from Rome.

   In fact, every center, every garden is lost; exile is synonymous with existence. Baudelaire, in analogizing himself to Virgil and Hugo (the poem's
epigraph is "A Victor Hugo"), hopes in "Le cygne" to achieve the modern
epic. Its hero is the dandy, who turns his eyes upward in anger, but who
learns that he may reknit the jagged holes that experience tears in creation.
The fabric will be loosely woven, but it will suffice. Where Gautier has not
yet learned the skill of surviving amid a humanly ordered chaos of analogy, where Barbey attempts such an existence "en l'air" but retreats to the
fortress of self, Baudelaire triumphs. So, too, will Cather and Nabokov
place the experience of exile at the center of their work. The world of "Le
cygne" is a labyrinthine world in which memory is the ball of yarn leading

the self to daylight, to the equivocal, the blurred, the made rather than the received. Analogy unmakes the world of absolutes even as it constructs the patterned chaos of beauty.

For the artist who would move from infantile encradlement in the *mundus muliebris* to the unmaking and remaking of the world by the power of analogy, suffering and memory will never be enough. By telling his story, the speaker in "Le cygne" redescribes his world and thus transforms it. For Barbey's Brummell, the demi-actions of heightened sensibility matter most; for the Baudelairean dandy artist, they cannot suffice. Baudelaire adamantly insists on artistic creation as willed action following upon thought and feeling. For his lessons in rebuilding every lost center, with an emphasis on will rather than memory's delicate layering and shading, he turned to a painter and theoretician of the modern, Eugène Delacroix.

L'HOMME UNIVERSEL: DELACROIX'S ANALOGY

During the twenty most fertile years of Baudelaire's artistic life, he found in Eugène Delacroix—in the actual presence of the man, the idea of the man, and his paintings—the very image of artistic dandyism. Writing of him, Baudelaire offers perhaps his most expansive portrait of the dandy, gathering all his thoughts in the great essay of 1863, "L'oeuvre et la vie d'Eugène Delacroix." This is hero worship of the most intelligent sort, for Baudelaire sets out to learn everything he can from Delacroix, on whom he lavishes his major terms of praise: genius, cosmopolitan, perfect gentleman, true artist. That Baudelaire sees Delacroix as a dandy there can be no doubt: "parce qu'il était un homme de génie complet, [il] participait beaucoup du dandy" (*OC* 1130; because he was a man of complete genius, he had an interest in the dandy). Delacroix's dandyism has to do not only with his youthful posturing (he told others he had labored with his English friend Richard Parkes Bonington, the painter, to introduce the English cut in shoes and clothing to his stylish friends) but with the more spiritual posturing that prevailed in his maturity. Delacroix appeared cold and affected, but this "manteau de glace" covered "une pudique sensibilité et une ardente passion pour le bien et pour le beau" (*OC* 1129; "icy mantle . . . modest sensitiveness and an ardent passion for what is good and beautiful" [*SW* 375]). He appeared egotistical, but he was actually devoted to friends and ideas. His manner was that of the subtle and polished man of the world: "une certitude, une aisance de manières merveilleuse, avec une politesse qui admettait, comme un prisme, toutes les nuances, depuis la bonhomie la plus cordiale jusqu'à l'impertinence la plus irréprochable" (*OC* 1130; "a self-confidence, a wonderful ease of manner, and with them a politeness that emitted, like a prism, every shade from the most cordial bonhomie to the most irreproachable brush-off" [*SW* 377]). Selecting his manner from a spectrum of tones, Delacroix had, according to Baudelaire, at least twenty different ways of saying "mon cher monsieur."

In the end he was "trop *homme du monde* pour ne pas mépriser le monde" (*OC* 1132; "too much a man of society not to despise society" [*SW* 379]). Resigned, cold, skeptical, and aristocratic, Delacroix was himself physically beautiful in an exotic and ardent way. Baudelaire saw in his olive skin, glossy hair, and dramatic features a king of ancient Mexico who lived and painted in modern France. He hid within him a spirit of domination, a volcanic crater that could erupt at any time. Surely Delacroix inspired Baudelaire's description of "Le dandy" in "Le peintre de la vie moderne" as a man with "une physionomie distincte" (*OC* 1177), "un feu latent" (*OC* 1180), "pleins de fougue, de passion, de courage, d'énergie contenue" (*OC* 1179; a distinctive physiognomy . . . a latent fire . . . full of spirit, passion, courage, controlled energy). Yet if the dandy must be "un Hercule sans emploi" (*OC* 1180; an unemployed Hercules), Delacroix is no dandy. I would argue the opposite: that in all the glory of his oeuvre, in his heroic creative impulse, exacting daily discipline, and select society of writers, musicians, and painters, Baudelaire's Delacroix enlarged the idea of what a dandy might be. His praise of Delacroix the man and his praise of the paintings are inseparable, because Delacroix ensured that they would be. He is a dandy because self and works are translations of each other. As Delacroix's journals reveal, he imagined himself into being as carefully as he imagined his paintings. At Delacroix's feet, before his paintings, Baudelaire schools himself in dandyism.

It is in contemplation of Delacroix's paintings that Baudelaire fully develops his notion of an imagination that, rather than piercing through the physical world to capture a glimpse of a distant ideal, creates instead its own world of resonating analogies. From early on, Baudelaire calls him "a harmonist" ("Salon of 1845"), but by 1863 this term has expanded to encompass not just the paintings, but the man himself, his "elect" audience, and the very fabric of the universe as well. For in Baudelaire's eyes, Delacroix succeeded in reconstituting the *mundus muliebris*.

The 1863 essay on Delacroix makes clear that Baudelaire himself wishes to be included in Delacroix's world, a cosmos ordered by Delacroix's imagination rather than by God. Like Barbey, who wished to live his life "en l'air," fluently translating self into and out of the selves of other people,

Baudelaire wants to incorporate Delacroix's vision and technique into his own artistic creation. What saves Baudelaire's lavish praise of Delacroix from insincerity is its very intensity: Baudelaire wants to be everything Delacroix is, to disappear into him, while remaining Baudelaire (just so does Nabokov pursue Pushkin). He is also aware that, by writing this essay, energy flows in the other direction: Delacroix will live on in Baudelaire's words, perhaps longer than in his own fragile canvases: "Cette friabilité de l'oeuvre peinte comparée avec la solidité de l'oeuvre imprimé, était un de ses thèmes habituels de conversation" (*OC* 1140; "This friability of the painted work of art, compared with the solidity of the printed work, was one of his habitual themes of conversation" [*SW* 388]). Baudelaire quotes himself at length in this essay, repeating part of an earlier essay on Delacroix, but he quotes a passage he claims had originally been written "presque sous la dictée du maître" (*OC* 1119; almost at the master's dictation). Is such a passage "by" Baudelaire, or Delacroix, or both?

At the same time as the essay offers a translation of Delacroix's person and oeuvre into Baudelaire's words, it is itself about translation. A painter who took his themes and subjects from literature, Delacroix "translated" the works of Shakespeare, Dante, Byron, Ariosto into "images plastiques." He moved easily among the worlds of painting, poetry, music, and mathematics because he understood "les parties concordantes de tous les arts et les ressemblances dans leurs méthodes!" (*OC* 1122; the concordant parts of all arts and the similarities in their methods!). Further, Baudelaire sees in his work analogies to other painters, especially such great colorists as Rubens, Raphael, Veronese, Charles Le Brun, David, and Rembrandt.

As the essay proceeds, we come to realize that, in capturing the truth of Delacroix, Baudelaire will stop at nothing less than a wholly analogized universe, called into being by the power of Delacroix's imagination. For Delacroix harmonizes, that is, draws intimately into his sphere (or, alternatively, widens his own sphere to contain) not just himself and other artists, but himself and his audience. He is the most suggestive of painters, which means that he makes us think, causes us to remember "le plus de sentiments et de pensées poétiques déjà connus, mais qu'on croyait enfouis pour toujours dans la nuit du passé" (*OC* 1117; "the greatest sum of poetic feelings and thought already experienced, but believed to have been engulfed forever in the night of time" [*SW* 361]). He taps into the vast knowledge that lies buried in each of us, our memories answering to his art, which is thus "une espèce de mnémotechnie de la grandeur et de la passion native de l'homme universel" (*OC* 1117; a mnemonic device of the greatness and the inborn passions of universal man). With such an art, "l'homme universel" becomes a possibility, as none of us is irretrievably lost within the limits of his own mind and spirit. That which is impalpable, invisible within each of us, may be called forth by a painting, meeting there with the expression of what is impalpable, invisible within its creator, his very nerve and soul. "Je veux illuminer les choses avec mon esprit et en projeter le reflet sur les autres esprits," Delacroix tells Baudelaire (*OC* 1122; "I want to illuminate things with my mind and cast its reflection on other minds" [*SW* 367]).

But what, precisely, is required of the artist who would translate on such a grand scale: among art forms, among artists, between artist and audience, artist and world? And would he not risk the loss of self in the process? What is required is simple: will, specifically the will to work. But the visionary impulse finds such a will antithetical to its very existence. Surely in order to possess in the first place that impalpable, invisible self of soul and nerve, temperament and vision, one must *feel* intensely. If melancholy is a source of beauty, one must nurture such an emotion in a sensitive abandonment to the feelings. The Romantic phantasmagoria has its uses. Yet it stops short of execution. The opium dream, paralyzing the dreamer, is a perfect image of the limitations of experiencing the Romantic *gouffre*—for all its vivid particularity, it may lead to no work of art. The vision alone suffices, or so the visionary feels. At best he will produce but a fragment of the dream.

By imagining Delacroix, Baudelaire solves the dilemma of imagining a practicing Romantic, one who creates works of art as "complete" as classically balanced, intensely executed sculptures. He had a dual character: "Une passion immense, doublée d'une volonté formidable, tel était l'homme" (*OC* 1119; "An immense passion, reinforced with a formidable will, such was the man" [*CS* 308]). Here was a man who worked in a frenzy, who channeled Romantic abandon by electing to be possessed by the activity of work, the application of will itself:

> La vérité est que, dans les dernières années de sa vie, tout ce qu'on appelle plaisir en avait disparu, un seul, âpre, exigeant, terrible, les ayant tous remplacés, le travail, qui alors n'était plus seulement une passion, mais aurait pu s'appeler une fureur.   (*OC* 1134)

> The truth is that during his later years everything that one normally calls pleasure had vanished from his life, having all been replaced by a single harsh, exacting, terrible pleasure, namely *work*, which by that time was not merely a passion but might properly have been called a rage.   (*CS* 327)

This dandy engages in orgies, not of drink, opium, or pride, but of disciplined artistic creation. Even his studio strikes Baudelaire by its "solennité sobre et par l'austérité particulière de la vieille école" (*OC* 1133; "sober solemnity and by the classic austerity of the old school" [*CS* 325]). If one is to live, create, and communicate in a world of analogies, Baudelaire implies, one had better learn to impose one's will on this, the most ambitious of projects. What the swan lacks, what the speaker in "A une passante" denies, what the child bathed in the *mundus muliebris* cannnot even imagine, Baudelaire's Delacroix erects as the ultimate standard for the artist. Technique and control now become as important as vision.

Through work, technique, and control, the artist who might otherwise lose himself in the vast analogies he weaves is recentered, "centralized" as Baudelaire calls it. The artistic self, existing in relation to audience, grows stronger, not weaker:

> Ce qui marque le plus visiblement le style de Delacroix, c'est la concision et une espèce d'intensité sans ostentation, résultat habituel de la concentration, de toutes les forces spirituelles vers un point donné. *"The hero is he who is immovably centred* [*sic*]*,"* dit le moraliste d'outre-mer Emerson.   (*OC* 1126)

> The most obviously characteristic features of Delacroix's style are conciseness, and a kind of intensity without ostentation, the usual type of thing arising from concentrating the whole of one's spiritual powers on a given point. "The hero is he who is immovably centred," says Emerson.   [*SW* 372]

The concentration of all the spiritual energies toward a given point: with this phrase Baudelaire marks the paradox at the center of his essay on Delacroix. The given point is nothing less than a canvas filled with the shimmering of light, the vagueness of dream, the beauty of sad women.

Delacroix translated his dreams into paintings; Baudelaire translated those paintings into essays and poems. What, then, did he see in a painting by Delacroix? Let us "read" one of Delacroix's tone poems, itself a translation of a literary text, Ovid's *Tristia*. The painting is *Ovid among the Scythians*. Delacroix painted a number of versions, the latest in 1862. The painting captures Ovid as he rests within view of the Black Sea, in Tomis, where he had been exiled in A.D. 8 by the emperor Augustus. The circumstances of the exile are not known; classicists surmise that his love poetry had angered a ruler who wished to raise the moral tone of Rome.

Here, then, is Ovid among the barbarians. Ovid has, in *Tristia*, compared the scene of parting from Rome to another such scene, "If I may be permitted in a smaller affair to use larger / Examples, the scene had the likeness of Troy when that city fell" (3.1.26). Like Baudelaire in "Le cygne," Delacroix portrays the artist in exile. And what an exile. Baudelaire's swan may languish, his Andromache may weep, but Delacroix's Ovid reclines, the perfect cosmopolitan gentleman, at home anywhere.

Eugène Delacroix, *Ovid among the Scythians*.
Courtesy of The National Gallery, London

The painting is a dream of repose, plenitude, ardent sorrow which nurtures its own pleasure. Taking Baudelaire's advice and allowing the painting's atmosphere, rather than its subject matter, to strike us first, we realize that *Ovid among the Scythians* is about a state of mind and spirit: somber yet luminous, tranquil, arrested by a magic spell. Ovid may have complained wittily enough of his exile from "Troy" in *Tristia*, but this "Aeneas" has come home. He takes his place in an undulating line of figures which extends across the foreground of the painting. Delacroix has painted an entire society, into which Ovid appears to be utterly welcomed: he is offered gifts, food, and gentle attentions. In the background, a hut stands ready to offer shelter; beyond it hazy blue and brown hills encircle a bit of the sea; beyond the hills the painting intimates more hills, and then a cloudy sky. Delacroix, like Baudelaire in "Le cygne," resolves his painting in the vagueness of a daydream.

Perhaps the first two figures we notice after we locate Ovid are those of the young woman in purple at the center of the canvas, and the horse, the largest and most intensely colored of the figures. Ovid's face is the delicate face of a woman; his pale hands rest delicately upon the rich stuff of his robes. The woman's back is to us, with a luxuriant arabesque of black hair falling over a shoulder far paler than the dark reddish tones of her legs and of all the other Scythians' bodies. That shoulder, that softly glistening hair, that purple robe meet Ovid's delicacy of feature, languor of posture, soft greenness of robes in a richly analogical moment. The moment reverberates within the painting's timeless dream medium to include, one by one, each of the other figures.

Centered once again in the young woman in purple, the eye moves to the mare, the only figure in the painting looking at the viewer. And with what an eye: large, dark, limpid, intelligent. This horse is no barbaric war machine; it personifies a poetic intelligence that has moved beyond wit to a sincerity without sentimentality. Again and again the viewer's eye rides the gentle wave of forms. All melt into a world of reclaimed unity. Ovid has found a refuge, barbarians have found an object of veneration, and Delacroix has imagined a world in which all the categories—of age, gender, nationality, species—offer themselves in full relatedness to one another. The painting taps the memories we are unaware we have, memories of the garden. By a sustained act of will, infused with passion, Delacroix has recaptured the lost world of feminine connection and moved it beyond the easy distinctions of gender and species. Ovid has a gentle woman's air; his "female" cupbearer has the broad, muscular legs of the masculine and savage world. The mare has a sweep of dark soft hair, a strong and broad back, and a human eye. Andromache, le cygne, la négresse, le mangeur, la passante: all the lost dandies have at last, in exile, come home. Memory, the satisfaction of desire, impelled by will, has created the work of art, the world of analogy. One last project remains for the analogist: to find such relatedness amid the jostling crowds of the modern city.

LA MÉMOIRE DU PRÉSENT

What if we should awaken from Delacroix's dream world to find that women, men, horses, children, barbarians, and poets really had escaped their categories? However difficult it may be to conceive of a world in which sharp distinctions of gender, species, age, nationality, and profession no longer apply, Baudelaire makes just that effort in "Le peintre de la vie moderne" (1863). Imagining himself within the *coincidentia oppositorum*, he finds he has imagined nothing less than a personal apocalypse in which the self is destroyed so that it may be born anew. And, as we shall see, Baudelaire feminizes such an act, finds his inspiration for it in the world of woman's dress and makeup.

To achieve this experience of an analogical "totality," the artist needs a kind of energy we have not yet seen in Baudelaire's meditations. The swan languishes, the opium eater dreams and suffers, Delacroix works as a man possessed. In "Peintre" Baudelaire attempts to place a new force in the artist's emotional palette—enthusiasm, even joy. Baudelaire seeks the grand gesture: not the futile flapping of wings, not darkly convoluted, internalized visions of harmony within human memory, not the subtle layering of color that makes of Delacroix's painting a dream world. Baudelaire seeks as well "un mélange de gloire et de lumière" (*OC* 737; a mingling of glory and light).

He creates such a mélange in "Peintre." The essay gathers its energies in order to disperse them with éclat; if "Peintre" is an explosion, the fuse lies buried in chapter 9, "The Dandy," with its by now familiar anatomy of the dandy as the figure who creates himself, who flaunts the artificiality of identity. His pose is meant to keep us honest, to remind us that we exist in a series of changing "relations to" rather than in a set of fixed "attributes of." "Le dandy" is meant as well to convey an aesthetic position, for Baudelaire's dandy, like Gautier's and Barbey's, impersonates certain artistic assumptions.

If we question the notion that the sonnet or painting or aria is a world the artist has fashioned from buried memories, inner fires, temperament, accumulated bric-a-brac of experience, we are also questioning a certain notion of identity. That is, such a view of art implies a self that is a deep, dark receptacle, a mysterious center out of which the created object emanates. This is the notion of identity Baudelaire infers from De Quincey, Delacroix, and Poe. He has reflected this image in "A une passante," in which his speaker never ventures wholly outside himself, never loses himself in the passerby. Even his moment of rebirth seems bogus: it leaves him more, not less, involved in his inner drama. The same notion of identity's center develops in "Le cygne"; in remembering, the speaker learns, is his salvation. He may exist in analogy to the swan and Andromache, but the analogy itself flows from the dark, interior springs of meditation and memory.

In "Peintre" Baudelaire asks a new question. What if the artist were fully to recognize, instead of interiority, the daylight world outside the artist? Then he may begin to imagine a self that expands, "vaporizes" into this world in order to host the workings of vast forces, vast patterns, a sort of "son et lumière" of the universe played out upon the individual spirit. This is an extreme of the Romantic image of the self as lyre, played upon by the winds of divine inspiration. Here, the self dies into expression, losing its boundaries. Such a concept of identity is the ultimate version of the dandy's contingent identity: the self lives on only in relation, "vaporized," its core gone.

When Baudelaire follows Guys through a day of walking about the city, we must realize then that what Guys sees is what he *is* as he avidly absorbs the non-*moi*:

Il jouit des beaux équipages, des fiers chevaux, de la propreté éclatante des grooms, de la dextérité des valets, de la démarche des femmes onduleuses, des beaux enfants, heureux de vivre et d'être bien habillés; en un mot de la vie universelle. . . . Un régiment passe. (*OC* 1161)

He enjoys handsome equipages, proud horses, the spit and polish of the grooms, the skilful handling by the page boys, the smooth rhythmical gait of the women, the beauty of the children, full of the joy of life . . . in short, life universal. . . . A regiment marches by. (*SW* 401)

What these carriages, women, soldiers are, Guys in the transports of receptivity becomes. Baudelaire has prepared us well for this moment. Beginning with memory's power to connect disparate experiences, he has repeatedly led us through the undulating fields of translation and analogy: Levana's child as king of the world, the dandy as a work of art, Baudelaire as De Quincey when he writes *Mangeur*, the passerby as a dandy, the new

Troy as the "real" Troy, Delacroix's paintings as poems, and implied in all of these examples, the artist as Creator. The analogy under which all of these instances are subsumed but never completed must be that of *moi* and non-*moi*. For Baudelaire there is no longer a dichotomy between self and world. Surely chaos must reign. The analogy from which Gautier fled in panic, the analogy with which Barbey flirted continually, Baudelaire now embraces. Call it the *coincidentia oppositorum* or the *mundus muliebris*, the "bain de multitude" or the "domain of the crowd," in this world self must give way to non-self, solitude to an ultimate dwelling in otherness.

As the evening comes, the man of the crowd seeks the final flickers of energy in the city. Then, in one final paragraph of this tale (itself a retelling of Poe's "Man of the Crowd"), Baudelaire chronicles the end of Guys's day. He returns to his room, and, possessing "la puissance d'exprimer" (the power to express), he takes up pencil, pen, or brush to fence with the images still vibrating in his mind, to thrust and parry them onto paper or canvas:

> Et les choses renaissent sur le papier, naturelles et plus que naturelles, belles et plus que belles, singulières et douées d'une vie enthousiaste comme l'âme de l'auteur. La fantasmagorie a été extraite de la nature. Tous les matériaux dont la mémoire s'est encombrée se classent, se rangent, s'harmonisent.
>
> (*OC* 1162)

> And things seen are born again on the paper, natural and more than natural, beautiful and better than beautiful, strange and endowed with an enthusiastic life, like the soul of their creator. The weird pageant has been distilled from nature. All the materials, stored higgledy-piggledy by memory, are classified, ordered, harmonized.
>
> (*SW* 402)

The *moi* returns to rescue the non-*moi*; the dark world of memory takes control. Like Delacroix, whose technique and discipline enable him to capture the teeming images in his mind, Guys is able to transfer the energy that his soul, like a vast solar cell, has accumulated all day, to the work of art. Content takes on form. Works of art and self are reborn simultaneously from a primal chaos. All is well; the Dionysian "hawk of the mind," as Yeats would call it, has been called in. Identity is still a safe concept, creativity still operates from a center, the self sits proudly ensconced upon the throne of memory.

"Pour tout dire en un mot, notre singulier artiste exprime à la fois le geste et l'attitude solennelle ou grotesque des êtres et leur explosion lumineuse dans l'espace" (*OC* 1169; "To sum it all up, our strange artist expresses both the gestures and attitudes, be they solemn or grotesque, of human beings and their luminous explosion in space" [*SW* 409]): with these words, Baudelaire brings to a close the first movement of "Peintre" in which he has attempted to describe the theory and practice of modern beauty. With these words he alludes to what is for him the central mystery of identity, captured in the credo with which he opens his private journal, *Mon coeur mis à nu*: "De la vaporisation et de la centralisation du *Moi*. Tout est là" (*OC* 1271; Of the vaporization and centralization of the *Self*. There is everything). "Peintre" offers us a choice. We may read chapter 9, "Le dandy," as its compact statement of what the dandy is, or we may trace the dandy through every line of the larger work, seeking him in a luminous expansion throughout the essay. I choose the latter way, because chapter 9 itself, with a tremendous centrifugal force, seems to insist on it.

Such an expansion has as its ultimate goal in "Peintre" women themselves. Analogy, for Baudelaire the method of the *mundus muliebris*, leads inexorably to the dandy's entry into a female space where the distinctions between male and female are at last wholly vanquished. However masculine the *moi*, however feminine the non-*moi*, the world of modern beauty is that of a movement between the two, a flux so complete as to vanquish not just the categories of gender, but category itself. Once again, the most powerful explosion occurs within the stronghold of gender. It is to the women of "Peintre," "Les femmes et les filles," that we must, finally, turn.

"LES FEMMES ET LES FILLES": THE *MUNDUS MULIEBRIS* RECAPTURED

At last the paradox at the heart of dandyism emerges fully. The dandy defines himself by both rejecting woman and embracing her so fully that dichotomous gender melts into analogous gender. For Baudelaire, the cold and even sadistic dandy, women are stupid beasts, unfit to express themselves, and unworthy of artistic expression by men. Woman is, quite simply, "le contraire du dandy." Yet woman also supplies the dandy with his very artistic powers: "Enfin, je veux dire que le goût précoce du *monde* féminin, *mundi muliebris*, de tout cet appareil ondoyant, scintillant et parfumé, fait les génies supérieurs" (*OC* 445; In a word, I mean that the precocious taste for the feminine *world*, *mundi muliebris*, for all that undulating, scintillating and perfumed display, makes superior geniuses).

Far from passively providing the male artist with inspiration, Baudelaire's woman embodies and communicates the enigma that defines Baudelaire from first to last: that identity exists in both concentered self and ethereal cloud, in both marble and air. In contemplating female beauty, Baudelaire can draw no absolute distinction between the female body and its ornamentation. Woman herself embodies the *moi* as non-*moi*:

> Tout ce qui orne la femme, tout ce qui sert à illustrer sa beauté, fait partie d'elle-même; et les artistes qui se sont particulièrement appliqués à l'étude de cet être énigmatique raffolent autant de tout le *mundus muliebris* que de la femme elle-même.   (*OC* 1181–82)

> All the things that adorn a woman, all the things that go to enhance her beauty, are part of herself; and the artists who have made a special study of this enigmatic being are just as enchanted by the whole *mundus muliebris* as by woman herself.   (*SW* 423–24)

"La femme elle-même," the *mundus muliebris*: who can say where one ends and the other begins? This is more than just a question of skillful ornamentation, of jewelry and clothing so luminous or diaphanous as to create a feminine aura inseparable from the luminosity of delicate skin, shining hair, "floating" carriage. Rather, if "women" cannot be absolutely distinguished from their immediately surrounding aura (clothing, jewelry, all adornment), how can they be absolutely distinguished from the next "layer" of their surroundings? Is the cushion into which a languorous woman melts distinguishable from her garments and those garments from her skin? For Baudelaire, to question woman's integrity is to question human identity itself.

As Pichois (156–62) has argued, *mundus muliebris* is a legal term from Justinian's *Code* which Baudelaire would have known from his own brief legal studies or from the conversation of friends, many of whom were law students. The legal term serves to distinguish the property that aids woman in her personal grooming—mirrors, perfumes, bath utensils, and so forth—from property that is purely ornamental: jewels, ribbons, wigs, etc. What the law has separated into two categories, Baudelaire has joined. Far from wishing to distinguish perfume from jewel, he will not distinguish either perfume or jewels from the body of the woman herself.

Indeed, the force of Baudelaire's three chapters about women in "Peintre" is an etherealizing force that works at first to make of women a cloud similar to Barbey's "nuée," but eventually to *unmake the world of defined entities*. In this way, Baudelaire is the student of Delacroix. When he first approaches the subject of "la femme," Baudelaire wholly objectifies her: she is a source of joy, an object of duty and attention, the being "par qui" artists and poets compose. As an object—and this is the familiar misogynist's tale—woman is divinity and star, but also "la femelle de l'homme," a stupid idol, an inferior being.

Yet Baudelaire's object soon begins to lose her outline, as he warns us she is not just an animal whose limbs furnish a perfect example of harmony, not just "le type de beauté pure, tel que peut le rêver le sculpteur" (the type of pure beauty, such as the sculptor can imagine). Baudelaire must move beyond the Parnassian, Winckelmannian ideal. Instead, woman has a "mystérieux et complexe enchantement" (*OC* 1181).

Not only does woman's "self" blend into her aura, and her aura into the world at large, but the harmony of that self has been constructed across categories. The complexity of the woman exists in the movement of her body, in the layers of filmy stuff with which she envelops herself, even "le métal et le minéral" that "serpentent" about her arms and neck (*OC* 1182; metal and mineral . . . wind). She is a being who combines several orders—human, animal, vegetable, mineral—and she does so deliberately, in the act of "maquillage."

Baudelaire devotes an entire chapter (11) to the praise of makeup. In an analysis borrowed in part from Joseph de Maistre's descriptions of original sin, he argues that nature, far from being innocent, is fallen and depraved. Only civilization, artifice—best exemplified in a woman's makeup—can save us from the law of the jungle. The chapter is a celebration of "la haute spiritualité de la toilette" (*OC* 1183; the high spirituality of dress, of grooming), an elevated spirituality that comes naturally to those in love with the intense sensation of the moment: the woman, the savage, and the infant. These three types of people display, in their desire to decorate their bodies, "le goût de l'idéal" (the taste for the ideal), which "la mode," the idea of fashion itself, captures and reproduces.

Women, chief devotees of *la mode*, in the act of making a harmony of themselves begin to rescue the world from depravity and disorder. It is their right and duty to appear magic, supernatural. In thus legitimizing makeup as an emblem of culture itself, Baudelaire imagines a superior being who need not necessarily be female. Indeed, anyone who, like women, possesses a bit of "ce feu sacré dont elles voudraient s'illuminer tout entières" (*OC* 1185; that sacred fire by which they [women] would like to illuminate themselves entirely), who wields artifice as a weapon against nature, may aspire to (female) divinity. Divine she must be, for she challenges God's creation. The name we would most commonly give to such a being is "dandy." The movement is thus paradoxically double: woman creates herself as a harmonious "whole" so that she may float outward into a glowing haze. She deliberately creates what may not be successfully deliberated upon: a sense of enigma and mystery. Out of the ephemeral, she creates a timeless beauty which is that of the modern moment, of *la mode* perpetually renewed. And the woman who effects this magic, who performs herself, is one of the dandies, "ces êtres [qui] n'ont pas d'autre état que de cultiver l'idée du beau dans leur personne" (*OC* 1178; those beings [who] have no other purpose than to cultivate the idea of the beautiful in their person). Woman is thus (male) dandy. Or, dandies can no longer be considered male. The point is, once again, that dandies are not men who dress with the harmonizing passion and imagination of stylish women. They are not male "androgynes." Rather, within the world of "Peintre," as Baudelaire has described "le dandy" and "la femme," they share so many crucial characteristics that the very dichotomy of male and female no longer serves to hold them in two separate categories. We must read "la femme" as a dandy, and "le dandy" as a woman, just as we must see in Baudelaire's dandy a soldier, and in his soldier a dandy. The world of categories is slowly unmade as it is rewoven into a world of analogy. And in his chapter titled "Les femmes et les filles," Baudelaire, from deep within this feminine world, once again describes the *mundus muliebris*. It is no longer a lost world, an ultimate encradling by multiple mothers, but a recaptured world in which the viewer can remake every lost connection. Nor is it a world of infantile innocence: the stuff of experience itself is held in the intimacy of analogy.

Baudelaire presents "Les femmes et les filles" (*OC* 1186–90) as his translation of Guys's drawings and paintings of women made during Guys's forays into the "tourbillon" of the city. In seeking "la beauté dans la *modernité*," Guys seeks women who are "très-parées et embellies par toutes les pompes artificielles" (*OC* 1186; "women in all their finery, their beauty enhanced by every kind of artifice" [*SW* 428]). Their artificial pomp links them to the military life (which Baudelaire has described under the chapter heading "Pompes et solennités"); indeed, like soldiers, the women of the city participate in that paradoxical phenomenon, the costumed corps of vivid individualists, the sisterhood of unique characters. As they are alike, so they differ: this is the paradox that informs the painting of modern life. Here is a world in which the energy of the city invades the mind and spirit so that even the organizing, idealizing power of memory cannot fully quell the popular insurrection of the "foule d'impressions" (mob of impressions). Even the basic organizing device of night and day is gone. The opening chapters of "Peintre" depict the artist who by day gathers impressions in his "bain de multitude" (bathing in crowds) and by night brings the organizing power of memory to bear upon them. Here the artist begins by observing bourgeois women in the comfortable light of afternoon, but slowly moves into the artificial, lurid lighting of cafés, theaters, darkened streets, the pit. The artist absorbs "une lumière infernale" (*OC* 1187; a hellish light), the darkened, sulphurous version of Guys's city of light.

Within this world even the distinction between translator and translated slowly disappears. We begin with the assumption that "Les femmes et les filles" is Baudelaire's translation into words of Guys's translation into images of the electrical impulses of "le nouveau." Yet the links of the chain, melted by the overheated imagination, no longer articulate clearly. For this stroll through an infernal city is not what we have expected of Guys; "le beau dans l'horrible" (*OC* 1190; beauty in the horrible) seems more Baudelaire's notion than his. Further, the tone and pace of the chapter, lingering briefly on one type of woman just long enough to convey the deep strangeness of her beauty, convey not the control of a scene twice translated by an idealizing memory, but the immediacy of a demented mind which roves from one woman to another as Poe's madman, "The Man of the Crowd," roves slavishly from one part of the city to another, propelled by an absolute and unrefined need. As readers, we wonder how much of this phantasmagoria is Guys's and how much Baudelaire's, but we wonder only to realize that the two artists are no longer two, though not yet one. In fact, the two artists are three, and more, for the presence of Honoré Daumier, or any of the other caricaturists Baudelaire so admired, is undoubtedly here: "Tout ce qu'elle renferme de trésors effrayants, grotesques, sinistres et bouffons, Daumier le connaît" (*OC* 1004; "All the fearful, grotesque, sinister, and ludicrous treasures [a great city] gathers together, Daumier knows them all" [*SW* 221]). Poe is here, counseling Baudelaire that "even out of deformities [the Imagination] fabricates that Beauty which is at once its sole object and its inevitable test" (Poe 155–56). The concept of "the creator" of the work has given way to the paradoxical concept of multiple creators—Guys, Daumier, Poe, Baudelaire, and others speaking through one pen.

Just as the chapter has been written by the one and the many, so the concept of "subject" gives way to a Paterian shower of atoms. Subjects there doubtless are: women, in all their particularities of facial expression, posture, clothing, ornamentation, and setting. These subjects are ranked from high to low, beginning with "des jeunes filles du meilleur monde" and ending with "une grosse megère" whose head is "serrée dans un sale foulard qui dessine sur le mur l'ombre de ses pointes sataniques" (*OC* 1189;

"a fat shrew, her hair tied up in a dirty silk scarf, which throws on the wall the shadow of its satanic points" [*SW* 432]). Although Baudelaire refers to a ladder down which he moves, the chapter in fact removes every rung until Baudelaire admits, close to the end, that we have been descending a spiral. In this world, there are no steps, just the endless circling of resemblance. Young girls resemble mothers. Actresses wear "travestissements absurdes" (*OC* 1186; absurd disguises). The fop's mistress resembles a great lady and the fop himself. In the gambling halls, women "passent et repassent, ouvrant un oeil étonné comme celui des animaux" (*OC* 1187; come and go, opening an amazed eye like those of animals); the line between them and "l'image variée de la beauté interlope" (the varied image of shady, suspect beauty) cannot be drawn. Beauties "teintée d'une fatigue qui joue la mélancolie" (tinged with fatigue that resembles melancholy) look like beasts of prey (*OC* 1187–88). *Courtisanes* resemble *commédiennes*, prostitutes strike "des poses d'une audace et d'une noblesse qui enchanterait le statuaire le plus délicat" (poses of a boldness and nobility that would enchant the most discerning sculptor). And so the dreadful parade continues, past expressions of ennui and "cynicisme masculin," past "nymphes macabres et des poupées vivantes" (macabre nymphs and living dolls), past shadows and gleams of satin, velvet, glass, past vapors of alcohol and tobacco, past inflamed flesh and adipose flesh. Although the passage is filled with the terminology of classification—types, levels, groups—the only organization is that of a deliberately shocking pulsation, the intense, periodic assault on the senses coupled with the dizzy feeling of a circling fall. The shadows gather, the gleams appear more lurid; experience resembles innocence, sensation resembles morality. Baudelaire has recovered the *mundus muliebris*. He has sought, within the world of feminine experience, which is the dandy's world of analogy, a release from the fixities of classification and hierarchy. Decades in advance of his time, Baudelaire's bursts of light, however lurid, illuminate the new century and the New World. London and Paris give way to Lincoln and Hartford and New Wye. Cather, Stevens, and Nabokov, dandies themselves, practice an art of dandyism in which Baudelaire's dandy, along with Gautier's and Barbey's, lives again.

5

ON THE DIVIDE

⟨⟨⟨⟨⟨⟨⟨⟨◆⟩⟩⟩⟩⟩⟩⟩⟩

CATHER'S DANDY

A TWICE-WRITTEN SCROLL: SENSATION AND SYMPATHY

The search for modernism's dandy in twentieth-century American literature is a search for translations—American dandies rendered from the
French—translations whose originals have gone largely unremarked. The
afterlives of French dandies in their American reincarnations, their very
passage from French to (American) English prose, demonstrate a continuity of the dandy tradition, for dandies have always been creatures of
translation. Crisscrossing the channel, nineteenth-century dandies required continual translation between French and English culture; Barbey's George Bryan Brummell and Lady Hamilton, and Baudelaire's
Thomas De Quincey and Edgar Allan Poe, mark the Anglo-Saxon as the
center, not the periphery, of the "French" phenomenon of dandyism.

Willa Cather (1873–1947) imported the literary type of the dandy from
the French tradition, which she knew well and admired lavishly. That we
seldom find the word "dandy" in her prose and that we find no essay on
dandyism per se in her writings should not disturb us, for these facts, too,

are part of dandyism's characteristic pattern. Like Gautier's, Barbey's, and
Baudelaire's dandies, Cather's dandies appear in other guises and under
assumed names; like their French ancestors, Cather's American dandies
subtly grow to compelling maturity in the very style and rhetoric of her
work taken as a whole, not just in her many fictional figures who are recognizably of the "type": aloof, elegant, sensitive, aristocratic, artistic.

Cather's biographers mention her knowledge of French literature and
the pleasure with which she read it among friends, at the University of
Nebraska, and during her years as a writer. In reviews she comments on
or alludes to a wide range of French writers, including Gautier (*Mademoiselle de Maupin*, she writes in one of her short stories, is secretly sold in
paper covers throughout Illinois); Baudelaire; Barbey (however indirectly,
through her knowledge of Clyde Fitch's *Beau Brummell*); Dumas *père*
and *fils*, Gustave Flaubert, Paul Verlaine, Emile Zola, Alphonse Daudet,
Guy de Maupassant, and others. Furthermore, she absorbed the French
tradition of literary dandyism when she read such English writers as Byron, Walter Pater, Algernon Charles Swinburne, and Wilde.[1] Cather mentions French literature most often in moods of hyperbolic praise or enthu-
siastic prescription. If French culture were to disappear, she says, "there
would not be much creative power of any sort left in the world" (*WP*
1:223). Mark Twain's "ignorance of French literature is something ap-
palling. . . . it is as necessary for a literary man to have a wide knowledge
of the French masterpieces as it is for him to have read Shakespeare or the
Bible" (*WP* 1:150).

For all her praise of French literature, Cather felt uneasy about it. Her
reservations appear not so much in direct attack as obliquely. She criticizes
the doctrine of *l'art pour l'art* by attacking Wilde's, not Gautier's, aestheticism. She criticizes Verlaine's morals, but ends by praising his aesthetic
genius. Knowing full well that midcentury French literature, blooming
with Baudelairean perversity, led to the decadences of the turn of the century, she chooses, for the most part, not to attack "degenerate" art but instead to praise its opposite: good, wholesome, "moral" art. The search for
a French style that is morally sound informs Cather's review essays. Predictably, the quest for a "moral aestheticism" enmeshes her in the self-
contradictions of her critical pieces. But in the realm of fiction, in the figure of the dandy, in a rhetoric of difficulty, hiddenness, even impertinence,

[1]See Clements for a thorough discussion of Baudelaire's influence on nineteenth-
century English writers.

her inconsistency takes the flexible form of metamorphosis, her contradictions achieve the condition of paradox.

To understand Cather's dandy, we must trace the trajectories of two central concerns in her work.[2] First is the issue French aestheticism raises: whether the work of art and the artist himself[3] should exist as exquisite concentrations of private sensation, sheltered from other people and the world, or whether the artist and his work should take their place within a social and moral community. This is a central issue of aestheticism, but it is a question the nineteenth-century dandy in particular engaged his creative energies in posing, a question he claimed as his own by literally embodying it. Should the dandy live before the mirror, maintaining an Olympian superiority, or might he look about him to seek faces that are interesting and important even though they are not his own? The second issue for Cather is that of gender. Is it absolute, inborn, a necessary categorization of male and female in two distinct groups? Or is it open to revision, subject to the fascinating power of self-presentation? This issue arose early for her, as she cross-dressed and signed herself Wm Cather Jr., W. Cather, William Cather, Jr. It persisted as she faced the question of every woman writer: in her words, "Has any woman ever really had the art instinct, the art necessity?" (*KA* 158). This chapter traces the trajectories of these two problems, aesthetics and gender. In simplest terms, Cather makes use of nineteenth-century French conceptions of gender in order to solve the aesthetic problem that haunted her. We will watch aesthetics and gender intersect, intertwine and separate, noticing how implicit in both of them is the presence of dandyism, a legacy Cather claimed by the appropriation of French novels and plays in her own fiction.

Cather adopted dandyism as a literary mode because its nineteenth-century creators addressed themselves, as passionately and thoroughly as she could wish, to her two issues: gender and what I call, for brevity's sake, the issue of (public, shared, moral) "sympathy" versus (private, immoral, or amoral) "sensation." Gautier, Barbey, and Baudelaire presented Cather with a potent literary strategy: that of creating characters who, while interesting in and of themselves, allegorically represented aesthetic positions. Gautier poses d'Albert's embodiment of the pure but deathly separation of art from life, a life of "sensation," against Madeleine's fluid,

---

[2]I am indebted to Kelly for the term "trajectory of gender."

[3]The masculine pronoun, because Cather in her criticism dismisses all women writers except Sappho, Jane Austen, George Eliot, George Sand, and Judith Gautier.

"sympathetic" ability to read herself into and out of others, to know herself in relation to them. For Barbey's dandy—part catatonic mental patient who knows others not at all, part aristocratic woman who turns a cold glance on her inferiors, part self-absorbed Christian martyr—knowing others, much less caring about them or the moral issues arising from a life of shared experience, seems unlikely. He may use, may "appropriate," others, certainly, but respect them, never. Although Barbey portrays Brummell as living, at least in part, in "sympathetic" relation to his society, the essay "Du Dandysme" is a cautionary tale of the mortal dangers attendant upon a life, or an art, so situated. For Baudelaire, sympathy and sensation merge: when the artist makes connections with others, the intensity of private sensation reaches explosive levels. The speaker of "Le cygne," Delacroix, and Guys discover their own means of weaving the self into the fabric of the world; only De Quincey, the tortured dandy, is self-involved, an addict of a crippling solitude.

Although Gautier, Barbey, and Baudelaire explore both how the individual may live in relation to others and how art may exist in relation to social claims (and for the dandy, self-creator, the two lines of inquiry converge), their aestheticism limits the breadth of these issues. They recognize the dandy's need for audience, for foil, for "material" for his art; they adumbrate the various arrangements by which the aloof but passionate figure may find his own best place in the scheme of things. Cather attempts to pursue the inquiry further, without sacrificing the love of pure form, of intense sensation, which draws her to French literature in the first place. Though she may praise French passion and precision, she steadily explores the (for her "American") question of caring, of action with or for others in addition to self-presentation before them.

Cather's short story "A Wagner Matinee" (1904) sets the terms that see us through the central novels of this study, *The Professor's House* and *My Ántonia*. In this story she asks whether art can be cultivated apart from life and answers by creating two contrasting dandies and passing judgment on them. "Life" in "A Wagner Matinee" presents claims of duty calling for self-sacrifice, claims of verisimilitude, sympathy, sincerity, work. Aestheticist art presents conflicting claims of independence, "delicious decline rather than wholesome growth" (Ellmann 269–70), sensual languor, self-absorption, lies and masks. Of the intersection of this aesthetic trajectory with that of gender I have more to say later.

The plot sketches the reunion of a Nebraska farm-boy turned Boston aesthete and the elderly aunt who reared him on the prairie. Aunt Georgiana has come to Boston to collect a small inheritance; her nephew Clark reminisces, during an afternoon spent with her at the opera, about their lives and the turns in their respective fortunes. Aunt Georgiana had been a teacher at the Boston Conservatory when, at the age of thirty, she married a farmer of twenty-one and followed him to a homestead. There she has performed crushing physical labor for over thirty years, sacrificing her art in the process. As a child, Clark had ridden herd for Georgiana's husband and received as much of an education in high culture as Georgiana could manage. Clark, having since made his escape from the farm, now lives the life of a cultured bachelor on Newbury Street. He feels sorry for Aunt Georgiana, whom he sees as "pathetic and grotesque," and feels pleased with his own life. At matinee's end, she is sobbing, "I don't want to go, Clark, I don't want to go!" Clark states, as the story's conclusion,

> I understood. For her, just outside the door of the concert hall, lay the black pond with the cattle-tracked bluffs; the tall, unpainted house, with weather-curled boards; naked as a tower, the crook-backed ash seedlings where the dish-cloths hung to dry; the gaunt, molting turkeys picking up refuse about the kitchen door.   (*SF* 242)

On its face, this is a tale about the crushing quality of life and the fragility of art, a portrait of a pathetic old woman who can hardly bear to be reminded of the world of beauty she has sacrificed through marriage and homesteading. It echoes Cather's insistence, in one of her reviews, that "an author's only safe course is to cling close to the skirts of his art, forsaking all others, and keep unto her as long as they two shall live. An artist should not be vexed by human hobbies or human follies; he should be able to lift himself up into the clear firmament of creation where the world is not" (*KA* 407). Yet by story's end, we have been asked to entertain two rather unsettling ideas: that aestheticist beauty inheres only within the moral world of work and suffering, and that Boston aesthete and frontier farm-woman are both dandies who serve to challenge sharp distinctions between art and life, male and female.

Aunt Georgiana has engaged in the human follies of marriage and homesteading, and she has paid the price. Clark remembers her telling him, when he is discovering music, "Don't love it so well, Clark, or it may be taken from you. Oh! dear boy, pray that whatever your sacrifice may be, it be not that" (*SF* 237). The work will never be perfected, Cather warns, if life robs the artist of solitude and energy.

Such an interpretation of "A Wagner Matinee" is unsettling, because Cather disliked didacticism in art. When she wanted to preach, she did so directly and fiercely—in her reviews and essays. She reserved her fiction for more subtle efforts. A second reading of the story reveals that this scroll is twice written, that Cather offers us an alternative to her tale of life's brutal victory over art.

To do so, Cather draws on the tradition of dandyism. Clark is not just a city man glad to have escaped the farm, not just a patron of the arts, but a dandy-aesthete. When we meet him, he already wears the dandy's mask, but Cather allows us fleeting glimpses of the man behind the mask. There is no mention in Clark's portrait of wife or friend, indeed of any human connection other than his landlady. We gradually realize that Clark utterly denies such connection; although he mentions repeatedly that he loves Georgiana and owes her a great debt, his aloofness is such that he has not communicated with her in many years, possibly not since he left the prairie. Not only is his own life free of contamination by other people, but, dandy that he is, he disapproves of love in general, finds it embarrassing and vulgar. Here is his description of Georgiana's courtship, which ended in a long, loving, and fruitful partnership: "she had kindled the callow fancy of the most idle and shiftless of all the village lads, and had conceived for this Howard Carpenter one of those extravagant passions which a handsome country boy of twenty-one sometimes inspires in an angular, spectacled woman of thirty. . . . the upshot of this inexplicable infatuation was that she eloped with him" (*SF* 236). Like Barbey's Brummell, Clark avoids women. His dandylike tone, supercilious and patronizing, colors the entire story. A dandy who lives before his mirror, Clark can narcissistically assign to Georgiana his feelings on hearing the Wagner, but it never occurs to him to resonate with hers: "I could feel how all those details sank into her soul, for I had not forgotten how they had sunk into mine when I came fresh from ploughing" (*SF* 239). But then how could he sympathize with his aunt? She is so ugly, so poorly dressed, so ill. His tailor is so obviously superior to hers. He is so shielded from fatigue, so busy capturing the most fleeting of sense impressions, entering a Paterian flux in which he dissolves people in order to appreciate pure sensation, life framed as art:

> The matinee audience was made up chiefly of women. One lost the contour of faces and figures . . . there was only the colour of bodies past counting, the shimmer of fabrics soft and firm, silky and sheer; red, mauve, pink, blue, lilac, purple, ecru, rose, yellow, cream and white, all the colours that an impressionist finds in a sunlit landscape.   (*SF* 238)

Clark, we gradually see, has re-created himself by affirming sensation's allure, denying the value of work, denying the beauty of nature, and, until Aunt Georgiana actually appears, denying his past altogether. Clark has, like every dandy, created the fiction of himself. He is someone new, someone who has always lived on Newbury Street; Aunt Georgiana's sudden appearance there cracks his mask.

In this second reading of the story, Cather suggests that there is something wrong with Clark. She reveals the limitations of the dandy-aesthete's values by allowing us to see Clark's misreading of Aunt Georgiana. When she cries during the performance of the "Prize Song," he fails to see that she cries for a lost connection, an old German tramp cow-puncher who used to sing it on the farm before he disappeared forever. Georgiana cries for a memory of a song and a person, a situation in which art and life intertwined—and not for lost Beauty in the abstract.

Cather saves her most damaging judgment for the close of the story. Aunt and nephew listen to Siegfried's funeral march. Clark admitting, finally, that he doesn't know what Georgiana feels, imagines that the music carries her out to "some world of death vaster yet, where, from the beginning of the world, hope has lain down with hope and, . . . renouncing, slept" (*SF* 241).

For him, the funeral march, and indeed all art, is ultimately about death and renunciation, because he has denied loving connection, the essence of life. For Aunt Georgiana, the world is still beautiful. She sobs pleadingly at music's end, "I don't want to go, Clark, I don't want to go" (*SF* 241). He assumes that she doesn't want to return to her harsh existence, but he has utterly missed her point. She doesn't want to *die*, because she has always surrounded herself with beauty—a moral aestheticism. The hardest years were, for her, the best years—she fed weakling calves, sang and played the piano, nurtured Clark, read Shakespeare, worked like a beast of burden. She broke the "inconceivable silence of the plains" (*SF* 239) with the complex composition of her life.

"A Wagner Matinee" suggests two divergent readings. In the first, Cather demands the perfection of the work and portrays life as a trap for the artist. Here, the leisured and aloof dandy is free to create himself the livelong day. In the second, Cather questions the value of a life that denies human connection. The two readings cannot be resolved into one, for the issue was too vital, too agonizing for Cather in 1904. At this time in her life, she was devoting or dissipating (and that is the issue) most of her energies to teaching, journalism, and Isabelle McClung. It will be five more years before she resigns her job and centers herself in her art.

In the meantime she published "A Wagner Matinee," in which the figure of the dandy appears, and then reappears. For Cather doubles her tale in another way. Aunt Georgiana herself is something of a dandy, for all her ill-fitting clothes and false teeth. She, too, is a superior being, a Boston musician who re-creates herself as a pioneer woman. She is run out of her New England town by a vulgar mob of friends and relatives who disapprove of her marriage to a younger man. She, too, is sublimely impassive after all the long years of struggle:

> She sat looking about her with eyes as impersonal, almost as stony, as those with which the granite Rameses in a museum watches the froth and fret that ebbs and flows about his pedestal—separated from it by the lonely stretch of centuries. I have seen this same aloofness in old miners who drift into the Brown hotel at Denver . . . conscious that certain experiences have isolated them from their fellows by a gulf no haberdasher could bridge.   (SF 238)

Her superiority and individuality, created by a lifetime of sympathetic connection to others, find their fullest expression in intimacy which paradoxically yields distance. The impersonal, buddhalike dandy, heir to Barbey's Brummell or Baudelaire's opium eater, might, Cather suggests, represent the apotheosis of the human community, not its denial. While Gautier's d'Albert aspires to the impersonality of glowing white marble, Cather imagines a granite Rameses—as opaque, mysterious, and beautiful as the very texture of everyday life.

Although the story at first appears dichotomously as two stories—Georgiana's tale of sympathy, Clark's tale of sensation—the meditative reader eventually comes to see a less polarized pattern. This movement begins, perhaps, in our attempts to understand Cather's message in terms of gender, and gender in terms of roles: in the culture she describes it is most commonly the woman's part to sympathize with others, the man's part to strive for solitary self-realization, and self-aggrandizement even at the expense of others. The female dandy will "of course" be more connected to others—women are that way. This view is consonant with, for example, Gautier's association of sympathy and fluidity of identity with Madeleine, narcissism and impersonality with d'Albert, or Barbey's association of a fierce, self-serving aloofness with Lauzun, a passionate insistence on intimacy and marriage with la Grande Mademoiselle.

Yet Aunt Georgiana and Clark are notable in one particular way when we consider their gender: our attribution of maleness to Clark and femaleness to Aunt Georgiana seems almost beside the point. It is not just that their sexuality is attenuated, though it is true that Clark seems bodiless, more interested in impressionistic hues of clothing than actual women's bodies, and that Georgiana is more a crooked frail creature than a sexually desirable or desiring woman. Beyond our inability to ascribe gender to them on the basis of sexuality is Cather's insistence on Georgiana's female life cycle—young womanhood, marriage, procreation, old age—and female body as against Clark's disembodiment, his denial of life's stages now that he is "safe" in his frozen life as a Newbury Street aesthete. We come away from the story with a sense not of dichotomous gender, not of a female versus a male tale, but of a feminized world of landladies and farm women through which nephews, husbands, and cowpunchers merely pass.

At the same time as we recognize Cather's lopsided engenderment of her tale, we begin to see that Clark and Georgiana fail to represent two opposed and distinct categories, sympathy versus sensation. Not only are both of them types of the dandy, but just as dandies themselves traditionally embody in one person contradictory, even paradoxical characteristics, so Clark and Georgiana, like d'Albert and Madeleine, provide the two related halves of one dandy. That is, Georgiana is not just a loving, sympathetic farm woman; she is a loving, sympathetic farm woman with the soul of a gifted pianist, the exquisite sensibility of the artist. Similarly, were Clark only a delicate register for sensation, we would find him uninteresting. It is his passionate, heartfelt need for beauty (so deep a need that he is still running from what was for him the intolerable ugliness of the plains) which distinguishes him from a mere fop. The two characters can overlap in our minds because Cather sets up opposing positions of gender and of aesthetics, only to collapse them. As the categories of gender dissolve, aesthetic categories follow. "He," "she," "sensation," "sympathy" flow, one into the other, in a movement of completeness which is nevertheless not synthesis. This pattern shapes *My Ántonia* and *The Professor's House* as well. It is at the heart of Cather's dandyism.

GENDER IN THE WINGS: CATHER'S PRAGMATIC AESTHETICS

When Cather writes of aesthetic issues in her reviews, we can discern the intertwining trajectories of gender and aesthetics at work in a similarly unsettling way. On the one hand, she associates certain aesthetic positions with certain genders: as we shall see, the French, aestheticist power of sensation belongs to women; the American, moral power of sympathy belongs to men. Aesthetics and gender are matters of polarization. Yet when Cather offers examples of specific artists and their contrasting aesthetic positions, she deliberately contrasts on aesthetic grounds woman artist with woman artist, or male artist with male. Aesthetic differences remain, but they may no longer be charted against the axes of male and female. Cather thus signals a practice she is to transfer from her criticism to her fiction: creating "men" and "women" whose gender, on closer investigation, has been absorbed into aesthetic meaning. That is, Cather makes use of nineteenth-century French writers' wresting of gender from two distinct, fixed, and essentialist categories in order to explore a similarly pragmatic approach to aesthetics. Such an exploration enables her to conceive of what I call the "romance of temperament"—a new form for the novel. But at this point examples from Cather's criticism illuminate the characteristic movement of gender from center stage to the wings in the self-announced drama of dandyism.

The aesthetic contrasts first. Here, Cather begins by using gender to point out radical differences in artistic practice. Women write one way, men another: "Women are so horribly subjective and they have such scorn for the healthy commonplace." Someday, perhaps, women will purge themselves of the overly subjective and write "a story of adventure, a stout sea tale, a manly battle yarn" (*KA* 409). Cather the critic repeatedly associates women artists not with sympathy, as our cultural stereotypes lead us to expect, but with the overly subjective, self-enclosing life of sensation. Thus women writers are guilty of Wilde's sin—insincerity, distance from life. The popular novelist Ouida, for example, "was misled into thinking that words were life . . . a life that only imagined and strained after effects, that never lived at all; that never laughed with children, toiled with men, or wept with women; of a lying, artificial, abnormal existence" (*KA* 409). Into the "female" column, then, Cather tends to place the self-centered, even the degenerate. She quotes Daudet approvingly when he personifies the life of sensation as a woman-beast, the aesthetic whore of Babylon: "Come to me! I am the immediate sensation, I am the pleasure of all time" (*KA* 227). However great her adoration of all things French, French decadence, French intensity, and French beauty are female, and thus suspect. Into the "male" column Cather places the "manly" battle yarn or stout sea tale, the cleansing barbarian energy of the Anglo-Saxon and Germanic races, the beauty of a football game well played, and the artist's direct, healthy association with life.

Leaving aside the rich implications of these statements when we attempt to read them as part of Cather's half-revealed lesbian narrative,[4] we still confront a dichotomized system which fails from its inception because of the sheer weight and complexity it is asked to bear. Terms twist and

[4]See Sedgwick and O'Brien (117–41) for discussions of this narrative.

slide. The male artist, to escape a damning female subjectivity, must "lift himself up into the clear firmament of creation where the world is not." He should be among men but not of them, "in the world but not of the world" (*KA* 407). This sounds suspiciously like Gautier or Flaubert, not like the "manly romance" or the "common sorrows of the common man," "heart rather than temperament" which would place the male artist solidly in the masculine aesthetic world of sympathy. Such crossovers, such transvestite aesthetics, are common enough in Cather's criticism to erode, slowly and unsurely, her dichotomous aesthetics. But this conflation occurs more strikingly when she reviews particular artists.

In her drama reviews, instead of contrasting female with male—in parallel to sensation and sympathy—she contrasts female with female, and then male with male. Discussing the contrasting claims of life versus art (read sympathy versus sensation, or health versus decadence, or common concerns versus elitist values, etc.), Cather seizes on two pairs of artists as illustrative of aesthetic principles. She contrasts two actresses—Eleanor Duse versus Sarah Bernhardt, and two actors, Richard Mansfield versus Joseph Jefferson. As chief drama critic for the *Nebraska State Journal*, she has several occasions on which to discuss these stage artists, and the contrast is that of "A Wagner Matinee," between sympathy and sensation. She establishes terminology by mentioning three names wholly familiar, even sacred, to nineteenth-century French dandyism: Napoleon, Byron, and Poe. The first two are, for Cather, men of action and achievement (in our terms, men of "sympathy"), the latter a man of style, or "sensation." That Byron is preeminently a figure who combined action and style in the minds of Gautier, Barbey, and Baudelaire immediately signals the difficulties Cather is about to encounter in her system of classification.

Yet on she goes. Duse is an artist of extremely aloof elegance—her talent is the ability to create dramatic parts by hiding utterly what she is. Thus she, like Barbey's Brummell or Baudelaire's Delacroix, creates art out of her very solitude: "The great art of other women is disclosure. Hers is concealment. She takes her great anguish and lays it in a tomb and rolls a stone before the door, walls it up" (*KA* 119). She is "utterly alone upon the icy heights where other beings cannot live" (*KA* 153). Again and again Cather writes of Duse, in open admiration of her self-effacement, self-sublimation. Like Clark of "A Wagner Matinee," Duse leads a life of private sensation, aloof from others. While Duse's "acting has been done in marble," Bernhardt's is "done in color" (*WP* 1:207). Art is Bernhardt's "dissipation," as it is Duse's "consecration." Lest we find Bernhardt lacking in comparison to Duse, Cather writes repeatedly of our need for artists who appeal with warmth and color to our common humanity, who win a place for themselves in the hearts of the people. We want, she advises, the tragedy and comedy of life as we find them, in familiar clothes and language. Bernhardt's warmth of personality and power of sympathy assure us that she is on our level, that beauty itself may be found as we dwell among common things rather than pose on icy peaks.

The entire contrast unfolds once again, in parallel fashion, with Richard Mansfield and Joseph Jefferson. Mansfield, who played Beau Brummell magnificently because he was, like Brummell, cold, "self-contained and self-sufficient" (*WP* 1:55), is a "supersensitive," nervous fellow. He ignores the audience, playing "for the play and for himself" (*WP* 1:55). He has a "wonderful aptitude for the bizarre, the unusual, the abnormal" (*WP* 1:440). Jefferson, of course, is just the opposite. He creates the art of the people from his "fresh, childlike perceptions" (*WP* 1:423); he loves the world rather than suffers at its hand; he is a man of compassion, generosity, warmth, rather than of jarring nerves and superior distances.

Thus the "female" mode of French refinement and sensation is the mode of Duse and Mansfield; the "masculine" mode of sincere, energetic simplicity is that of Bernhardt and Jefferson. Not only do gender and aesthetics diverge, but gender, it seems, is secondary to aesthetic issues in distinguishing one artist from another. Indeed, the very categories of male and female are called into question when "male" aesthetics are assigned to a woman (Bernhardt) and "female" aesthetics to a man (Mansfield).

Dandies, actors on the stage of public life, have always donned two masks: the mask of self-announced artifice, coldness, elitist distance, and the mask of passionate impulse, seething ardor, fraternal bonds. Cather imagines her way toward a figure complex enough to encompass both these types. Such a dandy—for, seen in the light of the nineteenth-century tradition, such a figure would be a dandy—cannot rest within a dichotomous system of gender. But that is applying a nineteenth-century conclusion to a twentieth-century conundrum. By the time Cather writes, gender in literature has already escaped its categories; Cather absorbs in her reading Gautier's transvestite, Brummell's effeminacy, and Baudelaire's *mundus muliebris*. For Cather the issue is not the freeing of identity from two strict categories of gender, but the artistic *use* she can make of such freedom, inherited with the tradition of dandyism. Gender in her novels, as we shall see, often symbolizes aesthetics, and beyond aesthetics, metaphysics. Such has always been the dandy-artist's special obsession: to trace through the ambiguous shapes of male and female a universe of beauty and truth which, if it does not command absolute authority, will do what is more valuable in the modern era—suffice us in our conflicting needs for order and chaos.

THE PROFESSOR: "BEAU, ÉLÉGANT, CORRECT COMME LE GÉNIE"

Dandyism allows, even invites, the manipulation of gender, for the (male) dandy is an effeminate, wasp-waisted "damoiseau" who lives before the mirror, and the prose of dandyism tends to be, like Barbey's "Du Dandysme," "un babiole," "un morcelet d'histoire . . . bon à mettre, comme une curiosité, sur la toilette d'or des fats de l'avenir" (DD 217; a bauble, a morsel of history good for putting, like a curiosity, on the golden washstand of future snobs). According to Barbey, elegance, the dandy's distinguishing characteristic, is but the feminine "petit sexe" of (masculine) Beauty. It was, in fact, in an attempt to describe a peculiarly modern beauty that nineteenth-century French writers began to experiment with notions of gender. Gautier's Madeleine announced to the world "her" uncomfortable freedom from the categories of gender, a statement that caused Gautier to remove her from the scene, abruptly ending his novel. Barbey, apologist for the forces of reaction, seemingly could not stop himself from speaking, however indirectly, the woman's part, swathing it in layers of linguistic preciosity, burying it beneath layers of masculine portraits, but allowing it nevertheless to glimmer in the very clouds surrounding, embodying his dandies, "ces dieux" (these gods). Baudelaire, too, rabid misogynist, discovered that the source of modern beauty lay in the *mundus muliebris*; the feminine mode of analogy determined the very weave of his artistic world.

Cather constructs in *The Professor's House* a novel that traces the dichotomies of French and American, female and male. Her central character, Professor St. Peter, encompasses by his dandyism both sympathy and sensation, American and French values. She then introduces an American, sympathetic (and therefore comfortably male) character, Tom Outland. Their story, which I trace along Cather's trajectories of aesthetics and gender, is the familiar story of categories only apparently fixed, but actually in metamorphic motion. In this most Gautierian of Cather's novels, we continue our search for modernism's dandy. What we discover is Cather's "romance of temperament"—an androgynous literary form, a form centrally in the tradition of dandyism which Cather invents in an attempt to infuse the fluidity of gender, inherited from her French precursors, with aesthetic meaning.

In Napoleon Godfrey St. Peter, professor of European history at Hamilton College, Cather creates an intense Francophile. Born of French Canadian and American parents, St. Peter's only intimate friends, until Tom Outland arrives, are the sons of the Thierault family of Versailles, for whom he served as tutor in his younger days. During the years of his strenuous professional life, which began in the 1890s, St. Peter has relaxed by cultivating his "French garden," "a tidy half-acre of glistening gravel and glistening shrubs and bright flowers" (*PH* 14), all arranged as symmetrically as the gardens at Versailles. St. Peter prefers his roast lamb *saignant* and his wines, as well as his novels, French.

St. Peter's grandfather is only one of his French ancestors, however; another is the notable Gallic American Edgar Poe. Cather shared with Baudelaire a fascination with this strange child, adopted by the Allan family, this spiritual foundling whose truest roots, at least by the dictates of poetic justice, are French.[5] In 1895 Cather read a paper on Poe to the joint meeting of the University of Nebraska literary societies (*KA* 380). Her essay presents a neurasthenic genius, an artist not only at odds with American society, but crushed by it. She places Poe squarely in the French tradition, even if her undergraduate grasp of dates is whimsical: "Poe belonged to the modern French school of decorative and discriminating prose before it ever existed in France. He rivalled Gautier, Flaubert and de Maupassant before they were born" (*KA* 382). Her essay, written to be performed, makes one deep impression: that of Poe as a dramatic character imaginable, like Barbey's Brummell or Baudelaire's "Dandy," only in the realm of contradiction. He is a "handsome, pale fellow, violent in his enthusiasm, ardent in his worship, but spiritually cold in his affections" (*KA* 381). Cather evokes the paradox of the fevered state—burning with chills—as well as the irony of Fortune—the young man destroyed by the very gift of genius—for a double purpose: to re-create Poe while attacking American values.

Cather's Poe, the "child-man" who is "nervous, egotistic, self-centered" (*KA* 381), echoes an earlier portrait of Poe, an essay that presented the American writer to a French audience. In 1856, Baudelaire's translation of Poe's *Histoires extraordinaires* appeared, with his introductory essay, "Edgar Poe, sa vie et ses oeuvres" (*OC*, Raymond ed., 713–37). If Baudelaire's dandy is a palimpsest—created by superimposing portraits of such figures

---

[5]For an account of the "re-creation" of Poe as a French writer, see Quinn.

as Andromache, Alcibiades, De Quincey, Delacroix, and Guys—Poe's face, taut and elegant, glimmers throughout this composite portrait. Baudelaire, too, sees in Poe a genius in agony,

> un de ces illustres malheureux, trop riche de poésie et de passion, qui est venu, après tant d'autres, faire en ce bas monde le rude apprentissage du génie chez les âmes inférieures.   (OC, Raymond ed., 715)

> one of these illustrious unfortunates, too loaded with poetry and passion, and born to suffer the harsh apprenticeship of genius here below amidst the crowd of mediocre souls.   (SW 163)

Baudelaire's essay, like Cather's, combines an angry survey of materialist American culture with an anatomy of the man himself. Like Cather, who later claims that "Our Lady of Genius" selected Poe for greatness, Baudelaire presents Poe as both darling and victim of a diabolical Providence which first endowed him with a spiritual nature and then cast him into hostile surroundings. Just as Poe possesses, for Cather, "fine harmonies of . . . fancy" (KA 385), he has, for Baudelaire, "une finesse de goût que tout, excepté l'exacte proportion, révoltait" (OC, Raymond ed., 717; "refinement of taste that everything apart from exact proportions shocked" [SW 166]).

For Baudelaire and Cather, Poe is a dandy because he becomes the object of his own exquisite taste, creates the character who is, paradoxically, himself. Baudelaire sees in him the studied pose of a man "beau, élégant, correct comme le génie" (OC, Raymond ed., 722; handsome, elegant, correct as genius). Cather's Poe wanders out of the theater of his imagination onto the stage of American life: "His speech and actions were unconsciously and sincerely dramatic, always as though done for effect" (KA 381). Correct genius, sincere dramatization: both Baudelaire and Cather edge toward oxymoron. In a second essay, "Notes nouvelles sur Edgar Poe" (1857; OC, Raymond ed., 738–56), Baudelaire makes explicit what he only implies in the previous essay, that his "beau et élégant," his posing prodigy, exemplifies a type: the dandy-artist.[6] He is a collection of contradictory qualities, all of which Cather, too, will brandish in her version of Poe. Baudelaire's dandy-artist is superior, but a failure; cold, but ardent; drunken but exquisitely aware; gifted by the gods but tortured by them as well; victim and executioner at once. Poe develops as a dandy in "Notes nouvelles" not only because he plays the part of himself, but because he

---

[6]For a discussion of the gradual identification of the dandy with the priest and then the artist, see Moers (254–83).

scorns the American public. In Baudelaire's first essay, Poe is wholly victim; in the second he fights back with sarcasm, impertinence. Baudelaire
quotes approvingly from Poe's *Marginalia*: "The nose of a mob is its imagination; by this at any time it can be quietly led" (*SW* 191). Master of the
dandy's barb, Poe is no longer merely a victim of American brutality, no
longer just a starving alcoholic with a grotesquely refined sensibility, but
the very type of the modern dandy-artist, strong in his weakness. Baudelaire allows Poe to speak for himself:

> *Genus irritabile vatum*! That poets . . . are a *genus irritabile* is well under-
> stood, but the *why* seems not to be commonly seen. An artist is an artist only
> by dint of his exquisite sense of beauty, a sense affording him rapturous en-
> joyment, but at the same time implying or involving an equally exquisite
> sense of deformity, of disproportion. Thus a wrong—an injustice—done to
> a poet who is really a poet excites him to a degree which to ordinary appre-
> hension appears disproportionate with the wrong. . . . But one thing is clear,
> that the man who is not "irritable" (to the ordinary apprehension) is *no
> poet*.   (*SW* 201)

The dandy-artist is no longer to be a victim of his own hypertrophied
nerves, seeking oblivion in debauchery; he is the proud creator who draws
back from common life, repelled by an ugliness only he can see: "Ainsi
parle le poète lui-même, préparant une excellente et irréfutable apologie
pour tous ceux de sa race" (*OC*, Raymond ed., 750; "Thus speaks the poet
himself, preparing an excellent and irrefutable apology for all members of
his kin" [*SW* 210]). Assuming the erect posture, defensively aggressive, of
the dandy, Baudelaire's Poe arms himself with his own fragility. Philistia's
victim becomes Philistia's enemy.

For Cather as well, the memory of Poe stands as a reproach to American society: "We lament our dearth of poets when we let Poe starve" (*KA*
387). He is a man whose strength issued from French nerve endings, not
American muscle: "His discrimination remained always delicate, and
from the constant strain of toil his fancy always rose strong and unfet-
tered" (*KA* 385). Elegant, aloof, armed with exquisite values: with this
manner of strength will Professor St. Peter, too, confront his small-town
enemies. In his irritability lies, perhaps, his victory.

Critics have long struggled to like this irritable man and the novel in
which he appears, *The Professor's House* (1925), more than they actually do.
Appearing when Cather's reputation was well established, the novel received, on the whole, a friendly critical response (Woodress 366), but the
book immediately seemed to call for explanation. So much about it is negative in a peculiar way. Certainly book 1 presents a bleak view of human

relations, but critics find it difficult to judge the evidence, because the Professor himself is so difficult to fathom.[7] Is St. Peter simply getting crotchety, or is he experiencing a nervous breakdown, or is he a misanthropist at heart? Are his measured responses to his family's internal battles loving and careful, or coldly judgmental and disapproving? Critics have tended to look for explanations in Cather herself: perhaps the book reflects her personal fatigue and ill health, or the crisis of middle age, or her loss of Isabel McClung (Woodress 371). The book is uncomfortable to read not just in its characterization and tone, but in its very structure. Tom Outland's story, inserted into the flow of the Professor's story, seems to vie with it for importance. Book 3, far briefer than the other two books, seems half afterthought, half key to the mystery. Its meditative tone breaks the book's dramatic pace without offering a wholly acceptable resolution.

It is with the reader's difficulties that I must begin, for as I demonstrate, the novel is a dandy's work, and dandies entertain others only begrudgingly, never giving themselves wholly away. St. Peter is difficult to grasp, to judge, because Cather means him to be. The novel's tone and structure puzzle us, because Cather intends to let us languish in uncertainty, not glory in negative capability. *The Professor's House*, like *Mademoiselle de Maupin*, or "Le peintre de la vie moderne," presents not only the figure of the dandy, but his disappearance into Cather's narrative texture and his reappearance in her aesthetic allegory. St. Peter is, like Baudelaire's dandy-artist, Poe, "une vérité habillée d'une manière bizarre, un paradoxe apparent, qui ne veut pas être coudoyé par la foule" (*OC*, Raymond ed., 741; "a truth clothed in a strange habit, an evident paradox, refusing to be elbowed by the crowd" [*SW* 191]). We, as readers, are part of that crowd. St. Peter successfully repels us; behind him stands Cather herself, equally unwilling to be elbowed by the crowd, producing a novel her public can read but never fully possess.

Perhaps the Professor's eeriest—and most dandylike—characteristic is his apparent respect for social convention, coupled as it is with his profound social rebellion. One sometimes feels that only St. Peter's hatred of social form fuels his exquisite social correctness; on the other hand, this view of St. Peter as cynic often leads to a glimpse of the Professor as aristocrat, hallowing, by an innate nobility, the very concept of social form. He sincerely strives to meet all his social obligations, benevolently guiding

[7]Stouck, among others, takes the reader's uncertain reaction to St. Peter as the very point of Cather's characterization: "Surely it is precisely because the Professor's depression and despair are not literally accounted for . . . that they assume the dimension of a universal experience" (99).

family members, working diligently at the university, respecting the needs
of others in the community. At the same time he is often mocking, silent,
insulting, or deliberately, if quietly, challenging, with his French tastes and
his belief in his utter superiority as a scholar. In turn-of-the-century Illinois, he seems to see himself as a king incognito, and he expects no one to
confuse his noblesse oblige with democratic egalitarianism. Baudelaire describes the dandy's passion as "avant tout le besoin ardent de se faire une
originalité, contenu dans les limites extérieures des convenances" (*OC*
1178; "the burning desire to create a personal form of originality, within
the external limits of social conventions" [*SW* 420]). St. Peter's character
vibrates strangely because Cather has fired him with this same controlled
desire. Creating a "personal form of originality" means rejecting the persona others would impose upon him; thus, for example, St. Peter fulfills
the duties of devoted husband while shrinking from his wife. He is, to our
discomfort, at once a loving and forgiving father, a harsh judge, and a distanced observer of his family. Even before he is seized with a deepening
fatigue and world-weariness, St. Peter has tended to retreat from the family and see it in framed tableaux. Calculating his responsibilities, he enters
into the family's activities at selected hours according to a rigid weekly
writing schedule. He has practiced, like every good dandy, "une espèce de
culte de soi-même, qui peut survivre à la recherche du bonheur à trouver
dans autrui, dans la femme, par exemple" (*OC* 1178; "a cult of the ego
which can still survive the pursuit of that form of happiness to be found
in others, in woman for example" [*SW* 420]). Like Gautier's d'Albert or
Barbey's Brummell, St. Peter has meant to preserve his ego without re-
sorting to that final defensive tactic, leaving the social world altogether.
His attic study connects to the rest of the house, even if Cather implies,
in a contradiction she savors, that the gap between levels is absolute,
unbridgeable.

For all his coldness, St. Peter suggests passion; indeed, his passions, like
his fine wine, are all the more convincing for the many years during which
he has reserved them. In order to write his eight-volume work, he has had
to deny claims on his emotions; his is the "cold exterior resulting from the
unshakeable determination to remain unmoved" (*SW* 422), but the fire is
there nonetheless, for all its latency. Cather paints it in his physical presence, his passion for swimming in Lake Michigan:

> his arms and back were burned a deep terra-cotta from a summer in the lake.
> His head and powerful reaching arms made a strong red pattern against the
> purple blue of the water. . . . his head looked sheathed and small and in-

tensely alive, like the heads of the warriors on the Parthenon frieze in their
tight archaic helmets.   (*PH* 71)

Baudelaire names generals—Caesar, Catiline, Alcibiades (*OC* 1177)—as
examples of the earliest dandies; in his journal titled "Mon coeur mis à
nu," he writes, "il n'y a de grand parmi les hommes que le poète, le prêtre,
et le soldat" (*OC* 1287; the only great men are the poet, the priest, and the
soldier). St. Peter's physical and spiritual superiority mingle as they do in
Baudelaire's dandy-soldiers, for "le Dandysme est le dernier éclat d'héroïsme dans les décadences" (*OC* 1179; "Dandyism is the last flicker of heroism in decadent ages" [*SW* 421]). St. Peter shares the dandy's military uni-
formity of expression—his manner seldom gives him away—as well as the
dandy's goal, "satisfaire [ses] passions, de sentir et de penser" (*OC* 1178;
"satisfying [his] passions, of feeling and thinking" [*SW* 419]). Reserved
and passionate at once, St. Peter lives austerely, in a rundown house, without even a proper stove to heat his study; at the same time he is "terribly
selfish about personal pleasures, fought for them" (*PH* 26). Like d'Albert,
he glories in a voluptuous asceticism, and like Baudelaire's dandies, he
practices "spiritualisme" and "stoicisme" (*OC* 1178). St. Peter finds joy in
a rejection of most worldly "necessities" in favor of a few luxuries. His goal
is a triumph over, not in, the world.

St. Peter is a Baudelairean dandy in the contradictions with which
Cather invests his character: his simultaneous regard for social convention
and attack on it, his emotional connections to the human community and
his cold withdrawal from it; the volcanic passion smoldering inside the
controlled and controlling exterior; the voluptuous asceticism, the feeling
and thinking masked by a soldier's schooled resignation. He is, perhaps,
most a dandy, however, in his artistic achievements. His unflagging pursuit
of beauty and rejection of triviality; his passionate desire to write *Spanish
Adventurers in North America*; the courage with which he has faced two
ways at once, toward the oeuvre and toward the human family: all these
qualities have won him a dandy's credentials.

In "Le peintre de la vie moderne," an extended meditation on the
draughtsman Constantin Guys, Baudelaire, as I discussed earlier, describes his ideal artist. In this essay Baudelaire makes explicit what he has
implied with every phrase of his earlier essays on dandies: that the type of
the dandy and the type of the modern artist are, for him, one:

> Je le [Guys] nommerais volontiers un *dandy*, et j'aurais pour cela quelques
> bonnes raisons; car le mot *dandy* implique une quintessence de caractère et
> une intelligence subtile de tout le mécanisme moral de ce monde. (*OC* 1160)

I would willingly call him a dandy, and for that I would have a sheaf of good
reasons; for the word "dandy" implies a quintessence of character and a subtle understanding of all the moral mechanisms of this world.   (SW 399)

Yet, Baudelaire writes, Guys "se détache violemment du dandysme," because "le dandy est blasé, ou il feint de l'être," and Guys's "passion insatiable, celle de voir et de sentir" removes him from the dandy-brotherhood
(OC 1160; "parts company . . . with dandyism . . . the dandy is blasé, or
affects to be . . . insatiable passion, that of seeing and feeling" [SW 399]).
Since Baudelaire's essay is itself a dandy's work, we may not accept this
judgment naively. In essay after essay, Baudelaire has praised the dandy's
vast energy, which is suppressed, controlled, even temporarily negated in
the holy war on vulgarity. In fact, this act of control, culminating in the
dandy's blasé manner, is crucial to the dandy's audacious self-creation. A
precise parallel to the act of creation in general, the dandy's self-creation
involves a period of passionate seeing and feeling, experienced in the
world at large, and then distilled in solitude to the work of art, himself.
Guys creates art as Baudelaire's dandy creates himself; after roving in the
crowd, absorbing its electricity, Guys returns to his room and re-creates,
through the selective power of memory, the essence of what he has seen.

His drawings are as alive as his own soul. And, circularly, in creating his
drawings, Guys creates the only self capable of making those drawings.
His distillation of the crowd's electricity, a process that takes place in solitude, results in two works of art: both the drawing and the renewal of that
"quintessential" self which can pass invulnerably through the crowd, to
return, unscathed, to the solitude necessary for creation. It is his personal
power to "voir le monde, être au centre du monde et rester caché au
monde" (OC 1160; "to see the world, to be at the very center of the world,
and yet to be unseen of the world" [SW 400]), that protects him as an artist.
The dandy who paradoxically holds himself apart from the crowd even as
he constitutes its center, Guys is also the artist, capable of capturing life
rather than being captured by it.[8]

In creating Spanish Adventurers in North America, St. Peter has re-
created himself. Like Guys, he has traveled about the world—Spain,
Mexico, France—but "the notes and the records and the ideas always
came back to this room. It was here they were digested and sorted, and
woven into their proper place in his history" (PH 25). And it has been in

[8]Cather also had Delacroix in mind when she created St. Peter; see Bohlke's study of the
parallels between the two.

this attic study that he has gradually fashioned the dandy's mask of imperturbability and superiority which has made his forays into social life possible.

The act of writing the history has been one of high artifice: "The hand, fastidious and bold, which selected and placed—it was that which made the difference. In Nature there is no selection" (*PH* 75). Echoing the rhetoric of "Le peintre de la vie moderne," Cather characterizes St. Peter by describing *Spanish Adventurers*, and describes *Spanish Adventurers* by recounting St. Peter's most deeply felt memories and experiences. Here is Cather's circular description:

> his little brig, *L'Espoir*, sailed out of the new port with a cargo for Algeciras. The captain was from the Hautes-Pyrénées, and his spare crew were all Provençals. . . . On the voyage everything seemed to feed the plan of the work that was forming in St. Peter's mind; the skipper, the old Catalan second mate, the sea itself. One day stood out above the others. All day long they were skirting the south coast of Spain; from the rose of dawn to the gold of sunset the ranges of the Sierra Nevadas towered on their right, snow peak after snow peak, high beyond the flight of fancy, gleaming like crystal and topaz. St. Peter lay looking up at them from a little boat riding low in the purple water, and the design of his book unfolded in the air above him, just as definitely as the mountain ranges themselves. And the design was sound. He had accepted it as inevitable, had never meddled with it, and it had seen him through. (*PH* 105–6)

Cather paints both the man and the work of art in striking contrasts: the high, sculptured, inhuman peaks, crystal and topaz against the sky, set against the little boat, riding low in the water with its vulnerable human community. The Parnassian ideal of sculptured objectivity once again describes, as it does in *Mademoiselle de Maupin*, both a work of art and a way of being—the "French" life of sensation and self-absorption which admits of no human sympathy. This ideal is challenged, fertilized, by an ideal of sympathy, of wisdom created by human beings rather than delivered from snowy peaks. St. Peter is strange and unsettling as a character only if we insist on the primacy of his psychological portrait, only if we insist on his subjective view of the world as the key to his character. Like his work of historical art, he, too, has a wholly objective, elevated, self-absorbed element in his character. He is as much "about" mountain peaks as little boats. And as a dandy, he is an impersonator of abstraction, a figure of allegory, embodying just those issues of aesthetics and gender most on Cather's mind.

THE PROFESSOR'S HOUSE:
THE EFFEMINATE ROMANCE OF TEMPERAMENT

That the Professor's life's work combines the worlds of sympathy and sensation, action and sensitive reaction, suggests that his gender, too, might
combine the categories of male and female. Certainly the Professor's
world of marriage and family (the institutions that often serve to support
a polarized view of gender) is a sphere he finds painful, repellent. Marital
discord, sibling jealousy (and joined by the institutions of the university
and the federal bureaucracy), hypocrisy, sloth, and greed thrive in their fixities of category.

To imagine an alternative, Cather introduces a character, Tom Outland,
who explodes all the novel's carefully constructed categories, most notably
those of gender and aesthetics. The Professor's integrity as a character and
his identity are "vaporized," to use Baudelaire's term. The novel itself, appearing at first in three distinct books—three separate rooms—loses its
architectural solidity. And when the pieces come to rest again, they do so
in a new form, the "romance of temperament," which reveals that the
masculine friendship of St. Peter and Outland exists analogically, neither
wholly male nor wholly female. This "romance" develops in the following
way.

"Pour tout dire en un mot," Baudelaire writes of Guys, "notre singulier
artiste exprime à la fois le geste et l'attitude solonnelle ou grotesque des
êtres et leur explosion lumineuse dans l'espace" (OC 1169; "To sum it all
up, our strange artist expresses both the gestures and attitudes, be they solemn or grotesque, of human beings and their luminous explosion in space"
[SW 409]). The dandy-artist sees in his characters both their core of identity
and their diffusion into their surroundings, an echo of his own rhythm of
solitary self-creation and foray into the crowd. Behind St. Peter, aloof, superior, lapidary, stands Cather; she hesitates not at all in scattering her character to the four corners of the novel. The light of "Tom Outland's Story,"
that immense, pure radiance, is both the light of the New Mexican landscape and the light generated as St. Peter's definite outline, his Parnassian
integrity, expands and explodes. As Baudelaire writes in the opening lines
of his journal, "de la vaporisation et de la centralisation du *Moi*. Tout est
là" (OC 1271; of the vaporization and centralization of the Self. There is
everything), so Cather practices the simultaneous "vaporisation" and "centralisation" of her characters. *The Professor's House*, like *Mademoiselle de
Maupin*, is a novel of flux, of images placed in motion by many mirrors.

St. Peter the dandy stands before Tom Outland as before his mirror image; indeed, all of book 1 finds its reflection in book 2. The reader cannot fully grasp St. Peter because he exists in the elusive, metamorphic texture of the dandy's novel, in which the fixities of plot and character are continuously made and unmade. We can locate the figure of the dandy in its "vaporized" form—however fleetingly—by examining the novel's structure.

Book 2, "Tom Outland's Story," is a tale of adventure, what Cather calls in her criticism a "romance." As a tale inserted into the novel, however, it raises some questions. Cather gave as an explanation for the "experiment in form" her desire to suggest a Dutch painting in which the viewer's eye moves from an overstuffed interior, through a painted open window, toward a "stretch of grey sea." Thus book 1 suggests the stuffy room where Cather would "open the square window and let in the fresh air that blew off the Blue Mesa" (Woodress 370).

That "fresh air" would be, for Cather, the fresh air of romance. From the first, Cather associates romance with masculinity, with American sympathy and clean living. Such an atmosphere would allow men to "love and work and fight and die like men" (*KA* 232), rather than to flounder in petty emotions, as they do in Hamilton. The term "romance" has a special meaning for Cather; she defines it frequently in her journalistic articles. It refers to a rousing tale in the literary tradition of *The Prisoner of Zenda* or *The Count of Monte Cristo*, and its primary creators are Robert Louis Stevenson, Stanley Weyman, Dumas *père*, Anthony Hope [Hawkins], and Alphonse Daudet. These tales, Cather tells her newspaper and magazine audiences, are heroic, colorful, action-filled. Stevenson's romances, the best of the genre, "g[i]ve the world an outlook beyond the rigid horizons of social life, of something new, fresh, unheard of, full of brilliant color and rugged life" (*WP* 1:136). The romance is, for Cather, "the highest form of fiction," and one to which the novel returns after it shakes off its turn-of-the-century torpor and pessimism.

On its face, "Tom Outland's Story" is a manly and rugged romance. Appearing in the novel after the strained nerves of book 1, "The Family," it does "open the window and let in the fresh air." Outland's youth, his strength of character, his adventurous exploration of the Blue Mesa despite everyone's discouraging advice: all of these attributes make him a hero of romance. After the clumsy structures of Hamilton, the stony beauty of the Cliff City appears as a kind of moral cleansing at the heart of the novel.

The contrast between books 1 and 2 would be striking were romance a simple and straightforward genre for Cather. It is not. For every passage in which she asserts the simple, manly, direct strength of romance, Cather adds a passage casting that very simplicity, that very masculinity, into doubt. She praises Stevenson for allowing "not a jot of morbid introspection, not a shadow of pessimism" to enter his works, but she states that he was himself an "overworked invalid . . . sick unto death and exiled to the South Seas" (*KA* 314). As ill as his characters are healthy, he is also as effeminate as they are masculine. Cather approvingly quotes William Low on Stevenson's personality: "the personal charm of that woman-man was the sweetest experience I have had" (*WP* 2:562). Hawkins, too, is "feminine . . . girlish" and "wrote those stories for the sake of the women in them" (*WP* 2:569). Stevenson has a "quaint quiet style" (*KA* 312). Romance, then, is a "manly" genre written by effeminate men. But the *writing* of romance itself is an antiromantic, effete activity; art does not belong to the world of action.

Time and again Cather judges the values of romance as the truest and best values, all the while praising the creators of romance who have chosen lives that can only be called degenerate by the standards of their art. To justify this inconsistency, Cather has two options. First, she might take a leaf from Baudelaire's essay, "Le peintre de la vie moderne," in which he argues that convalescents and children have an especially fresh and passionate, rather than weak or unformed, perception of life. Thus, Cather might argue that the childlike or effeminate men who create romance possess a special kind of strength. Second, she might come to see more complex qualities within the romance heroes themselves, discovering more sensation, refinement, and Poesque irritation, less sympathy, action, and strength. Cather, in fact, elects both of these rationales. Stevenson, for example, "had the clean grit of the Scots certainly, if he did not have their robust physique" (*KA* 314). Cather claims as heroic Stevenson's very act of writing: "If Mr. Stevenson had been a strong man in the days when men acted he would have sailed the seas under the black flag with a cargo of wine and Spanish gold. As he was a weak man in the days when men reflected, he was a romanticist. . . . he was a man of pure invention whom the world could ill afford to lose" (*WP* 1:136–37).

From the delicate heroism of the creator of romance, Cather moves to the delicacy of the romance hero himself. She mentions on a few occasions Stevenson's "underrated" *Prince Otto*, which "contains . . . his only weak hero, and shows that he understood and sympathized with weakness and inertia, though he preferred strength and action" (*WP* 1:137). Prince Otto, or Prince Featherhead as his subjects call him, is a "butterfly," an ineffectual ruler who loses his kingdom. Stevenson portrays him variously as fop, childish man of undeniable charm, eunuch, and victim of a conniving society. If Cather mourns the passing of the Napoleonic era, "when one man controlled the world and made the world's history" (*WP* 1:353), she also celebrates dreamers and abdicators.

Cather admires the manly romance of action, of "hearts and hands instead of nerves and inherited tendencies" (*KA* 231), but she herself writes the demasculinized romance of nerves and sensation, or, to use Poe's term, the romance of "irritability." She quotes Henry James's comments on another of these romances of decay, loss, stasis—Daudet's *Kings in Exile*, "a book that could have been produced only in one of these later years of grace. Such a book is intensely modern, and the author is in every way an essentially modern genius" (*WP* 2:575).

The Professor's House, like "A Wagner Matinee," is a twicetold tale. By Cather's revised standards for romance, "Tom Outland's Story" is still a masculine romance, but so, too, is St. Peter's story. The Professor's tale is one of self-absorption and irritation, but it is also a tale of the heroic act of dwelling in exile (from France, his spiritual home), and writing a vast and beautiful work. He is both virile of body and delicate of sensibility; in fact his heroism inheres more fully in that sensibility than in his physical prowess. Once again Cather shows us Poe's artist as hero rather than victim, or rather as heroic even in his victimization by the lesser souls surrounding him.

While the Professor's tale is a romance of sensation by Cather's own complicated standard, Tom's tale is equally an effeminate romance of sensation and irritability which only appears at first to be a tale of "fresh air" and simple action. Tom discovers the Blue Mesa when he has been sent out to the range to convalesce after pneumonia. His feelings about the Mesa are more important to him than all his acts of exploration, his fine horsemanship, and physical courage. He seeks, on the Blue Mesa, not power, but solitude. His irritability and romantic vision cause him to lose Roddy, his best friend. His failure in Washington, D.C., is the paradoxical success-in-failure of the aesthete in the lion's jaw of philistine culture. If book 2, the second movement in Cather's Whistlerian symphony in red and purple, is a "fresh air" romance, it is also a romance of sensation; like the butterfly dandy Prince Otto, like Daudet's Queen Frédérique, Outland loses the kingdom but claims his soul.

The Professor's House is metamorphic in its mirrored worlds of "masculine" and "feminine" romance, in its characterization of Tom and St. Peter, and in its continuously shifting moral atmosphere as the bonds between Hamilton and the Blue Mesa cross and recross. Cather plays off within this metamorphic texture not just the aesthetic issues of sympathy and solitude, art involved in "life as we know it" and *l'art pour l'art*, but, in tandem, the "manly" versus the "effeminate." It is the effeminate which carries the day. While Tom Outland's virile fresh-air romance slowly metamorphoses into a troubled romance of sensation, culminating in his defeat, death, and legacy of pain, the Professor's romance of sensation never achieves simple, robust vitality. "American" fresh-air virtues do not ventilate the novel: Augusta can save the Professor, but not the novel, from a suffocating atmosphere.

The novel presents a drama of gender in which Cather challenges the dichotomy of male and female by softening them into "manly" and "effeminate" and suggesting that the effeminate—nerve endings rather than muscles—matters more. Her "romance of temperament," born of the metamorphic interplay of (male) sympathy and (female) sensation, in the end leans toward the world of sensation—Poe's world, the dandy's world—of irritability, victimization, and equivocal victory. Cather has feminized the masculine world of romance, but she has done so not to reverse the hierarchy of male over female. Instead, Cather reveals that her search for a moral aestheticism has entailed the creation of a feminized form which challenges the very notion of hierarchy itself. The romance of temperament exists on the divide between the genders, a feminized space that paradoxically challenges the very notion of "the female" as a category. Why, then, does Cather insist on hierarchy when she closes the novel with a literal act of salvation supplied by the orthodox Augusta, the keeper of category and hierarchy?

The Professor's House is an angry and bitter book; like Delacroix's landscapes of massacre, "tout cet oeuvre . . . ressemble à un hymne terrible composé en l'honneur de la fatalité et de l'irrémédiable douleur" (*OC* 1132; "the whole work . . . is like a terrible hymn composed in honor of fate and inescapable grief" [*SW* 378]); and it is so in part for reasons biography can supply. But it is so, too, because of Cather's adoption of the dandy's tradition. For she had, seven years earlier, in completing *My Án-tonia* (1918), accepted the demise of stable categories of gender, and thus brought French and American aesthetic modes into intimate relation. To do so, she had to sacrifice not just her notion of gender's fixity, but her notion of a fixed order of things. Her success, which we shall now examine, was perhaps harder to bear than failure. *The Professor's House* is a strange, stiff, angry novel in part because it is the lid Cather places upon *My Án-tonia*. In writing that earlier, seemingly most accessible, expansive, and "sympathetic" of works, Cather raised some disturbing possibilities which she attempts to quell within *The Professor's House*. It is, finally, to *My Ántonia*'s sweetnesses and terrors—chief among them, the display of gender's insignificance—that we must turn.

JUST GOOD FRIENDS: DANDYISM ON THE DIVIDE

As I note in my introduction, the Divide is the rich farmland between the Republican and Little Blue rivers in Nebraska; in its fictional form, it provides the setting of many of Cather's prairie tales. As a divide, it is not a line separating one area from another, but a locus of interminglings. *My Ántonia* is the novel in which Cather most subtly and most forcefully creates the divide as the only area in which her characters can live, always and only analogically, as men and as women, as creators of books and as creators of people, as dandies and as farmers.

Cather places at the center of this fictional divide two friends, Jim and Ántonia. Like the romance of temperament, friendship can challenge the categories of gender, as it can cross the lines of many categories: age, nationality, religion, race, even temperament. Friendship is the human relationship dangerously prone to sentimentalization which Cather explores more boldly than any other. *The Professor's House* offers as an antidote to the social ills it portrays—epitomized by the Great War, which claims Tom Outland—the grace of friendship. Any discussion of friendship in *My Ántonia* must eventually face two related questions. First, why don't Jim and Ántonia claim each other fully, becoming lovers and mates rather than "mere" friends? (Jim tells Ántonia's children, "You see I was very much in love with your mother once.") And second, why does Cather conclude her novel by enthroning Ántonia as earth-goddess? Ántonia's strength and simplicity give her the power to challenge modernism's very modes: irony, narcissism, doubt, difficulty. Is Ántonia an exercise in nostalgia or wish fulfillment? Is she even convincing?

The answers lie in the experiments of Cather's literary dandyism. I begin with the most apparent figure of the dandy in Cather's novel, Jim Burden. The parallels between nineteenth-century French dandies and Cather's character immediately appear, if not in Jim Burden's clothing and personal elegance, then in his spiritual and aesthetic superiority. He experiences the world about him with the dandy-artist's distinctive sensibility. A parallel with Baudelaire will perhaps help here. Baudelaire summarizes the reactions of three artists, Hector Berlioz, Franz Liszt, and himself, to Richard Wagner's music:

la sensation de la *béatitude spirituelle et physique*; de *l'isolement*; de la contemplation de *quelque chose infiniment grand et infiniment beau*; d'*une lumière intense* qui réjouit *les yeux et l'âme jusqu'à la pâmoison*; et enfin la sensation *de l'espace étendu jusqu'aux dernières limites concevables*.   (*OC* 1214)

the sensation of *spiritual and physical beatitude*; of *isolation*; of the contemplation of *something infinitely big and infinitely beautiful*; of an *intense light*, which is a joy to *eyes and soul to the point of swooning*, and finally the sensation of *space, extending to the furthest conceivable limits*.   (*SW* 332)

Jim Burden experiences just these sensations as he roams the prairie. His exile from Virginia is an exile to an original unity—"that is happiness, to be dissolved into something complete and great"(*MA* 18)—the *coincidentia oppositorum* Nebraska-style, which the farming community busily destroys, and which it is the work of Cather's novels to reconstitute. Like Baudelaire's dandy De Quincey, Jim seeks expansion and intensification of sensory experience, waits for the landscape to reveal magnificent horizons, whether it be a plow against the sun or a particularly magical cast of light. Jim is from the first a dandy-aesthete in his willingness to turn away from his human companions in order to savor his surroundings with special powers of attention and discrimination: "I used to love to drift along the pale-yellow cornfields, looking for the damp spots one sometimes found at their edges, where the smartweed soon turned a rich copper colour" (*MA* 29). Ántonia's family, the Shimerdas, may worry about earning a living; Jim appreciates the growing intensity with which the landscape speaks directly to him. While the figures about him toil, Jim, in the finest tradition of the dandy's nonchalance and languor, soaks in sensation and reflects on it: "I kept as still as I could" (*MA* 18).

As a child, Jim lives partially in the magnificent near-void of the outdoors; like Levana's child, he is close to paradise, but not in it. He lives, too, in the *mundus muliebris* of his grandmother's kitchen. His lone forays into the measureless prairie end in the intimate female world of warmth and nourishment behind the stove, at the dinner table, in the bathtub, or in bed. If, as Baudelaire believes, "genius is no more than childhood recaptured at will," this young aesthete is well on his way to the dandy-artist's practiced acuity of perception, sense of superiority to others, and grandness of vision.

As Jim matures, he develops some of dandyism's harsher social attitudes: the Shimerdas' difficulties in coping indicate to him their inferior class status; the streets of Black Hawk irritate him as he nervously paces, waiting to escape to a world more consonant with his superior vision and power. The masks begin to appear: a public face of languorous inactivity (Baudelaire's "unemployed Hercules") hiding his solitary grind at college-preparatory studies; the persona of the young boy who will take on the "real women," a Brummellesque sexual posturing half revealing a sexual fear and coldness at the core. For Jim is a dandy in the distance he maintains between himself and the novel's women. Although it is Ántonia who rejects his sexual advances, Jim stops pursuing her, especially after Lena appears in his dreams, carrying a reaping hook. While he remembers this as a pleasant dream, his waking self counsels distance from the dangers of women. Like d'Albert dreaming of marble statues, Jim does not claim any of the pioneer women precisely because they are flesh and blood. Passions are ugly: witness his assault by Wick Cutter, the sordidness of Donovan's treatment of Ántonia, and Ole Benson's foolish pursuit of Lena. Jim finds several occasions resolutely to separate himself from Ántonia in disappointment or disgust, all the while counting on her admiring attitude when he chooses to return. Like Barbey's correspondent Trébutien, Jim's Ántonia ("My" Ántonia) *is* his admiring audience. Faithfully observed by her, always welcomed back with no questions asked, Jim might echo Barbey, "je me vois vu." Jim, like Barbey, silences his subject; Brummell does not speak for himself, nor does Ántonia. She speaks the words Jim needs her to speak: the Bohemian words of a not-yet-naturalized American, the sisterly words of a sexually off-limits woman, the idealized words of an earth-goddess.

Jim is most a dandy when, in his growing need to bring will to bear upon memory, he writes his story of Ántonia. Like Baudelaire, who sees in memory an idealizing power, Jim understands the need to move beyond the lush drama of memory he shares with Ántonia to the creation of art through an act of Delacroixian artistic will. Jim is an American man of French sensation; a man of sensation experienced in solitude rather than sympathy, of long periods of disappearance rather than intimacy. Like Mr. Shimerda, he never belongs in prairie society; but in contrast to him, he will, with the dandy's ferocity, press back against reality rather than submit to its crushing force.

Once again, Cather rethinks issues of both aesthetics and gender by layering another dandy's portrait over that of the first. If Jim is a male dandy with Parnassian tastes, a child-aesthete who matures to live aloofly in the world of sensation, then Ántonia completes the portrait of dandyism.

For all her fecundity, Ántonia practices the dandy's hieratic function: her love, her industry flow out to others in a kind of religious benediction. After one brief period of hedonism in Vanni's tent, Ántonia continues the habits of childhood in womanhood: a stoical bending to necessity para-doxically joined with an epicurean delight in the physical world. That she is joyful, warm, vivid, does not alter the fact that her joy lies in self-effacement, in a sympathetic lending of self to the sustenance of others. It is Ántonia who disappears into the kitchen in the middle of parties to bake a cake. Like the "Painter of Modern Life," she disappears into the scene rather than dominating it; it is Jim who counts on being valedictorian, who would impose his superiority upon prairie society.

The source of Ántonia's warmth is the dandy's inner fire which Barbey and Baudelaire depict; the warmth grows because, like Baudelaire's swan and Andromache, Ántonia solaces herself in exile from the Old World by forming connections, creating a center in the new. Ántonia is a full-scale American heroine, we feel, doubting all the while the possibility of such a creature. Cather invites us to imagine her rather as Baudelaire invites us to imagine his Indian, savage dandy, full of vigor although the tribes may be the "remnant of great civilizations of the past" (SW 421). Ántonia is the last in the line of old-country nobility; as such, it is fitting that she reject Jim, the crude, uncultured American boy. Ántonia lives the dandy's pro-gram of combatting and destroying triviality: "she still had that something which fires the imagination, could still stop one's breath for a moment by a look or gesture that somehow revealed the meaning in common things" (MA 353). Her gift is precisely that of the dandy's—to rise above, to pre-sent a new standard based on her personal gifts.

Ántonia's final appearance in Jim's memoirs and Cather's novel con-firms her as the ultimate dandy, the self-created person who has wholly merged with the chosen mask of selfless love, industry, simplicity. "The greatest perfection a work of art can ever attain is when it ceases to be a work of art and becomes a living fact" (WP 1:44): Ántonia as Cather's dandy of "vaporisation," sympathy, moral action, and health has, in book 5, inhabited dandyism in its deepest Baudelairean potential. Master of the analogical, she has re-created the mundus muliebris within the confines of her earthly estate, created a unified world apart, but wholly connected to nothing less than the universe. One feels the chord, not the individual notes: her children are as animals; her husband is as a son, a father, and a friend; the food preserved in barrels glows as ripe food on the vine; past is as present; old-country values and language are as new. At this pitch of emotional intensity, Ántonia's personal, sympathetic self reaches the con-dition of impersonality, and the chapter of exile is complete. Like Ovid among the Scythians, the Bohemian woman among her children and friends has come home.

Cather asks us to take Jim and Ántonia together, as metamorphic versions of each other, as layers in her palimpsestic creation of the dandy. By Cather's critical scheme, Ántonia represents masculine virtues of sympathy and action, Jim the feminine virtues of aesthetic acuity and self-absorption. Against Ántonia's masculinity, her relish for life, her thick neck and strong shoulders, we balance Jim's femininity, his delicacy, his virtually invisible body. Against Ántonia's romance of action—farming, childbearing—we balance Jim's romance of sensation. Yet the trajectories of aesthetics and gender do not, in this novel, end in a sweeping circularity, Jim's arc joining Ántonia's to form a novel in which we, as readers, find emotional shelter. Cather is, after all, herself a dandy-artist, careful to maintain an adversarial as well as sympathetic posture toward her readers. Cather tells in *My Ántonia* another tale of gender's fluidity, one far more threatening to her traditional ideas of order than this tale of a manly woman and a womanly man.

AFTER GENDER: ALLUSION AND ANALOGY IN *MY ÁNTONIA*

The trajectories of aesthetics and gender in *My Ántonia* extend beyond the novel itself to gather in much of Cather's own reading. The outline of the novel is permeable, indistinct, shifting. Like Barbey, Cather appropriated in vast sweeps the images with which she surrounded herself as a passionate reader. The very vagueness characterizing the relationship of Jim and Ántonia summons the ghosts of other literary pairs: Tom and Maggie Tulliver, Petrarch and Laura, Poe and Virginia, to name but a few. Two pairs, in particular, claim a vivid presence in the novel: Ovid's Diana and Actaeon of the *Metamorphoses*, and Dumas *fils*'s Marguerite and Armand, of *La dame aux camélias* (which Cather knew better in its English translation, *Camille*).

To trace the presence of these works in Cather's novel is to make clear that *My Ántonia*, apparently so simple and transparent a work, so lovingly realistic and sympathetic an account of pioneer life, is itself the work of a dandy-artist. Reader beware. Far from being an account, straight from the heart, of regional beauty, this novel of the American frontier only half hides a modernist sophistication. It is a collection of the stories of various speakers, transcribed by Jim Burden, but it is also a series of half-spoken tales, whispers and distant calls, which unmake the certainties on which the narrative pronounces its claim to realism: the cycle of the seasons, the domestication of the wilderness, the established cultural rituals surrounding birth, education, procreation, and death. To read *My Ántonia* across Ovid's and Dumas's works is to discern a world in which Cather, by disrupting the familiar arrangements of gender, by challenging our assumption that each character is either male or female, has created the only world that will suffice her as a modern artist. Her subtle undermining of the novel's apparent certainties places Cather and the reader in an adversarial relation, reminding us that the dandy-artist withholds, misleads, and that the reader of this tradition must be, like the reader of Barbey's "Du Dandysme," distrustful. While nineteenth-century fictions of dandyism present us with a difficult surface, Cather, in *My Ántonia*, presents the opposite: a straightforward, "human" memoir of life on the prairies. However loose its construction, it invites us to settle into its cycles; however gorgeous its language, it allows us to take its world as comfortably "real," a world resembling the one we live in, only simpler, truer. Yet the novel also requires us to pit our quickness of eye against Cather's sleight of hand: look again, and this is a novel not of American sympathy, but of French subtlety.

Lest we miss the challenge altogether, Cather sets up the Nebraskan frontier version of the myth of Diana and Actaeon in a rather obvious fashion. It is no accident Cather has chosen a myth about seeing and being seen, for, like her predecessors in the tradition of dandyism who rewrote Ovid, she has chosen a dandy's myth, a story of spectator and audience. Ovid's Actaeon, tired of hunting, tells his friends to "give up the labor,/ bring home the nets" (*Metamorphoses* 3.51–52). Strolling without employment, like any good dandy, Actaeon accidentally comes upon the sacred grove of Diana and sees the goddess bathing, surrounded by her nymphs. Diana, alerted by her screaming attendants and wrathful at the intrusion, sprinkles water upon Actaeon, transforming him into a stag with a human mind but an inability to express himself. When Actaeon hesitates, his own hounds, whom he is incapable of calling off, attack and slay him.

Cather retells Ovid's tale in a cubist fashion, rearranging its parts, multiplying its dramatic roles, and redistributing them freely among her own characters. Jim plays both of the principal roles on that summer's day when he and four of the pioneer girls agree to meet at the river for a picnic. Like Actaeon, Jim is a hunter: "Charley Harling and I had hunted through these woods, fished from the fallen logs, until I knew every inch of the river shores" (*MA* 233). But, as Diana, he is the surprised bather. Ovid's "secret grotto made by no art" becomes the "pleasant dressing room [Jim] knew among the dogwood bushes" along the wooded shore of the river (*MA* 233). Like Diana, the naked Jim is witnessed—but by the girls "peering down at me like curious deer when they come out of the thicket to drink" (*MA* 234). They are both Diana's shrieking nymphs and Actaeon after his metamorphosis. The pieces of Ovid's myth thus scrambled, Cather seems to transform the Ovidian tale of accidental lapse and gory punishment into a summer's idyll. Jim and the girls laugh at one another because the change in roles strikes them as funny: (male) seer is now himself vulnerable, "seen"; the hierarchy of power has been challenged. The world, for one lighthearted moment, has been turned upside down; Ovid's tragedy collapses into Cather's comic interlude.

Yet the game of literary allusion allows Cather to mislead the reader by making a subtle, not so visible use of the appropriated myth. In fact, Actaeon's fate reverberates menacingly throughout Cather's novel. The tale of Diana and Actaeon is a tale of seeing and being seen, and the costs of both positions. For, however elusively and inconclusively, this story glosses Cather's decision to conclude her book with the image of an earth-goddess, gloriously immune to the treachery of language. Ántonia, as Actaeon, has been silenced as her punishment for seeing. Ovid's mute beast is Cather's fecund, pioneer woman: Ántonia produces a family and a farm, not a book. The book is Jim's; as Diana, he retains the power of public language which Ántonia/Actaeon has lost. As Diana, too, Jim rejects Ántonia, because he is wrathful. He punishes her, failing to rescue her during the hard time after she returns to Black Hawk, pregnant and alone. These Ovidian parallels do not provide "explanations"—psychological, spiritual, or social—of the behavior of characters; rather they are tints, fleeting images, ways of softening and complicating the clear outline of Cather's plot.

In order to hear and see this subtle story, we must recognize Jim's and Ántonia's gender as neither fixed nor, in the end, terribly important. Ovid's tale, for Cather, is not one of gender's stability, not a myth in which Diana's outraged feminine modesty adequately explains her actions. For Cather, it is a tale of seeing and silencing regardless of gender or sexual roles. Gender is for Cather like species for Ovid: free-floating, subject to metamorphosis. The myth of Diana and Actaeon is, after all, part of the same cycle of Ovidian myths as that of Tiresias, who, for the crime of seeing snakes, is changed into a woman. If in the *Metamorphoses* Actaeon can become a stag, so in *My Ántonia* a woman can take the male part—Ántonia (and her friends) can see the naked Jim. Gender, far from being an absolute, is here a matter of roles: Ántonia does not "become" male, she acts *as* a male. The difference is that between an absolute and an analogical concept of gender.

Yet even when we align genders, considering Ántonia as Diana and Jim as Actaeon, the myth continues to reverberate in the novel. Ántonia is, after all, a figure like Diana, a beautiful, proud woman whom Jim observes throughout the novel, from the first childhood encounter on the railroad siding to his final framed vision of Ántonia in her garden. Ántonia does not want to be viewed by such an appropriating eye ("My" Ántonia); she wants to see others, tell others' stories to her children, manage her own theater of memory with her own script and actors. *This* Diana punishes Jim/Actaeon, silencing him, causing him to string together others' stories when he writes his memoirs, to edit out much of his own story in writing hers. There is a reticence, a feeling of things not said in Jim's narrative, a silence Ántonia's "wrath" explains. And, like Actaeon, for whom mute hesitation spells death, Jim is all hesitation, waiting twenty years to return to Ántonia. His death, though not literal, is a death of the heart: a loveless marriage, a missed opportunity forever mourned.

Once again, the fluidity of gender allows the transformation of aesthetic categories, specifically, those of genre. Ovid's tragedy becomes both a brief idyll and the long history of Jim and Ántonia's relationship. Ántonia's sad downfall with Donovan is but a preliminary act to the comedy of her life. The silly melodrama of Wick Cutter and his wife becomes the tragedy of two twisted souls. And, before she is finished, Cather's central aesthetic dichotomy—the dandy's art of sensation, the dandy's art of sympathy—will collapse, not into identity, not into synthesis, but into a fully realized analogical relation.

To discern the hints of this movement, it is helpful to read *My Ántonia* across Dumas's *Camille*. Once again, the parallels are at first all too clear. Ántonia and Jim never claim each other as mates because Ántonia, like Marguerite, has given up her beloved. Both Ántonia and Marguerite, believing they are not of the correct class and background, sacrifice their own happiness in love: "The woman does not love the man she would degrade," Marguerite avows (Dumas 22). Similarly, Ántonia urges Jim to go off to college and make something of himself. Jim, like Armand, suffers, but rationalizes his abandonment of Ántonia by disgust at her association with Donovan: "I could forgive her, I told myself, if she hadn't thrown herself away on such a cheap sort of fellow" (*MA* 304). Thus Donovan parallels Dumas's Varville.

Yet, once again, the "fit" between Cather's novel and her borrowed text is not nearly so simple as it would first appear. Ántonia, having given up her beloved, not only does not die, but flourishes. Her dubious past, rather than haunting her, sustains her. In fact it is Jim who more nearly resembles Marguerite: the figure of the dandy, pristine, pure, too good for this crass world. Marguerite describes the camellia: "It is a strange flower, pale, scentless, cold; but sensitive as purity itself . . . wound it with a single touch, you never can recall its bloom, nor wipe away the stain" (Dumas 12). Like the woman of the camellias, Jim is simply too sensitive for this world; though he does not die, he appears to us as withered and pale, ruined in some way which is not fully articulated, especially in contrast to Ántonia.

Camille is a myth of the Romantic artist; Jim Burden is not the first sensitive young man to see his own story in Marguerite's feverish passion and early demise. As if to reassure himself of his own fixed place in a fixed system of gender, Jim muses at the intermission, "Lena was at least a woman, and I was a man." Yet, when the play is over, Jim sighs "with the spirit of 1840," with nostalgia for the past, because it is precisely this simple crossing of gender lines which is no longer available to him. That a man sees himself in a woman suggests, in 1840, that he is a man "completed" by female characteristics, another pseudoandrogyne. Jim writes his memoir with Cather's twentieth-century awareness of life as theater, gender as pose. In her novel it is Marguerite's role, per se, that Cather points out to us. Even though the actress who plays the part is mediocre, the "role," the lines themselves, save the play for Jim and Lena. For Cather, *Camille* is a play of roles, of types, easily assignable and reassignable to both men and women in her own fiction. For the Romantic artist (Jim has a "romantic disposition," we are told on the second page of the novel), a male may aspire to incorporate the female. For the modern artist, gender is but an aspect of a role, and not necessarily the most important one. Gender, interchangeable and dramatic in nature, is not only no longer fixed, it is no longer necessarily the central fact about a person.

Yet if the web of allusion, hint, and innuendo in *My Ántonia* suggests a radical revision of the nature and place of gender in our culture, we must still recognize the novel's strong claims for the opposite view: that gender is both absolute and absolutely important. We must account for book 5 and its depiction of a world in which men marry women, in which the reproduction not just of children, but of traditional concepts of male and female, holds triumphant sway. We must account for this solid world of order and plenitude, seemingly the most real world, of Cather's vision.

In her rewriting of Ovid, Cather scrambles gender; in her rewriting of Dumas, she suggests gender's dramatic quality, its genesis in self-presentation. It was never Cather's intention to jettison cultural forms; as a traditionalist she regarded the past as sacred, the present as degraded. Like Barbey, she wanted to revive the present by rediscovering the integrities of the past. Thus the Catholic Augusta and the earth-mother Ántonia guard the closing movements of the respective novels in which they appear. Gender may be in flux, but it is also fixed by tradition.

Cather wants to avoid the limitations of received forms which eventually restrict rather than enliven, yet she will not accept innovation as her salvation. Her solution is by now a familiar one: the analogization not just of male and female, sympathy and sensation, but of that most basic of polarities—order and disorder. To close the novel with the Ántonia of book 5 is to hold at bay the elements of chaos which the subtexts of her novel introduce. Yet it is important to see that Cather presents Ántonia in a double frame: she stands within the garden of her own innocence and goodness, but she stands as well within Jim Burden's tale. He is preeminently the figure who comes and goes, promises but reneges, offers respect but exacts homage. The novel ends with the solidity of Ántonia, the diaphaneity of Jim, and neither quality exists outside the ironic texture of the whole.

Read in one slant of light, *My Ántonia* is a novel of Anglo-Saxon rectitude, of laws made and obeyed, of sympathy and action and innocence. This is the world epitomized by Jim's grandparents and by Anton Jelinek with his "frank, manly faith" (*MA* 107). Read in another slant of light, the novel portrays a prairie society as cosmopolitan and as fallen as Baudelaire's Paris, a place in which Ántonia becomes the flower emerging from the evils of dislocation, poverty, even brutality. This is a place to which misfits such as Pavel and Peter may flee. Yet what Cather might have represented as a conflict of realities unfolding in time she instead offers at every moment as a matter of irony and even paradox.

The trajectory of aesthetics in the novel leads to a form familiar in the tradition of dandyism. Just as Cather's characters learn to create the forms of analogy—Ántonia *as* a sister, mother, wife—just as friendship is *as* love, without its deathly implications, so the novel itself is the work of analogy. We read it as a novel of decency, optimism, and action, but also as a novel of irritation, narcissism, sensibility, and paralysis.

My Ántonia both reveals the chaos and hides it. This is the dandy's novel of the twentieth century: actually written by a dandy-artist who is a woman, it masks her tale not in arrogance, but in simplicity. Her novel, accessible, simple, healthy, is also duplicitous, allusive, elusive. In it, the trajectory of gender—the protean patterns it traces—enables Cather to form the aesthetics of analogy. Ántonia's womanhood, so simply and grandly described—"She was a rich mine of life, like the founders of early races"—is subtly undermined by a resolutely modernist understanding in which male is as female, American is as French, sympathy is as sensation, and order is as chaos.

Cather, the only woman writer of my study, has perhaps a certain advantage in creating a modernist aesthetic. The *mundus muliebris* is not for her alien territory to be recaptured from memories of childhood and explored with trepidation, but her native ground. The divide of analogical gender is not a threatening place, but the territory of love such as Alexandra finds it in *O Pioneers!*

What does threaten Cather is the conclusion she reaches after exploring the divide. Once she frees gender from dichotomous categories, she has by implication called a truce between male and female. Both art and life lose the compelling plots of distance overcome, of struggle, of the search for completion as male and female engage in a time-honored cultural dance designed to culminate in the subordination of women. To analogize male and female is to call for wholly new plots. What enables Cather, elitist and cultural conservative, to entertain such a radical shift in the ways of art, is a feeling: that the impingement of the alien into accepted forms is the very source of modern beauty. Baudelaire insists that beauty always has an element of the bizarre. Cather's version of this modernist insight reveals that American beauty must incorporate the strangeness of French beauty. Within the realm of the French, chosen precisely for its "otherness," Cather finds a space as large and powerful as the Nebraska plains. Within that French space she may entertain the notion of profound cultural change—the waning of dichotomous gender—safely, for it is a space she can, as an American, exit from time to time. It is a promise, not a prison.

And so it will be for Wallace Stevens as well. His exploration of both the female and the French allows him to reshape the very culture he wanted so desperately to preserve. It is to this admiring reader of Cather, this American male who courts an interior paramour who is French and female, that I now turn.

6

THE INTIMIDATING THESIS

STEVENS'S DANDY

THE PATRIARCHS OF TRUTH

Late in 1898, Wallace Stevens (1879–1955) noted in his journal: "I wish that like Eugénie de Guérin I might write something about which I could say, 'Ceci n'est pas pour le public; c'est de l'intime, c'est de l'âme, c'est pour un'" (*SP* 20; "This is not for the public; it contains my inmost thoughts, my very soul; it is for *one*" [Arnold 83]). Stevens quotes the same Mlle de Guérin who so fascinated Barbey d'Aurevilly that he included her in his palimpsest of Beau Brummell. She provided for Barbey the exemplary figure of the dandy as aristocratic woman. And it was Mlle de Guérin who said that Barbey was "un beau palais dans lequel il y a un labyrinthe" (*M* 2:343; a beautiful palace in which there is a labyrinth), expressing for Barbey his need to hide himself, the minotaur, within a fortress of coldness, imperturbability, mystery, and even monstrous threat.

While we cannot say with certainty that Stevens knew either Barbey's "Du Dandysme et de G. Brummell" or Eugénie de Guérin's journal—it is more likely Stevens came across the Guérin quotation in Matthew Arnold's essay about her—his interest in the quotation reveals three central aspects of Stevens's dandyism. First, Mlle de Guérin's statement appears in Stevens's journal in the original French. Just as dandyism was for Barbey intrinsically English, so it was for Stevens most powerful when it was French. Second, Stevens quotes a woman. Barbey's more than effeminate Brummell takes form simultaneously with Barbey's creation of a female aesthetic of modern beauty (elegance is "le petit sexe" of beauty); and Stevens himself begins (and continues to begin) with the female in his efforts to grasp a fresh and vital notion of order. Finally, Eugénie de Guérin's statement "ceci n'est pas pour le public . . . c'est pour un" is that of a dandy, always calculating how much she may withhold from the public without disappearing from the public eye, yearning for the perfect audience of "one" with whom to share secrets, that one collapsing exquisitely but never fully into the dandy's own, better self. Stevens created the scenario of such a collapse repeatedly in his correspondence, as we shall see, but he dramatized it as well in his poetry.

Imagining an aristocratic woman's presence within the dandy enabled Barbey to conceive of the dandy as artist. Stevens, too, wanted throughout his life to imagine a superior figure who would be involved in the private life of the imagination, the world of poetry, rather than the public life of politics, although it was to politics he first turned in his search for that superior man:

> The other night I sat in my room in the moonlight thinking about the top men in the world today, people like Truman and Bevin, for example. That I suppose is the source of one's desire for a few really well developed individuals. What is terribly lacking from life today is the well developed individual, . . . or the *man who by his mere appearance convinces you that a mastery of life is possible*. (*LWS* 518, emphasis added)

The quotation ends with an eerily ambivalent statement about a master of life who was much in the news, Stalin: "The unfortunate part about [Stalin's contempt for the people] is that in the long run these people will hold him back, and, for my own part, I think they should."

The figure of the dandy has traditionally been, in his simplest definition, the "superior man," but superiority as a concept would not suffice for Stevens. His dandy would have to be, like dandies before him, a personification of contradiction and even paradox: superior without being elevated, effective without taking action, masterful without exercising actual force, the most private of public figures. If Stevens observed the waning of the Judeo-Christian patriarchal myth, if God was now subject to fictional making, there was no longer any compelling reason why male hegemony should inform any aspect of the fictions, supreme or otherwise, that Stevens willed into being. Pleasurable, abstract, changing, yes; male, no. The very concept of the "superior man" had been called into question. This is precisely the understanding Gautier, Barbey, and Baudelaire reached: the dandy was the name they placed on the "superior" figure who challenged hierarchy with the ideas of metamorphosis, paradox, and analogy. We must watch Stevens struggling with an innate conservatism, a desire not to jettison, but merely to reform, restyle, patriarchy. Yet his repeated acts of the mind gradually lead him, a Moses in reverse, to a vision of the land beyond patriarchy's borders.

This chapter frames Stevens's engagement, as a dandy-artist, with two forms, the French and the female, within which Stevens discovered the possibility of novelty, described in this way: "In spite of the cynicisms that occur to us as we hear of such things, a freedom not previously experienced, a poetry not previously conceived of, may occur with the suddenness inherent in poetic metamorphosis. For poets, that possibility is the ultimate obsession" (*OP* 231). This novelty, poetic grace, enabled Stevens to think beyond the patriarchal myths. Throughout his life, Stevens inhabited in paradoxical fashion two mutually exclusive spaces. He lived within the social reality of his day, within his culture's set of truths about real men and proper ladies, the importance of work and the family, the nobility of the soldier, and so forth. Yet he lived, too, within a monstrous space in which certainty metamorphosed to possibility, as "truth" changed and changed again. He was, like dandy-artists before him, deeply conservative and revolutionary at once, and his poetry is a record of the struggle within him. I will argue that his macaronic poetry and prose, English mixed with French, accompanied a growing macaronic sense of gender, of the female juxtaposed with the male rather than subordinated to it or (what amounts to subordination) blended with it. In writing into the French and the female, Stevens sought the space of monstrosity, the space of the failure of category, in which resemblance and analogy, not hierarchy, held sway. He wrote himself into his own version of the *mundus muliebris*; there dichotomous gender meets its end. This dandy-artist's passage beyond the "certainties" of gender, the creation of modern beauty, is the story I wish to tell.

Critics, from the first, have labeled Stevens a dandy and found his poetry dandified. This view colored the first ten years of Stevens criticism, probably because *Harmonium* lent itself to terms like "precious" and "artificial." As critical aperçus, the terms of dandyism were applied to Stevens's poetry primarily to mark its weakness.[1] Dandyism has been, and remains, a code word in criticism for overly precious, decadent, silly, or shallow. Even the critics who demonstrated a deeper understanding of the literary tradition of dandyism sometimes faulted Stevens for adopting the dandy's persona.[2] Critics of Stevens's dandyism thus divide into two groups: the many who are put off by the dandy's poetic tactics—which they can see only as so many frivolous pirouettes—and the few who understand some of the complexity and suggestiveness of the full range, political and aesthetic, of his posing, pirouetting, hiding, attacking.[3]

In an early (1900) journal entry, Stevens criticizes and trivializes his own dandyism as mere foppishness:

> Sometimes I wish I wore no crown—that I trod on something thicker than air—that there were no robins, or peach dumplings, or violets in my world—that I was the proprietor of a patent medicine store—or manufactured pants for the trade—and that my name was Asa Snuff. But alas! the

[1] Morton Dauwen Zabel perhaps best characterized this view when he wrote in 1931, "Dandyism is style without significant motive or conviction" (Brown and Haller 49). This derogatory, reductive view of dandyism spans the criticism, however; Buttel writes of Stevens's movement beyond "mere dandyism" (170); in an otherwise useful essay on "Le Monocle de Mon Oncle," Maccaffrey writes of "a willingness on the part of the poet to appear foolish, precious, dandified, superficial" (Bloom, *Stevens*, 118). Stevens's biographer Joan Richardson (1988) writes of Stevens's critics that to them "he seemed a leftover aesthete, a dandy" (34), questioning their assessment of Stevens but not their understanding of what dandyism is. These are but a few examples of a widespread critical misunderstanding of dandyism.

[2] In his essay "The Dandyism of Wallace Stevens," Gorham Munson writes an acute sketch of the phenomenon: "In the dandy of letters, impeccability is primarily achieved by adding elegance to correctness. Yet life is disturbing and horrifying as well as interesting and delightful: one is inevitably tossed by the 'torments of confusion'; and the dandy, if he would maintain his urbane demeanor, must adopt protective measures. The safeguards . . . are three: wit, speculation, and reticence" (Brown and Haller 42). Yet Munson faults Stevens for his "well-fed and well-booted dandyism of contentment" (Brown and Haller 44), linking it with "the America that owns baronial estates."

J. V. Cunningham in 1960 places Stevens in the tradition of dandyism which stresses its aggressive defensiveness, suggesting that he, unlike most critics of Stevens, is familiar with some of the central documents of dandyism when he writes that it has "its private ritual and its air of priesthood—*odi profanum vulgus et arceo*, 'I despise the uninitiated crowd, and I keep them at a distance'" (Brown and Haller 125). See, too, Eda Lou Walton's 1931 review of Stevens's poetry in the *Nation* (reprinted in Doyle 91–92) for an astute account of dandyism.

[3] Along with Cunningham (Brown and Haller) see, for example, Benamou, Buttel, and Bates (97–126) for a richer account of dandyism.

tormenting harmonies sweep around my hat, my bosom swells with "agonies and exultations"—and I pose.   (*LWS* 48)

But Stevens also understood and documented the dandy's utter serious-
ness, his flight from, rather than toward, triviality, his need to conceal and
defend and attack in order to make a place for himself in a world of philistines. He sees a fellow soul in Willa Cather, who also writes in a concealed manner, although she chooses the mask of simplicity, the better to
please an unsophisticated audience while speaking in code to the sensitive
and literate. "We have nothing better than she is. She takes so much pains
to conceal her sophistication that it is easy to miss her quality," he writes
(*LWS* 381). Stevens attests to his reading in the tradition of dandyism
when he mentions in passing Stendhal, Delacroix, Pierrot, Alcibiades, and
Byron. He sees the artist as a figure of will and energy with a fierceness
reminiscent of Barbey: "One thing about life is that the mind of one man,
if strong enough, can become the master of all the life in the world. To
some extent, this is an everyday phenomenon. Any really great poet, musician, etc. does that" (*LWS* 360). And, as his earliest letters reveal, Stevens
is aware from childhood of his own tendency toward artificiality and coldness, the dandy's defense against a hostile world.[4]

Stevens, like Cather, stepped into the dandy's pose not because he directly imitated nineteenth-century French writers, but because he needed
and loved French culture in a general though intense way. It afforded him
his principal means of pressing back against the "pressure of reality";
things French—books, paintings, words—were talismans against philistine American culture. Stevens's motions are sometimes parallel to, sometimes derivative of, the French writers he enjoyed reading, and it is often
difficult to say with certainty which ideas he borrowed, which he developed independently.

Yet Stevens's dandyism was the product of Reading, New York City,
and Hartford, not Caen, Paris, or Brussels. It developed in the countryside
around those cities or in their parks, in a way that French dandyism, a phenomenon of city streets and cafés, never did. Stevens's dandyism requires
a peculiarly American posture of languor and elevation, a solitude not
within the crowd, but away from it. Heir to the Romantic poets, but not a
Romantic himself (though he does borrow a boat and row self-consciously
"up the Schuylkill . . . into a world of wild solitude and back again" [*SP*
57]), Stevens is a fresh-air dandy, a figure who seeks the heights of "Levana" as Baudelaire has described them through De Quincey's dream vi-

---

[4]See Ellmann's essay in Doggett and Buttel (149–70) for a convincing account of Stevens's awareness of his traits of coldness and artificiality.

sion. He frequently hikes to a place distant from the city, climbs a hill, and glories in the situation away from and above all things vulgar. He stretches out on a high ledge—dandies cultivate leisure as a fine art—even sleeps, to awaken: "I looked straight ahead from under my eyelids—nothing but clouds and clouds" (*LWS* 59). Although the dandy, the dissatisfied man, creates his own satisfaction, such an elevation holds always Levana's threat of ultimate homelessness, displacement.

Like Gautier's, Barbey's, and Baudelaire's literary dandyism, Stevens's dandyism is a phenomenon of rebellion against the vulgar certainties of his day: "Being rebellious is being oneself and being oneself is not being one of the automata of one's time" (*OP* 250). Like dandy-artists before him, Stevens seeks to re-create himself in order to gain freedom from the set of clichés by which he feels continually bound. He engages in a most American struggle for self-definition; but in order to struggle, he must re-think style, manner, vocabulary, language—and he must do so in a way that repels the very culture threatening to circumscribe him. Son, brother, husband, father, poet, lawyer, American, male are so many constructions against which the power of the mask and the stylized pose must suffice. Stevens often refers to the poet as scholar or rabbi; like Cather's scholarly St. Peter, Stevens himself is paradoxically both casual and passionate defender of, casual and passionate traitor to, the shared values and dominant myths of his day. A genuine change of style, the dandy's chief way of defending himself against philistine culture, is not just a change of subject, as Stevens so often instructs us. A true change of style implies the ability of genius to see, and by seeing to create, one novel step beyond the farthest reaches of culture. Reactionary and revolutionary, wearing his dark gray suit as a badge of both participation in and mourning for his culture, Stevens strolled impeccably toward, and occasionally beyond, the limits of that culture.

The doubleness of cultural participation and rejection, his stance as insider (home on Westerly Terrace, professional career, family life) and outsider (books and paintings, solitude, life of sensation)—this doubleness Stevens described in himself by describing another. Stevens was fascinated by John Crowe Ransom's "ferocity" toward the Tennessee land he loved, by Ransom's demand that his land "surrender, reveal, that in itself which [he] love[d]" (*OP* 248). Men who both love and demand understanding of love risk a loss of innocence; once they understand their emotion, "it may be said that they cease to be natives. They become outsiders. Yet it is certain that, at will, they become insiders again. In ceasing to be natives they have become insiders and outsiders at once" (*OP* 248). Stevens felt both inside and outside not just his native land, Pennsylvania, but the native land of "reality," the world. I wish to trace his position inside and outside of two native cultural forms: his gender, male, and his language, English. Throughout his writing, as I have mentioned, Stevens examines two changes of style, the female and the French. Superficially, both place him in the realm of dandyism: the picture of the effeminate, pomaded male wearing fashionable clothing, dropping French phrases and trilling French *r*'s, is perhaps one of the strongest American clichés of the dandy, along with that of the British gentleman. This "mere" dandyism, is, then, a phase best "gotten over," as Stevens appears to have done by publishing the socially engaged *Ideas of Order* after the precious *Harmonium*.

Stevens writes in a tradition that is anything but "mere" when he chooses to inhabit the French and the female as postures enabling him to stand, however shakily, abstractly, sporadically, outside the native soil of American, patriarchal culture. Stevens's poetry is a continuous, self-referential process of translation, a process that never reaches completion. Gautier chose Madeleine, a woman, to cross-dress, to "translate" herself into masculinity, and then put into motion an escape not just from femininity, but from the native land of gender, fixed and dichotomous. Barbey looked outside his culture to England for "true" dandyism, and embodied it in Brummell, a man existing only in the act of translation, an Englishman whom he made out of French words, but also out of women, madmen, tortured saints: all silent, all alarmingly eloquent in their silence. Baudelaire turned to a translation and re-creation of the American Poe and the English De Quincey, alcoholic and opium addict respectively, before creating "Le peintre de la vie moderne" as a true, "centerless" cosmopolitan, inside and outside of many places.

Stevens, too, used foreign languages and the threatening shapes of silenced others, foreigners to American cultural norms, to create his dandyism. Let us begin with two especially rich texts of the alien, Baudelaire's "La belle Dorothée," and Stevens's own play, *Bowl, Cat and Broomstick*. In these works we may linger, accumulate a sense, however impressionistic, of the shape of the space in which Stevens frames his own dandyism. Stevens, as I argue at length, did not write about figures of women in order to achieve (pseudo)androgyny, "completing" himself with a female "other" in order to become a more-than-male. Nor did he explore the female because he had no choice, since his society characterized any poet as feminine.[5] Rather, he wrote into the female realm because there he found

---

[5]See my discussion, in Chapter 1, of Lentricchia's view of the feminization of literature. I argue that, rather than struggling against feminization, Stevens chose to address the female as a means of critiquing, surpassing, the very culture that devalued it.

the energy to explode the notion of two distinct genders. Through the female, Stevens moved beyond the female and the male, to reach a conception of modern beauty.[6] To prepare ourselves to see Stevens at work in this way, let us look, once again, at Baudelaire.

"La femme est le contraire du dandy": thus Baudelaire writes in his journal (OC 1272; woman is the opposite of the dandy). Yet the body of his work presents the airs of a woman and the airs of a dandy as indistinguishable; dandies are figures of modern beauty which is itself best captured in the mysterious and melancholy faces of women. Further, the female world, *mundus muliebris*, is the basis of an entire aesthetic. For Baudelaire, to make art is to create as a woman lives, by the intimacy of resemblances, analogies, connections, not by the hierarchical Symbolist method in which the artist discerns echoes here below of the superior forms of the ideal realm. If the female world is the world of creation, what then may we learn by examining a woman herself, the type of modern beauty, its source, its means, its most intense expression?

Let us choose, by way of example, Baudelaire's "La belle Dorothée," who appears in a prose poem (1863) of that name, one of the *Spleen de Paris*. The poem is too long to quote in its entirety (OC 266–67), so I will try to convey its distinctive imagery and tone. Although woman is the dandy's opposite, it is also true that Dorothée is a dandy: "Cependant Dorothée, forte et fière comme le soleil, s'avance dans la rue déserte, seule vivante à cette heure sous l'immense azur, et faisant sur la lumière une tache éclatante et noire" (Dorothy, however, strong and proud as the sun, moves up the deserted street, sole living creature at this hour under the immense stretch of blue, and forming a brilliant black mark against the light). Dorothée strolls abroad in a seaside town when the sun attacks the earth with such force that most people are annihilated into silence and sleep. She can, by sheer power, overcome the forces of nature; she is unnatural, even evil—"une tache éclatante et noire." She is a woman made of contrasts, a collection of self-contradictions: her slight upper body balances on large hips; her tight clothing reveals absolutely the shape of her figure, as if it were an animal's skin as well as a woman's silk dress. She carries a parasol, but rather than preserving her fine skin against the sun, it casts a red glow upon her face. She wears heavy earrings in tiny ears, carries a heavy, blue-black mass of hair on a delicate head, and walks triumphantly, but lazily. However animallike she may be, abroad in a killing sunlight, her limbs are

---

[6]See Jardine (1–102). I find her analysis of the female space in contemporary French criticism quite suggestive when held up against nineteenth-century and early twentieth-century literary texts of dandyism.

those of a marble goddess "que l'Europe enferme dans ses musées" (that Europe locks up in her museums). Is she prisoner or work of art? It is difficult to say. Although she is not a slave, she walks with a slave's bare feet. What is more, she seems fully to appreciate the extraordinary flaneur's portrait she presents. As vain as any Parisian dandy, "elle s'avance ainsi, harmonieusement, heureuse de vivre et souriant d'un blanc sourire, comme si elle apercevait au loin dans l'espace un miroir reflétant sa démarche et sa beauté" (she advances thus, harmoniously, happy to be alive and smiling a blank smile, as if she saw ahead in the distance a mirror reflecting her stride and her beauty). Her reasons for leaving the "parfait boudoir" where she is free to dream, smoke, preen, and eat are unclear. Perhaps she seeks out an officer for conversation, and perhaps she seeks him out for more. The poem ends in a paragraph of mysterious and sinister innuendo, suggesting that she has to earn money in order to support her "young sister," eleven years old but already mature.

The space Dorothée defines as she walks down a deserted street is the impossible space of the insider who is wholly outside her culture. She is an insider in her perfect adaptation to her brutal surroundings: no one could be more at home than she. Yet to the reader, nothing about Dorothée is comfortable, expected, even acceptable. Dorothée is a curious figure because she seems to exist primarily in order to challenge our world; that is, all of her qualities and contradictions disturb *us* quite a bit, Dorothée not at all. Most disturbing, in fact, is her power utterly to challenge the very emotions she causes in us. She is a tease on the grandest of scales. Her world is best defined as not-our-world, even though it bears a tormenting resemblance to it.

Dorothée's is a space Stevens tries to define within his own poetry. It is the space of an absence, a set of questions with no answers, but not the traditionally pure absence with which women have supplied patriarchal myth. Dorothée's is a paradoxically filled absence, a burgeoning absence of utter possibility, too many answers to unposable questions. As the locus of chaos, she represents another familiar side of the patriarchal construction of woman. She represents precisely that which cannot be grasped, objectified, analyzed, or categorized. If we were to speak to her, she would flirt and snarl. If we were to touch her, she would burn and chill. She is like an animal, but also like a robot, unsuffering in a terrible heat. She is like a naive coquette, a bourgeois woman, a prostitute, a free man, a criminal, a saint. The trajectory of her walk along a deserted street is not linear, but immanent. She gets nowhere, this hallucinatory figure of paralysis, but she has been, will be everywhere. Seen by no one in particular, this dandy arrests us by her bizarre beauty, her "excess" that obliterates our standards of measurement.

Reading, New York City, and Hartford did not yield such creatures, nor could Stevens's imagination place them there. Yet, in his own style, he looked for Dorothée and the space in which she walks, not in order to deride or control her, but to try to join her there. He sought, in women, the annihilation of category which Baudelaire expressed as monstrosity. Modern beauty, for Stevens, flowed from the powerful, confusing, or frightening auras of the women he portrayed in his poetry, but he did not have to work as hard as Baudelaire did to expand and burst categories, as if they were so many objects under a punishing sun. Stevens inherited a dandy's world of analogy, contradiction, resemblance, and paradox from the French writers he appreciated; the space of Dorothée's walk extended to Pennsylvania and Connecticut within the volumes of French novels, poetry, essays, and catalogues of art shows he read throughout his life. It is her space I explore in this chapter.

In a story published while he was at college, "The Nymph" (*Harvard Advocate*), Stevens describes a failed attempt to cross into such an alien space. After tramping for three days in "what seemed an unbroken wilderness," a young man meets a "tall slim girl of about seventeen" who announces she is the last nymph, tosses aside his pedestrian lunch, and promises to feed him blackberries and mushrooms, which she lists in French on her sketch pad. Their brief encounter consists primarily of pronouncing "mûres de ronce" and "champignons" to each other, and listening to the birds. She is finally called to rejoin her party, "the Eureka Camping Club of Billville, Mass." A few French words and mischievous smiles do not the alien make.

Eventually Stevens writes another work, this one about a truly alien French woman, not a weekend nymph with restaurant French. The action of *Bowl, Cat and Broomstick* (1917) (*OP* 168–77), like that of Baudelaire's prose poem, is simple. It is the seventeenth century, and three men with strange names and commedia dell'arte costumes attempt to translate and judge a volume of poetry by a French poet, Claire Dupray. Bowl can translate it only with difficulty for Cat. When Broomstick arrives on the scene, they all attempt to judge both the woman (making use of a photograph) and the poetry, and to clarify the aesthetic principles by which they do so. The play ends when they finally read the preface to the volume, discovering Claire Dupray's actual age and family background.

The play at first reads as a frivolously serious treatment of art as filtered through patriarchal values. Claire herself, the "maker," is absent, silent, and objectified in her book and by the way in which the play's three characters comfortably assume her to be an object upon which they can exercise masculine scrutiny. None of her poems is actually quoted, except for a brief passage, awkwardly translated, here or there. Judgment is the order of the day, and its mechanisms, its successes and failures, occur somehow independently of the phantom woman who created the text they admire. Yet the ironic action of the play slowly comes to dominate it; by no means is it a simple dramatization of male domination. It is a sendup of a Platonic dialogue, with Broomstick an unlikely Socrates. Like Dorothée, Claire is not graspable by the men, even through her book: she simply will not translate. Platonic irony takes on renewed energy.

At first it is her Frenchness, more than her femaleness (they debate whether to call her poet or poetess), that makes her foreign to them; as the play opens Bowl translates "rouge" as "tawny" (*OP* 168). The slippage between two languages is great; it functions as metonymy for ungraspable foreignness no matter what its form. Thus the "French" Claire herself seems to dissolve into shimmering layers and elusive versions as the play progresses. There is the "actual Claire," whoever *she* is, but there is also the Claire of her physical presence, of her hair as she combs it, "concealing in its arrangement the things it begins to disclose to her" (echoes here of Baudelaire's "La chevelure"?) (*OP* 169). Then there is the Claire of the photograph, who appears to be twenty-two, and the Claire of the present day, whom they eventually calculate to be fifty-three. Further, Claire's form dissipates as surely as Baudelaire's "Moi" "vaporizes" when we learn of the books she has read and of her Calvinist upbringing in Geneva, not the expected Catholic upbringing in France. Is she really French after all? As if Claire's own hazy quality were not enough, each character has, of course, his own version of Claire. And the poetry itself announces a radical questioning of order as it insists that familiar opposites such as sun and moon, day and night, cannot be neatly distinguished from each other.

Then there are the games. Claire has written a poem bearing the title of Stevens's poem "Banal Sojourn." Others appear to be "her" poems alone, except that their subjects and images sound suspiciously Stevensian. If Claire writes Stevens's poems, perhaps, and Stevens writes hers, if Broomstick pronounces Stevens's aesthetic beliefs, sometimes, what we have here is a dandy's play, not just in its utterly precious tone, but in the intense mirroring and posing that goes on. Stevens adopts different personae in the play, inhabiting first one character, then another, but the central mystery organizes itself about Claire Dupray, French and female. She clears the space within which the posing occurs, the space that artistic possibility, cultural novelty, requires. Claire defines not an emptiness, but, in the mode of Baudelaire's *mundus muliebris*, a proliferation of connection, analogy. Broomstick defines this as the space of comedy: "There's no truer comedy than this hodge-podge of men and sunlight, women and moonlight, houses and clouds, and so on" (*OP* 170).

"To be himself in his day" to avoid cultural hegemony, Stevens turns to an anarchical space that offers always to resolve itself into the beautiful chaos of the *coincidentia oppositorum*. Like Barbey, the monarchist and Catholic, Stevens clung to the very patriarchal myths whose demise he announced in "Sunday Morning." He is always the insider, Broomstick with the word of wisdom, however far his vision extends to the boundaries of his culture. The pagan masculinity of "Sunday Morning" is only a first, frightened step into the "outside," disordered world of Claire and Dorothée. It is the story of the unfolding comedy, the dandy-artist's step into the "hodge-podge," which I propose to tell in the following pages.

THE WELL-DRESSED MAN WITH A BEARD: STEVENS THE DANDY

For those who see in Stevens's poetry his "mere" dandyism, the Sylvia Salmi photograph of the *Collected Poems* must come as a surprise: this is Peter Parasol? Yet the austere clothing, the aloof stare which challenges us to imagine the gorgeous language swirling behind the brow, the aura of self-sufficiency and elitist independence tempered by a sense of strain, a hint of martyrdom: these are the marks of the true dandy. If Stevens is the "Brahmin on the mountain-slope" (*SP* 211) in this portrait, he is also the too-solid man of business, always on a reducing diet. Stevens the conservative lawyer and Stevens the avant-garde artist are one, sheltered by the dandy's parasol.

Stevens was a dandy because his relation to the world and to other people—meaning the clichéd workaday world and vulgar people—troubled him. "Reality" is for him a subject of meditation in part because reality needs amendment. Although it has become fashionable in Stevens criticism to ask questions taking us beyond the overworked categories of reality and the imagination, I must return for a moment to this dichotomy, so insistently presented by Stevens himself. These were his terms for organizing a world into vulgar and refined, natural and artificial. While Stevens is a Keatsian and Wordsworthian poet of nature, he is also a poet of nature in a Gautierian and Baudelairean vein: the natural is evil, fallen, instinctive; the artificial is beautiful, civilized, redeemed.

When José Rodríguez Feo, one of the young aesthetes with whom Stevens corresponded over the years, writes to express his uncertainty about a life of refinement and the "monotony of elegance" (Coyle and Filreis 59), Stevens replies that reality is "the great *fond*" (62). Such a French reality seems somehow already a bit artificial, but there is more to come. He replies that fatigue and the need for beauty lead a man toward a more artificial existence of "Berlioz and roses." The "real" in this discussion is not the redemptive beauty of nature; it is the real of "the office" and worries and garden weeds, the workaday real which it is the business of art to transform. Stevens concludes with a quotation from Henry James: "To live *in* the world of creation—to get into it and stay in it—to frequent it and haunt it—to *think* intensely and fruitfully—to woo combinations and inspirations into being by a depth and continuity of attention and meditation—this is the only thing" (Coyle and Filreis 62). This is the dandy's life: to be in the world but not of it, to carry out demi-actions: frequent, haunt, think; to live in relation to a society as Barbey's Brummell lived in relation to English society—to woo, attend, meditate. In short, one must live in the world, but live there as a cerebral, sensitive, inner being, a stronghold of independent sensibility. The dandy transforms by being, not doing.

This is a hidden kind of life, and indeed Stevens depicts himself, as Baudelaire before him, as a king incognito, a regent of the spiritual realm who only appears to be a salaried man, but issues at night, like his "Ordinary Women," disguised, for a second life. "Observe how the things around one cease to stimulate after a while. (That is why kings are bored—and like Haroun-al-Raschid assume nocturnal disguises)" (*SP* 239): Stevens's nocturnal pose as poet involves the simultaneous creation of both poetry and self, a distinguishing mark of the dandy-artist. Stevens from the first "nurse[s] an aristocratic feeling" (*SP* 95), usually in reaction to Sunday feelings of ennui, self-loathing, nerves and hangovers and tobacco-induced tremors, of drowning in the commonalty he experiences in New York City. He takes pride in his cultivation of an impersonal manner in the face of the city's pathetic sights; he fastidiously edges away from, while appearing to ignore, the Italians and Jews and shopgirls and laborers the city thrusts into his path, onto his seat in the train, beside him in museums and concerts. He sees himself as flaneur when he walks along the wharves of West Street, and in the best Parisian tradition he experiments with the Epicurean life: "My idea of life is a fine evening, an orchestra and a crowd *at a distance*; a medium dinner, glass of something cool and at the same time wholesome, + a soft, full Panatella" (*LWS* 74).

Increasingly he elects a dandy's solitude, elevating the loneliness born
both of necessity and choice to an aesthetic principle: "Personality must be
kept secret before the world," especially in writing. An essay he reads is too
personal, it "should have been written by nobody at all: it should have been
absolutely impersonal" (SP 82). Stevens wishes to be wholly invisible himself: "How one wishes one could pass through life unnoticed" (SP 183).
The mix of arrogance and defensiveness is unmistakably the dandy's—
not to be sullied by the public's eye resting upon one, not to risk adversity
by the sheer state of visibility, writing as one lives, impersonally, ranging
incognito through the crowds, avoiding sabotage of one's individuality—
yet insisting, always insisting upon one's utter superiority. Faced with the
"teeming streets" which "make Man a nuisance—a vulgarity, and it is impossible to see his dignity," Stevens reacts by raising a high personal standard: "I feel, nevertheless, the overwhelming necessity of thinking well,
speaking well" (SP 217). And indeed, throughout his life, people noticed
his refined manners and appearance: "He was a very smooth man. He had
a soft voice, and his diction was beautiful" (Brazeau 37) or, "Just one act of
courtesy after another. He was just a fine gentleman" (45). For every person who remembers his grace and refinement, there is another who comments on his "caustic tongue" (31), his "arrogance . . . just plain coldness"
(29). Speaking well can serve to distance vulgar people indirectly, by creating a distance between one's own impeccable style and their crude
expression, as well as directly, by hurtful words.

Stevens rejected the masses as audience; like every dandy he professed
an obliviousness of their attentions. He insisted throughout his life that he
wrote poetry only for himself, or for abstract reasons—"I write it because
for me it is one of the sanctions of life" (LWS 600)—and he copied into
his journal a passage from Sully Prudhomme, in a language only the privileged could understand:

> This for heartsease.
> L'art pour l'art est aristocratique. . . . [L'artiste] se replie sur lui-même, s'en-
> ferme dans son argueil [sic] et son individualisme. Il dédaigne la foule et les
> genres littéraires qui lui plaisent, comme le théâtre: il se met au-dessus d'elle,
> elle n'est que la matière vile dont il tirera l'oeuvre d'art.
> Journal des Savants, Juillet, 1907. (SP 185)

Art for art's sake is aristocratic. . . . [The artist] encloses himself in his pride
and his individualism. He disdains the crowd and the literary types that
please it, such as drama: he places himself above it [the crowd], it is only the
base matter from which he will draw the work of art.
Scholars' Journal, July, 1907.

When the effort of holding himself above the crowd, that base substance, became too tiring, Stevens retreated to the countryside, to detoxify himself with long hikes, during which he posed as Byron (*LWS* 177).

The figure of the dandy as it emerges from Stevens's letters and journals is familiar enough to recall the dandies of the French tradition; Stevens portrays himself in terms similar to those with which Baudelaire, for example, portrays Delacroix: "sceptique et aristocrate . . . haïsseur des multitudes . . . parfait gentleman . . . froideur apparente, légèrement affectée . . . manteau de glace recouvrant une pudique sensibilité et une ardente passion pour le bien et pour le beau . . . esprit de domination" (*OC* 1128–29; skeptic and aristocrat . . . hater of the multitudes . . . perfect gentleman . . . apparent coldness, lightly affected . . . coat of ice masking a chaste sensibility and an ardent passion for the good and the beautiful . . . spirit of domination).

This figure appears qua dandy most obviously in Stevens's early poetry: the "Snow Man" is cold not just to make an epistemological point, but because Stevens as dandy wears a "manteau de glace." Crispin of "The Comedian as the Letter C" (*CP* 27–46) is the complete cosmopolitan, aesthete, flaneur of the world's climates, superior man, his goal "to drive away / The shadow of his fellows from the skies, / And from their stale intelligence released, / To make a new intelligence prevail." We may even seek in "Comedian" a second and third dandy—the speaker and, half hiding behind this verbal mask, Stevens himself. All Crispin's adventures in self-exploration and world exploration pale in contrast to the vividness of the poem's arch and difficult manner, its dense verbiage and somewhat tedious plot, its teasing toward a climax that never happens, its world-weary tone even as it narrates a tale of exploration and change. It is, far from being a comic poem, a poem of ennui not unrelated to "The Man Whose Pharynx Was Bad," whose speaker, the alter ego of the loquacious speaker of "Comedian," is "too dumbly in [his] being pent" (*CP* 96). Then there are the dandy's poems of seeing and being seen: "Peter Quince at the Clavier," "Tea at the Palaz of Hoon," or the dandy's poems of contempt for the vulgar, unimaginative masses, "Disillusionment of Ten O'Clock," "Gubbinal." Dandy-spotting in Stevens's early poetry seems to lack all sport.

Yet surely the author of *Ideas of Order* or *Transport to Summer* is no dandy, even if we can see his shape in "The Man with the Blue Guitar." Here we must carry our exploration of Stevens's dandyism one crucial step farther, past the collection of dandy's attributes (cold, superior, aristocratic, defensive, etc.) to the dandy's characteristic movements and gestures toward other people. Stevens worried about a life and an art divorced from the common reality of other people. By temperament a man who simply would not operate in any sphere more public than the workplace (for him, of course, a private office), Stevens sought the "common reality" in its least common form: he sought an audience of elect spirits in communion with whom he might be able to "bring the world round," to revise the common reality according to his own, superior vision.

I refer to Stevens's solution to the problem of solitude, for purposes of brevity, as the "Trébutien solution." Guillaume-Stanislaus Trébutien was the Norman bookseller, antiquarian, and publisher with whom Barbey engaged in an intense correspondence spanning some twenty-five years. This was no ordinary exchange of letters between close friends; rather Barbey engaged in nothing less than the appropriation of Trébutien's work, talent, and even personality into his own identity. In repeated acts of self-aggrandizement, captured in the correspondence for all to see, Barbey claimed Trébutien as audience, factotum, intimate friend, blood brother, wife, mirror, business partner, ghostwriter. To generalize this extraordinary performance, I would say that, fearing utter solitude, too wide and irrevocable a separation between himself and others, the dandy-artist takes action. He narrows the gap by creating an impersonal intimacy—the oxymoron is deliberate—with a few other people. Dandyism exists powerfully not just as a series of characteristics separating the dandy from others, but in a highly choreographed series of pas de deux, special, artistically created relationships. To see the dandy, then, we must watch his audience and its engagement with him.

Stevens had his Trébutiens. Among them were his wife, Elsie, and his correspondents José Rodríguez Feo, Tom McGreevy, and Peter Lee, figures who could be dominated by virtue of their age, gender, social standing, distance. Although Stevens never took advantage of these people in as monstrous a way as Barbey did of Trébutien, he did appropriate them in order to construct himself. For the self, like other abstract concepts, is no longer a given for Stevens; if "the death of one god is the death of all" (OP 191), it is equally true that the death of one god is the death of all abstract certainties. If "the final belief is to believe in a fiction," if "the exquisite truth is to know that it is a fiction and that you believe in it willingly" (OP 189), meditation will eventually suggest that "I" is no more a figure of fixed truth than "God." The new man, the maker of fictions, wills himself to believe not just in God, but in himself. The dandy is the figure who acted on the hypothesis of the fictionality of self before he "proved" it, willed it into truth.

Stevens began posing, he tells Elsie, simply because "I like to be anything but my plain self" (Richardson, *Early Years*, 291); soon he is gener-
alizing, though still clinging to the notion of a fixed, "basic" identity:
"There is a perfect rout of characters in every man—and every man is like
an actor's trunk, full of strange creatures, new & old. But an actor and his
trunk are two different things" (*SP* 166). Eventually he comes to see that
the self, the "guerilla I," is part of the "dead romantic," a falsification. To
create poetry is to create one's sense of the world, and to create oneself as
well. In the end, trunk and actor are indistinguishable. Without controlling fictions, anarchy might reign. Dorothée is for Baudelaire a personification of such a fear, a self-portrait of the dandy standing outside society's
prefabricated personal identities. Dorothée is an ever-expanding set of
possibilities, some of them even inhuman.

Stevens begins the task of self-construction in the journal in which he
wrote and erased, crossed out and rewrote.[7] He extends the process to include the self he creates in his letters and the self he creates in the recipients of his letters: his correspondence, in certain cases, becomes an act of
manipulation of others in the name of self-construction, "Be thou me." He
creates himself as a palimpsest of *people* he knew, out of the *things* he
causes these people to send to him, as well as the *places*, the worlds in
which they live or visit. Readers of the letters have seen Stevens claiming
the men, aesthetes one and all, foreign, who pass the "Stevens barrier" by
being young, literate, well versed in French literature, and eager to share
the details of their daily lives. Stevens claims their mules and their climates, their mothers and their native languages, their political positions
and family histories, always increasing thereby the "rout of characters" in
his trunk, always experiencing the supreme frisson: that of feeling inside
and outside at once. A personal visit, which all the young men propose
sooner or later, is anathema. To see them in the flesh would be to challenge
one's own carefully pastiched self. It is no wonder that one of Stevens's favorite works of fiction is Robert Louis Stevenson's "Silverado Squatters"
(*SP* 77); every character in the tale is an eccentric, and the narrator lives in
a ramshackle structure hanging off the side of a mountain, in danger of
being blown away or (as happens) dispossessed. The entire tale is a tone
poem of the fragility of personhood, the wonderfully fictive nature of "I,"
even if such an "I" risks being blown out like the candle flame in the wind
at the tale's end.

[7]See Bates's introduction to Stevens's *Sur Plusieurs Beaux Sujects* and Holly Stevens's editorial comments in *Souvenirs and Prophecies*.

Along with letters to aesthetes whose very foreignness allows Stevens to feel "inside" a reality to which he is really an outsider, go letters requesting that people send him things. The thrill is partly Parnassian: the object, beautiful in itself, arrives from Ceylon or Japan or Paris, its very foreign beauty as he uncrates it at the office evoking a deeper frisson. But the real thrill is in the process: the creation of a relationship that will yield, eventually, such spoils. To travel in order to buy his own *objets* would spoil the fun, not just of creating and advising a network of agents, but of feeling the objects as truly foreign. Marking the travels of his friends, seldom traveling himself, Stevens follows Baudelaire, who traveled only rarely, but who put at the center of his "Le peintre de la vie moderne" Constantin Guys, the man who had been everywhere.

Categories begin to dissolve as Stevens the dandy controls his intimate experience of the world: things, people, places, and events enter one texture, that of Stevens's imagination. It is this quality, of palimpsest and relation, multiple selves and worlds, reflected in the poetry, which makes the text of dandyism a far subtler thing than the rehearsing of a central pose of aloof superiority. "And out of what one sees and hears and out / Of what one feels, who could have thought to make / So many selves, so many sensuous worlds" (*CP* 326): when Stevens confronts within the female a monstrous world of metamorphosis and potential, he recognizes it for what it is because he has been creating it on his own, in parallel, all along.

As the boundaries between inside and outside, self and other, collapse, always to be rebuilt by the dandy who can exist only in the land of difference, the dandyism of relation makes itself known. This dandyism, for Stevens, is created most intensely in the two realms we have still to explore at close range: the difference that is French, and the difference that is female. It is to these that we finally turn.

THE FACULTY OF ELLIPSES: LANGUAGES AND GENDERS

"I lay on the edge of the Palisades basking on a rock and I thought of the top of the Pinnacle—and then of the panorama below" (*SP* 224), Stevens writes of one of his treks into nature. He liked the feeling of the ground between Pinnacle and valley floor, not because he was especially interested as a poet in heights and depths, but because he was interested in places that were neither here nor there. To read of Rodríguez Feo's mule, to gaze on a painting sent from Paris, to eat dried fruit from Oregon was to be neither in Hartford nor out of Hartford, or, to take a different vantage point, to be inside Cuba, Paris, Oregon while remaining outside. This is the dandy's place, a place that is a relation, not a fixed point. Stevens rehearsed the inhabiting of this relation not just in his correspondence, not just in his poetry which described exotic places he had never actually visited, but also in the very Gallic texture of his syntax and diction, the haze of faint but continual allusion to nineteenth-century French literature throughout his writing.

Stevens wrote in French as part of an effort to "pass from the created to the uncreated" (*NA* 174); this most civilized, elegant language was for him also, paradoxically, an element of chaos. The French in his poetry—witness the annoyance of his critics at this foppishness—refuses to blend invisibly into an American whole. Life as a perpetual invitation to translation: this was a mode that had fascinated Barbey, too, for the modern beauty that it yielded, a beauty of strangeness, of resemblance that cannot collapse into identity. Stevens's use of French titles for his English poems, his lines of poetry in which words of Anglo-Saxon origin, Romance origin, and pure French pedigree mingle, bear witness to a taste for distinct cultures brought almost into harmony.

Stevens liked the dissonance between French and English, Latinate and Anglo-Saxon, because it imitated, at a linguistic level, the acts of appropriation he carried on at a personal level. French words and syntax in American poetry were akin to the *objets d'art* arriving in his office from correspondents in other countries. Once again, it was the aesthetic jolt—the feeling of being insider and outsider at once—that he cultivated.

In a description of his late friend Henry Church, Stevens describes by implication himself, the man who needed to exist between categories:

> in New York, he seemed to be essentially of Paris, and, very likely, in Paris, he seemed to be essentially of New York. He was a simple man who had little interest in things that were not complex. . . . Because of the existence in him of these opposites, two things followed, one, that he seemed often to be an enigma and, the other, . . . that *he was always a potential figure.* Here was an American who lived in France, or, say, a Frenchman who made long visits to America.   (*LWS* 570–71, emphasis added)

As Barbey's Brummell existed between France and England, so Henry Church existed somewhere between France and America. Stevens existed as a man between business and art; his poetry existed between French and English. This liminality made of him and his poetry alike a "potential figure." Potentiality defined a space for novelty, for creation outside the dominating myths of his day. Far from being entrapped by those myths, he, like Gautier, Barbey, and Baudelaire, radically challenged them.

But what did he know of these French writers? Stevens insists on the general quality of his association with French literature, "I was the youthful general reader" (*LWS* 636), and his borrowings were unconscious, he claims.[8] He mentions having read Stéphane Mallarmé, Paul Verlaine, Jules Laforgue, Paul Valéry, Gérard de Nerval, and Baudelaire, among others, and although we might go influence-hunting, such is not my aim here.[9] The evidence is usually at best circumstantial. Did Stevens write "it is necessary to any originality to have the courage to be an amateur" (*OP* 195) because he read Baudelaire's "Salons" in which he praises the amateur? Perhaps—we know that Stevens liked the genre of art catalogues. Where Baudelaire railed against the "poncif," "le résumé des idées vulgaires et banales" (*OC* 925; the summary of vulgar and banal ideas), Stevens defined throughout his oeuvre the "true romantic" in opposition to the false, outmoded, or sentimental romantic. Branch and stem, or parallel branchings? Stevens's borrowings of French nineteenth-century literature are so many and so utterly diffuse that discerning points of origin can become reductive.

Instead, I want to note Stevens's general use of French echoes. Like Cather, he is drawn to French not as a literary source book, but primarily because it is, quite simply, French. As an American, he carried within him an outsider's ideal of beauty which he identified as French, and expressed by a bit of French syntax here, "of a port in air," a French word there, "panache," a strong hint of Baudelaire, "Esthétique du Mal," a weak hint of Baudelaire, "ennui of apartments," occasionally entire lines of French, as in "Sea Surface Full of Clouds." At least one-third of the entries in his commonplace books contain French passages, and many more contain passages translated from French or refer in English to French subjects.

French enabled Stevens to write impersonally, not just because he echoed Parnassian impersonality—he did from first to last in his poetry—but because it allowed him to escape from who he was, to escape the "gue-

---

[8]I believe that the best statement of influence was made by Stevens himself, in response to a query by René Taupin, who wrote *"L'influence du symbolisme français sur la poésie américaine (de 1910 à 1920)"*: "La légèreté, la grâce, le son et la couleur du français ont eu sur moi une influence indéniable et une influence précieuse" (quoted in Buttel 276; The lightness, gracefulness, sound, and color of French have had on me an undeniable influence and a valuable influence). Stevens loved, above all, the sound of French. This is not to denigrate the important work of Benamou and Buttel in tracing actual French sources for Stevens's works.

[9]For example, Stevens strongly implies having read Poe's "Man of the Crowd": "Poe liked to analyze his feelings in crowds (*LWS* 759). This was a work which in part inspired Baudelaire's great essay on the dandy, "Le peintre de la vie moderne." But how much, precisely, to make of such a connection?

rilla I," the male, American, hegemonic self, in ways similar to his correspondence with young, foreign poets. French enabled him to pose linguis-
tically. Although Stevens appears to be a dandy because he preciously
sprinkles French words and constructions throughout his writing, Stevens's "French" dandyism is more profound. It is a locus of paradox: "Il
faut être paysan d'être poète," he writes (*LWS* 461). To be a peasant and a
cultivated French speaker at once (like Broomstick of *Bowl, Cat and
Broomstick*, a coarse aesthete) is to be both insider (native) and outsider at
once. From this position which is nowhere on the current map of culture,
Stevens may plot the impossible, a fresh look at culture.

It is the relatedness but disparity between French and English on which
Stevens depends. He sees the linguistic gap, the "ellipsis," in geographical
terms: for years he writes to his Parisian art agents, the Vidals, in English,
and they reply in French. In the gap, a fictional Paris develops for Stevens,
a place he has no intention of exploring in any but the most abstract way.
For Stevens, linguistic space is an analogy to geographical space, and both
are analogous to cultural space. Based on difference and hiatus, French
words and fictions may have begun as a background of the ideal for the
poet's American meditations; but these words and fictions became the crucial other ground upon which his dandyism flourishes.

Gautier's Madeleine forsakes home and gender in a quest that leaves her
with no place in which to be; Brummell's exile from masculinity and London, home turf, is a death sentence; but Baudelaire's swan learns that every
center is a place of exile, that it is the process of making a nowhere a somewhere that defines the movements of modern beauty. Delacroix's *Ovid
among the Scythians* teaches Baudelaire the possibility, the *potential,* for
creating truth and beauty by decreating the world, unmaking its categories.[10] In the space between French and English, Paris and Hartford, Stevens, like Delacroix's Ovid, feels at home in an exile that is a homecoming.
He expresses this position by contradicting himself: "French and English
constitute a single language" (*OP* 202) he writes; then, comparing Paris
and New York, "the accents of one are not the accents of the other and,
however much alike they may be, there is a difference and the difference is
not to be bridged" (*LWS* 697).

As language, so gender. Female and male exist in Stevens as one language that is two. Among the rout of characters in Stevens's poetry,
women figure largely: "she" of "Sunday Morning," the singer of "The

---

[10]It is not my intention to examine Stevens in light of deconstructionist theory, but to
explain why he was attracted in the first place to Weil's notion of decreation, whatever its
relation to deconstructionist theory. For an account of the deconstructionist interpretation
of Stevens, its frustrations, victories, and *longueurs*, see Schaum (100–128).

Idea of Order at Key West," Nanzia Nunzio of "Notes toward a Supreme Fiction," Mrs. Alfred Uruguay, the mother of "Auroras of Autumn," Penelope of "The World as Meditation," to mention but a few of his major female figures. Since Stevens is an artist and since most of these women are involved, however abstractly, in the issue of creation, the obvious question has been the relation of male writer to female subject, this subject herself a creator with a subject of her own. In other words, it is the cross-gender *mise en abyme* which announces itself in any study of gender in Stevens.

Read as a poem about artistic creation, "The Idea of Order at Key West" (*CP* 128–30) presents us with Stevens's dilemma of gender in a clear form. "She was the single artificer of the world / In which she sang. And when she sang the sea, / Whatever self it had, became the self / That was her song, for she was the maker": or so it seems. For the poem soon turns, and it is the hinge here that squeaks, alerting us to "problems" of gender: "Ramon Fernandez, tell me, if you know / Why . . . the glassy lights . . . / Mastered the night and portioned out the sea, / Fixing emblazoned zones and fiery poles, / Arranging, deepening, enchanting night." Things are amiss here, we feel. The woman has been silenced, like Wordsworth's "Solitary Reaper": we hear of her, but we don't hear her.[11] Instead we hear another speaker, provisionally male, and behind him, Stevens's own voice. In a poem about a woman maker, the last word in making is given to "we," and couched in the masculine rhetoric of power and glory, "Mastered . . . portioned . . . fixing," even if Stevens does modulate (too late, the jury has already heard the damning evidence) to "ghostlier demarcations." And certainly Stevens himself, the male artist, has appropriated, silenced this woman, repeating on aesthetic ground the solution he has found in his daily life for living with others. It is Stevens's song, not hers, we hear; the woman as maker, is, alas, woman as muse.

A few escapes from the dilemma of the silenced female artist suggest themselves. Perhaps we simply need to read further in Stevens's oeuvre until we find a woman who stands and speaks for herself. Here we encounter the difficulties of Stevens's "independent women": they often seem evil or frightening, even odious. Perhaps, instead, we need simply to reinterpret "The Idea of Order" itself: Stevens as male writer acknowledges here his indebtedness to his anima or some related creature, the female principle without which he cannot create. Or perhaps, fearing to be called effeminate because he is a poet in America early in the late-capitalist twentieth

---

[11] For a discussion of Wordsworth's, Coleridge's and Stevens's muting of female voice in "The Idea of Order," see Santos (152), who argues that "musing the obscure ultimately entails muting the muse."

century, Stevens creates this artist/muse specifically in order to silence her. Such is his patriarchal prerogative in a dog-eat-dog world. Here we find ourselves at an impasse. At worst Stevens subordinates and silences woman; at best he makes use of her, internalizes her in order to be more of a poet. Yet the poem speaks, in some mysterious way, beyond these discomfiting claims. To learn its language, I propose asking different questions: in what sense *is* it a poem about gender, and what does the concept of gender mean to Stevens? To answer these questions, we need a running start from far beyond the borders of the poem itself.

GENDER AS ADULT MAKE-BELIEVE

Gender in Stevens is tied intimately, irrevocably, to the power of imagination. On the one hand, Stevens believed in social "truths" and institutions: the desirability of monogamous marriage, for instance, or the necessity of formulating moral principles and acting in accordance with them. On the other hand, Stevens distrusted the foundation upon which this version of reality, these citizen's virtues and sanctions, rested. He questions the notion of rules obeyed because they have been carved in stone by some authority. Stone carvings too rapidly lose their power, become part of the false Romantic, the detritus of the world. Instead, he claims that "the structure of reality because of the range of resemblances that it contains is measurably an adult make-believe" (*NA* 75). Not just a relative truth, but playful "adult make-believe," that is, our beliefs, values, institutions— roughly speaking, "the structure of reality"—are abstract, pleasurable, and subject to change. To follow this observation to the subject at hand is to explore the notion that gender arrangements, "gender" itself, is adult make-believe, a construct of the imagination like any other, and thus subject to change. Certainly a poet who analyzed the Judeo-Christian patriarchal myth, insisting on its "fictional" quality, attempting to re-imagine it in a new style—the style of ourselves, the style of our era—certainly such a poet acted, however unintentionally, to upset the gender arrangements accompanying that myth.[12] In "To the One of Fictive Music" (*CP* 87–88), Stevens even demonstrates an imaginative construction of a female figure

[12]Consider, for example, this statement by Paul Elmer More which Stevens copied into his journal in 1909, suggesting that he was already taking a critical look at gender in religious myth: "It was the mission of the new faith to promulgate the distinctly feminine virtues in place of the sterner ideals of antiquity—love in place of understanding, sympathy for justice, self-surrender for magnanimity,—and as a consequence the eternal feminine was strangely idealised" (*SP* 220–21).

in whom we may believe. The poem chronicles a "making," the process of willing into existence two entities: this particular woman, and the female itself. The title, so suggestive of French translated into English, and the body of the poem, so suggestive of Mallarmé's "Sainte," creates the space of French difference as it goes, unfolds a space within which Stevens imagines the novel figure. She is defined equally by her gender and by her spiritual status: she is adored because she is extravagantly female (the poem names one female role after another), and she is female because she is extravagantly adored (how else, the poem seems to ask, could we describe the feeling of care with which a beloved spiritual figure enfolds us?). Gender and spirituality go hand in tender hand here.

"The operation of the imagination in life is more significant than its operation in or in relation to works of art" (*NA* 146), Stevens assures us. In writing "To the One of Fictive Music," he reveals the imagination at work creating a form that, like Mallarmé's "Sainte," is simply a beautiful instance of the purity of art, the occasion for pleasure in words, rhythms, images. Yet he also reveals the imagination as it creates two of life's forms: those of religious belief and gender. The poem reveals that we necessarily exercise imagination in creating cultural form: to "make believe" in a virgin born of earth, not sky, is to create what all along has been created by people rather than presented to them by immutable divine revelation. To "make believe" in the female is likewise to create what has all along been created by people rather than presented by immutable divine or biological revelation.

If Stevens writes poems in which he creates religious myth, he also writes poems in which he mocks moribund myth. In two poems about bodies after death, he questions existing religious belief, and gender crumbles, literally. "Cortège for Rosenbloom" (*CP* 79–81) mocks male apotheosis; Rosenbloom is carried to the sky, but remains just a corpse. Buried high in the sky, he is neither elevated nor transfigured. While "Cortège" mocks the sky as locus of patriarchal authority—God's place—"The Worms at Heaven's Gate" (*CP* 49–50) upsets patriarchal hierarchy in another way. The princess Badroulbador achieves apotheosis, but, like her metaphorical brother Rosenbloom, she fails to reach "elevated" status. She is transfigured by those worms; heaven's gate, earth itself, is as much of heaven as she shall know. Both poems are about disintegration—of religious "certainties" as well as human bodies. The disintegration of the categories of heaven and earth in "The Worms at Heaven's Gate" parallels the disintegration of the categories of male and female; both in the end must rot, return to the common clay they are.

"To the One of Fictive Music" and "The Worms at Heaven's Gate," however, take us a step farther than "Cortège." Both female figures represent the accomplishment of a gaiety that is lacking in the stiff scenario of failure in "Cortège" as the "infants of nothingness" carry Rosenbloom upward. Just as Stevens repeatedly writes "in French" in his poetry, he writes "in female": through images of the female he creates and inhabits a female space in the poetry. But entering that space, he discovers that it is vast, incapable of organization by two finite categories, male and female. *The female paradoxically denies the female, and the male along with it.* "Cortège" suggests that apotheosis apart from earth is but tinny fantasy, "jangle" and "jumble," but the two poems about women replace the *poncif* with the myth of a new style. And that style is androgynous, not in the sense that anima meets animus and all is well, but in the more confusing sense of "adult make-believe," the comic "hodge-podge" of *Bowl, Cat and Broomstick*, that we stand among crumbling categories. Stevens experiments with his own version of the *mundus muliebris* in "To the One of Fictive Music," the oceanic embrace of the "sister and mother and diviner love," gently speaking a world of additive relation even as it purports to arrange a new hierarchy:

> Most near, most clear, and of the clearest bloom
> And of the fragrant mothers the most dear
> And queen, and of diviner love the day
> And flame and summer and sweet fire. . . .
> (CP 87)

All the "ands" add up not to one towering figure, but to a feeling of nearness: they extend into the embrace of the fragrant mother, the patient relation of like to like which eventually must include us all, both male and female.

But Stevens, it might be argued at this point, is a great poet of patriarchy, of the superiority of male gender. To see that gender results from an act of imagination is only to free Stevens to create a men's club of earthly apotheosis: "the hero," "major man," "the miraculous man," "the highest man with nothing higher," "the youth, the vital son, the heroic power," "the clairvoyant men that need no proof," and so forth. To note the instances of these related figures is simply to chronicle Stevens's particular change of style, which is a change of belief: he did not jettison the Judeo-Christian myth (although he tried to, for example, in the paganism of "Sunday Morning") but transformed it incrementally. Stevens's figure of belief may be male, but Stevens's poetry of the act of transformation is female-centered, and that act displays the pragmatic nature of belief. We believe as we need to believe, creating the truth as we find what will suffice rather than discovering it, fully formed and immutable in quality. If "truth" changes, Stevens's insistence in the 1930s and 1940s that it must be embodied in a male figure is itself subject to change. Not only is religious truth mutable, but insofar as religious truth is linked to gender—and it always is, "for the style of the gods and the style of men are one" (*OP* 262)— then gender itself is subject to change. Our belief that men are men and women women, that what biology decrees society enacts, is as timebound a belief as any other.

For every poem in which Stevens insists on the superiority of a male figure—and the dandy's innate conservatism, his reverence for traditional forms, is relevant here—we may find a poem in which the very distinctions we make between male and female begin to blur—the dandy's desire to escape the stale intelligence of his time is relevant here. He fashions his escape in many ways. In "The Wind Shifts" (*CP* 83), for example, the word "her" stands at the poem's very center, yet the poem insists throughout on "human" rather than male or female. Had Stevens substituted the word "him," the poem would mean something different—but the point is that in a poem about human beings, Stevens deliberately rejects the notion of male gender as the "standard" human gender. Often, in poems of the impersonal "I," such as "Two Figures in Dense Violet Night" (*CP* 85), we simply cannot determine the gender of the speaker, although critics have assumed masculinity in the absence of a gender tag.[13] Or again, Stevens frequently writes poems in pairs, one about a male, one about a female, in which the parallelism of experience acts to weaken the distinctions of gender. "Woman Looking at a Vase of Flowers" (*CP* 246) and "The Well Dressed Man with a Beard" (*CP* 247) are versions of each other. "She" experiences something like "an act, / An affirmation free from doubt"; he experiences the possibility of "One thing remaining, infallible . . . / Out of a thing believed, a thing affirmed." The poems cannot be absolutely distinguished from each other; their crucial overlap extends to their central figures, undermining the absolute dichotomy of male and female. "Tea" and "To the Roaring Wind" appear to be a female and male matched set of poems, yet, as John Hollander reminds us, "Figures of persons, things, or activities in Stevens are always full of shadows and echoes of other figures" (Doggett and Buttel 235). Umbrellas in Java unfurl in "the distances of sleep," and roaring wind finds its lost syllable, perhaps, in the word "tea." It is as if Stevens were searching for a way out of gender's dichotomous

---

[13]See, for example, Ehrenpreis (Doggett and Buttel 226).

hold by writing his/her poems which are versions of each other. The movement appears to take us from male *versus* female to male *and* female (and eventually, as I must demonstrate, to male *as* female.)

Again, Stevens challenges the absolute distinction between genders when he places a man and a woman in a single scenario whose importance overwhelms the distinction of gender: "Anatomy of Monotony" may appear at first to be a poem about mother earth and father sun; yet the mother's deathly coldness and the father's life-giving warmth alike exist against a background that cancels distinction—"that fatal and that barer sky" (*CP* 107–8). One could never complete a definitive list of such examples; once we see that Stevens challenges not only archetypal but even less rigid methods of distinguishing between male and female, we are well on our way to comprehending the quarrel Stevens holds with himself on the subject of gender. Gender in his poems is no longer a matter of contraries, but of ever finer distinctions and harmonies which shade beautifully toward chaos.

"Things are because of interrelations and interactions" (*OP* 189); poetry itself for Stevens is a matter of capturing the relations between things in motion. Certainly Stevens repeatedly makes discriminations along gender lines; sometimes he sees the imagination as feminine, elegant, euphuistic (*NA* 78), sometimes as masculine, virile, even violent. The true artist, however, is usually male: "The artist, that is to say, the man of imagination . . . the ethereal compounder, pater patriae, the patriarch" (*LWS* 372). Although he clings to old myths of gender in his letters and journals, "moral qualities are masculine; whimsicalities are feminine" (*SP* 114), all of them argue for fixity, "a *is* b"; and fixity was the one quality Stevens could never tolerate.

Gender is one of the keys in which Stevens plays variations on the nature of poetry and the identity of the poet; if the artist is male, he is, as poetic subject, transformed like every other poetic subject. If male in "reality," he might well experience re-creation in the imagination as female. Here, Stevens's dandyism makes itself felt; for one who appropriates others in his correspondence, for one who feels the self to be multiple, the relations between things and their interactions include the relation between selves and their interactions. I speak not of the mating of male and female, but of the metamorphosis of male into female, female into male, which begins in the finding of resemblances and ends in the making of an analogical world— male as female and female as male, not male *or* female. Like Cather, Stevens imagines gender in geographical, spatial terms; he, too, imagines living "on the divide." Taking a stroll one evening, he reports,

I could not realize that it was I that was walking there. The boy self wears as many different costumes as an actor and only midway in the opening act is quite unrecognizable. Now and then something happens to me, some old habit comes up, some mood, some scene (both of the sun, and of the moon) returns, and I return with it. . . . Sometimes, just before I go to sleep, I fancy myself on a green mountain—Southward, I think. It's simply green, the grass,—no trees, just an enormous, continental ridge. (*LWS* 81)

Written when Stevens was a young man of twenty-five, the journal entry chronicles his loss of a sense of identity. When, in moments of recollection, identity returns, it comes in both traditionally masculine and feminine images, sun and moon. Just before sleep, however, he experiences the vast, empty beauty of the *coincidentia oppositorum*, in which all the different costumes and roles, and the two genders, are *as* one in an expanding vastness, not one converging on a central and fixed point. Even the youthful Stevens recognizes the temporal, multiple, changing nature of the self, the falsity that lies in fixity.

The dandy is the metamorphosist who traces not the circle of monism, the closed system of absolute truth, the absolute patriarchal tautology, "I am that I am," but instead inscribes the ellipse, the decreated circle. When Stevens speaks of the "faculty of ellipses and deviations / In which he exists but never as himself" (*CP* 493), he intends for us to notice two meanings of the word "ellipses": words removed from a grammatical construction (a silence, the dandy gone into hiding once again); and the geometrical figure, the "ellipse"—the deformed circle, the almost-circle. If the "guerilla I" is the self as closed circle, the dandy's identity is at any moment almost a circle, always a deviation from the self, subject always to change while remaining in part the same. Stevens the dandy must live in the self but outside existing conceptions of it, just as he must "live in the world but outside existing conceptions of it," just as his poetry must participate in a reality "outside existing conceptions of it." Self, art, and world provide the supreme analogy in the dandy-artist's practice: a core, paradoxically, made of change, a constant decentering. "I never feel that I am in the area of poetry until I am a little off the normal" (*LWS* 287), he confides in 1935; seven years later he adds, "let the imagination create chaos by conceiving of it" (*LWS* 403).

In the stale romantic, the existing conception of things, every woman is Eve, the locus of chaos, the destroyer of order, the pool of irrationality. We know that Stevens was not a churchgoer, and that he "gr[e]w infinitely weary of accepting things, of taking things for granted" (*LWS* 79). Stevens

escapes by changing his mind, and he changes his mind in the dandy's nar-
cissistic mode, by seeing in it a reflection of himself, his feeling that he is
multiple: "the various faculties of the mind co-exist and interact, and there
is as much delight in this mere co-existence as a man and a woman find in
each other's company." He imagines the mind not as a synthesis of male
and female, but as a process of "cross-reflections, modifications, counter-
balances, complements" (*LWS* 368). That is, he introduces the female into
the male mind in order to express the very idea of change and motion. As
he adds the female to the mind, he adds a series of "others" to his conception of self and world and poetry: he adds the notion of artifice to nature,
French to English, woodsman to city dweller, solitary walker to family
member.

Among these various spurs to the passivity of received wisdom, woman
is perhaps the most potent. After all, received wisdom has itself always
suggested woman's power to destroy culture; Stevens had only to seize on
the clichés and give them the brief twist of genius in order to arrive at the
space of novelty from which he created, in which he lived. If woman is
false and dangerous and witchlike, Stevens, like Baudelaire before him,
sees in her deceptiveness a critique of bourgeois truth, feels in the danger
an escape from ennui, portrays in the witch's profile the new lineaments of
nobility, the flowering of evil. Although he associates women with the
moonlike principle of change, he also twists that cultural topos, reinter-
prets instability as the principle of renewal and vigor, frightening but necessary if the world is to remain in motion. Women are sinister, blue, me-
tallic, as menacing as the nightmarish "Madame La Fleurie," who flowers
as "the bearded queen," the mother who feeds on her son (*CP* 507). Stevens
creates a drama: holding his belief in poetry's redemptive qualities as a sil-
ver cross, he repeatedly enters that dark chamber. When his eyes adjust he
sees nothing more or less than the figure of the poet. Let us turn to an example of the sinister female, Lady Lowzen of "Oak Leaves Are Hands,"
and then to her prosaic version in Stevens's essay of 1943, "The Figure of
the Youth as Virile Poet." Only then will we be prepared to return to the
singer by the sea and to parse her idea of order.

THE INTIMIDATING THESIS

Lady Lowzen of "Oak Leaves Are Hands" (*CP* 272), artist and dandy, is
worth encountering fully:

In Hydaspia, by Howzen,
Lived a lady, Lady Lowzen,
For whom what is was other things.

Flora she was once. She was florid
A bachelor of feen masquerie,
Evasive and metamorphorid.

Mac Mort she had been, ago,
Twelve-legged in her ancestral hells,
Weaving and weaving many arms.

Even now, the centre of something else,
Merely by putting hand to brow,
Brooding on centuries like shells.

As the acorn broods on former oaks
In memorials of Northern sound,
Skims the real for its unreal,

So she in Hydaspia created
Out of the movement of few words,
Flora Lowzen invigorated

Archaic and future happenings,
In glittering seven-colored changes,
By Howzen, the chromatic Lowzen.

Her name is a pun in German, Lady Lowzen of Howzen, "Lady Loose of
Trousers." Like the figure of Charlie Chaplin who appears in "Notes toward a Supreme Fiction," Lady Lowzen leads us once again to the comic
world of the hodgepodge. Here is Stevens's poetic equivalent of the letters
in which he, like Barbey before him, appropriates people, places, and
things. Lady Lowzen is a sinister figure not because she changes, but because she changes too thoroughly, and because she seems to feed on the
world as she "broods"—literally, thinks and births herself at once. She is a
spider, but she is also of Hyd-"asp"-ia; and we feel that she tricks us, takes
something, perhaps even our blood, for what she gives. What delicious
adult make-believe.

Lady Lowzen is an aristocratic figure by virtue of her title and her propensity for change—for nobility, as Stevens instructs us, "resolves itself
into an enormous number of vibrations, movements, changes. To fix it is
to put an end to it" (NA 34). She is a dandy because she poses, creating and
re-creating herself as a work of art, now as this figure, now as that, and she
is a dandy in her ability at once to hide and reveal her whereabouts, her

disguises. Furthermore, in her power to deny reality, like any circus side-show, she becomes a figure of the poet as Stevens constructs him in "The Noble Rider and the Sound of Words":

> Suppose we try, now, to construct the figure of a poet, a possible poet. . . . He must have lived all of the last two thousand years. . . . He will consider that although he has himself witnessed, during the long period of his life, a general transition to reality, his own measure as a poet, in spite of all the passions of all the lovers of truth, is the measure of his power to abstract himself.   (*NA* 23)

Both Lady Lowzen's immoral and immortal qualities, her "lying" exis-tence, mark her measure as a poet. Stevens chooses, in "Oak Leaves Are Hands," to personify the power of the male imagination as female and un-controllable, to characterize the necessary power of the possible poet as fe-male. The very falsity of Flora's existence suggests truth: the "glittering seven-colored changes" of the "chromatic Lowzen" find an echo in a 1946 essay, "Rubbings of Reality," in which Stevens muses that the writer needs to "proceed from the chromatic to the clear, from the unknown to the known" (*OP* 245). Lady L's quick-silvered existence puts her in the run-ning for truth.

The poem's speaker, aesthete, dandy, and detective in the best tradition of Sherlock Holmes or Hercules Poirot, has solved her mystery—knows her methods, her hideouts, her various aliases. The poem's two dandies, subject and speaker, mingle and separate throughout the poem, one or the other subtly claiming the limelight: now it is the speaker's precious games with the letter *h* or *f* we hear most clearly, now it is Lady Lowzen her-self—whoever that is—who demands our attention. The poem is a dan-dy's paradox: where the speaker is, Lowzen is not, and vice versa; yet the two cannot ever be separated. Like Barbey and Brummell, Stevens's speaker and Lady Lowzen are engaged in a struggle for the limelight. Re-lation is all; biography is butterfly quarry and butterfly pursuer.

Lady Lowzen and speaker are dandies, too, in their willful destruction of category. The poem is one of Stevens's great Ovidian occasions, a tale in Arachne's tradition, "weaving and weaving many arms." Like Ovid's Arachne, who depicts the gods in their all-too-human deficiencies, Stevens challenges the gods by pointing out their origins in the human imagina-tion. Because she dares to challenge the hierarchy of gods and men, Arachne is punished by a metamorphosis downward in the scheme of things. She lives on in Stevens's poem to challenge the very idea of hierarchy, and its corollary, category. The beauty of Arachne's weaving is the beauty of the analogical, difference shading into likeness:

> . . . From the dark purple
> The threads shade off to lighter pastel colors,
> Like rainbows after storm, a thousand colors
> Shining and blending, so the eye could never
> Detect the boundary line, and yet the arcs
> Are altogether different.
>
> (*Metamorphoses* 6.58–63)

This is the analogical beauty of "the chromatic," Lowzen's "glittering seven-colored changes."

In "Oak Leaves Are Hands" Stevens feminizes the dandy by insisting on Lady Lowzen's gender. Yet he tells us as well that she has been and will be "he"—Mac Mort, florid bachelor as well as Flora. Now she gestures like Botticelli's Venus, but who knows about those future happenings, or even all the archaic ones? Lady Lowzen, like Baudelaire's Dorothée, is a figure of sinister energy, invigoration. She threatens and mystifies. She lures us to her place, always "the centre of something else"—the perpetual decentering which is an image of decreation. But, and this is the poem's intimidating thesis, we cannot name her, either by patronymic or by pronoun. She is neither Lowzen nor Mac Mort; in fact, she is not even she. Mademoiselle de Maupin would know just how Flora Lowzen must feel.

Lady Lowzen is above all a figure who flaunts her powers. Her continual self-creation challenges not only our concept of personal identity— certainly, we change, but there are limits—but our understanding of the poet as mirror or lamp. Both of these roles imply that the artist is a creator of form and meaning, one who bestows on the world a truth he has grasped by one means or another. Stevens, with figures like Lady Lowzen, reimagines the poet as one who never arrives, who clears away (stale) truth in order that the process of truth-making may proceed. Lady Lowzen, creating herself as art, continually creates and decreates herself; she makes rather than receives or mirrors a completed truth.

But why personify truth-making in a devious woman? Perhaps Stevens begins with the notion of muse, the female "genius of poetry," helpmeet to the male poet. He describes such a figure when he accepts the Gold Medal of the American Poetry Society in 1951:

> Out of that which is often untutored . . . insensible to custom and law, marginal, grotesque, without a past, the creation of unfortunate chance, she

> evolves a power that dominates life, a central force so subtle and so familiar that its presence is most often unrealized. Individual poets, whatever their imperfections may be, are driven all their lives by that inner companion of the conscience which is, after all, the genius of poetry in their hearts and minds. I speak of a companion of the conscience because to every faithful poet the faithful poem is an act of conscience.   (*OP* 253)

Perhaps the ponderous public occasion of this statement explains its marginality to Stevens's own views. Seldom does he speak of poetry as an act of conscience. Here is a figure of the muse who directly challenges the powers of Claire Dupray, Dorothée, and Lady Lowzen. The "genius of poetry" reads out the rules that transform the "marginal, grotesque" into the central. The dangerous woman, on the other hand, decreates the rules, embodies the monster who leads us to the margins. Which figure would Stevens have the poet follow? Let us ask the poet himself, or, rather, "The Figure of the Youth as Virile Poet."

Soon after "Oak Leaves Are Hands" appeared in *Parts of a World* (1942), Stevens delivered a talk at a conference, the Entretiens de Pontigny. The essay that issued from the talk is daunting in the magnitude and number of issues it addresses: the relation between poetry and philosophy, between the poet's personality and his poetry, between imagination and reason, fact and imagination. Metamorphosing relentlessly from one topic to another, the essay displays what we knew all along, that Stevens is in the end the least dichotomous of thinkers ever to arrange his issues in opposing pairs, for he poses them thus only in order to upset the distinctions in a meandering but deceptively powerful current of resemblance and analogy.

The figure of the virile poet first appears in the fifth section of the essay, which begins, "The centuries have a way of being male" (*NA* 52). Strong male philosophers and poets, Stevens claims, have always dominated their centuries, giving them a masculine identity. Certainly Bowl, Cat, and Broomstick have suggested as much: Claire Dupray has not only failed to define the seventeenth century but has fallen prey to the stultifying effects of her day. She or he who does not conquer the century is conquered by it, the play implies.

The youth Stevens describes and then sets speaking later in the essay is also a figure of the seventeenth century, though male and English, not female and French:

> When we look back at the face of the seventeenth century, it is at the rigorous face of the rigorous thinker and, say, the Miltonic image of a poet, severe and determined. In effect, what we are remembering is the rather haggard background of the incredible, the imagination without intelligence, from which

a younger figure is emerging, stepping forward in the company of a *muse of its own*, still half-beast and somehow more than human, a kind of sister of the Minotaur. This younger figure is the intelligence that endures. It is the imagination of the son still bearing the antique imagination of the father.

(*NA* 52–53, emphasis added)

This figure appears as a savior, rescuing us from our leaden times as Brummell rescued his puritanical society from its own failure of the imagination. Barbey, thanks to Eugénie de Guérin, characterized himself as inhabiting a fortress within a labyrinth; he must be the minotaur lying in wait to destroy the world in order to defend himself. But Stevens's youthful figure, not a monster himself, is accompanied by a figure doubly monstrous: "still half-beast and somehow more than human, a kind of sister of the minotaur." Cow to the minotaur's bull, woman to the minotaur's man, she gives monstrosity a new dimension. But when she appears, she is already syntactically involved with the virile youth. Midway through the quoted passage, pronouns lose clear antecedents. And "a muse of *its* own" depicts the youth as neither male nor female, and perhaps not even human. Not a muse of "his" own, she is a kind of sister to the virile youth as well as to the minotaur. Like her, the virile youth is monstrous because outside the categories—even if only for the fleeting space of one indefinite pronoun. We return to the essay's title: the *figure of* the youth *as* virile poet: in the quoted passage we see the figure for the split second before he is named as masculine, for virile means, in addition to "maturely masculine, procreative," simply "masculine, male." The figure of the poet moves from sexless or weakly sexed puerility to virility in the space of the title's "as"; we tend to shove him into the virile category, but he does not fully belong there.

Stevens gingerly enters a world of disengenderment, the space for which he has cleared in a way quite familiar to us by now: the essay's continual juxtaposition of French writers and English writers, quotations in French paired with quotations in English. The essay's macaronic quality acts as a kind of turbine, an engine that blows away the miasma of cultural forms and allows Stevens to see, through the clearing mists, the "unremembered forms" of chaos. The essay diverges from the standard—American, virile, normal—to explore the French, female, monstrous, and then tries to take back the solid ground it has, however briefly, abandoned. Thus speaks the virile youth: "*No longer do I believe that there is a mystic muse, sister of the Minotaur. This is another of the monsters I had for nurse, whom I have wasted. I am myself a part of what is real, and it is my own speech and the strength of it, this only, that I hear or ever shall*" (*NA* 60, emphasis in original). No monster speaks to *his* inner ear, that is, he is no monster himself. Yet the rejection of this monster seems to have been too costly to sustain; the "real" seems to him to eliminate imagination, so he amends his statement by simply adding to it, à la Brummell, *"And I am imagination, in a leaden time and in a world that does not move for the weight of its own heaviness"* (*NA* 63).

The amendment, however, has come too late, for Stevens has already destroyed a crucial distinction, that between fact (part of "reality") and imagination: "it is no doubt true that absolute fact includes everything that the imagination includes. This is our intimidating thesis" (*NA* 60–61). Intimidating, indeed, and in more ways than one. For to conflate absolute fact (i.e., fact cleansed of stale imagination, something like the thing seen freshly, the Stevensian *Ding an sich*) and imagination is to conflate reality and imagination and, in turn, "real" (male) poet and "mystic" (female) muse—the monstrous figure of imagination run rampant, Lady Lowzen and all her sisters. This thesis, striking to the heart of gender, one of our most powerful of adult make-believes, is directly expressed in the virile poet's final apostrophe, overheard rather than spoken, as if he had already become his own interior paramour: *"Inexplicable sister of the Minotaur, enigma and mask, although I am part of what is real, hear me and recognize me as part of the unreal. I am the truth but the truth of that imagination of life in which with unfamiliar motion and manner you guide me in those exchanges of speech in which your words are mine, mine yours"* (*NA* 67).

My conclusion is this: although Stevens may appear to speak from the "centrality" of American social forms, he has entertained the monster and found her sympathetic. She has not made him more or less of a man, but she has enabled him to think *as* a man rather than as a *man*. She has shifted the emphasis from category to relation, a shift the French writers so beloved of Stevens had prepared long ago and far away. The new emphasis falls on the constructing of gender, an imaginative form like any other, or perhaps even a premier imaginative form, along with the idea of god. The monster has allowed Stevens to solve gender's problems—its propensity to entrap, its ability to frighten—by providing the space into which he may exit from clichéd forms, of "male" versus "female." Gender, like religion, is now an imaginative process, not a fixed idea. A corollary: although we must examine the female figures in the poetry in order to reach this conclusion, we must, paradoxically—like the defiant readers of dandyism we have become—accept the fading of gender throughout Stevens. Women and men in his poems often are neither women nor men: they are as women, as men, and as each other. Stevens's world of resemblances, of the beautiful chaos of the diminished categorical, is just the place for his walker by the sea to sing a song beyond gender, and so she does.

"The Idea of Order at Key West" presents us with the task of construing the relations among the woman singing, nature, and the (assumed) male speaker, the "me" of "Ramon Fernandez, tell me." "Behind" all three elements stands Stevens, the male artist. If a study of Stevens's dandyism is to have any value, it must help explain the poetry to us, not exist merely as a label to be placed on a style or a figure. I initially read "The Idea of Order" as a poem extending the tradition of dandyism because I see in it the dandy's figure. Stevens, as I have noted, was a fresh-air dandy, one who liked to be alone before nature as a way of escaping the trivial, besmudged world, and so, it appears, does his singer. Perhaps she issued in part from a bit of Stevens's experience—a trip to the seashore, not a place he really liked. Feeling alone, he was actually glad to learn that he had company: "Two women—one dressed in yellow, one in purple moving along the white sand—relieved the severity of the prospect" (*LWS* 60). Such women remind the dandy of his need for others, of the limits of his solitude, surely an issue in "The Idea of Order." Or perhaps his singer issued in part from an artificial world. On a visit to the American Art Gallery he admires a painting: "There was an Israels that I thought well of: a girl knitting by the sea. I liked her bare feet and the ordinary sand and the ordinary water. But what I liked best was that she was not dreaming. There was no suggestion even of that trite sorrow" (*LWS* 88). Such a girl erases the *poncif romantique*; Stevens would hope to do the same in his portrait of a woman by the sea.

The shift from journal to poem is subtle enough: in the journal the dandy-aesthete takes the measure of female subject; in the poem the female subject becomes the dandy herself, taking the measure of her own scene. She is, throughout the poem, wholly aloof from others: she does not notice the speaker; she is unaware of his (and Stevens's) acts of description, of all their questions about her. The situation is parallel to that of Baudelaire's sonnet, "A une passante," in which the male dandy picks a stranger out of the crowd, reacts strongly to her, and then loses sight of her. All the while, she proves the superior dandy by remaining wholly unmindful of him. The singer of "The Idea of Order" is simply vision-proof. The desire to characterize her as "the artist" remains his alone, and because this is so, because she cannot be manipulated, will not play Trébutien to his Barbey, she is both the seer (of the ocean) and the seen, the unclaimable superior figure, the dandy herself.

From the speaker's point of view, the aim must be appropriation of some sort, and in fact it is on the assumed grounds of *his* and Stevens's appropriation of her that much criticism of the poem has rested. Perhaps a look at another poem in which a man looks at a woman, "The Apostrophe to Vincentine" (*CP* 52–53), will help us address this issue of appropriation:

> I.
> I figured you as nude between
> Monotonous earth and dark blue sky.
> It made you seem so small and lean
> And nameless,
> Heavenly Vincentine.
>
> II.
> I saw you then, as warm as flesh,
> Brunette,
> But yet not too brunette,
> As warm, as clean.
> Your dress was green,
> Was whited green,
> Green Vincentine.
>
> III.
> Then you came walking,
> In a group
> Of human others,
> Voluble.
> Yes: you came walking,
> Vincentine.
> Yes, you came talking.
>
> IV.
> And what I knew you felt
> Came then.
> Monotonous earth I saw become
> Illimitable spheres of you,
> And that white animal, so lean,
> Turned Vincentine,
> Turned heavenly Vincentine,
> And that white animal, so lean,
> Turned heavenly, heavenly Vincentine.

The poem at first appears a pendant to "To the One of Fictive Music," an account of the apotheosis of a woman: "And that white animal, so lean, /

Turned Vincentine,/Turned heavenly Vincentine." But we are troubled: why "that white animal"? Who *is* this speaker?

We tend to assume that he is male, but "he" is in fact without gender, perhaps a potential member of that genderless "group/Of human others" he so woodenly describes. Or perhaps there is a gender tag, his power over Vincentine. Let us leave the question open. The poem describes the speaker's acts of appropriation of Vincentine: "I figured you. . . . I saw you. . . . What I knew you felt. . . . I saw become." But Vincentine is not the French, female, form of Vincent, "conqueror," for nothing. She rules the poem by her sheer obliviousness of, her safety from, the grasping and apotheosizing power of the speaker, because she exists outside his world. Like Baudelaire's "passante" and Dorothée, Vincentine has achieved the dandy's impermeability, his armor of personal superiority. In rebuffing the speaker, she calls into question a set of assumed relations: male superior to female, heaven superior to earth, heavenly woman superior to lean animal. And she does so not on the speaker's terms, those of hierarchy, but simply by remaining wholly unconscious of him and his terms alike. Like Dorothée, she appears to define a new game, a new adult make-believe, even if we cannot tell what the rules are. She takes no power over the speaker; she simply exists outside his scheme altogether. Like Hoon of "Tea at the Palaz," she is the world in which she walks, but utterly unlike him, she does not feel elevated. She does not feel anything we can know. By imagining a Vincentine, Stevens pushes toward an effacement of two dichotomous genders. Not only are speaker and group of human others unsexed, as it were, but if the speaker's appropriation of Vincentine is only a private fantasy—the insistence on turning suggests that the speaker is still working at apotheosis—then perhaps the speaker's more basic act of appropriation, labeling her a woman, is "make-believe" as well. As "To the One of Fictive Music" has revealed, gender and religion are equally constructs in poems of female apotheosis. The speaker figures her as, sees her as, sees her become. The dandy, attempting to appropriate another, challenges the very categories he appears to celebrate, including those of female and male, "you" and "I."

Here is the dandy's primal scene—that of "A une passante," "La belle Dorothée," "Apostrophe to Vincentine": the speaker sees a woman who does not see him, thus adjusting the balance of power, not to female over male, but to somewhere off-center, outside the arena of hierarchy altogether. And it is of course the scene of "The Idea of Order at Key West." The poem is so complex because it is a palimpsest of poems. At one level, perhaps the least satisfying, it is a dramatic lyric in which the speaker sees a woman who is for him an emblem of the artist. He silences her by the very act of reportage. This reading implies that Stevens depicts two genders in the poem (and he does) and arranges them hierarchically (and he does).

Yet if we read a different level of the palimpsest, a different idea of order emerges, the beauty of decreated, decentered order, the beauty of controlled chaos. In this reading, the singer is a figure of mystery and power over whom the speaker simply cannot achieve a firm grasp. He does not report the words of her song because he is incapable of distinguishing them. The poem consists primarily of unanswered questions and a plethora of hypotheses, even if it is couched in a rhetoric of statement. The poem displays, in fact, a rhetoric of re-statement, a moving about a central mystery in order to try to see it.

"She" and the sea are involved in a way that appears to exclude the speaker precisely because he cannot sort out a relation of dominance. It is akin to a game of twenty questions: did the water form to mind? did the mind form to water? The speaker fails to assign the genesis of the sound he hears, the relation between singer and sea, because his primary subject, whether he knows it or not, is the failure of his sorting devices. The confusion increases exponentially when "we" enters the equation of singer and sea. Answers can only be tentative: "If it was only . . . if it was only" or, sublimely vague, "But it was more than that,/ More even than her voice, and ours, among/ The meaningless plungings of water." The rhetoric is analytical, but the manner is wholly impressionistic. The scene, relentlessly about *she*, moves through the female to the inchoate which lies at the end of the artist's song.

"She," the single artificer, is woman, sea, and us—not a comforting union of the three, but a confusion of them, a comic hodgepodge reminiscent of Claire Dupray's poetry. The singer's private world, nature, and our common world are one because literally indistinguishable. Far from being a poem in which male speaker, male poet, dominates female by appropriating her powers, this is a text in which a vast confusion overtakes everyone and everything alike. For all the mastering and portioning that occurs at poem's end, what is fixed is ever-changing fire, what is arranged is mysteriously deepened, enchanted. The power of resemblance, the power of "as," reigns, but never "over," only "toward." This is a dandy's poem not just because it is about a superior, aloof woman for whom creation of art and creation of self are one. It is so because it announces, through the female, a world beyond, a new myth of gender. The *coincidentia oppositorum* is a world of "ghostlier demarcations"; among the "keener sounds" is perhaps that "scrawny cry from outside" (*CP* 534), heard in March, when the frozen certainties of winter melt to release spring's liquid beauty, the chaotic newness of the modern itself.

The search for modernism's dandy, then, has led us directly to Wallace Stevens himself and to his poetry of elegant, precious, posing male figures. Yet having arrived there, we are confronted by the dandy's disappearance into verbal bon ton, his metamorphosis into the frightening female figures of Baudelairean perversity, his paradoxical position as reflection and annulment of his creator. For Stevens's imagination situated him between categories: attorney and aesthete, American and Frenchman, believer and skeptic, male and female. If his poetry reveals its meaning only in its difficulties and reticences, such is the dandy's prerogative. Stevens has achieved what few dandies and fewer poets have: the creation of an audience that finds itself naturalized in his imagination, peering out from behind his mask, to see the world as he mirrored it, as he re-created it, in an elegant chaos which is something new.

7

THE ABYSSINIAN MAID

NABOKOV'S DANDY

For Vladimir Nabokov (1899–1977) time's line forms a spiral, as readers of *Speak, Memory* know. It is thus fitting that my study, which begins with *Mademoiselle de Maupin* (1835), should find its completion in a twentieth-century rendering of a work of the early nineteenth century, Aleksandr Pushkin's novel in verse, *Eugene Onegin* (first published 1825–32). Pushkin (1799–1837) was Nabokov's chief literary passion, the writer whom he most admired and most yearned to know fully, and *Eugene Onegin* was the work by Pushkin which Nabokov not only read, translated, annotated, and interpreted, but continuously rewrote throughout his own fiction. Pushkin's character Onegin is a dandy who dresses in the London fashion, speaks impeccable French, and poses in imitation of Byron and Brummell. That Nabokov's precise yet extravagant version of *Eugene Onegin* itself constitutes a central text of twentieth-century dandyism it is the aim of this chapter to establish. Translating Pushkin's novel into English as a four-volume (Bollingen Press) cultural artifact was for Nabokov only the central act of translation of that work; all Nabokov's stories and novels translate Pushkin's sacred text into the Nabokovian vernacular.[1]

I place the translation of *Eugene Onegin* at the center of Nabokov's oeuvre as did Nabokov himself, claiming, "I shall be remembered by *Lolita* and my work on *Eugene Onegin*" (*SO* 106). Yet Nabokov's work joins other studies of dandyism in denying the very concept of center. Once we have followed Nabokov in his relentless push toward the elusive center of Pushkin's "truth," once we have experienced a commentary so rich and complicated as to approach monstrosity, we must confront what Nabokov himself finds: a darkness. Not even Nabokov, perhaps the most impassioned and painstaking of Pushkin's translators, can fully capture the poem and effect its metamorphosis from Russian to English. The dark portion of the untranslatable can be measured only through the looking glass: slight, but vast. The darkness in Nabokov's translation of *Eugene Onegin*, abstract enough, also takes form. Nabokov gives it a figure. He places at the very locus of paradox, the center of his scholarly work and a lifetime's worship of Pushkin, a black African woman, "Gannibal's sister." She (about whom much more) is a descendant on time's line, but a sister on time's spiral, of Baudelaire's "négresse" in "Le cygne":

> Je pense à la négresse, amaigrie et phthisique,
> Piétinant dans le boue, et cherchant, l'oeil hagard
> Les cocotiers absents de la superbe Afrique
> Derrière la muraille immense du brouillard,
>
> A quiconque a perdu ce qui ne se retrouve
> Jamais, jamais!   (*OC* 83)

[1]For an excellent discussion of Nabokov's version of *Onegin* see Clarence Brown, "Nabokov's Pushkin and Nabokov's Nabokov," in Dembo (195–208). Not only does Brown give a brief account of the controversy surrounding the translation, but he also points out that the commentary is as important as, or more important than, the translation itself. Brown also argues that the study of Pushkin is in fact "the culmination of that unique thing which he has been doing all along, with remarkable consistency, in fact with almost monomaniacal persistence, in *The Real Life of Sebastian Knight*, *The Gift*, *The Eye*, *Pale Fire*, *The Defense*, and so on" (200). In these novels, Brown explains, Nabokov concerns himself with two lives which "coalesce," and "the relationship between Nabokov's translation of *Eugene Onegin* and his commentary on *Eugene Onegin* is exactly the same as the relationship that we have seen in these other cases" (206). I agree with Brown's preliminary insight, and take as my task the explanation of why and how Nabokov sets up this pattern in his fiction and in his commentary to *Onegin* alike.

I think of the negress, emaciated and consumptive,
Treading in the mud, and seeking, with haggard eye
The absent coconut palms of superb Africa,
Behind the immense rampart of the fog,

Of anyone who has lost that which is found
Never, never!

Like "la négresse," Gannibal's sister Lahann exemplifies the loss of home, family, center. Like "la négresse" and all the others who will never fully retrieve their own "superbe Afrique," whatever its form, Lahann represents the transformation of hierarchical category, centered in patriarchy, into a decentered analogical weave. Yet at the same time, to draw a parallel from another of Nabokov's beloved authors, she brings to mind Proust's hawthorn blossoms, on which the young Marcel locates "little patches of a creamier color, beneath which I imagined that [their] fragrance must lie concealed" (Proust 123). Located wherever the center is not, Lahann paradoxically marks, for Nabokov, the very imagined essence of Pushkin's genius, issuing as it does from a mysterious Abyssinian ancestor.

Familiar elements of dandyism hover about her: her dangerous but attractive femaleness which beckons to a deathly land beyond gender; her paradoxical nature; her place in a work of literary translation. Translation is by now a familiar subject in the world of dandyism, where it is a special case of metamorphic transformation and self-creation. We have seen it, for example, in Barbey's Brummell, the Englishman who exists between French and English, the man made out of words written as Barbey recreates himself.

The story of Nabokov's approach to this dark woman, both in his edition of *Eugene Onegin* and throughout his fiction, is the final account of dandyism and gender I offer. The story begins in Nabokov's own youthful dandyism, but extends to his lifelong appropriation of Pushkin. I trace this appropriation in two stories, "Spring in Fialta" (1938) and "Mademoiselle O" (1939), in the translation of and commentary on *Eugene Onegin* (1964), and finally in *Pale Fire* (1962). I present a sketch, not an exhaustive account, of the dandy—figure and texture—as he and she appear in Nabokov's seductive, repellent fictions. Dandies define their audiences, and Nabokov is no exception. Sleuths seeking telling details and aesthetes savoring impressions, we defiant "criticules" and yielding readers must begin.

A CRASH BEYOND FIALTA: THE BIRTH OF TEXTURE

Nabokov began his life as a dandy, or rather a brittle young fop, in Russia: "I wore spats and a derby. The cane I carried, a collector's item that had belonged to my Uncle Ruka, was of a light-colored, beautifully freckled wood, and the knob was a smooth pink globe of coral cupped in a gold coronet" (*SM* 243). Whether or not it is this cane Nabokov later gives to so many characters, including Aunt Maud and John Shade in *Pale Fire*, its gold coronet serves as an emblem of the aristocratic past from which he was exiled. Dandies have long imagined themselves as kings incognito; Baudelaire's De Quincey learned the fascination of passing unremarked but with inward superiority among the crowd; Stevens imagined himself as Haroun-al-Raschid. Nabokov experienced an actual fall from an exalted stature. The roll call of dandies in exile—Gautier's Madeleine, Barbey's Brummell, Baudelaire's swan, Delacroix's Ovid, Cather's Ántonia—reaches with Nabokov its most compelling name. Like the artists who imagined their own exile, feeling themselves abstractly separated from the ideal, Nabokov, who experienced actual political exile, cultivated homelessness until it yielded art.[2] Paradoxically, this most artificial of dandy's lives was in fact generated by "actual" events. Baudelaire, at home in Paris, imagined himself through Guys, "man of the world," but Nabokov was a true cosmopolitan: "I am an American writer, born in Russia and educated in England where I studied French literature, before spending fifteen years in Germany" (*SO* 26). He actually lived a Stevensian "hodgepodge." The dandy believes that philistine society is hostile: "On peut dire que toute la société est en guerre contre lui" (*OC* 1140; One could say that all of society wages war against him). Nabokov fled actual revolution and war.

Nevertheless, he chose the dandy's and not the war refugee's enemies. While deeply concerned by the actual horrors of the day, he battled them on aesthetic grounds.[3] He was at war with mediocrity, not a specific gov-

---

[2]Nabokov is of course not the only writer to experience actual rather than imaginary exile. From Ovid to Dante to Joyce to Solzhenitsyn, writers have been forced to leave their countries. Dandy-artists, however, often stay at home yet imagine themselves in exile from their "true" home, always a spiritually or aesthetically superior locale.

[3]Ellen Pifer, throughout *Nabokov and the Novel*, argues correctly that Nabokov's artifice does not oppose life but "is deployed by Nabokov to renew the reader's perception of reality—by estranging that perception from habitual formulations" (25). She convincingly argues for the morality (without didacticism) of Nabokov's aestheticism.

ernment; his enemy was the vulgar mob in all its guises. "Real-life" enemies he characterized in the time-honored terms and tones of dandyism,
speaking, for example, of "that trite *deus ex machina*, the Russian Revolution" (*SM* 229). The Soviets were vulgarians, people of failed imagination, the worst philistines of all.

Yet Nabokov's fictional heroes sometimes lose their minds in the sadness
of exile rather than finding there the impetus to creation. The mad Brummell in Caen is their spiritual ancestor. Choosing sanity, Nabokov chronicles the formation of a saving persona, transforming loneliness and up-
rootedness through a pose of superiority, complete with special clothing
and gestures. Here is a self-portrait of the young Russian at Cambridge:
"Aloof, solitary, impassive, the crack goalie is followed in the streets by entranced small boys. . . . His sweater, his peaked cap, his kneeguards . . . set
him apart from the rest of the team. He is the lone eagle, the man of mystery, the last defender" (*SM* 267). The tone is self-mocking, since a safely
ironic distance must be maintained, even from oneself. The pose continues: "I would . . . think of myself as of a fabulous exotic being in an English footballer's disguise, composing verse in a tongue nobody understood
about a remote country nobody knew" (*SM* 268). Never a team player, Nabokov has not yet translated his poetry or his self into an adopted language. But he has learned to pose—the dandy's necessary, if not sufficient,
skill—and he has learned to insist on his own superiority and aloofness.
Exile has taught him to ignore his audience—he lives, with other émigrés,
"among perfectly unimportant strangers, spectral Germans and French-
men in whose more or less illusory cities we . . . happened to dwell" (*SM*
276). Exile has taught him as well the counterrhythm to ignoring the
masses, the search for a perfect audience in whose eyes he may seek a self-
enhancing reflection. And he was admired, as Sirin, the young writer here
described in 1932 by Andrei Sedykh: "The curious will see a thirty-three-
year-old young sportsman, very slender, nervous, and impulsive. [One no-
tices] his graceful manner and elegant speech with slightly rolled r's . . .
distinguished features. . . . Sirin speaks quickly and with enthusiasm, but
a certain sense of restraint keeps him from talking about himself" (Field
156). It is as if Nabokov, who most enjoyed life when it imitated art, lived
out the poses of literary dandyism in reality. Like Barbey, Baudelaire, and
Stevens, he lived palimpsestically—Russian aristocrat, awkward Cambridge student, writer, lepidopterist, impoverished tutor, family man. His
life had the quality of artificiality as he constructed a self from many layers. Whereas Barbey fought to acknowledge and celebrate a multiplicity of
selves, "cette vie en l'air," Nabokov took such multiplicity for granted and

sought to bring it under control. The solution was homeopathic: the only approach to a life made out of various personae was yet more fiction.

Nabokov's dandyism makes itself felt most powerfully as a pose constituted by countless details in his writing. We all use the term "Nabokovian" to characterize that pose, but to see Nabokov as part of the literary tradition of dandyism enables us to anatomize the Nabokovian. Here, for example, is Baudelaire's Delacroix, recognizably a brother to Nabokov's Nabokov as he appears in his interviews, autobiography, and essays:[4]

> Eugène Delacroix était un curieux mélange de scepticisme, de politesse, de dandysme, de volonté ardente, de ruse, de despotisme, et enfin d'une espèce de bonté particulière et de tendresse modérée qui accompagne toujours le génie.
>
> (*OC* 1128)

> Eugène Delacroix was a curious mix of skepticism, politeness, dandyism, ardent will, ruse, despotism, and finally of a particular type of kindness and of restrained fondness which always accompanies genius.

Anyone who has read *Strong Opinions* sees a Nabokov who is closely akin to this portrait. The precise and cutting views of that collection, what Baudelaire called "son esprit de domination" (*OC* 1129; spirit of domination), are views Nabokov developed out of a sense of innate superiority and an understanding that exile provides a clear choice: purposeful self-creation or defeat by external events.

Nabokov adopts poses throughout his life, but he presents us with a few qualities that seem stable enough across time. Aloofness, a refusal to join clubs, groups, schools: like Baudelaire, he aspires "être un grand homme et un saint *pour soi-même*" (*OC* 1289; to be a great man and a saint *for oneself*). A moral aesthetic: he believes that "one day a reappraiser will come and declare that, far from having been a frivolous firebird, I was a rigid moralist kicking sin . . . ridiculing the vulgar and the cruel" (*SO* 193). A deliberate deviation from the "average" and the "commonsensical." A Barbeyan disdain for his readership, "my proud and disinterested and even contemptuous attitude toward the *fata* of my books" (*Selected Letters* 264), coupled with a contradictory belief that he deserves the admiration of posterity and relief from financial troubles. An antibourgeois sense of play coupled with a "volonté ardente," a will to accomplish, the two qualities mingling in butterfly collecting in which the perennially young boy clambers over the countryside while the serious scientist proudly affixes his name to a subspecies after dissecting butterflies under the microscope.

---

[4]I borrow the phrase "Nabokov's Nabokov" from Brown in Dembo (195–208).

Early in his academic career Nabokov expresses a dandy's view of the artist as one who must escape the vicious mob: "And the more brilliant, the more unusual the man, the nearer he is to the stake. *Stranger* always rhymes with *danger*" (*Lectures on Literature* 372). "Let us bless the freak," he intones, let us "supplant . . . the dominant vulgarian" (372). Most important in this battle is the detail. Beau Brummell lived for detail: different glove-makers worked on separate parts of each of his gloves. So Nabokov counsels the "supremacy of the detail over the general, of the part that is more alive than the whole, of the little thing which a man observes and greets with a friendly nod of the spirit while the crowd around him is being driven by some common impulse to some common goal" (373).

Certainly Nabokov would be the last figure to approve of labeling: to call him a dandy is useless except insofar as it allows us to notice, with renewed vividness and understanding, details of the man and his art. That he fits the profile of the dandy tradition, itself a shifting and nebulous silhouette, is a beginning. Only what he makes of dandyism matters.

Let us begin, then, with detail, a portrait of Nabokov's first dandy, Uncle Ruka:

> Then in June again, when the fragrant *cheryomuha* (racemose old-world bird cherry or simply "racemosa" as I have baptized it in my work on "Onegin") was in foamy bloom, [Uncle Ruka's] private flag would be hoisted on his beautiful Rozhestveno house. . . . on small, mincing feet in high-heeled white shoes [he] would lead me mysteriously to the nearest tree and delicately pluck and proffer a leaf, saying, "*Pour mon neveu, la chose la plus belle au monde—une feuille verte.*"
>
> (*SM* 69)

Uncle Ruka, we learn, is a homosexual who embarrassingly fondles and croons over the young Vladimir. He speaks French, Italian, and English better than he speaks Russian, and he spends a portion of every year in France. These details of dandyism in fact carry within them, like Proust's little Japanese paper bits that expand in water, the vast structure of Nabokov's recollection. He mentions his work on *Onegin* not just as a casual gloss on this childhood scene, but to indicate that, within the translation of *Onegin* itself, especially the "Commentary," he writes another autobiography, the story of the growth of his imagination. Uncle Ruka's achieved Frenchness is echoed in Nabokov's insistence that the greatest of Russian poets, Pushkin, wrote a masterpiece in heavily Gallicized Russian. Many of Pushkin's words, constructions, and idioms, so Nabokov's argument goes, arise directly from French translations of English, German, and Italian classics, as well as directly from French novels and "mediocre" French poetry of the eighteenth century. For Nabokov, as for Cather and Stevens, dandyism is related to French language and literature. Like Uncle Ruka, who spoke Russian only imperfectly and preferred a macaronic language, Pushkin's "Russian" is made in part of French.

The lesson Uncle Ruka teaches the young Vladimir is not, then, the sentimental cliché (a simple green leaf is the loveliest thing in the world) but the mysterious interest that lies in existing between categories—male (uncle) and female (mincing feet in high-heeled shoes), Russian and French. Nabokov conveys this interest by texture and allusion, Uncle Ruka's preciosity not quite concealing the powerful machinery of Nabokov's four-volume *Onegin*; the double duty of the French phrase, characterizing as it does both Ruka's and Pushkin's sentimental sources, the derivative nature of their originality. Finally, there is a little joke for the elect: Nabokov identifies in *Eugene Onegin* Pushkin's long digression on the "little feet" of women; Uncle Ruka's feet are not his own, but imported directly from the land of Pushkin's art. Worthy readers will enjoy this fact; other readers are of little interest to Nabokov.

While Nabokov lived a dandy's life, he, like other dandy-artists before him, defined and expanded in his art the meaning of such a life. Uncle Ruka provides us with a key: the passages describing him in *Speak, Memory* are as powerful in their texture of juxtaposition, allusion, pastiche, and tone as they are in their figuration of a dandy in his setting. If it is important to note the shape, color, and habitat of the butterfly, it is equally important to study the very pattern on its wing, *as* pattern, not wing. Before we can fully appreciate Nabokov's translation of *Eugene Onegin* and the tale of gender and aesthetics it tells, we must examine two stories in which Nabokov reveals the crucial source of his art: the defeat or death of women and their literary resurrection in the very texture of the work of art itself.

The subject of texture is a familiar one in the history of literary dandyism. Gautier's d'Albert, for example, seeks a marble, Parnassian surface, while Madeleine seeks truth in a woven tapestry picturing process, incompletion itself. But a return to the footnote of Barbey's "Du Dandysme et de G. Brummell" with which I began my study of his art is perhaps the best place, once again, to begin:

C'était précisément sous Brummell. Ils [dandies] étaient à bout d'impertinence. . . . Ils trouvèrent celle-là, qui était si *dandie*! . . . de faire râper leurs habits, avant de les mettres, dans toute l'étendu de l'étoffe, jusqu'à ce qu'elle ne fut plus qu'une espèce de dentelle,—une nuée. Ils voulaient marcher dans leur nuée, ces dieux! L'opération était très délicate et très longue, et on se ser-

vit pour l'accomplir, d'un morceau de verre aiguisé. Eh, bien, voilà un véri-
table fait de Dandysme! L'habit n'y est pour rien. Il *n'est* presque *plus*.

(DD 307–8, n. 2)

It was precisely under Brummell. They [dandies] had run out of impertinence. . . . They found that which was so "dandy" . . . to tear their clothes
before putting them on, the entire length of the cloth, until it was nothing
more than a sort of lace,—a cloud. They wanted to walk in their cloud, those
gods! The operation was very delicate and very long, and to accomplish it
they used a piece of sharpened glass. And, well, there's a true example of
Dandyism! The clothes themselves are not important. They practically no
longer *exist*.

Nabokov knows the facts about Beau Brummell and uses them to gloss
dandyism throughout *Eugene Onegin*. But at this point I am more interested in the strong parallel between Barbey's "espèce de dentelle" and the
weblike texture in Nabokov's fiction. Barbey describes the transformation
of cloth into lace, of the dandy into a god, by the process of picking out a
pattern with a piece of sharpened glass.

My claim about gender in Nabokov's work can be at first only baldly
stated: Nabokov, too, sees the necessary transformation of clothing into
lace, of plot, character, setting, etc., into pattern, but during the dangerous
operation, women figures die. Their death, however, is not final; they are
resurrected in the very *texture* of his prose, its most important quality. Nabokov, who may appear to tell traditional tales of fixed and dichotomous
gender, of marriage and infidelity, tyranny and madness, in fact writes
through the female into a world in which categories and hierarchies of
gender achieve the analogical truth of pattern, of texture itself. Just as Stevens writes into the female realm in order to gaze beyond established cultural forms, so Nabokov creates women who die at the level of characterization and plot in order that Nabokov's feminized story of detail and
texture may be told, a tale that radically challenges accepted cultural notions. Lest this strike us as one more example of the oppression of women,
of their use as a means to an end, I hasten to point out that, in the four cases
I have chosen to examine—"Spring in Fialta," "Mademoiselle O," *Eugene
Onegin*, and *Pale Fire*—women are bearers of truth, equal or superior to
the men who judge them, and perhaps most important, visionaries who,
moored in reality, see beyond this patterned world to the infinitely patternable worlds of the modern understanding. So inspired are they that
they fear neither the loss of category nor the loss of the world as we know
it (the tired story of dichotomous gender is but one of its chapters). Such a
loss is perhaps best expressed as death and rebirth, and although men die

throughout Nabokov's oeuvre, women die with alarming (and sometimes, it seems, wholly gratuitous) frequency.

One of these women is Nina, of "Spring in Fialta" (*Nabokov's Dozen* 13–38), whose death in a car accident outside Fialta inspires the narrator, Victor, to write the story of their long, inconclusive love affair. Victor has slowly grown to see their sporadic affair as sad and hopeless: "I grew apprehensive because something lovely, delicate, and unrepeatable was being wasted: something which I abused by snapping off poor bright bits in gross haste while neglecting the modest but true core which perhaps it kept offering me in a pitiful whisper" (*Nabokov's Dozen* 31–32). We soon realize that neither Nina nor the affair is whispering of any "true core." Nina is sexy, elusive, disorganized, and curiously impersonal—it's not so much that she "uses" Victor as that she operates in a realm of impersonality in which no one's emotions matter much. Their affair parallels Baudelaire's "A une passante," in which a Parisian dandy sees, romanticizes, craves, and rejects a woman dandy in the space of one sonnet, while the woman herself appears not even to notice him. Victor, determined never to disrupt his bourgeois marriage, thinks he is always in the process of craving and rejecting Nina when in fact she, like the "passante," never really *sees* him: "Every time I had met her during the fifteen years of our—well, I fail to find the precise term for our kind of relationship—she had not seemed to recognize me at once . . . and then she uttered a cry . . . and, in the middle of the street, with merely the frank impulsiveness of an old friendship . . . she kissed me thrice with more mouth than meaning" (16). This text of dandyism is by now a familiar one: Victor tries to tell the clichéd, vulgar tale of infatuation, marital infidelity, and parting, but Nina's implied motto, *nil mirari*, prevents him from doing so while supplying him with no other equally comfortable cliché as substitution: "I fail to find the precise term for our kind of relationship." Nabokov's hints and statements of artifice (e.g., their affair has a "plot," the "theme of a snowball fight started in the dark," "her small, comfortable body folded in the form of a Z," "She hurriedly appeared in the margins of my life, without influencing in the least its basic text," etc.) in fact constitute the story. It is as if Victor, who at the level of plot cannot understand his situation, could, within the texture of his/Nabokov's style, understand perfectly the "true" story of his affair—its status as artifice, as a made thing, as a series of details carefully placed upon paper. Nina's body is compared to a Z because it is a body composed of letters and words, not skin and bone.

In fact the entire story, as commentators have amply recognized, is a web of repeating images, a patterned confection (like the candy of Fialta) that *has* no core, however fervently Victor might wish to find it.[5] But most important, it is Nina's death which enables Victor to produce this literary texture. As Nina drives off to her death, Victor writes,

> suddenly I understood something I had been seeing without understanding—why a piece of tinfoil had sparkled so on the pavement, why the gleam of a glass had trembled on a tablecloth, why the sea was ashimmer: somehow, by imperceptible degrees, the white sky above Fialta had got saturated with sunshine, and now it was sun-pervaded throughout, and this brimming white radiance grew broader and broader, all dissolved in it, all vanished, all passed, and I stood on the station platform of Mlech with a freshly bought newspaper, which told me that the yellow car I had seen under the plane trees had suffered a crash beyond Fialta.   (*Nabokov's Dozen* 38)

Nina's death, its enlightening "brimming white radiance," itself *effects* the telling of this tale as texture, as a pattern of artifice so complex and controlled that it calls up in us a series of unruly emotions: amusement, regret, yearning, irritation. Nina exists only and always in self-announcing arrangements of words. With her death Nabokov destroys one major dichotomy—that between artifice and reality, "art" and "life"—after which all the others follow. Nina takes her place in the tradition of dandyism not just because she sees and refuses to see Victor, but because, like any good self-creating dandy, she challenges the line between art and life. Dressed in Barbey's lace, her body is visible only as it shines through the filaments of art. In the same way, Nabokov's deeply artificial story paradoxically enables the real world to shine through. Nina's death elevates her not to the pedestal of dichotomous gender, the false elevation of women in a system in which men are always superior, but to the vivid colors and forms of earthly life in patterns: violets, yellows, blues, mountains, skies. While the monstrous female orchestra of Fialta plays on, Nina is resurrected in Nabokov/Victor's perfect cadences.

Like any detail in Nabokov's fiction, this orchestra merits close attention. It is "composed of half a dozen weary-looking self-conscious ladies interlacing mild harmonies on a crammed platform and not knowing, as he [Nina's husband, Ferdinand] put it, what to do with their motherly bosoms, quite superfluous in the world of music" (26). The butt of Ferdinand's humor, they push their instruments away "like so many pieces of furniture" when they finish. Personifying the narrator's gross and "growing morbid pathos" as he slowly realizes Nina is not to be tamed, they par-

---

[5]See, for example, Barbara Heldt Monter, " 'Spring in Fialta': The Choice That Mimics Chance," in Appel and Newman (128–35).

ticipate in Fialta's lugubrious atmosphere. As part of the texture of the tale, however, they represent once again the feminization of art. Earthbound, clumsy, pathetic, they are the graceful Nina's sisters of the mirror. Further, they resemble other ugly or pathetic objects in the story—the model of Mount St. George, the "little street on crutches" (32), the "hen clucking madly as it raced for its life" (33). Nabokov is careful to avoid the enticements of pure fantasy in his transformation of text to texture: the enigmatical Nina, artist of the quicksilver appearance, another "Lady Lowzen," depends on the bosomy, failed female orchestra. Although Nabokov's tale avoids allegory, it suggests the heavy, the sad, the untransformable stuff upon which art merrily announces its playful, hopeful *programme*. These women (and hens and cheap mementos) are the textual equivalent of *Grund*, that which keeps the web of meaning from floating away in the breeze of artistic self-indulgence, of pure fantasy. Such a *grund* never reveals meaning, only the promise of meaning.[6]

"Mademoiselle O" (*Nabokov's Dozen* 177–96) is a fuller portrait of such a sad woman, and it is important to see that if women die into analogical texture, their mirror images survive in, or rather, *as*, the quiddity of the world. "Mademoiselle O," the first chapter of Nabokov's autobiography to be written, appeared in Paris in *Mesures* (1936). Perhaps the most often read section of the autobiography, it demands explanation: why does an artist who rejected vulgarity, misfortune, and self-pity present "Mademoiselle O" as the germ of his autobiography? The answers are many, but related to one another, and they concern the engendering of the dandy-artist's persona. For in Mademoiselle O we recognize Nabokov's self-portrait, once we accept the fact that Nabokov's dandy, like Barbey's and Baudelaire's, is a palimpsest. In fact, if we review the major exemplary figures in Barbey's dandy, we see that Nabokov recognizes in Mademoiselle O's irritating, bulky, self-pitying figure the very lineaments of dandyism in its darker transformations. Mademoiselle O's principal characteristic for Nabokov is her self-enclosed sadness, just like the "l'intensité surhumaine de la douleur" (*M* 3:61) that Barbey notes in his study of the catatonic madmen. Unable to learn Russian, hard of hearing, always the victim of

---

[6]For an excellent discussion of "the earth" in Nabokovian representation, that which "has no intrinsic meaning, is a nulliverse or black backdrop upon which unexpected illuminations, miracles of insight take place," see Albright on Nabokov (52–94). His discussion of the "rift experience" is especially germane to my understanding of the death of women in Nabokov's work. As I argue at length, Nabokov's women often serve to point to the rift through which our culture might be led to an understanding of the *coincidentia oppositorum*.

misfortune and cruelty, Mademoiselle O makes her own bad luck. Like Barbey's St. Sebastian, who suffers "le supplice sans le supplice," she has been injured, but it is hard to say exactly how and why. Her station in life is a kind of debased martyrdom. She resembles, too, Barbey's Mlle de G..., not in physical appearance, but in the wasted quality of her life, the sense that an inner demon consumes her while she merely waits, lost in a frozen country far from home. And, finally, like Barbey's self-portrait of the dandy among provincials, she is a superior being who struggles to communicate that superiority to Russian barbarians who will not, cannot, see it. Her superiority lies precisely in her French:

> And really, her French was so lovely! Ought one to have minded the shallowness of her culture, the bitterness of her temper, the banality of her mind, when that pearly language of hers purled and scintillated, as innocent of sense as the alliterative sins of Racine's pious verse? . . . her tongue's limpidity and luster . . . had a singularly bracing effect upon me. . . . This is why it makes me so sad to imagine now the anguish Mademoiselle must have felt at seeing how lost, how little valued was the nightingale voice which came from her elephantine body.   (*Nabokov's Dozen* 192–93)

Here, then, is the image the male dandy sees in the dark mirror of reversal—the mad and the sad which we recognize in such figures as Humbert Humbert, Charles Kinbote, and Vadim Vadimovich. Here, too, is the world's imperfection, upon which the artist turns his back at his own risk. Here is the woman who, in her heavy sadness, embodies the difficulty of transformation, of translation of either self or language. She is the perpetual exile (back in Switzerland, retired, Mademoiselle O sentimentalizes Russia "as if it were her own lost homeland") who produces nothing, who embodies the impossibility of recentering, precisely the impossibility on which Nabokov's art of texture depends. For, if Baudelaire's swan and Andromache learn the necessity of working analogically to make a new center of their exiled position, dandies a century later work analogically without trying to reestablish center. The full transformation of the romantic to the modern has occurred.

Nabokov, like Barbey and Baudelaire before him, includes a woman in his palimpsest of the dandy, thus beginning the process of challenging dichotomous gender. Nabokov begins his autobiography with Mademoiselle O because he begins with a self-portrait. Arrogant, contained male dandy is vulnerable, pathetic woman. But beyond this initial move toward androgyny and the weakening of category, we must see Mademoiselle O as the French-speaking beauty disguised, hidden in layers of banality and flesh. The tutor who finally drives Mademoiselle away from the Nabokov home is named Lenski, changed from Pétrov and Orlov in previous versions (Grayson 149). Nabokov borrows the name from Pushkin—Lenski is one of the three major characters of *Onegin*. This link to Pushkin is tiny, but it illuminates a major link: Nabokov's principal claim about *Onegin* is that it can only be translated and understood by one who sees and hears Pushkin's borrowings from the French. Out of the pen of the colossus of Russian poetry glitters the French language, artfully interwoven into the Russian. Nabokov gives Mademoiselle O a lovely French voice in an elephantine body in part because he wishes to personify the nearly silenced (but now amplified by Nabokov) French voice of its greatest poet. He imagines himself as both Mademoiselle O and as Pushkin.

Women as airy texture, women as bottomless *Grund*, women as French: it is with these three ideas in mind that we may now turn to Nabokov's translation of *Eugene Onegin*.

THE SERVILE PATH: NABOKOV TRANSLATES PUSHKIN

Pushkin is for Nabokov "a colossus who bears on his shoulders our country's entire poetry" (PRP 41). In an effort to know Pushkin's works and to reconstruct imaginatively Pushkin the man, Nabokov produces not only a four-volume translation of *Eugene Onegin* with commentary but also a body of fiction into which he translates Pushkin. Just as Barbey translated an actual man, George Bryan Brummell, into words, so Nabokov translates Aleksandr Pushkin and his works into the words of *Speak, Memory*, *The Gift*, *The Real Life of Sebastian Knight*, *Lolita*, and *Pale Fire*, to mention only the most obvious examples.

The sheer fact of translation carried immense weight for Nabokov. It is Nabokov's major contention, as I mentioned above, that Pushkin himself depended on French translations of the works underlying *Onegin*: "the St. Petersburg fashionable, the ennuied Hussar, the civilized squire, the provincial miss in her linden-shaded chateau of painted wood—all read Shakespeare and Sterne, Richardson and Scott, Moore and Byron, as well as the German novelists (Goethe, August Lafontaine), in French versions, and French versions only" ("Servile Path" 97–98). Several consequences flow from this first principle, not the least of which is the exalted status given to the French translator himself: "Shakespeare [for the educated nineteenth-century Russian] is really Letourner, Byron and Moore are Pichot, Scott is Dufauconpret, Sterne is Frenais, and so on" (98). A moment's meditation suggests another pair who must have been on Nabokov's mind as he wrote these lines after translating *Onegin*: for the discerning twentieth-century English reader, *Pushkin is really Nabokov*.

The tradition of dandyism helps us know the significance of such paired translator and translated: Baudelaire and Poe or De Quincey come to mind, as do Barbey and Brummell. For in characterizing the great man in question, Baudelaire, Barbey, and Nabokov create themselves as artists. Once again, we watch the "appropriation" of the great man by the dandy-artist. Bits and pieces, nuances and atmospheres, methods and means of Pushkin's *Eugene Onegin* appear throughout Nabokov's works. Fialta, to mention one of these bits, suggests Yalta in part because Nabokov and his family spent a brief part of their exile there, but also because Pushkin, ex-iled to the Crimea as well, alludes to the fact within *Eugene Onegin* (Comm 2:428). This matter of exile is a coincidence on which Nabokov self-consciously draws in order to see his and Pushkin's lives as mirror im-ages of each other.

But Nabokov cannot stop there, at the level of coincidence. He uses this coincidence and others (e.g., Pushkin is thought to have fought a duel on what became a Nabokov family estate, Batovo) as springboards for trans-lation, the transformation of Pushkin the artist into Nabokov the artist. Once we see this major principle at work in Nabokov's works, we see fully the hall of mirrors in which he writes. We cannot separate the instances in which Nabokov patterns himself on Pushkin from the instances in which Nabokov patterns Pushkin on Nabokov. For example, Nabokov writes in his "Commentary" to *Onegin*, "It has become a commonplace with com-mentators to deplore Pushkin's 'exile.' Actually, it may be argued that dur-ing those six years he wrote more and better than he would, had he re-mained in St. Petersburg" (Comm 3:151). So, too, would Nabokov claim that his years of exile and eventual repatriation in the United States helped his art, perhaps were the making of him as an artist. Did he make this claim as the successor to the "translated" version of Pushkin? Or did he interpret Pushkin in the light of his own experience, bringing the Push-kinian translation ever closer to the Nabokovian original? No one, perhaps least of all Nabokov, can tell us.

Yet Nabokov was quite self-conscious in his reconstruction of Pushkin. In a talk delivered in Paris in 1937, recently translated as "Pushkin, or, The Real and the Plausible," we see Nabokov setting forth the Pushkin agenda which was to serve him, with various modulations and metamorphoses, for a lifetime. Here Nabokov presents himself as a religious disciple of

Pushkin's: "To read his works, without a single exception . . . and to re-read them endlessly is one of the glories of earthly life" (PRP 39). To know Pushkin means to know his works and to yearn endlessly to know the man behind them:

> those of us who really know him revere him with an unparalleled fervor and purity, and experience a radiant feeling when the richness of his life over-flows into the present to flood our spirit. Everything about it is a source of joy, everyone of his enjambments . . . the most minute details of his exis-tence, even the names of those who passed close to him, for an instant blend-ing their shadows with his. (PRP 39)

But, as Nabokov explains in his Paris talk, one can never know the "real" Pushkin; one is thrust back upon the inevitably fictional nature of one's account of him. The solution to this frustration is beautifully, arrogantly elegant: to erect one's own fiction of Pushkin (necessarily superior to those of hack biographers, ignorant translators, and vulgar readers of Pushkin) as supreme. But if to write of Pushkin is to write a fiction, Nabokov takes one more syllogistic step which it is crucial to perceive. For Nabokov, *to write fiction is to write of Pushkin*, always and inevitably. Lest this seem too broad a claim, I will describe the ways in which the Nabokovian novel is "about" Pushkin. Certainly we may successfully go allusion hunting in *The Gift*, *Lolita*, *Ada* (or, as I intend to do, in *Pale Fire*).[7] But beyond such individual details as a tutor's name or an uncle's feet, we must see that Na-bokov's entire, complex pose of artistic dandyism is an appropriation of Pushkin's masquerade and method.

Pushkin himself is a man of poses and masks for Nabokov: "It is but imagination that bestows a certain elegance on Pushkin, who, incidentally, in keeping with a whim of the period, liked to disguise himself—as a gypsy, a cossack, or an English dandy. A fondness for the mask, let us not forget, is an essential trait of the true poet" (PRP 40). Pushkin's artistic method rhymes with his posing: it is, for Nabokov, a matter of artifice, parody, pastiche. In short, of texture. The "radiance" he reports feeling

---

[7] See Priscilla Meyer, "Nabokov's *Lolita* and Pushkin's *Onegin*: McAdam, McEve and McFate," in Gibian and Parker (179–211). Meyer demonstrates that "*Lolita* represents a free translation through space and time of a Russian literary monument of the 1820's into an American one of the 1950's." She sees Nabokov's novel as a parody of paraphrastic trans-lation, the bête noire of Nabokov's "Commentary."

I wish to extend Meyer's compelling argument to include Nabokov's entire oeuvre; to do so I demonstrate that Nabokov parodies Pushkin's methods as well as his images, char-acters, and plots. Meyer's anatomy of literary languages in *Onegin* is especially relevant to my analysis.

when reading Pushkin is the "radiance" the transfigured Victor experiences on Nina's death into texture in "Spring in Fialta." Nabokov explains Pushkin's method with passion, acuity, and single-minded persistence in his commentary on *Onegin*. For example, Nabokov describes Onegin as

> a character borrowed from books but brilliantly recomposed by a great poet to whom life and library were one, placed by that poet within a brilliantly reconstructed environment, and played with by that poet in a succession of compositional patterns—lyrical impersonations, tomfooleries of genius, literary parodies, and so on.   (Comm 2:151)

From his juvenilia to *Look at the Harlequins!* Nabokov impersonates Pushkin, who himself impersonates other writers (pastiche, parody, tomfoolery) in his creation of Onegin, a wholly artificial character borrowed from books. For Pushkin, such artificiality is never barren, since "life and library were one."

We must learn to appreciate Nabokov as a man who is engaged in creating himself, simultaneously with his re-creation of Pushkin, in fictions made out of words. Nabokov has decided opinions on how to translate *Onegin* and Pushkin (the man and his works are, for Nabokov, inseparable) from Russian into English. He explains and defends the process at length;[8] it is itself deeply paradoxical and centrally located in the tradition of dandyism. For in explaining the theory and practice of translation, Nabokov creates a persona for himself. Paradox: on one hand, he intends to translate the poem with "absolute accuracy," to provide a trot of the poem in which the reader can easily match English word with Russian original. But this literal accuracy, it gradually becomes apparent, must rest upon a vast reservoir of context. Lexical word-for-word translation fails utterly. When Pushkin uses a word, Nabokov explains, the truly scientific translator must understand the context in which Pushkin chose the word, in order to make the proper parallel choice in English. Only an understanding of what and whom Pushkin knew, how he felt, what (and in which particular translations) he was reading, where he was when he wrote, and how each of his words fits into the line, the stanza, the poem, Russian literature and all of European literature—only such a knowledge can ensure the proper choice of English word, and the full "translation" of Pushkin's art.

---

[8]Nabokov's major discussions of translation appear in "Problems of Translation," "The Servile Path," "The Art of Translation" in *Lectures on Russian Literature*, the "Translator's Introduction" to Pushkin's *Onegin*, and within the "Commentary" to *Onegin*.

So the trot, while sacrificing rhyme, avoiding paraphrase, rejecting false elegance, only at first appears literal, accurate, if pedestrian—or, as Nabokov himself describes it, "honest and clumsy, ponderous and slavishly faithful" (*SO* 7). Only a translator who has imagined himself into Pushkin's world, only a translator who feels Pushkin's truth within him ("there was not a single moment when Pushkin's truth, as indestructible as conscience, ceased to glitter somewhere. I feel it within me now" (PRP 42), only a translator who translates himself into and out of Pushkin, can do the job. This is the largest implicit claim of Nabokov's method. The "literal trot" is accompanied by long, authoritative notes that attempt to flesh out, make public, Nabokov's appropriation of Pushkin. Their scholarly depth and creativity are beyond question, even by those who disagree with him about the fundamental theory behind the translation. I examine both the poem and the notes more fully, but here it is useful to take the larger view. What pose does Nabokov strike in translating *Onegin*?

Like most dandy's poses, his is created in layers, shades, tones. There is the pose of nonchalance: this is joyful play. Obviously the product of a Napoleonic research campaign fueled by an already vast erudition, the translation must never smell of the battle. For example, Nabokov tells us that he can mention only a few Gallicisms casually jotted down as he read. Such "casual" reading includes works by Clément Marot, Guillaume de Chaulieu, Voltaire, André Chénier, and Charles Hubert Millevoye. Although Nabokov suffered a near nervous collapse at one point during the research and writing, individual notes sail nonchalantly into playful surmise, the final precision in the dandy's world of paradox. Then there is the armor of nastiness, aggressiveness: Nabokov frequently stops in his explication of Pushkin's poem to launch vicious attacks on other translators who have committed howler after howler because their method has been wrong.

In the end, however, the only "method" that works is *to be Nabokov*, to have his ear, his knowledge, his soul. The pose is one of immense pride. The pride is both tempered and enhanced by another paradox: the more Nabokov researches, explains, explicates, the richer and more mysterious the poem becomes. His very thoroughness ensures his failure to grasp the poem once and for all. Poem is as elusive as poet. Nabokov's notes act most often to "vaporize" the poem, to borrow a term from Baudelaire. This vaporization occurs principally as a result of one of Nabokov's major theories about Pushkin: that he wrote deeply allusive verse, and that the body of literature he alluded to was written in French. By displaying with specificity and thoroughness the source of many of Pushkin's Gallicisms in the

"mediocre" French poetry of the eighteenth century, he demonstrates that
"Russian" is not really Russian, but French/Russian. Even the verse form
of *Onegin* is, Nabokov claims, derived from the French.

Like Cather and Stevens, Nabokov locates a special truth in French language and literature. They provide him with a free zone in which metamorphosis (Pushkin/Nabokov, Russian/English) may freely proceed. This
free zone, however, opens the way to chaos, for once we see that a "Russian" word is but a version of the "original" French word, itself often originally English, the entire weave of the poem is loosened. Russian cloth becomes a dandy's French lace; artifice reigns. It is with some satisfaction
that Nabokov announces, for example, that

> an interesting situation arises when, in alluding to an author, Pushkin uses a
> phrase which constitutes a parody of that author's diction. Yet even more in-
> teresting are such passages where the aped phrase is found to occur in the
> Russian version of the French translation of an English author, so that in re-
> sult Pushkin's pastiche (which *we* have to render in English) is three times
> removed from its model!   ("Servile Path" 102)

Translations of translations interest him because they are what he, Nabokov, writes, as we shall see when we take up the matter of *Pale Fire*. Translations of translations interest him too because they throw into question
the ability of category (here, linguistic category) to contain the transformations of genius. Nabokov's notes to *Onegin* playfully create a macaronic
universe in which, for example, Nabokov turns to an English text (Byron)
to reflect back on a Russian text (*Onegin*) in which a French meal is at issue
(*EO* chap. 1, st. 16; p. 101). Where Pushkin defends the Gallicization of
Russian, Nabokov, like Stevens before him, defends the comedy of the
hodgepodge itself. And, as I shall argue, not just the French, but the female, guides him to its very centerlessness.

A COMPLETE LEXICON OF WORDS IN VOGUE: DANDIES IN PUSHKIN'S *EUGENE ONEGIN*

With Nabokov's translation of *Onegin* we enter a true *mise en abyme*. Nabokov, the dandy-artist, holds the commentator's mirror up to Onegin, a
figure who already exists *before* a mirror (he is a dandy) and *in* a mirror
(Pushkin's verse of parody, pastiche, tomfoolery).

Pushkin's *Eugene Onegin* is on its face a verse novel about a dandy:
"Now my Onegin is at large: / hair cut after the latest fashion / dressed like

a London Dandy" (*EO* 1.4; p. 97). Like all responsible creators of dandies, Pushkin sends his to French lessons: "and finally he saw the World./In French impeccably/he could express himself and write" (*EO* 1.4; p. 97). Onegin in town lives the life of a *fashionable* much like that of Rodolphe in Gautier's "Celle-ci et celle-là": he rises late, dresses, strolls, stops for idle chat, dresses for dinner, attends the theater, womanizes. His truest dandyism, however, resides not in his standardized activities, but in his Brummellian *relation* to society, the cumulative effects of his poses. Pushkin lists the varieties of his relations to his society: he amazes, alarms, amuses, catches, conquers, waits, begs, demands, eavesdrops, pursues, obtains. Most of these verbs relate him to women; like Rodolphe, Onegin has yet to learn that he is caught in a clichéd romantic plot.

Onegin begins as a clothes-wearing man, ambiguous in gender:

> He three hours, at the least,
> in front of mirrors spent,
> and from his dressing room came forth
> akin to giddy Venus
> when, having donned a masculine attire,
> the goddess drives to a masquerade.
>   (*EO* 1.25; p. 106)

But Pushkin gradually complicates and deepens his dandyism at the level of language itself. The combed and curled, Anglicized and Gallicized Onegin presents Pushkin with the opportunity to make his own verse as self-conscious, as precious as the character, just as Barbey has described his account of Brummell as "un morcelet d'histoire," "cette babiole" (DD 217, 215; a morsel of history, this bauble). Onegin's clothing becomes doubly artificial when Pushkin points out that it is made of foreign words as well as foreign fabrics and patterns:

> I might before the learned world
> describe here his attire;
> this would, no doubt, be bold,
> however, 'tis my business to describe;
> but "pantaloons," "dress coat," "waistcoat"—
> in Russian all these words are not;
> whereas, I see (my guilt I lay before you)
> that my poor style already as it is
> might be much less variegated
> with outland words . . .   (*EO* 1.26; p. 106)

Onegin is foppish in clothing; Pushkin is foppish in his adaptation of English and French words.

Onegin is a character not only dressed in foreign words, but, as Nabo-kov points out, made out of foreign literary characters: Chateaubriand's René, Byron's Childe Harold, Benjamin Constant's Adolphe, and so forth. As time passes, he suffers increasingly from ennui; the "child of pastimes and of luxury" learns that he is to suffer from the disease inherited, as it were, through the ink of Pushkin's pen as he deliberately constructs One-gin from other fictional people, some of the very figures, as it happens, who were to provide Baudelaire as well with his notion of the dandy. Like Childe Harold, Onegin finds that "nothing moved him / he noticed noth-ing" (*EO* 1.38; p. 112). He decides to leave the *beau monde*; he tries and fails to become a writer, and is rescued from debt when his uncle dies, leav-ing him a country estate. By now he has become a more "mature" dandy, one who understands the emptiness of life and the need to struggle against, rather than participate in, constricting cliché. Yet he succeeds only in substituting a new set of *topoi* for the old: he now practices a Barbeyan violence, cold and bitter. "Pushkin," his "pal" who meets him just as he leaves the beau monde, describes him:

> I liked his traits,
> to dreams the involuntary addiction,
> nonimitative oddity,
> and sharp, chilled mind . . .
> . . . .
> At first, Onegin's language
> would trouble me; but I grew used
> to his sarcastic argument
> and banter blent halfwise with bile
> and virulence of gloomy epigrams.
>   (*EO* 1.44, 46; pp. 114–15)

Slowly he shades into the darknesses of dandyism which we have seen threatening Gautier, Barbey, and Baudelaire. Onegin's changing emo-tions, like his clothing, are thus stylized; he puts on Childe Harold's (or Adolphe's or the Wandering Jew's, etc.) emotions as adeptly as he changes his clothes.

What plot there is in the verse novel appears to be a vehicle for present-ing Onegin's metamorphoses from shallow fop to cold dandy to volcanic, passionate lover. Tatiana falls in love with him but his dandy's coldness causes him to reject her; he kills Lenski, his friend, in a duel because he imagines himself a figure beyond the moral code.

Pushkin cynically denies him the possibility of sincerity; once one un-derstands the "made" quality of identity, one cannot return to the notion of a "sincere" life without pose—even sincerity is a pose. Onegin cannot be rescued from his modern sensibility:

> Is he the same, or grown more peaceful?
> Or does he still play the eccentric?
> Say, in what guise has he returned?
> What will he stage for us meanwhile?
> As what will he appear now? As a Melmoth?
> a cosmopolitan? a patriot?
> a Harold? a Quaker? a bigot?
> Or will he sport some other mask?
>
> (EO 8.8; p. 285)

It is Pushkin who sees that Onegin will not be redeemed by love; Onegin understands his own metamorphoses only imperfectly. For Onegin is doubly derivative: creator of himself in a series of metamorphosing poses, he is also created by Pushkin as a series of types borrowed from English, French, and German literature. Living by the pose and killing (Lenski) by the pose, he never sees that his eventual yearning for Tatiana cannot be satisfied in the borrowed plots within which Pushkin places him. A fop may choose to mature into an honorable married man, but a demon-driven dandy, never.

Onegin, in his urge to transcend his own literary type, meets not his creator Pushkin, but merely another character, Tatiana. With her, Pushkin simply reinforces the plot of dandyism, creating Tatiana as a posing woman who herself learns to exercise the dandy's cold powers. She develops from a moonstruck, posing girl to an austere, cool, dandy-figure when Onegin rejects her. If he is cold, she must know why, and she learns by visiting his house, searching his library in his absence, reading his books, and learning of dandyism's darker and colder figures: "the pensive Vampyre, / or Melmoth, gloomy vagabond, / or the Wandering Jew, or the Corsair, or the Mysterious Sbogar" (EO 3.12; p. 155). So fully are Tatiana's and Onegin's psychologies a matter of fictional *topoi* that, for both of them, to read is to pose is to become.

Once again, categories of gender weaken when female and male figures alike discover within the dandy's pose the artificiality of identity in all its aspects. Tatiana learns to understand Onegin by reading his "modern" books, but in reading them, she crosses the line between his self and hers; she takes on not only his quality of gloomy coolness, but the very (itself compromised) masculinity of Melmoth, Jew, Corsair with which he has constructed his persona.

Thus Pushkin prepares the "primal scene" of dandyism, the scene in

which a male dandy pursues a woman who ignores him because she herself has learned the defensive posture of cold, aristocratic elegance. The
scene of Baudelaire's "A une passante" appears in parallel in Pushkin's
Onegin as Tatiana "cuts" the recently returned and suddenly smitten
Eugene:

> She does not notice him,
> no matter how he strives—even to death;
> receives him freely at her house;
> elsewhere two or three words with him exchanges;
> sometimes welcomes with a mere bow,
> sometimes does not take any notice:
> there's not a drop of coquetry in her,
> the high world does not tolerate it.
> Onegin is beginning to grow pale;
> She does not see or does not care. . . .
>
> (*EO* 8.31; p. 296)

Pushkin stresses Tatiana's lack of coquetry, her intrinsic elegance, yet the
greatest pose of all is to appear natural: "without those little mannerisms, /
without imitational devices . . . / All about her was quiet, simple. / She
seemed a faithful reproduction / *du comme il faut* . . . (. . . forgive me: / I
do not know how to translate it)" (*EO* 8.14; p. 288). Tatiana knows that she
poses, but she does not understand the full extent of her artificiality. She
seems a faithful reproduction "du comme il faut" without fully appreci-
ating her own derivative status, just as she has almost glimpsed the fact of
Onegin's condition as a man made out of fictions. Reading Onegin's books
she only begins to see what the novel's narrator does see:

> Can it be—[Onegin] an imitation,
> an insignificant phantasm, or else
> a Muscovite in Harold's mantle,
> a glossary of other people's megrims,
> a complete lexicon of words in vogue?
> Might he not be, in fact, a parody?
>
> (*EO* 7.24; p. 262)

Might she not be, as well, a parody?

Eugene Onegin, a *mille-feuille* of poses, does not leave us here, with the
returned dandy, Onegin, spurned by the dandy Tatiana, "this stately, this
nonchalant / legislatrix of salons" (*EO* 8.28; p. 295). Since we have observed this scene in *Mademoiselle de Maupin*, "A une passante," *My Ántonia*, and "Apostrophe to Vincentine," we must, once again, pursue the

question of gender it raises. If Tatiana, who has first translated herself into the French of "du comme il faut," acts *as* Onegin, if she imitates male fictional models, is gender not, once again, in flux? Tatiana and Onegin join other pairs—Gautier's d'Albert and Madeleine, Cather's St. Peter and Outland, Ántonia and Jim, Stevens's "The Well-Dressed Man with a Beard" and "Woman Looking at a Vase of Flowers"—in a highly patterned process of mutual mirroring, male to female, which works to break down the dichotomous categories of gender. Tatiana cools as Onegin begins to feel passion; Tatiana writes a letter in French to Onegin; he reciprocates much later with a letter in Russian; Onegin moves from the city to the country, and then travels, while Tatiana moves from the country to the city, and remains there, and so on.

Pushkin offers in *Eugene Onegin*, however, one striking example of the potential fluidity of all category. He gives Tatiana a belief in "the lore / of plain-folk ancientry, / of dreams, cartomancy / and the predictions of the moon" (*EO* 5.5; p. 205). Thus she puts a mirror under her pillow and "dreams a wondrous dream." It reveals primarily a chaos of the transspecies variety: a bear follows, woos, then carries her from the world of fixed category to a hut where she witnesses a party of monsters: "one horned, with a dog's face, / another with a cock's head; / here is a witch with a goat's beard; /. . ./ there is a windmill the squat-jig dances" (*EO* 5.16–17; p. 211).

To Tatiana is given the terrible nighttime vision of the monstrous juxtaposition and blending of species. In light of her dawning understanding of Onegin as a creature of other people's whims, she seems perfectly placed to understand gender, too, as a kind of fiction, the daytime world of gender's hierarchical categories giving way to the nighttime *coincidentia oppositorum* of juxtaposition and analogy. If men and women can be dandies, and dandies are creatures of changeable pose, then perhaps gender is but part of self-creation, not god-given and immutable but author-given and subject to change.

Yet it is precisely this set of realizations that Tatiana never reaches. Like d'Albert of *Mademoiselle de Maupin*, who dresses as a bear but fails to leave the world of fixed category, Tatiana "reads" the dream as a commentary on the daytime world of fixity. In the closing chapter of the verse novel, she reveals through tears that she still loves Onegin but intends to remain a virtuous wife.[9] That is, she remains true, as Nabokov points out, to the ro-

[9]Nabokov writes: "It should be noted, in relation to this and the other novels Tatiana read, that their heroines . . . remained as faithful to their respective husbands as Princess N. (born Tatiana Larin) will be to hers" (Comm 2:342).

mantic novels in which heroines adopt a "higher" stance within a fixed hierarchy, the pose of the faithful female spouse. She never allows herself to question the categories and institutions and plots of her waking world, not even after the dream reveals itself as clearly prophetic of her name-day party and Onegin's duel with Lenski. What is more, Tatiana feels the plot she has chosen as a natural, emotional choice, not an aesthetic decision. Tatiana cannot see herself as a fictional heroine, although Pushkin, Nabokov, and we ourselves can.

Nabokov sees the potential for beautiful chaos in Pushkin's poetry; indeed his commentary on the poem acts to define within it ever more layers, ever more centrifugal a force propelling it into a vast array of other languages, other people's books, "other people's megrims." In this exquisitely detailed commentary Nabokov gradually makes a powerful claim: that Pushkin grounds his complex method in the French and the female. We turn now from the poem, with its dual figures of dandyism—crossing and recrossing the lines of gender even as they cling to category—to Nabokov's "Commentary." There we seek the metamorphoses of Nabokov's dandy, the movement through the female to a world beyond the categorization of gender, the world of modern beauty itself.

A MAN WITH A WARDROBE: PUSHKIN'S DANDIES, NABOKOV'S DANDIES

Nabokov's "Commentary" to *Eugene Onegin* constitutes a major twentieth-century essay on dandyism, comparable in scope to Barbey's "Du Dandysme et de G. Brummell" and Baudelaire's "Le peintre de la vie moderne." Just as Barbey elevates the footnote to the status of art, Nabokov makes it an intrinsic part of his translation, as inseparable from the long poem it accompanies as, in the end, Nabokov is inseparable from Pushkin. Just as "Le peintre de la vie moderne" combines genres and subjects, so does Nabokov's "Commentary." It contains elements of autobiography, biography, literary criticism, history, linguistic and aesthetic theory, political and social history, and botanical and zoological observation. For the dandy-artist the fluidity of category must begin at home, in his conception of genre. When we shift from genre to style and tone, the complexity increases by an order of magnitude. Some notes are but a few words long; others are essays in their own right. Some feature a pointed "scientific" accuracy; others bounce or pirouette toward fantasy.

The "Commentary" addresses itself specifically and frequently to the subject of dandyism, since it glosses a poem about dandies. Beau Brummell makes several appearances, as Nabokov chooses him to personify the type of dandyism Onegin aspires to. Like Barbey, Nabokov uses Captain Jesse's biography as his source of information about Brummell.[10] Thus, for example, he glosses Pushkin's line "he's driving home to dress" (*EO* 1.22; p. 104) with " 'The beau of the times invariably went home to change . . . after the opera, previously to attending . . . either ball or supper' (see Captain Jesse's *Brummell*, II, 58)" (Comm 2:97). We learn about Brummell's album, toilette, clothing, and meals because they are, for Nabokov, the originals of which Onegin's are the translation.

Nabokov even concocts one of his own literary pastries for us, a dandy's *jeu d'esprit*, with the mirroring help of Brummell and *his* commentator and editor, Captain Jesse. Glossing lines in chapter 4 of *Onegin* about the siege of Izmail in canto 7 of *Don Juan*, Nabokov first connects Byron to Pushkin through the linguistic hodgepodge:

> In the jocular lines devoted to the siege of Izmail in can. VII of *Don Juan*, among bungled Russian names that had already been misspelled in their passage through German transliteration into French and English, names with ragged *w*'s and shoddy *sch*'s still hanging about them or, on the contrary, losing their *h*'s in Frenchified forms, there is, in st. XVII, a "Mouskin Pouskin" (Musin-Pushkin) rhyming with "through skin" and "new skin." (The Counts Musin-Pushkin are distantly related to the plain Pushkins.)
>
> (Comm 2:477)

As if this "distant relation" were not distant enough, bringing to mind some of Charles Kinbote's "free" reconstructions in *his* commentary, Nabokov slyly points to his own (mad?) tendency toward overreading, glossing this gloss with another:

> The name seems to have sorely puzzled Englishmen: "The author of the pretended tour is a Russian prince, Mouska Pouska . . . [nobody] could possibly equal his misrepresentations about English society." Thus writes George Brummell to a lady, from Caen, on Jan. 1, 1836, a year before he began losing his mind (quoted in Jesse, *Brummell*, vol. II, ch. 22).
>
> (Comm 2:478)

Here is the darkness of Brummell's madness transformed to a bright flickering of verbal stage business; Nabokov's mad heroes, dandies themselves,

---

[10]According to Field (54), Nabokov knew the Russian translator of Barbey d'Aurevilly, but I can find no evidence that Nabokov knew Barbey's "Du Dandysme" or used it in interpreting *Onegin*.

are related to the mad Brummell much as "Mouska-Pouska" is to Pushkin. Distantly, connected by a laugh.

Nabokov traces the development of the dandy as he metamorphoses subtly from the romantic hero. Onegin, Nabokov believes, differs from earlier models (such as Constant's Adolphe) in one crucial way: Onegin cannot have "true-to-life" emotions because the central point about him is his very counterfeit human existence:

> . . . Onegin . . . is seen to grow fluid and flaccid as soon as he starts to feel, as soon as he departs from the existence he has acquired from his maker in terms of colorful parody and as a catchall for many irrelevant and immortal matters. On the other hand, as a physical being, Onegin in comparison to the gray engraving of Adolphe, is superbly stereoscopic, a man with a wardrobe, a man with a set of recognizable gestures, a man existing forever in a local world colored and crowded with Pushkin's people, Pushkin's emotions, memories, melodies and fancies. (Comm 3:101)

In glossing the nature of Pushkin's dandy, Nabokov describes nothing less than the nature of his own fictional characters. Emotions in Nabokov's novel arise not from figures of psychological verisimilitude, whatever that is, but from the very patterns generated by details: clothing, weather, words spoken, songs overheard, colors. Nina's yellow scarf in "Spring in Fialta" for a moment carries her emotions; we will never ascertain them by seeking her "personality." Nabokov reads into Pushkin's method precisely what he reads out of Pushkin in creating his own novels. "Real life" gives way to a process of verbal construction; the dandy is both creature and creator in that process.

Just as Nabokov is derivative of Pushkin, so *Onegin* is "made" of other works of literature. To this Nabokovian principle we must add two corollaries. First, the dandy is for Nabokov a creature of (Baudelairean) "vaporization." The process of glossing Pushkin's poem of dandyism is a process of adding author upon author, of linking ever more texts, allusions, languages, facts, surmises. What Nabokov constructs, taking his cue from the very artificialities of the text he translates and studies, is an ever vaster context for Pushkin's work. Pushkin stands not at its center, for the very idea of center is one he rejects. If everything in *Onegin* is a translation of something else—feint, sleight-of-hand, nuance, parody, travesty—then direct meaning dissipates into texture. By glossing the poem and bringing to light ever finer patterns in the texture, Nabokov's mental connections are, as it were, woven into an already existing tapestry. He may deepen, intensify one of Pushkin's passages, or he may knit into it a passage from his own autobiography. Nabokov is aggrandized in his version of *Onegin*, but he is also, paradoxically, potentially lost. Where to touch down, if there is no center? What salvation in texture can there be?

To the principle of artificiality and the corollary of vaporization, we must add one final corollary, that of the necessity of the truly modern. Here we are on familiar ground: the dandy and the phenomenon of dandyism must change, must engage in metamorphosis. Artifice must be constantly renewed; left alone, it moulders into false romanticism, as much Nabokov's concern as it was Stevens's and Cather's. The fictional quality of our world, our very cultural constructions, must be constantly recast in new patterns as the old wear thin, or are claimed by the vulgar masses who want comfort rather than truth, common sense rather than sensitivity. Pushkin's poem is not an allegory, but it includes allegorical hints in its pastiche of types and modes. Tatiana reads the old-style romances and fails to (refuses to) transform herself into the more modern genre. Onegin is a bit more modern in style; the inconclusiveness of his life, the shadowy fragments of "Onegin's Voyage" and chapter 10, suggest that Pushkin recognized the necessity of transforming Onegin to the next stage, whatever that would be. Lenski dies because he insists on the dead romance of love and marriage. The truly artificial depends on process and change, and so Nabokov must search for an honorable way to bring his translation to a close. This he finds in the dark radiance of pure texture, the decentered, always provisional "truth" of Pushkin's genius as it issues from his mysterious black ancestor.

GANNIBAL'S SISTER: DYING INTO THE MODERN

In Appendix 1 to the "Commentary" to *Eugene Onegin*, titled "Abram Gannibal" (Comm 3:387–447), Nabokov attempts to rescue from legend Gannibal, Pushkin's black great-grandfather, although, as it turns out, neither his name nor his blackness can be established.   Nabokov tells us in *Strong Opinions* that "true art deals not with the genus, and not even with the species, but with an aberrant individual of the species" (155). Pushkin, for Nabokov, deviates from the norm by virtue of his poetic genius. His special nature is equally a matter of race, however, since race is a subspecies for Nabokov the lepidopterist, a means of classifying the aberrant individual.[11] Pushkin's racial background so fascinates Nabokov that

[11]William L. Brown, a professor of entomology at Cornell, reminisces in Gibian and Parker (224–25) about Nabokov's belief in naming ever more subspecies (races) within the

when he argues, in "Pushkin, or, The Real and the Plausible," that the poet can never be objectively rescued from the past, Nabokov begins his fictionalization in this way: "Here, then, is this brusque, stocky man, whose small swarthy hand (for there was something Negroid and something simian about this great Russian) wrote the first and most glorious pages of our poetry. Here is the blue fire of his gaze, in striking contrast with the dark chestnut hue of his frizzy hair" (PRP 40). The attraction is to contrast itself, to one man whose race in a Russian context renders him different from others of his species, and who himself embodies contrasting images, great Russian and Negroid, blue eyes and dark frizzy hair, human and simian. The implied racism of "aberrant" and "simian" is not to be ignored here—certainly the dandy tradition as I have sketched it includes racism.[12]

Nabokov, in writing "Abram Gannibal," continues a pattern he has established throughout the "Commentary" proper, that of questioning the strength of categories. The Russian masterpiece *Onegin* is made of French words, images, characters: the category "Russian" must expand to include, or melt into, the category "French." Similarly Pushkin is in his deepest self both Russian and Abyssinian, both white and black, both the center, the *fons*, the foundation, and—because of the problems in determining his history—the forever decentered, the unlocatable, that which cannot be known and cannot be ignored. "Abram Gannibal" concerns itself with the search for a man who will never be found; Gannibal is thus only an intensification of Pushkin himself, who can only be re-created, never known, who can only exist as a kind of "monstrous hoax" (PRP 40).

Gannibal suggests, too, again with the flavor if not the method of allegory, the very secret at the heart of Pushkin's genius as he expresses it in *Onegin*. Pushkin's "pre-life" is African; this biographical appendix captures and refracts the dark light emanating from the elusive cadences of Pushkin's poetry, its slippery, parodic, derivative manner which is, for Nabokov, its only subject. Like Barbey's "vie en l'air," Gannibal's life as Nabokov presents it is all construction from documents, all a deliberate fash-

---

butterfly species, which was his specialty. His scientific practice thus parallels his aesthetic preference for the detail over the type; it is often by microscopic detail that subspecies are established.

[12] All six of the writers featured in this volume wrote out their racism as well as their misogyny. The dandy's elitism exists at the expense of the "other," whether that other be defined in terms of sex, ethnicity, religion, or class. One motivation for this project was my desire to understand why otherwise admirable writers could so offend me by some of their social views.

ioning out of imperfect materials. And it is here that Nabokov finally lifts the lid of the "boîte de nuit" (PRP 40), the past itself, the truth of darkness, to reveal that white is as black and Russian is as French *because* male is as female. If Pushkin is the most profound source of Russian genius in poetry, if Gannibal is the profound, hidden source of Pushkin, Gannibal's sister Lahann and her *mundus muliebris* are the profound, hidden source of Gannibal's truth. Pushkin's is the house that woman built.

This is emphatically not, however, the story of the woman behind the man. For, as we shall see, woman's truth in "Abram Gannibal" is the truth of the drowning of the female and, in a watery element, its transformation into a world of analogical gender, male as female, female as male. Nabokov's apparent respect for dichotomous gender and its accompanying roles is the pose that enables him first to feminize literature and then to consider gender itself as mistlike, illusory, the very stuff of the fictional impulse and artifact. This is the story that Appendix 1, fittingly "other" than the main commentary, has to tell.

Why does Nabokov choose to research so thoroughly (there are seventy-two items in the bibliography to the appendix, many of them multivolumed) and write so painstakingly about the so-called Blackamoor of Peter the Great? In part because the text of *Onegin* demands it as gloss when Pushkin writes, "beneath the sky of my Africa . . . to sigh for somber Russia" (*EO* 1.50; p. 117). In part because Nabokov likes the chase, as he writes to Edmund Wilson:

> I have greatly enjoyed all that tremendous research. One of the most difficult clues to pursue proved to be the origin of Pushkin's Abyssinian ancestor. I do not know how many old and new maps of that country I have examined, and how many travels (Jesuits, Protestants, Bruce, Salt, etc.) I have studied in order to find "Lagon" (Logo), a town mentioned by "Gannibal" (that great-grandfather)—who in a certain fascinating sense was a descendant of Rasselas! (*Nabokov-Wilson Letters* 292)

But Nabokov writes "Abram Gannibal" in part, too, because it solves the problem of closure for the "Commentary": not only does an appendix respect the integrity of the main body of the text while challenging it, but this particular appendix takes as its subject inconclusivity itself. The evidence of Gannibal's life is simply inadequate to the task of recomposing that life, especially its earlier years. We might even say that "Abram Gannibal" parodies the "Commentary," where Nabokov adopts the persona of the passionately objective and erudite scholar while allowing himself some most unscholarly flights of fancy. Here, Nabokov must exercise the purest surmise; "Abram Gannibal" parodies the "Commentary" because it both identifies with and detaches itself from it.[13] Nabokov writes it as well because it is an exercise in genealogy; since he self-consciously creates himself as Pushkin's descendant, it would be well to know the very darkest sources of his own genius. And how conveniently life mimics life, for it happens that Pushkin's great-grandfather, like his distant descendant Vladimir Nabokov, suffered a world-shaking experience of exile, from Africa all the way to the tsar's court of Russia.

Finally, however, Nabokov writes "Abram Gannibal" for aesthetic reasons, as a means of exploring the death of the false romantic and its reemergence as modern beauty. "Abram Gannibal" is a bit of biography, but it functions for Nabokov as a parable about the true path of art. At its source is the episode of leave-taking, a moving into exile marked by a woman's death by drowning. Reconstructing Gannibal's story, Nabokov attempts to see beyond his culture by exploring the place of gender in his world.

Nabokov weaves "Abram Gannibal" of fact and surmise; it is a sign of Nabokov's genius that he manages almost to convince us that one is the other.[14] In his search for Gannibal, Nabokov gives names themselves a most compelling authority: that is, he wants above all to *name*—both this ancestor and the place from which he came. Only then, he implies, will the mystery be solved. In fact, he pins his entire web of surmise upon one name, that of Gannibal's sister. In the shadowy world of Africa, her name is the source that must illuminate all, and her death is the birth of the modern. It happens as follows.

Nabokov manages to piece together an outline of Gannibal's life from "scanty and conflicting data." We learn of his birth (1693?) in Abyssinia(?), his capture there, probably as part of the slave trade, his transport from Constantinople to Russia, his training as a military engineer in Russia and France. Significantly, Nabokov finds that during his stay in France Gan-

---

[13]As Frosch in "Parody and Authenticity in *Lolita*" (Rivers and Nicol 171–87) comments, "Nabokov uses the energies of his style—its parody, its centering of language, its flamboyant self-consciousness—first against the spirit of romance and then in behalf of it. . . . It [style] functions as a defensive strategy both against the romanticism of the material and against the anti-romanticism of the 'jury' " (184). In his romance of Pushkin, Nabokov defuses criticism by parodying his own method.

[14]Toker correctly argues that in Nabokov's biography of Abram Gannibal, historiography gives way to the creation of fiction and poetic "motifs." However, Toker does not examine Nabokov's process of self-creation in the fiction of Lahann, nor does she raise the issue of gender.

nibal (otherwise known as Avram Petrov) adopts as his name the Russianized form of the name Hannibal, a favorite French hero; thus he resembles one of Pushkin's Gallicized characters. We learn of Gannibal's successful career, two marriages, children—his son Osip is Pushkin's maternal grandfather—and his death on his estate, Mihaylovskoe, in 1781.

Nabokov begins rather nonchalantly, claiming that the appendix is the "outcome of a few odd moments spent in the admirable libraries of Cornell and Harvard universities," but before he finishes he argues with great intensity for one particular interpretation of the data. Not only is Gannibal's precise name unknown (obviously his original name is lost, but we have several versions of his European name to choose from), but even the color of his skin, his "Negroid" appearance, is uncertain. His German biographer refers to him as an "Afrikanischer Mohr" and a "Neger"; Nabokov interprets: his "type [Abyssinian] represents a Hamito-Semitic component of the Caucasian race; and a Negroid strain *may* so strongly predominate in *some* tribes that the term 'Negro' is in *such cases* applicable in a *general sense*" (Comm 3:396, emphasis added). To the ambiguity of his color Nabokov adds a set of possible names, all of which vary according to French and Russian spelling. Gannibal is a man who floats among names and races. And among birthplaces. The German biography is the principal source of both information and misinformation about Gannibal's life, and Nabokov describes it with characteristic venom:

> pompously worded in idiomatic but none-too-literate German . . . it contains certain details, such as a few names and dates that only Gannibal would have remembered; and . . . it also includes a number of passages, contradicted either by historical documents . . . or by plain logic, that were obviously inserted by the biographer with a view to pad the story, to span its gaps, and to give a eulogistic (but actually absurd) interpretation of this or that event in the hero's life.   (Comm 3:392)

A petition written by Gannibal himself (1742) states, "I was born in the demesne of my father, in the town of Lagona [or Lagono or Lagon]" (Comm 3:398), and in trying to establish the town's location, Nabokov depends on the very biography he despises: "On the strength of the German biography, I assume that this town is in Abyssinia" (Comm 3:398). Nabokov sorts through many travel accounts and maps documenting villages and towns in Ethiopia, before deciding to refer to the place simply as "L": "I would consider . . . the determination of 'L' as not settled at the time of writing [1956]; but I am inclined to assume that it was situated in the general region of northern Abyssinia" (Comm 3:405). One particular aspect of Lagona interests him. Since *g* and *h* are both transliterated by a Russian gamma, and since the locative case of Lagona does not "disclose the ultima of the nominative," Lagona might be Lagon, Lahon, Lagona, Lahona, Lagono, or Lahono. Thus, "the similarity between the name of the sister [Lahann] mentioned in the German biography and the name of the native town mentioned only in the petition is very disturbing. I have not found— within the limited scope of my reading—any instance of an Abyssinian child receiving the name of its birthplace" (Comm 3:399).

In fact, the name of the sister will be central to his interpretation of all the evidence before him, in this reconstruction of Abram Gannibal. Nabokov grapples throughout his study with the inferior German biography, the longest document pertaining directly to Gannibal. In most cases, he quotes a section in order to refute it at length. But in two cases he accepts its account. The first is, as I have mentioned, the German biographer's belief that Gannibal was originally Abyssinian. The other is its account of Gannibal's sister. The two are connected in Nabokov's mind through the Lagon/Lahann "coincidence." In the section of his appendix devoted to the sister, Nabokov quotes at length the German biography's mythology, at first, it seems, only because he enjoys it. The biography describes a world in which women wield oblique power: Gannibal's "father, according to the Moslem custom, had very many wives (even up to about thirty, with a correspondingly large progeny), the numerous old princesses and their children joined forces in the common intention of protecting themselves and their offspring." Why was Abram sent so young as hostage to Constantinople? "Since [Abram] was the youngest son of one of the youngest wives, who did not have at court as many supporters [as the elder princesses had], these contrived through trickery and intrigue, almost by force, to put him on a Turkish vessel and turned him over to the fate that had been assigned to him" (Comm 3:397–98). Gannibal, so the myth goes, was exiled from a world of women to the cruelties of the Russian court (where he would be regarded as a curiosity, like a dwarf or a jester) because women chose not to protect him.

Nabokov quotes at length the German biographer's account of the sister:

> His only full sister, Lahann, who was some years older than he, had yet sufficient courage to oppose this act of violence. She tried everything, but had to yield to number; she accompanied him to the very deck of the small ship, still nursing the hope that she might obtain by entreaties the freedom of this much beloved brother or purchase it with her jewels; but when she found that her tender efforts . . . remained fruitless to the last, she cast herself in

despair into the sea and was drowned. To the very end of his days, the venerable old man [Abram] would shed tears of the tenderest friendship and love as he recollected her; for although he was still very young at the time of that tragic event, yet whenever he thought of her this vague memory would become new and complete for him; and this offering [Abram's tears] was the better deserved by her sisterly tenderness since she had struggled so hard to free him, and since these two were the only siblings from the same mother.

(Comm 3:405–6)

The entire passage, arising as it does from the German text Nabokov regards as a "grotesque fabric," will of course, we believe, be dismissed. Quite the contrary. Here is Nabokov's gloss on it:

The receding ship, in whose wake swam—somewhat ahead of the romantic era—a passionate sister, might be easily condemned to dwindle to a reed raft on a seasonable river; indeed, the entire event might be dismissed by the cynic as one of those fairy-tale recollections that old age confuses with true happenings; but there is one reason it should command attention: the name "Lahann" is, I find, a plausible Abyssinian name.

(Comm 3:406)

Gannibal must be from Abyssinia because the German biographer (otherwise untrustworthy) tells us he is. Now we must believe this story—and none of the others from the same source—because this woman's name is a plausible Abyssinian name, and what is more, it coincides strangely with a possible name of Gannibal's village. The circularity of reasoning is so apparent as to seem impertinent.

Nabokov has *chosen* a center for Gannibal in Abyssinia and in his sister. Together they anchor his story. Nabokov never says that the story is true, only that it should "command attention." That is, it is a myth he finds interesting, useful. Why? Perhaps because he seeks a germ of truth, a fixed point, a concentration or essence in this excursion into the dark "boîte de nuit" of his own artistic past. He uses a woman's name to ground his entire Abyssinian surmise; at the dark heart of Pushkin's truth stands, first, a woman's world from which a man has been exiled (that womb from which each of us is exiled) and, second, a particular woman who allows us to locate the male before she drowns. She drowns as a figure of pre-romantic myth for Nabokov, but not before he has taken her name, Lahann, and transformed it from name to a loose set of associations, to etymological texture, to footnote:

In Turkish, a language that Gannibal must have been able to understand at one time, *lahana* means "cabbage" and *lahin* "note," "tone," "melody," "modulation," and "mispronunciation," and *layan* means "softness," "gentleness," *Zartlichkeit*. In several Oriental languages, the stem *lah-* is associated with "loose woman" (cf. the Russian *lahanka*, a slattern, Pskovan dial., and *lahudra*, an inferior whore).   (Comm 3:406, n. 20)

From the earthiness of cabbage, to harmony and gentleness, to fallenness, from the hodgepodge of Turkish to Arabic to oriental languages to Russian, Nabokov transforms Lahann, as we watch, from romantic type to modern abstraction. Just as Nina dies in "Spring in Fialta" (1938), Lahann dies in 1956 in Nabokov's scholarly fiction of Gannibal's origin. Like Barbey, pricking out the dandy's costume into ethereal lace, Nabokov uses the woman as a shard of glass with which to prick out the tired romantic (woman sacrifices herself for a man), to transform it to texture, even as he insists on the fiction he has constructed as, in some sense, "true."

It is, finally, the blending of the artificial and the natural, Nabokov's understanding that art and nature, fiction and truth, mirror each other in a vast post-Wordsworthian rolling translation, a deep reflexivity, which was his great contribution to twentieth-century art. He closes the appendix with a playful cadenza on the theme of women's song, quoting a passage from an Abyssinian travel account by Charles Poncet: "Certain women with tabors . . . began to sing . . . in so doleful a tone that I could not hinder being seized with grief," and executing a triumphant pirouette in which the facts of Gannibal's history and the images of Nabokov's poetic imagination spin into one blur:

> One's marginal imagination conjures up here many a pleasing possibility. *We recall Coleridge's Abyssinian maid (Kubla Khan, 1797)* . . . singing of "Mount Abora." . . . We may further imagine that Coleridge's and Poncet's doleful singer was none other than Pushkin's great-great-grandmother; that her lord, either of Poncet's two hosts, was Pushkin's great-great-grandfather; and that the latter was a son of Cella Christos, Dr. Johnson's Rasselas. There is nothing in the annals of Russian Pushkinology to restrain one from the elaboration of such fancies.   (Comm 3:441, emphasis added)

Gannibal, like Eugene Onegin, is a phenomenon of words and stories. His "real life" cannot be seized. What is left is the rich possibility of making connections, recombining, refashioning. This is, of course, a portrait of a method—Pushkin's and Nabokov's—and as a method it has an origin in the mythology of gender. What makes (male) artists capable of the modern is the drowned and resurrected women (count the instances of Ophelia in Nabokov's works), the sister whose name is the signpost, quickly removed, to the Nabokovian "divide" where art is as life, life is as art. Art itself is the reconstituted *mundus muliebris* for Nabokov as it was for Baudelaire. Not an androgyne, a man "completed" by a woman, Nabokov re-creates the dark woman at the heart of his own Pushkinian genius, the woman who lives again as his art and as his life. "Sirin" and "Vivian" Darkbloom alike know the attraction of the analogical, male as female, female as male.

Let us turn to the reflected glories of *Pale Fire*, a novel that again enacts the drowning of romance and its resurrection as high modernist art, the drowning of a woman and the renewed life of analogical gender.

MILLE DE MES LARCINS:
DANDYISM AND PUSHKINISM IN *PALE FIRE*

It is a critical commonplace that in *Pale Fire* Nabokov parodies his own scholarly edition of *Onegin*. Even Kinbote/Botkin seems strangely aware of the Nabokovian endeavor in which he participates, claiming, "I have no desire to twist and batter an unambiguous *apparatus criticus* into the monstrous semblance of a novel" (*PF* 54).

But *Pale Fire*, as a test case supporting my claim that Pushkin inspires Nabokov's oeuvre, must go beyond self-parody. It must in some way be about Pushkin as well—his subjects and methods and works. Here the difficulties begin: neither Shade nor Kinbote is a poet resembling Pushkin. Shade's poem "Pale Fire" is as nearly sincere in tone as *Onegin* is posing and precious. Only Shade's "conclusion" to his meditation on Hazel's death links him to Pushkin: "Just this: not text, but texture; not the dream/ But a topsy-turvical coincidence, / not flimsy nonsense, but a web of sense" (*PF* 44). Pushkin's reliance on tone and texture rather than plot and characterization, a reliance so convincingly documented by Nabokov's own scholarship, places him within mirror-distance of John Shade.

The relation of Pushkin to *Pale Fire* blossoms into complexity, however, only when we look at details of *Pale Fire*, for it is in its details, and the patterns into which Nabokov arranges them, that the meaning of the work inheres. I begin with one example, deliberately chosen for its slightness, for our tendency to overlook or dismiss it, as a way of fastening onto the gossamer threads of allusion which are the finest weave of *Pale Fire*. Kinbote glosses the passage in which Shade describes his parents, both ornithologists:

> The poet's mother, nee Caroline Lukin, assisted him in his work and drew the admirable figures of his *Birds of Mexico*, which I remember having seen in my friend's house. What the obituarist does not know is that Lukin comes

> from Luke, as also do Locock and Luxon and Lukashevich. It represents one
> of the many instances when the amorphous-looking but live and personal
> hereditary patronymic grows, sometimes in fantastic shapes, around the
> common pebble of a Christian name. The Lukins are an old Essex family.
> Other names derive from professions such as Rymer, Scrivener, Linner (one
> who illuminates parchments), Botkin (one who makes bottekins, fancy foot-
> wear) and thousands of others.   (*PF* 64–65)

What we recognize first is always what we expect to see: here, Kinbote's
excruciating exertions to bring Lukin around, finally, to the subject always
at hand, Botkin himself. But I submit that it is a deliberately created "coincidence" that in speaking of Shade's mother, Nabokov borrows from another study he has recently finished, about an old Abyssinian family related to Caroline Lukin's "old Essex family." Gannibal's sister and her
birthplace, the first location of Pushkin's genius, are also a matter of *L*'s:
"There is no reason why this Lahaina, rather than Logo or Logote, should
not have been the Lagona or Lahona of Gannibal's petition. . . . I would
consider therefore the determination of 'L' as not settled at the time of
writing. . . . The name 'Lahann' is, I find, a plausible Abyssinian name,"
and so forth (Comm 3:405–6).

What Nabokov parodies in *Pale Fire* is this scholarly tone poem in the
key of *L*, the sound of a list of names. And he slips into *Pale Fire* another
nearly private joke. "Lukashevich"—the final metamorphosis of Caroline
Lukin's "patronymic"—is a parodic conflation of "Luka Vladislavich," a
minor figure in Gannibal's drama (Comm 3:421–22). Such odd parodic details exist more often for Nabokov's private enjoyment than as a key to
meaning. He discusses in his introduction to *Bend Sinister* his propensity
for such camouflaged borrowings: "What pleases me most is the wayside
murmur of this or that hidden theme" (*Bend Sinister* xii). Such details
sometimes can, however, provide the key to patterns of meaning which are
important. If we can see a bit of the texture for what it is, then the entire
pattern shifts into focus.

But this should sound familiar, for Nabokov's claim for Pushkin's poem
is identical. That is, once we see that Pushkin borrows specific details,
words and phrases from French poets, then we can see exactly what Pushkin attempts in his poem: the creation of people made out of words, others' words. For example, Nabokov translates a few of Pushkin's lines as
"sometimes a white-skinned, dark-eyed girl's / young and fresh kiss" (4.39,
lines 3–4). He glosses these lines: "the translator is confronted with the fact
that Pushkin masks an autobiographical allusion under the disguise of a
literal translation from André Chénier, whom, however, he does not men-

tion in any appended note" (Comm 2:462). Pushkin deceives doubly. Not only must a good translator know the Chénier line "le baiser jeune et frais d'une blanche aux yeux noirs" (Comm 2:463) in order to see Pushkin's theft (or borrowing), but he must know Pushkin's life to understand that "our poet camouflaged in the present stanza his own experience, an affair he was having that summer at Mihaylovskoe [estate granted originally to Gannibal] . . . with a delicate-looking slave girl" (Comm 2:462).

I call Pushkin's unacknowledged translation of Chénier's line a theft because Nabokov sees it as such. In fact, he makes such plagiarism a central concern of *Pale Fire* when he alludes to the lines from *Timon of Athens* which give the novel its name.[15] But Nabokov does more than allude to such unacknowledged borrowing; he engages in it himself, as we shall see. *Pushkin's method becomes Nabokov's method*, articulated and blessed by none other than Chénier, in a poem Nabokov quotes in French in his "Commentary" and in English (his own translation) in "The Servile Path":

> A bumptious judge, scanning my works, denounces
> All of a sudden, with loud cries, a score
> Of passages, from so and so translated.
> He names their author, and on finding them,
> Admires himself, pleased with his learning: why
> Does he not come to me? To him I'll show
> A thousand thefts of mine he may not know.
>
> (109)

A thousand thefts—"mille de mes larcins": the dandy has always concealed while revealing. Such thefts are there for any poor critic-sleuth to discover. So nonchalant and impertinent is the dandy-artist that he will be glad to show the critic even the thefts she has not discovered. Chénier, Pushkin, and Nabokov are a law unto themselves, in the best of the dandy's tradition.

To discover Chénier's presence in *Eugene Onegin* is to discover a web of

[15]I'll example you with thievery:
The sun's a thief, and with his great attraction
Robs the vast sea; the moon's an arrant thief,
And her pale fire she snatches from the sun;
The sea's a thief, whose liquid surge resolves
The moon into salt tears; the earth's a thief,
That feeds and breeds by a composture stol'n
From general excrement. Each thing's a thief.
  (*Timon of Athens* 4.3.431–38)

allusion and meaning. Likewise, to discover one of Nabokov's thefts, the presence of Robert Louis Stevenson's novel *Prince Otto* in *Pale Fire*, is to move with stunning speed to a central pattern of the novel otherwise only fleetingly apparent. Nabokov's fascination with the fluidity of gender, his exploration of hierarchy and of dichotomous gender as it metamorphoses into analogical gender: this is the pattern revealed when we see the details of characterization, plot, and setting of *Prince Otto* making unacknowledged appearances in the prose of *Pale Fire*. At the moment we discover one of his "thefts," the half-buried *Prince Otto*, Nabokov moves one step closer to Pushkin himself, whose works also require such discoveries of its readers.

Putting Stevenson aside for the moment, let us look at the relation Nabokov creates between himself and his master. If Nabokov's appropriation of Pushkin's method in *Pale Fire* rests on such parallel thievery (Pushkin of Chénier, Nabokov of Stevenson), that appropriation is fired by a fierce pressure toward fictionalization itself. That is, Nabokov explores in *Pale Fire* the limits of "making up" Pushkin. In "The Real and the Plausible" he describes the necessarily imaginative, as opposed to "objective," re-creation of Pushkin. One begins to re-create the beloved figure by commenting on one of his masterpieces. Such work beckons with all the seductiveness of imaginative reconstruction. Not only does Nabokov allow himself from time to time within the "Commentary" a fillip of fantasy, but the very nebulous quality of Pushkin's text, the very weight of Nabokov's extraordinary knowledge about Pushkin, constantly urge him to read between the lines or beyond the verse novel's eight chapters. Even establishing the text presents problems. Should unpublished manuscript passages matter? Which ones might legitimately be included in the text?[16]

Nabokov models Kinbote upon himself. Just as Nabokov explains in his essays on translation the necessity of context to accuracy, so Kinbote breathily explains that "without my notes Shade's text simply has no human reality at all since the human reality of such a poem as his . . . with the omission of many pithy lines carelessly rejected by him, has to depend entirely on the reality of its author and his surroundings, attachments, and so forth, a reality that only my notes can provide" (*PF* 12). Kinbote's reliance on far more than the established text, his willingness even to fabricate passages on which he then comments, constitute a fictional postscript to Nabokov's essay on the art of creating a plausible Pushkin. The art is necessarily fictional, but *fantasy* is not good fiction. A spectrum of "Pushkin

---

[16]See Comm 3:166 for Nabokov's discussion of this topic.

reconstruction" forms: on one end, the "incorruptible," precise translator; toward the center the increscent novelist; at the opposite end the madman who believes that he can fully appropriate Pushkin, that "Nabokov is Pushkin." What saves the novelist from sliding into madness is precisely his own awareness of the artifice of what he does. So Nabokov deliberately plants within *Pale Fire* various "stolen" bits from *Prince Otto*. The act itself recaptures and appropriates Pushkin's method, but the cool deliberation with which it is carried out ensures that Nabokov remains in control of Nabokov. The dandy's joke must never be on himself.

Nabokov writes in the tradition of dandyism when he claims the writings of others as his own; it is not a simple case of plagiarism, but rather a sense perhaps expressed by the hero of Baudelaire's "La Fanfarlo" when he imagines claiming the work of others: "c'est donc de moi—il n'y a que l'espace d'un tiret" (*OC* 486; it's by me—there's only the space of a hyphen). Baudelaire translates De Quincey's *Confessions* but adds passages of his own, thus placing his mark upon it; he rewrites Poe's "Man of the Crowd" in "Le peintre de la vie moderne" without fully acknowledging his source.

Pale Fire claims Pushkin's *Onegin* doubly: first in its free "translation" of Eugene Onegin into Charles Kinbote, and then in its translation of Pushkin's allusive/plagiaristic method into Nabokov's own "borrowing" from Stevenson. Let us begin with the first, Kinbote as parody of Pushkin's dandy Eugene Onegin. Once again, it is the detail that reveals all. Here is "King Charles" in flight: "What is the time, ḳot or? He pressed his repeater and, undismayed, it hissed and tinkled out ten twenty-one" (*PF* 92). Readers of Nabokov's "Commentary" to *Onegin* know that Eugene Onegin wears, as part of his dandy's costume, a "Bréguet repeater" and that Nabokov writes a substantial note explaining just what this (French) watch is (Comm 2:69).

Such details, transposed from *Onegin* (both poem and commentary) to *Pale Fire*, are legion—I can mention only a few. Kinbote refers to himself ironically as a "beau ténébreux" (*PF* 108) because Nabokov refers to Onegin as such. Shade and Kinbote contrast with each other so fully because Lenski and Onegin differ: "They got together; wave and stone, / verse and prose, ice and flame, / were not so different from one another" (*EO* 2.13; p. 131). Kinbote's dream "poem" of Zembla's glory will never find an audience in part because of the lines of Evariste Parny which Nabokov quotes in the "Commentary": "Et mes vers une rêverie / Sans espérance et sans lecteur" (Comm 2:379; And my lines a reverie without hope and without reader). Or perhaps it is these lines by Pierre Lebrun, another French poet claimed by Pushkin, whom Kinbote parodies: "Martyr des maux rêvés plus que des maux soufferts, / Au gré d'une inconstante et sauvage tristesse," (Comm 3:85; Martyr of imagined ills rather than suffered ills, at the mercy of a changing and wild sadness). Kinbote's yearning, nostalgia, and even self-pity suggest that the same minor poets on whom Pushkin based his great poem lurk deep in the background of *Pale Fire*, too. Kinbote believes the poem "Pale Fire" to be a circle, its first and last lines identical, because Nabokov sees *Eugene Onegin* as a circle (Comm 3:300). Shade's images often mix artifice with reality—for example, "Whose spurred feet have crossed / From left to right the blank page of the road?"—because Pushkin's images have done the same: "Neater than modish parquetry, / the ice-clad river shines" (*EO* 4.42; p.194). Even Kinbote's rejection by the people of New Wye has a source in Pushkin's rejection by a woman he loved, who writes in her diary: "A Negro profile acquired from his maternal generation did not embellish his face. Add to this . . . affected manners, an arrogant way of looking at the women he chose to love, the oddities of his natural character and of his assumed one, and [his] boundless *amour-propre*" (Comm 3:202). Every misunderstood, maligned, and "difficult" exile is for Nabokov a type of the black outsider, the African in Russia.

Kinbote is a dandy: he removes his gloves finger by finger, buys chocolate-coated cookies and caviar, rejects the forms of bourgeois marriage, considers himself superior to almost everyone, adopts a mask of insolent composure and exquisite good manners. He is most intensely a dandy in his very eccentricity shading into freakishness and madness.[17] Like Brummell in exile, Kinbote has failed in translation. He wants above all for Shade to recognize him. "Je me vois vu" (*L* 4:102), Barbey tells his Trébutien—but Kinbote never considers himself "seen" by his Shade.

Like Barbey, who feels his life "bifurque et trifurque de tant de côtés . . . cette vie en l'air" (*L* 1:239; bifurcate and trifurcate in so many ways . . . this life in air), Kinbote lives two or three lives, Charles-Kinbote-Botkin at once. And like Barbey, who feels that "à un certain degré dans le désir, la force de l'imagination corporise, et il y a possession réelle" (*L* 2:299; at a certain pitch of desire, the intensity of imagination corporealizes and there is actual possession), Kinbote believes he can make Zembla live again.

When the dandy goes mad, what becomes of dandyism? Barbey writes tauntingly, defensively, "Je ne suis point un sage, non! Morbleu! mais la

---

[17]Nabokov discusses dandyism and eccentricity at length in his note to *EO: 1.27* (Comm 2:110–11).

folie incarnée. . . . Je trouve une volupté dans la déraison, et le diable m'emporte" (*M* 2:252–53; I am not a sage, no! for God's sake! but madness incarnate. . . . I find sensual delight in insanity, and may the devil take me). As the dandy fragments and embraces madness, dandyism bursts the bounds of the dandy's figure to enter into the very texture of the literary. A life "in air" is a series of transformations, collages in progress, palimpsests, constructed of trickery, ruse, caprice. Let us turn, then, to the caprice of the "larcin," *Prince Otto*.

PRINCE OTTO IN PALE FIRE: "A WRENCH, A RIFT"

Grunewald, Prince Otto's kingdom, is a doubly imaginary state; not only is it presented in legendary terms—its location distant, its streams pure, its people brave—but, having been decreated by the diplomats at the novel's end, it "vanished like a morning ghost" (*PO* 3) and now exists, like Zembla, only in texts, *Prince Otto* chief among them. Grunewald's topography as well as its legendary status remind us immediately of that mythical land of Zembla because, in fact, Nabokov has parodied Stevenson's kingdom. Both countries consist of mountainous sections and plains, and both possess only two main roads. In fact, Nabokov simply places Grunewald's roads upon Zembla's terrain. Grunewald has a "wide imperial highway" which "descended the slopes obliquely and by the easiest gradients" and a second road running "like a fillet across the very forehead of the hills, dipping into savage gorges" (*PO* 5). Zembla, likewise, has an older road which "shirks difficulties" and "the newer one, an elaborate, twisting, marvelously graded road" which "traverses the range westward . . . and is termed in tourist booklets a 'scenic drive'" (*PF* 91).

After sketching in Zemblan topography, Nabokov populates his kingdom with some of Grunewald's own inhabitants. Principal among the translated characters is Prince Otto himself, misruler of Grunewald, who reappears in *Pale Fire* as King Charles. Since King Charles rules mirrorland, it is only fitting that, in reflecting Prince Otto, he present us with a reversed image. Prince Otto is king *malgré lui*; he wants to escape from the "toy kingdom" Stevenson has created for him and become an actor free to choose his own roles. Charles Kinbote, conversely, is not a king and longs to be one; he searches for an artist who will realize him in print, make him, in the eyes of a persecuting world, a real king.

Kinbote imagines that he is a dethroned king in part because Nabokov, like Cather before him, must have enjoyed Stevenson's tale of Prince

Otto's downfall. Otto is irresponsible, hedonistic, foppish—anything but serious about running his kingdom. His disgusted subjects are up in arms. Nabokov weaves Prince Otto's characteristics into both Kinbote and Charles. Ever busy with the young boys in the boudoir and true son of the absurd King Alfin, Charles could easily share Prince Otto's labels, "hereditary fool," (*PO* 7), "featherhead," (108), "Prince Puppet" (67). Prince Otto is a "plexus of weaknesses" (78, 91) who is mocked in song by his subjects; within Nabokov's "plexed artistry" (*PF* 37), King Charles is also the butt of a ballad, the insulting "Karlie-Garlie" (*PF* 69). Kinbote, as well as Charles, is an agent of misrule—his private life is a sad shambles, and his eccentricities and spells of madness cripple his attempts to function as teacher, colleague, friend, and lover. Like Otto, he adopts the dandy's mask. With foppish disdain Kinbote speaks of the "tedious and unnecessary Zemblan Revolution" (*PF* 73), even as he invests it with enormous importance. Kinbote feigns urbanity, a mask that repeatedly slips, to the amusement and annoyance of the community of New Wye.

There are other mirrorings, coincidences, echoes too numerous to discuss at length: for example, Otto's friend and confidant Gotthold (a private tippler like Shade) metamorphoses (and multiplies) into the bookish Conmal and the loyal Odon. Nabokov mirrors Sir John Crabtree, who writes a nasty exposé of Otto's kingdom, in John Shade, who will not chronicle Zemblan history. Gondremark lends his heavy, clumsy, bilious body and his rough shave to the villain Gradus. Countess von Rosen, the scheming, promiscuous, but good-hearted courtesan who saves Otto, becomes Sylvia O'Donnell of the checkered past and multiple husbands who finds Kinbote (Botkin) an academic post in America. Colonel Gordon lends his name to the young Gordon metamorphosing at the Villa Libitina. Finally, Nabokov pays special and direct homage to Stevenson and the tradition of romance by conflating and parodying two scenes from *Prince Otto*. In the long note that chronicles King Charles's escape over the border (*PF* 90–97), we find, *detail for detail*, Prince Otto's temporary escape with which *Prince Otto* opens and Seraphina's escape with which it closes: a secret passage, a king incognito, a night with a peasant family, a morning interview with the daughter of the family, the struggle to reach the mountain pass. Acknowledging his own parodic act of "blue magic," Nabokov closes the performance with a verbal tip of the hat: "I trust the reader has enjoyed this note" (*PF* 97). Once we see the structure of resemblance between *Pale Fire* and the work Nabokov almost hides within it, the issue of significance arises. What does *Prince Otto* have to tell us about *Pale Fire*?

Stevenson's novel provides Nabokov with Kinbote's homosexuality and the means of interpreting it. Otto himself, not a homosexual, is a rather impotent fellow. We learn that Otto's "one manly taste is for the chase" (*PO* 78), that he was "born incapable of inspiring" Princess Seraphina's love (203), that he is "not manly" (63), and that his love is "slavish and unerect" (294). Otto is popularly (though incorrectly) regarded by his subjects as a cuckold who is "so little of a man . . . that he holds the candle" while his wife takes lovers (19). Intertwined with the innuendoes of impotence are, however, suggestions of homosexuality. Otto's inability to express physical love for his wife, Stevenson hints, might be tied to a preference for men.

What is whispered in *Prince Otto* is spoken in *Pale Fire*. We gradually learn that Kinbote's feelings of persecution stem in part from his homosexuality as well as from his unassuageable feelings of loneliness in exile. Intermittently striving to keep up heterosexual appearances in New Wye, Kinbote transfers his fantasies of sexual freedom to Zembla, where homosexuality is condoned so long as the king manages to father an heir.

Prince Otto's effeminacy has two related meanings within Stevenson's novel. The first has to do with a failing masculinity: "That these intermarriages [Otto's descent through the king of Bohemia] had in some degree mitigated the rough, manly stock of the first Grunewalds, was an opinion widely held within the borders of the principality" (*PO* 4). The sovereign race has "soft character and manners" (*PO* 5). Otto "dresses very prettily—which is a thing to be ashamed of in a man—and he acts plays" (*PO* 14).

To lose one's manliness, to have it degenerate into a soft effeminacy, describes both Otto's sexuality and his political authority and power. To lose one's manliness is to be unable to manage the affairs of state, to call down chaos upon the heads of his subjects precisely because the loss calls hierarchy itself into question. Otto's very fluidity, his decline from the state of manhood, compromises his ability to enforce hierarchy and category themselves. The peasant Fritz must remind a forgetful Otto that "you know very well that a man is a man, and a woman only a woman" (*PO* 37). Stevenson makes explicit the connection between Otto's sexual and political "falls".

Surprisingly the plot of the novel chronicles Otto's loss of the throne, but not his loss of the kingdom of gender and order. The "Republic" is declared at novel's end, monarchy is fallen, but Otto has learned how to be a husband/man and Seraphina a wife/woman. Their hardships throw them back upon one another and the old forms. The plot of the novel, however, is not the final word on the issue of gender and power. Even though Otto and Seraphina reaffirm their marriage vows, what triumphs in the end is *not* category and hierarchy but artifice itself, associated with both Otto's effeminacy and Seraphina's femininity: "Her manners, her conversation, which she interlards with French, her very tastes and ambitions, are alike *assumed*" (*PO* 79). Otto and Seraphina, exiled from Grunewald, reemerge as paper figures, the only evidence of their existence a book of French poetry they write together. Like Kinbote, who continues his own story in the index to *Pale Fire*, they turn up in a "Bibliographic Postscript" to the novel—people, finally, made of words. Here is a familiar story: Nina, of "Spring in Fialta," dies into print as Otto and Seraphina are exiled to the land of French poetry. Gender in that land is but a turn of phrase, not a matter of immutable hierarchy and category and the forms of power attending those arrangements. Once again, the female and the French provide the space within which gender may at last float, free to form analogical connections.

Varieties of sexuality in *Pale Fire* span Shade's craggy heterosexuality, Sybil's traditional feminine heterosexuality, Maud's lesbian proclivities, Kinbote's homosexuality, and Hazel's apparent asexuality. But, as in Grunewald, so in New Wye and Zembla: different expressions of sexuality imply different understandings of what gender itself might be. And, as in Fialta and Abyssinia, so in New Wye and Zembla, women's deaths provide the means by which the tired romantic myths may metamorphose into the modernist myth of texture, tone, manner, analogy. Female gender, seen as fixed and dichotomous, must die, preferably by drowning, in order that a world of gender fluidity may be born.

Four women—Disa, Sybil, Maud, Hazel—inhabit what appear to be the margins of *Pale Fire's* major drama, the transformation of Shade's poem into Kinbote/Botkin's world of fantasy. Each of these four women in her own way creates, like Nina and Lahann, a space in which text may be transformed to texture. Their gender is the site upon which Nabokov transforms the false romantic to the modern. Like Baudelaire's Dorothée, like Wallace Stevens's Lady Lowzen, Nabokov's women in *Pale Fire* point the way to a place beyond Nabokov's cultural understanding, a place of monstrosity in which the hierarchies and dichotomies of waking life, patriarchal hegemony, no longer apply. To imagine that place is to imagine a kind of death, and all four of these women come to artificial life in a verbal pattern of images of death and dying.

Disa, for example, pines away in her futile love for Kinbote. She is often connected, at the level of the detail, to fluidity of gender. Charles first meets her in his Zemblan fantasy when she, like Mademoiselle de

Maupin, is cross-dressed, at a masked ball in which, for the space of an evening, role becomes identity: "She had come in male dress, as a Tirolese boy, a little knock-kneed but brave and lovely" (PF 115). She lives on the Côte d'Azur in a villa that carries both masculine and feminine names, Villa Paradiso and (in Zemblan) Villa Paradisa. Yet gender fluidity is Disa's curse, not her choice: she loves Kinbote as a good, female wife loves a profligate, male husband, and is humiliated by his homosexual adventures. Despite the sadness of the tale Kinbote tells—he can pity and love her only in his dreams—Disa indicates a world beyond the very gender arrangements that entrap her, a woman faithful to an "almost man," Kinbote/Botkin.

The "answer" to the dilemma of homosexuality for Kinbote lies in divesting his wife of her reality. Unlike Stevenson, who has Seraphina (whom Stevenson describes as a "breeze which blows out of paradise," hence Nabokov's "Para*disa*") plot her husband's overthrow, Nabokov chooses to submerge the tale of marital humiliation within his text. Disa appears only fleetingly and mysteriously. While Seraphina, through a weakness in Stevenson's art, is ill defined and incoherent as a character, Disa, completely under Nabokov's control, is shadowy, ephemeral. She epitomizes the shades, ghosts, mists, and hazes of Nabokov's novel, its turn to the incorporeal. Hazel communicates with ghosts; Disa is herself a ghostlike "almost-character" within the novel. We know her primarily through a letter she writes and a madman's dreams about her. Several removes from reality, she is always and only a part of the novel's texture, a poignant figure because we feel her absence.

Although Disa personifies the victimization inherent in clinging to the standard plot of cultural arrangements—dichotomous gender, heterosexual love, marriage, and procreation—she embodies, as a woman made out of words, first the disappointment of that plot and then its very dissipation, through the disembodiment of the female person. Sybil represents the countermovement to Disa's "vaporisation." Kinbote sees them as mirror images, because where Disa is all dream and "glancing reflection" (PF 140), Sybil is all bustling, real business, beloved and loving wife of the virile Shade. Together they appear to personify the strength of current arrangements of gender and marriage. Yet Sybil is a translator into French, and of poems about death at that. As present as Disa is absent, as loved as Disa is ignored, Sybil is a creature of pattern too, created to contrast with Disa as the Countess von Rosen contrasts with Seraphina in *Prince Otto*. And for Shade himself, searching for an understanding of his daughter's death, Sybil is a figure who points the way to texture rather than text:

And all the time, and all the time, my love,
You too are there, beneath the word, above
The syllable, to underscore and stress
The vital rhythm. One heard a woman's dress
Rustle in days of yore. I've often caught
The sound and sense of your approaching thought.
And all in you is youth, and you make new,
By quoting them, old things I made for you.

                                         (*PF* 40)

Sybil, too, makes new; her voice and her name suggest wisdom from beyond the tomb. Yet in the drama of textual death and resurrection, she is notable primarily as a foil to the two women whose deaths really do "make new" the old myths, Maud and Hazel.

From the first, Maud is associated with images of death. She is "A poet and a painter with a taste / For realistic objects interlaced / With grotesque growths and images of doom" (*PF* 17). She paints *Cypress and Bat*, her room contains "the forlorn guitar / The human skull," and Shade claims her cane, the sign of human infirmity, mortality. Maud's ghost, Kinbote suggests, comes back to haunt the household, and it is Hazel who receives her messages. "Dear bizarre Aunt Maud," urbanely framed by Shade, seems to elude his control, however, for she represents to him the rift into which he falls occasionally—as a child with seizures, as a man experiencing a heart attack, briefly dead to the world. "A wrench, a rift, that's all one can foresee. / Maybe one finds *le grand néant*; maybe / Again one spirals from the tuber's eye" (*PF* 31): whatever lies beyond life, it is the subject of Maud's art and the secret knowledge she hints at possessing.

Hazel is from the first determined to pursue that knowledge. Nabokov creates her as the type of the Romantic strangeling: "The theme of unsocial children of either sex was a commonplace of Romanticism" (Comm 2:282). Like Pushkin's Tatiana, Hazel is a child who never feels at home in her world. But unlike Tatiana, Hazel is gifted with an irritation at the received plots of courtship and marriage, so intrigued is she by the continuation of life's story past the borderline of death. While her parents' version of her death—pathetic, ugly, and disappointed, Hazel kills herself—has a partial validity, Kinbote and Shade unwittingly supply us with another tale about her.[18] Attuned to the spirit world, in communication with

[18]Kinbote and Shade project their values (lack of charm equals lack of worth) onto Hazel, argues Knapp. She reveals the shortcomings of the standard critical interpretation of Hazel, which uncritically accepts Kinbote's and Shade's judgments of the young woman. Nabokov gives us evidence that Hazel is a clever woman possessing insights and intuitions which the men choose to discredit.

Maud (*PF* 104), Hazel decides to walk into the very rift of death, so sure is she of another world awaiting her there: a "blurry shape stepped off the reedy bank / Into a crackling, gulping swamp, and sank" (*PF* 28). Like Lahann, Hazel participates in two stories. Lahann is the romantic sister who sacrifices herself in the name of love. But she also marks the place into which all Romanticism collapses, drowning with her, to be resurrected in the ever-expanding web of Nabokov's style. Hazel drowns because Lahann drowns; she *is* similarly resurrected in Shade's poem, not as a tired Romantic ghost, but as the "correlated pattern" of modern beauty itself:

> Not flimsy nonsense, but a web of sense.
> Yes! It sufficed that I in life could find
> Some kind of link-and-bobolink, some kind
> Of correlated pattern in the game,
> Plexed artistry, . . .   (*PF* 36–37)

The pattern of which Hazel's death is one link extends backward in time to Nabokov's first realization that Pushkin was for him not just a figure of aesthetic adoration, but also the prime mover behind Nabokov the world-maker. Hazel's death by drowning is prefigured in every instance in Nabokov's art in which plot and characterization metamorphose ineluctably into tone, manner, pattern. Her death links her to *Eugene Onegin*, where Pushkin's "essence" is dispersed, dislocated, by placing it in a black woman who dies. And, finally, Hazel's death links her to a long and rich tradition of literary dandyism in which the dandy, elegant man of the avenue, finds his own best expression in a constant weaving across a collection of lines that define a world: French and English, male and female, artifice and reality, self and other.

Kinbote is mad, and in his madness creates a world moving rapidly toward chaos. Zemblan itself is a linguistic hodgepodge that makes the hodgepodge of French, Russian, English, and such in *Onegin* appear orderly in contrast. People and places metamorphose too freely, as Kinbote merely fantasizes parallel worlds, Zembla and New Wye. He admires his uncle Conmal, whose translations, wildly off the mark, suggest only the freedom of ignorance. Within this context of mad freedom, cancerous metamorphosis, Maud and Hazel stand as markers indicating the very rift through which the sane might escape into a world in which fiction and

---

Knapp also points out that, in adopting Goethe's *Erlking* to his own purposes, Shade changes the gender of the child from male to female, "mirroring the awkward Zemblan translation of the 'pale fire' passage in *Timon of Athens*, in which the male sun becomes female and the female moon becomes male" (108). Such gender substitution in relation to Hazel indicates that part of what Hazel suggests is a state beyond stable gender.

reality are no longer opposed, but related. Their very pathos links them to the female orchestra of Fialta, to Mademoiselle O: they moor Kinbote's wildly multiplying fantasies to reality. As frightening as death itself—and therefore dying is a powerful metaphor for it—their world is also, paradoxically, precisely the world beyond the only world we know, the world of culture which surrounds us, entraps us. Only if we are visionaries of Nabokovian power can we, like Hazel and Maud, see the tunnel through which we might escape our given world. Through this rift lies the *coincidentia oppositorum*, a chaos that is the original order, the watery ground to which Hazel returns. If Nabokov as an artist does not travel there, he attempts to convey his vision of its quality in the very measured chaos of infinitely expanding patterns in words that are his—and Pushkin's—art.

Nabokov's dandyism reverberates throughout his works, not just in figures such as Kinbote, but in his very acts of translation, the "blue magic" he first learned to perform as an English-speaking child in Russia and then refined as an inhabitant of several countries and a writer in two languages. Nabokov translated far more than languages; he believed that the elements of his world—books and chairs, people and weather—were alike ripe for translation. The very act of writing consisted of translating the world into the Nabokovian vernacular, and he made of that act at once a scientific discovery, a game, and the creation of high art. His translation of Pushkin's *Onegin* allowed him to refine a principal notion about art—that it consists of the act of translating world into texture—but it allowed him as well to consider the original and ultimate translation, that of himself into another. Nabokov as Pushkin, Pushkin as Nabokov: thus the dandy-writer tips his hat as he disappears into his own mirrored texture of parody, pastiche, and plagiarism.

AFTERWORD

"With Fred I'd be Ginger, and with Ginger I'd be Fred"—thus reminisces Hermes Pan, rehearsal assistant to Fred Astaire and Ginger Rogers (Croce 96). Pan speaks matter-of-factly, assuming his ability to play the parts of others, regardless of their gender. With his statement, all the mirrors click into place, for the people he impersonates during rehearsal are themselves playing dandies who mirror each other when they dance. Astaire's costume (can a tuxedo be said to cling?) reveals a figure lithe but erect, delicate but strong, cool but passionate. He talks when he sings, sings when he talks. Rogers's chiffon swirls about, a cloud that almost hides her steely, concentered self. The tiny waist, slender arms, soft lashes somehow mock our every attempt to claim her as lovely lady: those heels, like Lauzun's, are made to wound. Fred and Ginger, Ginger and Fred: they tap and swoon their way past all our comfortable categories, instructing us in their ineffable superiority even as they try to please.

Astaire and Rogers suggest a question arising inevitably from this book: just how far and wide can one range in looking for the dandy? Certainly I could have doubled the size of the book by accounting for the tradition of dandyism in English literature. Byron and Wilde are the tutelary, if almost silenced, geniuses of my study. And certainly I could have chosen other artists as well: George Sand, Isak Dinesen, Rainer Maria Rilke, Louise Bogan, T. S. Eliot, among others. Nor is dandyism exclusively a verbal phenomenon: beyond writers, painters, sculptors, actors, directors, choreographers, dancers, composers, and musicians come to mind.

Is a tradition potentially this inclusive a tradition at all? I would answer that the very notion of tradition has been modified by the dandy-artist, whose goal in Stevens's words is "to pass from the created to the uncreated." Paradoxically, dandies create a tradition by dismantling the notion of tradition as patriarchal line in which one writer inherits or wrests from another the sacred torch or sanctified pen. Rather, in courting the *coincidentia oppositorum*, dandies teach us of sudden metamorphoses, of "a poetry not previously conceived of," of surprise and novelty which challenge orderly succession, neatly drawn lines, categorical exclusion and inclusion themselves.

Here I must pause to place this book more precisely in its historical moment. What attracted me to dandyism was its profound and intense *modernity*, and that word happened to carry with it at the time two critical resonances, feminist and post-structuralist. Writers in the tradition of dandyism suggest that we study how a culture understands femaleness in relation to maleness rather than focusing on the category of women as a discrete area of exploration. When Mademoiselle de Maupin announces that she is no longer a woman but not yet a man, she simultaneously heralds for the modern era the dismantling of polarized gender systems. Dandies further instruct us in the need to search for gender in art not just in the recognizable figures of men and women but in the very abstractions of literary texture, the methods of artists themselves.

Further, dandies reveal the nineteenth-century roots of some twentieth-century semiotic and post-structuralist understandings. For example, dandies flaunt what a culture usually attempts to ignore or hide, that the human body is never "natural," or naked of cultural clothing, but is instead a system of signification, a cultural construct. The dandy's clothing, bearing, makeup, and so forth announce the necessarily "made-up" quality of what we often take as one locus of unmediated nature, our own bodies. Once dandies discover the power of self-presentation, they can no longer imagine a self independent of cultural mediation. Their rebellious self-interpretation presses back upon the self presented to them by their society. For the dandy-writer, worlds are made of words, in styles, and so are people.

When dandies exhibit themselves as creatures seeking an audience, asking to be "read," they also exhibit a process of conflicting meanings. Texts of dandyism are striking in their complexity: it is not unusual for an artist who is herself a dandy (and thus self-imagined) to create a fiction of a dandy who is an artist, this "fictional character" then manipulating the mirrors of translation, imitation, parody. The ever-shifting, metamorphic *mise en abyme* is dandyism's native form. In fact, the critic's tendency to write about dandyism in a style of labyrinthine consciousness and precious tones, to toss her own views into the system of mirrors and wires, is hard to resist. The dandy teaches us to accept ambiguity, multiplicity, and contingency—the confusing but vital making of a world, not the exploration of a given world.[1]

Dandies, whether reactionary or revolutionary (or both at once, as it often happens), challenge the hierarchical arrangements of their societies. Demonstrating culture's artificiality, the possibility of its being *arranged* just as curls or facial expression or clothing is arranged, dandies attempt to change the world by redescribing it. They offer us a distance from accepted beliefs and a well-developed skepticism about such "givens" as truth, self, and language. Dandies aim to subvert existing social forms by the method of saying and unsaying established cultural "truths." If it is bourgeois consumerism they challenge, what better criticism than a celebration of its values turned, precisely, upside down? Thus dandies have "advertised"— by a quiet, nearly hidden series of gestures—leisure rather than industry, solitary passivity rather than group cooperation, "consumption" of form and style rather than goods and services, suspicion of scientific progress rather than its embrace.

Again, as precursors of the "post-modern," dandies attack reason as a fixed and abstract basis for human endeavor. In their war on reason, they often mount reason's own weapon, paradox. In place of their societies' utterly tiresome appeal to reason, dandies suggest a panoply of other activities: posing, hoaxing, jesting, lying, hiding, ignoring, condescending.

But perhaps most important for the purposes of my book, dandies dissolve the self. Barbey's view of "cette vie en l'air," of his self as multiple, contingent, volatile, and fragmented, augurs the deconstructionist view. The self is no longer seen as stable and coherent; in centralizing and vaporizing, it changes in its very quality. When Stevens, for example, chal-

[1]He or she gives temporary form to the "jouissance of semiotic mobility" (Moi 170). Throughout my discussion of dandies as precursors of post-structuralist thought, I am indebted to Moi, Flax, and Weedon for their complementary accounts of the relation of feminism to post-structuralism.

lenges the essentialism of the Judeo-Christian myth, he demonstrates that just as we will ourselves to believe in God, we also practice a Jamesian "will to believe" in all the important abstractions by which we live, including "self." Dandies are figures who will into existence the changing centers of their continually reconstructed selves. My six writers are critics as well as novelists and poets, and they think in profoundly theoretical ways about issues that continue to engage us, even as they send their dandies strolling on the divide between literature and criticism.

In a book that has taken as its subject dandyism—its fluidity of meta-morphosis, its continuous reflexivity of paradox, its ever-widening possi-bility of analogy—the afterword, the final word, is permissible only as an-other turn of the spiral. My subject, though seen, cannot be captured: the dandy as the riddle.

SELECT BIBLIOGRAPHY

Abel, Elizabeth, ed. *Writing and Sexual Difference*. Sussex: Harvester, 1982.

Albouy, Pierre. "Le myth de l'androgyne dans *Mademoiselle de Maupin*." *Revue d'Histoire Littéraire de la France* 72 (1972): 600–608.

Albright, Daniel. *Representation and the Imagination: Beckett, Kafka, Nabokov, and Schoenberg*. Chicago: University of Chicago Press, 1981.

Anderson, Jean. "Baudelaire misogyne: Vers une lecture féministe des *Fleurs du mal*." *New Zealand Journal of French Studies* 9 (1987): 16–28.

Appel, Alfred, Jr., and Charles Newman, eds. *Nabokov: Criticism, Reminiscences, Translations and Tributes*. Evanston: Northwestern University Press, 1970.

Armstrong, Nancy. *Desire and Domestic Fiction: A Political History of the Novel*. New York: Oxford University Press, 1989.

Arnold, Matthew. "Eugénie de Guérin." In *Essays in Criticism, First Series*, edited by Thomas Marion Hoctor, 76–95. Chicago: University of Chicago Press, 1968.

Asselineau, Charles. "Charles Baudelaire, sa vie et son oeuvre." In *Baudelaire et Asselineau*, edited by Jacques Crépet and Claude Pichois, 59–155. Paris: Librairie Nizet, 1953.

Aynesworth, Donald. "A Face in the Crowd: A Baudelairean Vision of the Eternal Feminine." *Stanford French Review* 5–6 (Winter 1981): 327–39.

Balakian, Anna. *The Literary Origins of Surrealism: A New Mysticism in French Poetry*. New York: New York University Press, 1947.

Barbey d'Aurevilly, Jules-Amédée. *Articles inédits (1852–1884)*. Edited by A. Hirschi and J. Petit. 2 vols. Annales Littéraires de l'Université de Besançon 138. Paris: Belles Lettres, 1972.

———. "Du Dandysme et de G. Brummell." In *Oeuvres complètes*, 3:205–330. Geneva: Slatkine Reprints, 1979.

———. *Le XIXe siècle: Des oeuvres et des hommes*. Edited by Jacques Petit. 2 vols. Paris: Mercure de France, 1966.

———. *Le XIXe siècle: Les oeuvres et les hommes: Mémoires historiques et littéraires*. Vols. 13–14. Paris: Alphonse Lemerre, 1893.

———. *Lettres à Trébutien*. In *Oeuvres complètes*, vols. 6–7. Geneva: Slatkine Reprints, 1979.

———. *Memoranda*. 4 vols. Reprinted in *Oeuvres complètes*, vol. 5. Geneva: Slatkine Reprints, 1979.

———. "Pensées détachées." In *Oeuvres complètes*, 3:153–204. Geneva: Slatkine Reprints, 1979.

———. *Premiers articles (1834–1853)*. Edited by A. Hirschi and J. Pétit. Annales Littéraires de l'Université de Besançon 143. Paris: Belles Lettres, 1973.

Barkan, Leonard. *The Gods Made Flesh: Metamorphosis and the Pursuit of Paganism*. New Haven: Yale University Press, 1986.

Barolsky, Paul. *Walter Pater's Renaissance*. University Park: Pennsylvania State University Press, 1987.

Bates, Milton J. *Wallace Stevens: A Mythology of Self*. Berkeley: University of California Press, 1985.

Baudelaire, Charles. *Baudelaire: Selected Writings on Art and Artists*. Translated by P. E. Charvet. Cambridge: Cambridge University Press, 1971.

———. *The Flowers of Evil*. Edited by Marthiel Mathews and Jackson Mathews. New York: New Directions, 1989.

———. *Intimate Journals*. Translated by Christopher Isherwood. San Francisco: City Lights, 1983.

———. *Un mangeur d'opium*. Edited by Michèle Wulf. In *Etudes Baudelairiennes*, vols. 6–7. Neuchatel: Editions de la Baconnière, 1976.

———. *The Mirror of Art: Critical Studies by Charles Baudelaire*. Translated and edited by Jonathan Mayne. New York: Phaidon, 1966.

——. *Oeuvres complètes*. Edited by Y.-G. Le Dantec and Claude Pichois. Paris: Editions Gallimard, 1961.

——. *Oeuvres complètes*. Edited by Marcel Raymond. Lausanne: Guilde du Livre Lausanne, 1967.

——. *Selected Letters of Charles Baudelaire: The Conquest of Solitude*. Translated by Rosemary Lloyd. Chicago: University of Chicago Press, 1986.

Benamou, Michel. *Wallace Stevens and the Symbolist Imagination*. Princeton: Princeton University Press, 1972.

Benjamin, Walter. *Charles Baudelaire: A Lyric Poet in the Era of High Capitalism*. Translated by Harry Zohn. London: NLB, 1973.

Berthier, Philippe. *Barbey d'Aurevilly et l'imagination*. Geneva: Librairie Droz, 1978.

Bloom, Harold, ed. *Charles Baudelaire*. New York: Chelsea House, 1987.

——. *Wallace Stevens*. New York: Chelsea House, 1985.

——. *Willa Cather*. New York: Chelsea House, 1985.

Bohlke, Brent L. "Godfrey St. Peter and Delacroix: A Portrait of the Artist in the Professor's House." *Western American Literature* 17 (1982): 21–38.

Bouchard, Ann. "Le masque et le miroir dans *Mademoiselle de Maupin*." *Revue d'Histoire Littéraire de la France* 72 (1972): 583–99.

Boyd, Brian. *Vladimir Nabokov: The American Years*. Princeton: Princeton University Press, 1991.

——. *Vladimir Nabokov: The Russian Years*. Princeton: Princeton University Press, 1990.

Brazeau, Peter. *Parts of a World: Wallace Stevens Remembered*. New York: Random, 1983.

Brogan, Jacqueline Vaught. "'Sister of the Minotaur'—Sexism and Stevens." *Wallace Stevens Journal* 12 (Fall 1988): 102–18.

Brombert, Victor. "Le cygne de Baudelaire: Douleur, souvenir, travail." *Etudes Baudelairiennes* 3 (1973): 254–61.

Brown, Ashley, and Robert S. Haller, eds. *The Achievement of Wallace Stevens*. Philadelphia: Lippincott, 1962.

Burnett, David G. "Sexual Rhetoric and Personal Identity in Théophile Gautier's 'Preface' to *Mademoiselle de Maupin*." In *Manifestos and Movements*, 38–45. French Literature Series 7. Columbia: University of South Carolina Press, 1980.

Buttel, Robert. *The Making of Harmonium*. Princeton: Princeton University Press, 1967.

Camus, Albert. *The Rebel: An Essay on Man in Revolt*. Translated by Anthony Bower. New York: Knopf, 1957.

Carassus, Emilien. *Le mythe du dandy*. Paris: Armand Colin, 1971.

Cather, Willa. *Collected Short Fiction, 1892–1912*. Lincoln: University of Nebraska Press, 1965.

——. *The Kingdom of Art*. Edited by Bernice Slote. Lincoln: University of Nebraska Press, 1966.

——. *My Ántonia*. Boston: Houghton Mifflin, 1977.

——. *The Professor's House*. New York: Random House, 1973.

——. *The World and the Parish*. Edited by William M. Curtin. 2 vols. Lincoln: University of Nebraska Press, 1970.

Cixous, Hélène. "The Laugh of the Medusa." *Signs* 1 (1976): 875–99.

Clements, Patricia. *Baudelaire and the English Tradition*. Princeton: Princeton University Press, 1985.

Colie, Rosalie. *Paradoxia Epidemica: The Renaissance Tradition of Paradox*. Princeton: Princeton University Press, 1966.

Cook, Eleanor. *Poetry, Word-Play, and Word-War in Wallace Stevens*. Princeton: Princeton University Press, 1988.

Coyle, Beverly, and Alan Filreis. *Secretaries of the Moon: The Letters of Wallace Stevens and José Rodríguez Feo*. Durham: Duke University Press, 1986.

Creed, Elizabeth. *Le dandysme de Jules Barbey d'Aurevilly*. Paris: Librairie Droz, 1938.

Croce, Arlene. *The Fred Astaire and Ginger Rogers Book*. New York: Galahad Books, 1972.

Davis, Natalie Zemon. "Women on Top." In *The Reversible World: Symbolic Inversion in Art and Society*, edited by Barbara A. Babcock, 147–90. Ithaca: Cornell University Press, 1978.

de Maistre, Joseph. *The Works of Joseph de Maistre*. Translated by Jack Lively. New York: Macmillan, 1965.

Dembo, L. S., ed. *Nabokov: The Man and His Work*. Madison: University of Wisconsin Press, 1967.

Dodille, Norbert. *Le texte autobiographique de Barbey d'Aurevilly: Correspondances et journaux intimes*. Geneva: Librairie Droz, 1987.

Doggett, Frank, and Robert Buttel, eds. *Wallace Stevens: A Celebration*. Princeton: Princeton University Press, 1980.

Douglas, Ann. *The Feminization of American Culture*. New York: Knopf, 1977.

Doyle, Charles, ed. *Wallace Stevens: The Critical Heritage*. London: Routledge and Kegan Paul, 1985.

Dumas, Alexandre, Jr. *Camille: Or, the Fate of a Coquette*. Translated by Matilda Heron. In *Modern Standard Drama*. New York: Samuel French, [1856?].

Eliade, Mircea. "Mephistopheles and the Androgyne: Or, the Mystery of the Whole." In *The Two and the One*, translated by J. M. Cohen, 78–122. London: Harvill, 1965.

Ellmann, Richard. *Oscar Wilde*. New York: Knopf, 1988.

Felman, Shoshana. "Women and Madness: The Critical Phallacy." *Diacritics* 5 (Winter 1975): 2–10.

Field, Andrew. *VN: The Life and Art of Vladimir Nabokov*. New York: Crown, 1986.

Flax, Jane. "Post-Modernism and Gender Relations in Feminist Theory." *Signs* 12 (1987): 621–43.

François, Simone. *Le dandysme et Marcel Proust: De Brummell au baron de Charlus*. Brussels: Palais des Académies, 1956.

Gautier, Théophile. "Celle-ci et celle-là: Ou la Jeune-France passionnée." In *Les Jeunes-France: Romans goguenards*, 96–200. Paris: Bibliothèque Charpentier, 1900.

———. *Histoire du Romantisme*. Paris: Bibliothèque Charpentier, 18—.

———. *Mademoiselle de Maupin*. Edited by J. Robichez. Paris: Imprimerie Nationale, 1979.

———. "Mademoiselle Fanny Elssler." In *Portraits contemporains*, 372–78. Paris: Bibliothèque Charpentier, 1874.

Gervaud, Michel. "Willa Cather and France: Elective Affinities." In *The Art of Willa Cather*, edited by Bernice Slote and Virginia Faulkner, 65–83. Lincoln: University of Nebraska Press, 1974.

Gibian, George, and Stephen Jay Parker, eds. *The Achievements of Vladimir Nabokov*. Ithaca: Center for International Studies, Cornell University, 1983.

Gilbert, Sandra M. "Costumes of the Mind: Transvestism as Metaphor in Modern Literature." *Critical Inquiry* 7 (1980): 391–417.

Gille, Pierre. "L'ambivalence chez Barbey d'Aurevilly: Structures, figures et genèse." *Revue des Lettres Modernes* 8.351–54 (1973): 39–74.

Gilman, Margaret. *Baudelaire the Critic*. New York: Columbia University Press, 1943.

Girard, Sylvie. *Le parfum du démon: Un écrivain nommé Barbey d'Aurevilly*. Paris: Hermé, 1986.

Grayson, Jane. *Nabokov Translated: A Comparison of Nabokov's Russian and English Prose*. Oxford: Oxford University Press, 1977.

Green, Martin. *Children of the Sun: A Narrative of "Decadence" in England after 1918*. New York: Basic Books, 1976.

Gubar, Susan. "Blessings in Disguise: Cross-Dressing as Re-Dressing for Female Modernists." *Massachusetts Review* 22 (Autumn 1981): 477–508.

Heilbrun, Carolyn. *Toward a Recognition of Androgyny*. New York: Harper and Row, 1973.

Hiddleston, J. A. *Baudelaire and Le Spleen de Paris*. Oxford: Clarendon, 1987.

Huyghe, René. *Delacroix*. New York: Harry N. Abrams, 1963.

Jardine, Alice. *Gynesis: Configurations of Woman and Modernity*. Ithaca: Cornell University Press, 1985.

Jehlen, Myra. "Archimedes and the Paradox of Feminist Criticism." *Signs* 6 (1981): 575–601.

Johnson, Mark. *The Body in the Mind: The Bodily Basis of Meaning, Imagination, and Reason*. Chicago: University of Chicago Press, 1987.

Kaiser, Walter. *Praisers of Folly: Erasmus, Rabelais, Shakespeare*. Cambridge: Harvard University Press, 1963.

Karlinsky, Simon, ed. *The Nabokov-Wilson Letters: Correspondence between Vladimir Nabokov and Edmund Wilson, 1940–1971*. New York: Harper and Row, 1979.

Kelly, Dorothy. *Fictional Genders: Role and Representation in Nineteenth-Century French Narrative*. Lincoln: University of Nebraska Press, 1989.

Kempf, Roger. *Dandies: Baudelaire et cie*. Paris: Editions du Seuil, 1977.

Kessler, Suzanne J., and Wendy McKenna. *Gender: An Ethnomethodological Approach*. Chicago: University of Chicago Press, 1978.

Knapp, Shoshana. "Hazel Ablaze: Literary License in Nabokov's *Pale Fire*." *Essays in Literature* 14 (1987): 105–15.

Laqueur, Thomas. *Making Sex: Body and Gender from the Greeks to Freud*. Cambridge: Harvard University Press, 1990.

Lemaire, Michel. *Le dandysme de Baudelaire à Mallarmé*. Montreal: Presses de l'Université de Montréal, 1978.

Lentricchia, Frank. *Ariel and the Police: Michel Foucault, William James, Wallace Stevens*. Madison: University of Wisconsin Press, 1988.

——. "Patriarchy against Itself: The Young Manhood of Wallace Stevens." *Critical Inquiry* 13 (1987): 742–86.

Levenson, Michael H. *A Genealogy of Modernism: A Study of English Literary Doctrine, 1908–1922*. Cambridge: Cambridge University Press, 1984.

Liedekerke, Arnould de. *Talon rouge: Barbey d'Aurevilly, le dandy absolu*. Paris: Olivier Orban, 1986.

Lloyd, Rosemary. "Rereading *Mademoiselle de Maupin*." *Orbis Litterarum* 41 (1986): 19–32.

——. "Speculum Amantis, Speculum Artis: The Seduction of Mademoiselle de Maupin." *Nineteenth-Century French Studies* 15 (Fall-Winter 1986–87): 77–86.

McGann, Jerome J. "The Dandy." *Midway* 10 (Summer 1969): 3–18.

Mack, Sara. *Ovid*. New Haven: Yale University Press, 1988.

Matoré, Georges. *Le vocabulaire et la société sous Louis-Philippe*. Geneva: Librairie Droz, 1951.

Mazzeo, Joseph Anthony. *Renaissance and Revolution: Backgrounds to Seventeenth-Century English Literature*. New York: Pantheon Books, 1967.

Miller, Nancy K., ed. *The Poetics of Gender*. New York: Columbia University Press, 1986.

Moers, Ellen. *The Dandy: Brummell to Beerbohm*. 1960. Lincoln: University of Nebraska Press, 1978.

Moi, Toril. *Sexual/Textual Politics: Feminist Literary Theory*. London: Methuen, 1985.

Montpensier, Anne-Marie-Louise. *Mémoires de Mlle de Montpensier*. Edited by A. Chéruel. Paris: Bibliothèque Charpentier, 1858.

Murphy, John J., ed. *Critical Essays on Willa Cather*. Boston: G. K. Hall, 1984.

Nabokov, Vladimir. "The Art of Translation." In *Lectures on Russian Literature*, edited by Fredson Bowers, 315–21. New York: Harcourt, 1981.

———. *Bend Sinister*. New York: McGraw-Hill, 1974.

———. "Commentary." In *Eugene Onegin*, by Aleksandr Pushkin, translated by V. Nabokov. New York: Bollingen, 1964.

———. *The Gift*. Translated by Michael Scammell and Vladimir Nabokov. New York: Penguin, 1963.

———. *Lectures on Don Quixote*. Edited by Fredson Bowers. New York: Harcourt Brace Jovanovich, 1983.

———. *Lectures on Literature*. Edited by Fredson Bowers. New York: Harcourt Brace Jovanovich, 1980.

———. *Lolita*. New York: Capricorn Books, 1955.

———. *Nabokov's Dozen*. New York: Doubleday, 1958.

———. *The Nabokov-Wilson Letters: Correspondence between Vladimir Nabokov and Edmund Wilson, 1940–1971*. New York: Harper and Row, 1979.

———. *Nikolai Gogol*. New York: New Directions, 1944.

———. *Pale Fire*. New York: Putnam's, 1962.

———. "Problems of Translation: *Onegin* in English." *Partisan Review* 22 (1955): 496–512.

——. "Pushkin, or, The Real and the Plausible." Translated by Dmitri Nabokov. *New York Review of Books*, 31 March 1988, 38–42.

——. *The Real Life of Sebastian Knight*. New York: New Directions, 1941.

——. *A Russian Beauty and Other Stories*. New York: McGraw-Hill, 1973.

——. *Selected Letters, 1940–1977*. Edited by Dmitri Nabokov and Matthew J. Bruccoli. New York: Harcourt Brace Jovanovich, 1989.

——. "The Servile Path." In *On Translation*, edited by Reuben Brower, 97–110. New York: Oxford University Press, 1966.

——. *Speak, Memory: An Autobiography Revisited*. New York: Putnam's Sons, 1947.

——. *Strong Opinions*. New York: McGraw-Hill, 1973.

——. *Tyrants Destroyed and Other Stories*. New York: McGraw-Hill, 1975.

Needham, Rodney, ed. "Introduction." In *Right and Left: Essays on Dual Symbolic Classification*, xi–xxxix. Chicago: University of Chicago Press, 1973.

Nelson, Lowry. "Baudelaire and Virgil: A Reading of 'Le Cygne.'" *Comparative Literature* 13 (1961): 332–45.

Nussbaum, Martha. *The Fragility of Goodness*. Cambridge: Cambridge University Press, 1986.

O'Brien, Sharon. *Willa Cather: The Emerging Voice*. New York: Oxford University Press, 1987.

O'Flaherty, Wendy Doniger. *Asceticism and Eroticism in the Mythology of Siva*. London: Oxford University Press, 1973.

——. *Women, Androgynes, and Other Mythical Beasts*. Chicago: University of Chicago Press, 1980.

Ortner, Sherry, and Harriet Whitehead. *Sexual Meanings: The Cultural Construction of Gender and Sexuality*. Cambridge: Cambridge University Press, 1981.

Ovid. *Metamorphoses*. Translated by Rolfe Humphries. Bloomington: Indiana University Press, 1955.

——. *Tristia*. Translated by L. R. Lind. Athens: University of Georgia Press, 1975.

Paglia, Camille. *Sexual Personae: Art and Decadence from Nefertiti to Emily Dickinson*. New Haven: Yale University Press, 1990.

Petit, Jacques. *Barbey d'Aurevilly: Critique*. Annales Littéraires de l'Université de Besançon 53. Paris: Belles Lettres, 1963.

Pichois, Claude. *Baudelaire: Etudes et témoignages*. Neuchatel: Editions de la Baconnière, 1967.

Pifer, Ellen. *Nabokov and the Novel*. Cambridge: Harvard University Press, 1980.

Plutarch. *The Lives of the Noble Grecians and Romans*. Translated by John Dryden and revised by Arthur Hugh Clough. New York: Modern Library, 1932.

Poe, Edgar Allan. *Marginalia*. In *Complete Works*, edited by James A. Harrison, vol. 16. New York: Crowell, 1902.

Prevost, John C. *Le dandysme en France (1817–1839)*. Geneva: Librairie Droz, 1957.

Proust, Marcel. *Remembrance of Things Past*. Translated by C. K. Scott Moncrieff and Terence Kilmartin. Vol. 1. New York: Random House, 1981.

Pushkin, Aleksandr. *Eugene Onegin*. Translated with a commentary by Vladimir Nabokov. 4 vols. New York: Bollingen, 1964; 2d ed., 1975.

Quine, W. V. *The Ways of Paradox and Other Essays*. New York: Random House, 1966.

Quinn, Patrick. *The French Face of Edgar Poe*. Carbondale: Southern Illinois University Press, 1957.

Richardson, Joan. *Wallace Stevens: The Early Years, 1879–1923*. New York: William Morrow, 1986.

———. *Wallace Stevens: The Later Years, 1923–1955*. New York: William Morrow, 1988.

Rivers, J. E., and Charles Nicol, eds. *Nabokov's Fifth Arc: Nabokov and Others on His Life's Work*. Austin: University of Texas Press, 1982.

Rorty, Richard. *Contingency, Irony, and Solidarity*. Cambridge: Cambridge University Press, 1989.

———. "Feminism and Pragmatism." *Michigan Quarterly Review* 30.2 (1991): 231–58.

Roth, Phyllis. *Critical Essays on Vladimir Nabokov*. Boston: G. K. Hall, 1984.

Rubin, Gayle. "The Traffic in Women: Notes on the 'Political Economy of Sex.'" In *Toward an Anthropology of Women*, edited by Rayna Reiter, 157–210. New York: Monthly Review, 1975.

Saint Mars, Gabrielle Anne. *Mémoires des autres*. Paris: A la Librairie Illustrée, [18——].

Saint-Simon, Louis de Rouvroy, duc de. *Mémoires: Editions au journal de Dangeau*. Edited by Yves Coirault. 8 vols. Paris: Gallimard, 1983.

Santos, Maria Irene Ramalho de Sousa. "The Woman in the Poem: Wallace Stevens, Ramon Fernandez, and Adrienne Rich." *Wallace Stevens Journal* 12 (Fall 1988): 150–61.

Savalle, Joseph. *Travestis, métamorphoses, dédoublements*. Paris: Librairie Minard, 1981.

Schaum, Melita. *Wallace Stevens and the Critical Schools*. Tuscaloosa: University of Alabama Press, 1987.

Schwenger, Peter. "The Masculine Mode." In *Speaking of Gender*, edited by Elaine Showalter, 101–12. New York: Routledge, 1989.

Sedgwick, Eve K. "Across Gender, Across Sexuality: Willa Cather and Others." *South Atlantic Quarterly* 88 (1989): 53–72.

Shakespeare, William. *The Life of Timon of Athens*. Edited by Charlton Hinman. In *William Shakespeare: The Complete Works*, edited by Alfred Harbage, 1136–68. Baltimore: Penguin Books, 1969.

Shaw, Annette. "Baudelaire's 'Femmes Damnées': The Androgynous Space." *Centerpoint* 3 (1980): 57–64.

Showalter, Elaine. "Feminist Criticism in the Wilderness." *Critical Inquiry* 8 (1981): 179–205.

——, ed. *Speaking of Gender*. New York: Routledge, 1989.

Smith, Albert B. "Gautier's *Mademoiselle de Maupin*: The Quest for Happiness." *Modern Language Quarterly* 32 (1971): 168–74.

Smith-Rosenberg, Carroll. *Disorderly Conduct: Visions of Gender in Victorian America*. New York: Knopf, 1985.

Springer, Mary Doyle. "The Feminine Principle in Stevens's Poetry: 'Esthétique du Mal.'" *Wallace Stevens Journal* 12 (Fall 1988): 119–37.

Starkie, Enid. *Baudelaire*. New York: New Directions, 1958.

Steiner, George. "Extraterritorial." In *Nabokov: Criticism, Reminiscences, Translations and Tributes*, edited by Alfred Appel, Jr., and Charles Newman, 119–27. Evanston: Northwestern University Press, 1970.

Stepan, Nancy. *The Idea of Race in Science: Great Britain, 1800–1960*. Hamden, Connecticut: Archon Books, 1982.

Stevens, Holly. *Souvenirs and Prophecies: The Young Wallace Stevens*. New York: Knopf, 1977.

Stevens, Wallace. *The Collected Poems of Wallace Stevens*. New York: Knopf, 1969.

——. *Letters of Wallace Stevens*. Edited by Holly Stevens. New York: Knopf, 1966.

——. *The Necessary Angel*. New York: Knopf, 1951.

——. "The Nymph." *Harvard Advocate* 67.6 (1899): 86–87. Signed John Fiske Towne.

——. *Opus Posthumous*. Edited by Milton J. Bates. New York: Knopf, 1989.

———. *Sur Plusieurs Beaux Sujects: Wallace Stevens's Commonplace Book*. Edited by Milton J. Bates. Stanford: Stanford University Press, 1989.

Stevenson, Robert Louis. *Prince Otto: A Romance*. New York: Scribner's, 1923.

———. *The Silverado Squatters*. In *The Travels and Essays of Robert Louis Stevenson*, vol. 15. New York: Scribner's Sons, 1900.

Stouck, David. *Willa Cather's Imagination*. Lincoln: University of Nebraska Press, 1975.

Stuart, Dabney. *Nabokov: The Dimensions of Parody*. Baton Rouge: Louisiana State University Press, 1978.

Toker, Leona. "Fact and Fiction in Nabokov's Biography of Abram Gannibal." *Mosaic* 22 (Summer 1989): 43–56.

Toussenel, Alphonse. *Le Monde des oiseaux, ornithologie passionelle*. Paris: Librairie Sociétaire, 1847.

Turner, Victor. "Betwixt and Between: The Liminal Period in *Rites de Passage*." In *The Forest of Symbols*, 93–111. Ithaca: Cornell University Press, 1967.

Vendler, Helen. *Wallace Stevens: Words Chosen Out of Desire*. Knoxville: University of Tennessee Press, 1984.

Virgil. *The Aeneid*. Translated by Rolfe Humphries. New York: Scribner's, 1961.

Vouga, Daniel. *Baudelaire et Joseph de Maistre*. Paris: Librairie José Corti, 1957.

Wagner, C. Roland. "Wallace Stevens: The Concealed Self." *Wallace Stevens Journal* 12 (Fall 1988): 83–101.

Weedon, Chris. *Feminist Practice and Poststructuralist Theory*. Oxford: Blackwell, 1987.

Williams, Roger L. *The Horror of Life*. Chicago: University of Chicago Press, 1980.

Wohlfarth, Irving. "Aspects of Baudelaire's Literary Dandyism." Ph.D. diss. Yale University, 1971.

Woodress, James. *Willa Cather: A Literary Life*. Lincoln: University of Nebraska Press, 1987.

INDEX

Albouy, Pierre, 29n, 48n
Albright, Daniel, 231n
Alcibiades, 10, 16
  in Barbey, allusion to, 60, 65, 84–85,
    92
  in Baudelaire, allusion to, 102
  as dandy:
    feminization of, 92
    general characteristics of, 4
  in Gautier, allusion to, 35, 38–40, 49
  and parallel in Cather, 157, 161
  in Stevens, allusion to, 184
Analogy, 4n, 11, 13, 19, 22, 24, 27, 136
  in Barbey, 68, 85, 88, 89, 96
  in Baudelaire:
    "Le cygne," 120, 122–27, 135
    as a female mode, 118–19, 137,
      155
    on Guys, 135–36

  "L'oeuvre et la vie d'Eugène
    Delacroix," 127–34
  "Le peintre de la vie moderne,"
    128, 129
  in Cather, 169, 172, 178
  in Delacroix's painting, 131–33
  in Nabokov, 243, 249, 255, 264
  in Ovid's *Metamorphoses*, 114
  in Stevens, 190–91, 206, 212
Androgyny, 6, 15n, 16, 47
  in Barbey, 84
  in Baudelaire, 117
  in Cather, 155, 177
  in Gautier, 47, 48
  and "pseudoandrogyne," 47, 116,
    177, 186
  and psychological androgyne, 47
  in Stevens, 204
Archaeology of women, 18–21

Armstrong, Nancy, 11n
Aynesworth, Donald, 115–17

Babcock, Barbara, 35n
Balakian, Anna, 107n
Barbey d'Aurevilly, Jules-Amédée, 17,
    22
  analogy in, 68, 85, 88, 89, 96
  and appropriation of others, 62, 65–
    73, 78–79
  and audience, relation to, 55, 70–71,
    76–77, 80–82
  and Brummell as self-portrait, 78–
    79, 81, 89, 92
  as dandy himself, 54
  and exemplary portraits, 57, 58, 72,
    81
    of Eugénie de Guérin, 61–65, 72,
      76, 86
    of madmen, 58–59
    of St. Sebastian, 59–62, 64, 65, 76
    of self, 62–65
  and feminization of dandy, 57, 61–
    62, 65, 86–92
  gender dichotomies challenged by,
    9, 73, 103
  genre fluidity in, 55, 90
  and identity, construction of, 56–85,
    89
  and literary texture in, 57, 227
  metamorphosis in, 56–57, 88
  and paradox, 56, 59, 67, 71–74, 78,
    87–91
  self-portrait of, 62–68, 71–73, 78–79
  and translation, 77–82, 85, 96
  and Trébutien. See Trébutien, Guil-
    laume-Stanislaus
  works:
    "Un Dandy d'avant les dandys,"
      2, 92–96
    "De l'élégance," 86–87, 92
    "Du Dandysme et de G. Brum-
      mell," 2, 7–9, 54–58, 67–70,

73–97, 101–2, 146, 155, 174,
    180, 227–28, 244
Barkan, Leonard, 39n
Bates, Milton, 183n, 196n
Baudelaire, Charles, 10, 17, 22
  analogy in, 106–10
  androgyny in, 117
  dandy:
    construction of, 100–104
    etiology of, 98, 99
    feminization of, 103–4, 187–89
    himself as, 110, 111
  exile in, 123–26
  gender dichotomies challenged by,
    103–4, 114, 117–18, 125, 137
  genre fluidity in, 244
  and identity, construction of, 137
  the ideal in, 106–9, 119, 122
  and literary texture, 110
  mundus muliebris in, 118–20, 126–
    28, 131, 136–42, 187
  paradox in, 111–13, 118, 140, 162
  patriarchy in, 188
  on Poe, Edgar Allan, 104–5
  translation in, 113, 128–30, 135, 141
  works:
    "A une passante," 114–18, 215,
      229, 242
    "La belle Dorothée," 186–89
    "La chevelure," 190
    "Le cygne," 109, 120–27, 221
    "Edgar Poe, sa vie et ses
      oeuvres," 156–58
    "La Fanfarlo," 259
    Un mangeur d'opium, 97–100
    "Notes nouvelles sur Edgar Poe,"
      157–58
    "L'oeuvre et la vie d'Eugène
      Delacroix, 127–34
    "Le peintre de la vie moderne,"
      3, 101–3, 111–14, 120, 128, 134–
      42, 159–63, 166, 197, 244, 259
Benamou, Michel, 183n
Benjamin, Walter, 5n

Bernhardt, Sarah, 153–54
Brown, Clarence, 221n, 225n
Brummell, George Bryan:
  biography of, 73–74
  as contradictory figure, 74–75, 84,
    86, 89
  death of, 82
  as feminine figure, 87–88
  as figure of influence, 77–78
  in Nabokov, allusion to, 245–46
  as self-portrait of Barbey, 78–79, 81,
    89, 92
Buttel, Robert, 183n, 199n
Byron, Lord George Gordon, 3, 84, 92
  as Barbey's hero, 80, 89
  and Cather, 144, 153
  and Delacroix, 129
  and *Eugene Onegin*, 220
  Gautier's admiration for, 26
  and Stevens, 184, 194

Camus, Albert, 10n
Carassus, Emilien, 10, 25n
Castiglione, 4, 5
Cather, Willa, 16, 17, 22
  aesthetics and gender, trajectories
    of, in, 145–46, 151–55, 173, 176
  allegory in, 145, 163
  analogy in, 169, 172, 178
  androgyny in, 155, 177
  dandy:
    Ántonia Shimerda as, 171–73
    characters as, 147–51
    Jim Burden as, 169–71, 173
    principal characteristics of, 154,
      159
    St. Peter as, 159–61, 162–63
    vaporization and centralization
      of, 172
  and exile, 172
  and French tradition, 143, 151–52,
    155–56, 179
  gender dichotomies challenged,
    151, 154, 164, 179

genre fluidity in, 165, 176
hierarchy and category challenged
  by, 154, 165, 166, 168
impersonality in, 172
metamorphosis in, 155, 167
and moral aestheticism, 22, 144,
  145, 149
and *mundus muliebris*, 170, 172, 179
Ovid alluded to, 174–76
and romance of temperament, 152,
  155, 164–68
Stevens on, 184
and sympathy versus sensation
  in drama reviews, 153–54
  in *My Ántonia*, 173, 176
  in *The Professor's House*, 164–66
  and St. Peter, 163
  in "A Wagner Matinee," 146–151,
    153
works:
  "Edgar Allan Poe," 156–59
  My Ántonia, 23, 169–79
  The Professor's House, 23, 155–69
  selected journalism, 151–55
  "A Wagner Matinee," 146–51,
    153
Chénier, André, 256–58
Cixous, Hélène, 15, 18, 19
Coincidentia oppositorum:
  in Baudelaire, 109, 134
  in Cather, 170
  in Gautier, 47
  in Nabokov, 268
  in Pushkin, 243
  in Stevens, 191, 207, 218
Colie, Rosalie, 75n
Creed, Elizabeth, 25n, 55n, 79n
Cross-dressing. *See* Transvestism
Cunningham, J. V., 183n

Dandy, the:
  anti-essentialism of, 2, 5, 13, 43
  feminization of, 4, 6, 8, 10, 11, 26,
    155

in Barbey, 61–62, 65, 86–92
in Baudelaire, 103–4, 137–40,
    187–89
in Cather, 147–51
in Gautier, 30, 32–34
in Nabokov, 230–33
in Stevens, 181–82, 186–91, 204,
    208–11
principal characteristics of, 3, 154
    in Barbey, 60–63
    in Cather, 154, 159
    in Gautier, 26–28, 30–33, 35, 37
    as patterned on Alcibiades, 4
    in Stevens, 181, 182, 184, 185,
        209–10
and women, 1, 6, 7, 31–33, 137, 148,
    171–73
Dandyism:
    and analogy, 11, 140, 142
    and criminality, 4n
    and French Romanticism, 26n
    history of, 1, 1n
    and literary tradition, 270
    and mirror images, 30, 34, 38, 40,
        67, 164–65, 190, 201, 238, 254,
        262
    and postmodernism, 270–72
    of Stevens, criticism of, 183n
    and texture, 38, 197
    vaporization and centralization in,
        3–4
        and Barbey, 57
        and Delacroix, 131
        in My Ántonia, 172
        and Nabokov, 237, 246
        in "Le peintre de la vie mo-
            derne," 135, 137
        in The Professor's House, 164–65
        and the self as labyrinth, 81–82
Dante, Alighieri, 38
Daudet, Léon, 167
Daumier, Honoré, 141
Davis, Natalie Zemon, 35n

Delacroix, Eugène, 101, 123, 127–36,
    162n, 225
    "Ovid among the Scythians," 131–
        34
De Quincey, Thomas, 97–100, 118
    works:
        Confessions of an English Opium-
            Eater, 97–100
        Suspiria de Profundis, 97–100
Divide, 24, 169, 206
Dodille, Norbert, 68n
Douglas, Ann, 19n, 20
Dumas, Alexandre, 176–77
Duse, Eleanor, 153–64

Eliade, Mircea, 47. See Coincidentia
    oppositorum
Ellmann, Richard, 184n
Elssler, Fanny, 48
Erasmus, 4, 75
Exile:
    in Baudelaire, 123–26
    in Delacroix, 131
    in My Ántonia, 172
    in Nabokov, 223, 223n, 224, 250, 253
    in Stevens, 200

Felman, Shoshana, 17
Feminization:
    of American culture, 20n
    of the dandy, 4, 6, 8, 10, 11, 26, 30–
        34, 155
        in Barbey, 61–62, 65, 86–92
        in Baudelaire, 103–4, 137–40,
            187–89
        in Cather, 146–51, 169–79, 171–
            73
        in Gautier, 30, 32–34
        in Nabokov, 230–33
        in Stevens, 181–82, 186–91, 204,
            208–11
    of literary culture, 24

of literary text, 19–21, 19n, 23, 134,
    151
Field, Andrew, 245n
Feo, José Rodríguez, 192, 195
Flax, Jane, 271n

Gautier, Théophile, 17, 22
    Alcibiades alluded to, 35, 38–40, 49
    allegory in, 27, 29
    analogy in, 27
    androgyny in, 47, 48
    classical objectivity in, 49–50, 52
    dandy:
        d'Albert as, 30–34
        expands notion of, 31–32, 34
        feminization of, 30, 32–34
        Madeleine as, 34
        principal characteristics of, 26–
            28, 30–33, 35, 37
    genre fluidity in, 22
    hermaphrodite in, 42–43, 46–47
    hierarchy and category challenged
        by, 39–42, 46
    impersonality in, 52
    metamorphosis in, 26–27, 33, 38–
        43, 45, 48, 53
    Ovid alluded to, 38–40, 43, 47
    paradox in, 49
    pragmatism in, 43
    romantic subjectivity in, 49–52
    texture in, 49
    transvestism in, 34–38, 40, 48
    works:
        "Celle-ci et celle-là," 27–29
        Histoire du Romantisme, 26, 47–
            49
        Les Jeunes-France: Romans go-
            guenards, 25–29, 51
        Mademoiselle de Maupin, 6, 11, 26,
            27, 28, 29–53, 144, 155, 159
Gender:
    and biological difference, 11–14, 14n

dichotomies challenged, 9, 11–14,
    11n, 17, 23, 116, 228
    by Barbey, 9, 73, 103
    by Baudelaire, 103–4, 114, 117–
        18, 125, 137
    by Cather, 151, 154, 164, 179
    by Delacroix, 133
    in Eugene Onegin, 241, 243
    feminism versus phallocentrism,
        15–16
    feminization of art, 19, 21
    by Nabokov, 249, 258, 264
    by Stevens, 186–87, 205–6, 214,
        217, 219
    and masculinity, construction of,
        14n
    as self-presentation, 12–13, 17, 36–
        37, 103, 117, 175
    and sex, 11–14, 114
Genre fluidity:
    in Barbey, 55, 90
    in Baudelaire, 244
    in Cather, 165, 176
    in Gautier, 22
    in Nabokov, 244
Gilbert, Sandra, 15, 17
Gilman, Margaret, 112n
Green, Martin, 4n
Gubar, Susan, 16n, 17
Guérin, Eugénie de, 61–62, 63, 180–81
Guys, Constantin:
    in Baudelaire, 110, 111, 113, 135–36,
        140–41
    paralleled in other writers, 146, 157,
        161–62, 164, 197, 223

Heilbrun, Carolyn, 15n
Hermaphrodite:
    in Gautier, 48
    in Mademoiselle de Maupin, 42–43,
        46–47
    in Ovid, 39, 43, 44, 46

Hoffmann, E. T. A., 38
Homosexuality, 10n, 35, 226, 262–65

Impersonality:
    in *Mademoiselle de Maupin*, 52
    in *My Ántonia*, 172

James, William, 9, 272
Jardine, Alice, 187n
Jefferson, Joseph, 153–54
Jehlen, Myra, 17, 18n
Jesse, Captain William, 71, 245
Johnson, Mark, 114n

Kaiser, Walter, 64n, 75n
Kelly, Dorothy, 145n
Kempf, Roger, 10n, 112n
Kessler, Suzanne, and Wendy
        McKenna, 11n, 103n, 117n
Knapp, Shoshana, 266n, 267n

Laclos, Pierre, 38
Laqueur, Thomas, 12, 13
Lentricchia, Frank, 18n, 19–21, 186n
Levenson, Michael, 50n
Lloyd, Rosemary, 30n, 38–39n

Mansfield, Richard, 153–54
Matoré, Georges, 13n, 25n
Mazzeo, Joseph, 4n
Metamorphosis, 12, 22. *See also* Ovid
    in "Du Dandysme et de G. Brum-
        mell," 57
    in *Mademoiselle de Maupin*, 26–27,
        33, 38–43, 45, 48, 53
    in Nabokov, 244, 246, 247, 258, 267
    in *The Professor's House*, 155, 167
    in Stevens, 197, 206–7, 210–11, 219
    and symbolist text, 45
Meyer, Priscilla, 235n
Moers, Ellen, 1n, 25n, 157n
Moi, Toril, 15
Monter, Barbara Heldt, 230n
Montpensier, Mlle de, 9

More, Paul Elmer, 202n
Mundus muliebris, 10, 18, 119–20, 154,
        155
    and analogy, 126–27, 137, 140, 142,
        155
    and appropriation of women, 19, 58
    in Baudelaire, 118–20, 126–28, 131,
        136–42, 187
    in Cather, 170, 172, 179
    Delacroix reconstitutes, 128
    in Nabokov, 249, 254–55
    in Stevens, 182, 191, 204
Munson, Gorham, 183n

Nabokov, Vladimir, 16, 17, 22, 22n
    analogy in, 243, 249, 255, 264
    and artifice, 229, 230, 238, 246–47,
        254, 259
    and attitude toward audience, 225
    and *coincidentia oppositorum*, 268
    as dandy himself, 223–27
    and exile, 223, 223n, 224, 250, 253
    and female characters, 6, 228–33,
        231n, 249, 264–68
    and feminization of dandy, 230–33
    in the French tradition, 227, 232–33,
        237–38
    and Gannibal's sister, 221–22, 247–
        55, 256
    gender dichotomies challenged by,
        249, 258, 264
    and genre fluidity, 244
    hierarchy and category challenged
        by, 222, 227, 232, 238, 243–44,
        248
    and identity, construction of, 224
    and metamorphosis, 244, 246, 247,
        258, 267
    and mirror images, 238, 254, 262
    and *mundus muliebris*, 249, 254–55
    paradox in, 230, 236–37
    parody in, 236, 238, 242, 244–47,
        255–68
    and patriarchy, 264

and plagiarism, 255–68
and Pushkin, special relation to,
    220–22, 226, 227, 233–38, 244–
    68
self-portrait of, 232–34, 236
texture in, 23, 227–31, 235–36, 246–
    47, 256–57, 265, 267
and vaporization, 237
on women, 23, 232, 249
works:
    Bend Sinister, 256
    Eugene Onegin, translation and
        commentary on, 23, 221–22,
        221n, 228, 233–61
    The Gift, 233
    Lectures on Literature, 226
    Lolita, 233
    "Mademoiselle O," 222, 231–33
    Pale Fire, 222, 233, 255–57, 258–
        68
    The Real Life of Sebastian Knight,
        233
    Speak Memory, 226–27
    "Spring in Fialta," 222, 229–31
Napoleon, 80, 84, 153
Needham, Rodney, 4n
Nelson, Lowry, 124n
Nussbaum, Martha, 85n

O'Brien, Sharon, 152n
O'Flaherty, Wendy, 4n, 7n
Olsen, Tillie, 18n
Ovid, allusions to:
    in Baudelaire, 109, 125
    in Cather, 174–76
    in Gautier, 22, 38–40, 43, 47
    in Stevens, 210

Palimpsest:
    in Barbey, 58–65, 67, 76, 83
    in Baudelaire, 104
    in Cather, 156, 173
    in Nabokov, 224, 231–32, 261
    in Stevens, 180, 196–97, 217–18

Pan, Hermes, 269
Paradox, 22, 75–77
    in Barbey:
        "Du Dandysme et de G. Brum-
            mell," 56, 59, 67, 74, 78, 89–91
        on elegance and beauty, 87
        exemplary portraits, 71
        on gender, 73
        on the self, 73
        and Trébutien, 71
    in Baudelaire:
        "A une passante," 118
        "Le Dandy," 111–13
        "Les femmes et les filles," 140
        "Le peintre de la vie moderne,"
            162
    in Gautier's *Mademoiselle de Mau-
        pin*, 49
    in Nabokov:
        Eugene Onegin, Translation and
            Commentary, 236–37
        "Spring in Fialta," 230
    in Ovid, 44, 46
    in Stevens:
        dandy personifies, 181
        interest in French culture, 200
        "Oak Leaves are Hands," 210
        personal style, 185
Patriarchy:
    in Baudelaire's poetry, 188
    challenges to, by literature of dan-
        dyism, 6, 14–21
    and feminist critics, 15
    in Nabokov, 264
    in Stevens, 203–7, 212
Pichois, Claude, 138
Pifer, Ellen, 223n
Plato, 4, 190
Plutarch, 4, 10
Poe, Edgar Allan, 104–5
    Baudelaire on, 156–58
    Cather on, 156–59
    Marginalia, 158
Proust, Marcel, 222, 226

Pushkin, Aleksandr:
  as creator of fictional dandies, 3,
    238–42
  Eugene Onegin, 3, 23, 220–22, 227–
    28, 233–34, 237–44
  and female character as dandy, 241–
    44
  Nabokov's relation to, 220–22, 226,
    227, 233–38, 244–68

Quinn, Patrick, 156n

Racism, 192, 248, 248n
Rorty, Richard, 7n, 76n
Rubin, Gayle, 15n

Saint-Simon, 8, 8n
Santos, Maria Irene Ramalho de
    Sousa, 201n
Schaum, Melita, 22n
Sedgwick, Eve K., 152n
Shakespeare, William, 4, 38
Showalter, Elaine, 14nn
Smith-Rosenberg, Carroll, 16n
Starkie, Enid, 107n
Stevens, Wallace, 9, 13, 17, 20, 22, 23
  and analogy, 190–91, 206, 212
  and androgyny, 204
  and audience, relation to, 193, 195
  on Cather, 184
  and *coincidentia oppositorum*, 191,
    207, 218
  and critics, 183n
  and cultural space, 190–91, 198,
    200, 204, 208, 213, 214
  as dandy himself, 182–85, 191–95
  and dandy's principal characteris-
    tics, 181–85, 209–10
  and deconstructionist theory, 200n
  and exile, 200
  and feminization of dandy, 181–82,
    186–91, 204, 208–11

  and French tradition, 184, 194, 197,
    199n, 214
  Eugénie de Guérin as influence,
    180–82
  and female, 181–82, 186–91, 204
  of nineteenth-century literature,
    184, 198–200
  and gender, construction of, 186–
    87, 201, 202–8, 202n, 214, 217,
    219
  hierarchy and category challenged
    by, 182, 203, 210, 217
  and identity, construction of, 195–
    97, 207
  and metamorphosis, 197, 206–7,
    210–11, 219
  and *mundus muliebris*, 182, 191, 204
  as outsider, 185–86, 188–89, 196,
    198, 199
  and paradox, 181, 185, 200, 210
  and patriarchy, 203–7, 212
  Poe alluded to, 199n
  and Ransom, John Crowe, 185
  and translation, 186, 198–200
  women as threatening, 189–91, 197,
    201–2, 208–11, 213
  works:
    "The Apostrophe to Vincentine,"
      216–17
    "Auroras of Autumn," 201
    Bowl, Cat, and Broomstick, 186,
      189–91, 212
    "The Comedian as the Letter C,"
      194
    "Cortège for Rosenbloom," 203
    "Disillusionment at Ten
      O'Clock," 194
    "The Figure of the Youth as
      Virile Poet," 212–14
    "Gubbinal," 194
    Harmonium, 186
    "The Idea of Order at Key
      West," 200–201, 201n, 215–19

Ideas of Order, 186
"Madame La Fleurie," 208
"The Man Whose Pharynx was Bad," 194
"The Man with the Blue Guitar," 194
"The Noble Rider and the Sound of Words," 210
"Notes toward a Supreme Fiction," 21, 201
"The Nymph," 189
"Oak Leaves are Hands," 208–12
"Peter Quince at the Clavier," 194
"Rubbings of Reality," 210
"Sunday Morning," 200
"Tea at the Palaz of Hoon," 194, 205
"To the One of Fictive Music," 204
"To the Roaring Wind," 205
"Two Figures in Dense Violet Night," 205
"The Well Dressed Man with a Beard," 205
"The Wind Shifts," 205
"Woman Looking at a Vase of Flowers," 205
"The World as Meditation," 201
"The Worms at Heaven's Gate," 203
Stevenson, Robert Louis:
and artifice, 264
works:
Prince Otto, 166, 258–68
"Silverado Squatters," 196
Stouck, David, 159n
Sully Prudhomme, Armand, 193

Texture:
in Barbey, 57, 227
in Baudelaire, 110
in Gautier, 49
in Nabokov, 227–31, 235–36, 246–47, 256–57, 265, 268
Thucydides, 4
Toussenel, Alphonse, 121–22
Translation, 22, 30
in Barbey, 77–82, 85, 96
in Baudelaire, 113, 128–30, 135, 141
in Nabokov, 220–22, 233–38, 236n, 257–59, 268
in Stevens, 186, 198–200
Transvestism, 16, 16n, 17
and Cather, 145, 153
in *Mademoiselle de Maupin*, 34–38, 40, 48
and pseudoandrogyny, 47
Trébutien, Guillaume-Stanislaus, 67–71, 74, 195
appropriation of, 67–71, 72
"Du Dandysme," correspondence on, 67–71
Turner, Victor, 36n

Van Dyck, Anthony, 59–61
Virgil, 123–26

Weedon, Chris, 271n
Wilde, Oscar, 3, 270
Woodress, James, 24
Woolf, Virginia, 24
Wulf, Michèle, 97n

Zabel, Morton Dauwen, 183n

LIBRARY OF CONGRESS CATALOGING-IN-PUBLICATION DATA

Feldman, Jessica R. (Jessica Rosalind), 1949–
    Gender on the divide : the dandy in modernist literature / Jessica R. Feldman.
        p.   cm.
    Includes bibliographical references and index.
    ISBN 0-8014-2790-8
    1. Dandies in literature. 2. Sex differences (Psychology) in literature. 3. Modernism
(Literature). 4. Literature, Modern—History and criticism. I. Title.
PN56.5.D34F45   1993
809'.93352—dc20   92-26193